Soirée musicale, a typical salon of the 1820's

FRITS NOSKE

French Song
from
Berlioz to Duparc

The Origin and Development of the Mélodie

SECOND EDITION

Revised by Rita Benton & Frits Noske

Translated by Rita Benton

Dover Publications, Inc. / New York

Published in Canada by General Publishing Company, Ltd., 30 Lesmill Road, Don Mills, Toronto, Ontario.
Published in the United Kingdom by Constable and Company, Ltd., 10 Orange Street, London WC 2.

French Song from Berlioz to Duparc, first published by Dover Publications, Inc., in 1970, is at the same time the first English translation and a new revised edition of the work originally published in French by the North-Holland Publishing Company, Amsterdam, and the Presses Universitaires de France, Paris, in 1954 with the title *La mélodie française de Berlioz à Duparc; essai de critique historique.* The present volume also includes several new sections: a preface; a postscript; an English "Prose Rendering of Poetic Quotations"; the "Remarks for the Second Edition" of the song catalogue; and a selection of illustrations.

Some of the musical examples reproduced in this book appear by permission of the following publishers: Heugel & Cie, J. Hamelle, Durand & Cie and Rouart et Lerolle.

Library of Congress Cataloging-in-Publication Data

Noske, Frits, 1920–
    [Mélodie française de Berlioz à Duparc. English]
    French song from Berlioz to Duparc : the origin and development of the mélodie / Frits Noske ; revised by Rita Benton & Frits Noske ; translated by Rita Benton.
        p.   cm.
    Translation of: Mélodie française de Berlioz à Duparc.
    "Song catalogue": p.
    Bibliography: p.
    Includes index.
    ISBN 0-468-25554-9 (pbk.)
    1. Songs, French—France—History and criticism. 2. French poetry—Musical settings—History and criticism. 3. Songs, French—France—Bibliography. I. Benton, Rita. II. Title.
ML2827.N613 1988   87-28962
784'.0944—dc19   CIP
                                                                          MN

Manufactured in the United States of America
Dover Publications, Inc.
180 Varick Street
New York, N.Y. 10014

PREFACE TO THE SECOND
REVISED EDITION

THIS STUDY WAS WRITTEN ORIGINALLY IN FRENCH AND PUBLISHED IN 1954 by the North-Holland Publishing Company in Amsterdam and the Presses Universitaires de France in Paris. It emanated from a casual comment made in 1947 by Professor K. P. Bernet Kempers, with whom I was studying musicology at Amsterdam University. Having heard some songs by Gounod on the radio, he expressed surprise that they had never been the object of scholarly research. Taking this as a challenge (but with moderate enthusiasm, since I was not strongly attracted to Gounod's music at the time), I started to prepare a paper on the subject. I soon realized that the task of providing the necessary historical background for Gounod's *mélodies* was virtually impossible because of the lack of literature about the entire history of French song from 1600 to about 1880. Only two books relating to the subject existed: Gérold's study of French vocal art during the seventeenth century and Gougelot's investigations of the romance during the Revolution and Napoleonic Empire.[1] Apart from a few minor aspects treated in scattered articles, the rest was *terra incognita*. Consequently I changed the topic of my paper to a survey of the development of French song during the seventeenth and eighteenth centuries. Although based principally on personal research, this student essay suffered from many deficiencies and to-day the manuscript, happily unpublished, still rests in my files. Nevertheless, the study served as an orientation for the historical background, enabling me to find a point of departure for starting this book as a doctoral dissertation in 1949.

Whatever the value of the present study, the importance of its

v

subject is surely beyond dispute. Such a vast fallow land is rare indeed in music history. Much has been written about the *mélodies* of Fauré, Duparc, Debussy, Ravel, and Roussel, but almost nothing about the origins of the genre they favored. The poets Baudelaire, Verlaine, Mallarmé, and their contemporaries have often been discussed in connection with French song, but musical scholarship has been silent about the earlier poetic generation that included Victor Hugo, Alfred de Musset, and Théophile Gautier. The genius of Gounod, Bizet, Delibes, and Massenet for opera and ballet and of Saint-Saëns, Lalo, and Franck in the field of instrumental music is conceded without question. But what about the talents of these same composers for song writing? And were French musicians of the mid-nineteenth century insensible to the seductive influences of contemporary German song and the music-generating verses of their own poets?

This study of the *mélodie*'s origins and early development attempts to fill a gap in our knowledge of French music history by answering these questions. The general plan is clear from the table of contents and requires only a few comments.

The first chapter, dealing with the *mélodie*'s origins, contains many quotations from nineteenth-century sources. Since the birth of "modern" song was a very complicated process, in whose earlier phases the social aspect was sometimes more important than the artistic, the superficial remarks quoted from the Paris musical press of the 1830's often give a truer and livelier picture than could ever be drawn by a modern hand.

In his review of the first edition Jacques Barzun questioned the need for the discussion of linguistic and literary problems that appears in Chapter II.[2] I cannot insist too strongly on its indispensability. Since song is the product of both poetry and music, the former must not be neglected in favor of the latter. No scholar, singer, or listener can grasp the essence of French song without some insight into the complex and hallowed traditions of its musical prosody. The same holds true for the subtle interrelationships between poetic and musical expression, an affinity that offers more problems in France, with its centralized culture and its constant concern with the beauties and refinements of language, than in other countries.

The remaining chapters deal with the songs of eighteen composers, including some born outside of France (e.g., Wagner, Liszt, and Franck) who made substantial or interesting contributions to the *mélodie* genre. Many more might have been selected from among the composers of the thousands of *mélodies* published between 1830 and 1880. But discussion of a larger group of composers would have turned this into a shallow enumeration lacking room for the extensive analysis of compositional techniques so necessary to the understanding and appreciation of the songs. I believe that this critical study of the output of eighteen composers provides a fairly complete picture of the historical development of the *mélodie*, without implying that some of the other figures (e.g., Thomas, Auber, Adam, or Clapisson) lack merit or importance; similar analysis of additional composers would have left the general image unchanged. On the other hand, composers like Reyer and Castillon, who more or less failed as song writers, have been included because the very reasons for their failure are historically important.

The present revised and translated edition leaves the structure of the book virtually unchanged, although a number of details have been corrected and some others added or omitted. Prose quotations from French or other non-English sources have also been translated; the reader who wishes to consult the original text is referred to the first edition. Foreign-language poetic quotations, however, have been left unchanged, with their English prose rendering appearing in Appendix V. Song titles have not been translated unless this was necessary for the meaning of the context in which they appear. Changes incorporated in the extensive song catalogue comprising Appendix VI are explained in the preface to that section. The bibliography, like that of the first edition, includes a few items not consulted for this work but nevertheless considered useful for the reader.

In addition to the acknowledgments mentioned in the preface to the original edition (not reprinted here), I wish to thank Rita Benton for her careful translation and her untiring labor in the preparation of the new edition. Every sentence was discussed between us, and I am indebted to her for many observations that show sound judgment and a thorough knowledge of French music history. We are both grateful to Paulène Aspel and Anne Funke for their review of the translated poetic texts appearing in Appendix V; to our colleagues at the Bibliothèque Nationale for their gracious assistance; and to Stanley Appelbaum of Dover Publications for his painstaking editorial work and patient coping with the delays caused by transatlantic collaboration.

This book was not written for scholarly purposes alone. It deals with an aspect of music history that has much to offer both professional and amateur musicians. Many of the songs discussed here have quite unjustly fallen into oblivion, particularly outside of French-speaking countries, in spite of the fact that most of them are still readily available from Paris music publishers. I cherish the hope that the enthusiasm transmitted through this effort will contribute to the extension of the singer's repertoire.

Leyden University   FRITS NOSKE
March, 1968

CONTENTS

LIST OF ILLUSTRATIONS

NOTE: The Bibliothèque Nationale, Paris, is abbreviated as BN.

The Origins of the Mélodie

THE FRENCH MÉLODIE EMERGED AS A DISTINCT TYPE OF COMPOSITION in the fourth decade of the nineteenth century as the result of various factors, among which three were especially important: the decline in the artistic level of the romance, with the resultant need for a substitute vocal genre; the introduction into France of Schubert's *Lieder*, which soon became enormously popular and influential; and the impact of the new Romantic poetry, supplying composers with inspiration and with literary texts that forced a renunciation of earlier compositional styles and techniques. These important phenomena, together with a brief history of the romance and a sketch of prosodic theory, will be explored before broaching the subject of the *mélodie* itself.

The Romance

The name "romance" originally referred solely to a literary form. The *Dictionnaire de l'Académie Française* (1718) describes it as "a kind of light verse, recounting some ancient story" but omits any mention of the fact that it was sung. This feature is indicated for the first time in the *Encyclopédie* (1765), although even there the literary aspect predominates: "An ancient tale, written in simple, easy, and natural verse. Naïveté is the principal characteristic. ... This poem is sung and French music, clumsy and inane as it is, seems quite suitable to the romance." The description in Rousseau's *Dictionnaire de musique* (1767) becomes clearer and more detailed, defining the romance as "An air to which is sung a short poem of the same name, divided into stanzas, [and] whose subject is usually some love story, often tragic." Rousseau emphasizes the need for simplicity:

> Since the romance should be written in a simple, moving, and rather archaic style, the air should correspond to the character of the words: no ornaments, nothing mannered, but a sweet, natural, rustic melody that produces its own effect regardless of how it is sung. ... An accurate, clear voice that articulates well and sings without affectation is all that is required for singing a romance.

From a purely musical point of view, the romance seems to have its origins in the *brunette*.[3] Whereas the romance was exclusively vocal, the *brunette* could be performed instrumentally as well as vocally, as shown by such titles as "Sarabande" and "Menuet" in the collections published by Ballard.[4] Toward the middle of the eighteenth century the melodic line became more appropriate for the voice, as shown in the piece by an unknown composer given in Example 1.

Example 1: *Brunette*

Although this air dating from about 1750 still bears the title "Brunette,"[5] a short time later the name "romance" began to be used and in Rousseau's *Dictionnaire* the word *brunette* no longer appears. The early drawing-room romance played only a modest role in musical life, but at the Opéra Comique its position was more important and through this intermediary the genre reached foreign countries. Some eighteenth-century English collections contain French songs. In Germany, Johann Gottlieb Naumann composed numerous vocal pieces to French words, calling them *ariettes* even though the pieces had the same general characteristics as the romance. In Vienna, where French comic opera was very popular, Karl Ditters von Dittersdorf introduced the romance into instrumental music in 1773, in his Symphony in E-flat major, Opus 7, no. 1.

The romance reached maturity as a separate composition when Martini (i.e., Johann Schwartzendorf) published his famous "Plaisir d'amour" in 1784, set to a text by Florian.[6] Whereas earlier romance accompaniments had consisted of a basso-continuo part played on the harpsichord, this piece is sung to a written-out piano part. The work is further notable for its rondo form, containing a prelude, several interludes, and a postlude. Martini may be said to have raised the artistic level of the romance, for after 1784 the distinction between popular and art song, still rather vague with Rousseau, Dezède, and Monsigny, is clearly marked.

The political events of the Revolution influenced the genre in both its musical and poetic aspects. The narrative romance began to deal with current events, some poets bemoaning the fate of the victims of the Terror, while others mocked them. Apart from this, romance texts were written in deliberate imitation of medieval troubadour verse. Thus the artificial forms of the *ancien régime* gave way to a true lyric style impregnated with a melancholy atmosphere. Pastoral poetry was relegated to a secondary place and disappeared entirely about 1830.

Henri Gougelot's important study of the romance describes the songs according to their content, style of presentation, and poetic form.[7] On the basis of subject matter, three types may be distinguished: historical, pastoral, and sentimental romances. The second criterion also furnishes three subdivisions: narrative, dramatic, and lyric romances. As might be expected, Gougelot does not attempt a breakdown in terms of musical properties, since an equally clear separation would be virtually impossible. Two types might nevertheless be distinguished on the basis of their musical attributes: first, the romance in which expression is the most important feature, where the vocal line is tied to the words and closely follows the text. In the middle of the stanza, the structure may sometimes be quite free, while chromatic notes, unusual modulations, and altered chords direct the attention to the piano part. In the second type of romance, the melodic line has a purely musical character and is detached from the text without being entirely inconsistent. The accompaniment, of which the harmony remains on an elementary level, is completely subordinated to the vocal part, merely supporting the voice with broken chords.

Thus the categories of expressive and "abstract" romance may be derived from the melodic character. The former type appears in the work of Adrien *l'aîné*, Méhul, and d'Ennery, all showing some degree of German influence. The abstract romance was closer to the Italian style and was written by Plantade, Blangini, Boieldieu, d'Alvimare, Pradher, and especially Carbonel. Both types are among the romances of Joseph Denis Doche, Gabriel Lemoine, and Sophie Gail. During the Revolution the expressive romance was dominant; it was gradually replaced during the Empire by the romance with "abstract" melody and practically disappeared after 1815.

The romances of Spontini require a separate category. They exceed the limits of the genre by their richer, orchestra-like accompaniment, and rather resemble the *scène*. This type of composition, which may be said to have introduced opera into the salon, will be discussed later.

The romance attained full bloom during the Revolution and the Empire. Both music and poetry contained characteristic elements of pre-Romanticism; true Romanticism had not yet been achieved. Many poets found themselves unable to express emotions with old-fashioned means. Indeed, Marceline Desbordes-Valmore and Chateaubriand are the only writers of romance texts that have withstood the test of time. Composers in their turn struggled with the rigid structure imposed by the strophic form. The general feeling of obligation to conform to the established scheme is graphically described by Thiébault:

The structure of the romance is predetermined. The air of a romance cannot include more than one stanza, unless by successively using the minor and major modes, the composition is doubled in length. There are composers who have liberated themselves from this restriction by varying the tune for each stanza and joining them with more or less rich and complicated *ritornelli*. But only foreigners would have thus conceived of perverting the romance and transforming into a difficult study piece requiring long attention, that which is only meant to charm for a moment.[8]

In spite of its limitations the romance must nevertheless be credited with having given France, for the first time since the *air de cour* of the seventeenth century, a type of song of unquestioned artistic value, in which music and poetry filled roles of equal importance.

The Decline of the Romance

After 1815 the romance is named in various ways. Among the titles that appear are *barcarolle*, *tyrolienne*, *chansonnette*, *nocturne*, *tarantelle*, and *boléro*, all still collectively called romances. The significance of these names is determined either by the character of the music or by the literary subject, or both, as in the *barcarolle*. The *tyrolienne*, a sort of sophisticated *Ländler*, was born of purely musical needs. The name *boléro* or *tarantelle* would be chosen for poems dealing with Spain or Italy. The name *valse* appeared in song literature only after 1840, although numerous waltzes were composed earlier without being designated as such. A piece for two voices was inexplicably called a *nocturne*. The name *ballade* is not easily defined, since it was used for the most diverse types of romances. In any case, the French *ballade*, unlike the German, is only rarely a narrative type of composition. Finally, along with such less common titles as *élégie*, *fanfare*, and *cantatille*, appears the *chant*, applied chiefly to patriotic romances (e.g., *chant héroique*, *chant national*).

The *chansonnette*, a humorous or anecdotal little piece, contains elements of the romance as well as of the chanson. The many collections entitled *Romances et chansonnettes* indicate that contemporaries did not consider them identical.

In 1846 Antoine Romagnési, one of the best-known composers of romances during the Restoration, published a short treatise on "the art of singing romances, *chansonnettes*, *nocturnes*, and in general all salon music."[9] He divides these songs into five categories:

1. Sentimental romances
2. Dreamy and serious *mélodies*

3. Heroic *chants*, strongly rhythmic
4. Passionate and dramatic romances
5. *Chansonnettes*

Romagnési offers some interesting descriptive comments about the various types of drawing-room song. He considers sentimental and heroic romances the only true romances with respect to French taste and character. Tender and melancholy romances generally awaken the strongest response in the soul of the listener. The style of the *mélodie* is reminiscent of the German *Lied*. The *chansonnette* is graciously gay in character; although he does not consider it a romance at all, Romagnési nevertheless emphasizes the difference between the *chansonnette* and the chanson. Since the latter is "acted" rather than sung, he considers it beyond the scope of his treatise. Dramatic romances are also excluded, since their structure and accompaniment are similar to pieces sung at the theater. Here Romagnési is obviously referring to the *scènes* which were so popular until 1848. He gives this plausible explanation of their origin:

> They must have arisen as a kind of study for young composers, formed in our schools to become the mainstay of French opera. Finding it for the most part, however, almost entirely closed to them, they cast into the world works which are no doubt respectable, but which sometimes miss their effect because of not being performed in their proper place.[10]

In tracing the origins and development of the *mélodie*, one cannot disregard the *scène*, especially since it sometimes had a strongly expressive character, either in its entirety or in sections composed in romance style; but it differs from the romance chiefly in its free structure. The accompaniment imitates the orchestra, using frequent tremolos, while the vocal part is treated as either recitative or aria. Some longer *scènes* may be considered to be dramatic cantatas.

About 1825 appeared a new type, the *romance dialoguée*, for one voice, a melodic instrument, and piano accompaniment. Boieldieu, Garat, and others had already published romances for voice, violin, and piano during the Empire, but always treating the violin as an *ad libitum* part that could be omitted without great loss to the accompaniment.[11] In the dialogue romance, however, the instrument plays a role of equal importance with the voice, responding to sung fragments, while the accompaniment is left to the piano alone. Auguste Panseron, "the inventor of those dramatic romances in which the accompaniment of a flute, oboe, horn, violin, or cello arises from the subject itself and is an obligatory part of the composition," urged his text writers to use subjects that would furnish the opportunity for adding a second part to the voice. In his "Sainte-Cécile" (1833),[12] dedicated to the famous cellist Franchomme, the voice and cello are rivals in virtuosity (Example 2).

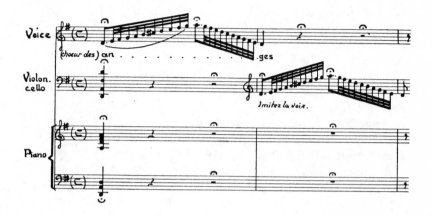

Example 2: Panseron, "Sainte-Cécile"

The choice of instrument can often be deduced from the title alone (e.g., "Le cor" [The Horn][13] or "Le songe de Tartini" [Tartini's Dream]). The latter piece, reported to have "all musical Paris in a flutter," was called "a true concerto" because of the difficulty of its violin part,[14] a not-unusual feature of the dialogue romance.

After 1815 the romance became an object of specialization for many composers. Romagnési and Pauline Duchambge (who wrote over 300 romances)[15] were the public's favorites during the first years of the Restoration, although Charles Plantade and Pradher were also popular. By 1825 these composers were dethroned by others: Panseron, who in the years preceding the July Revolution of 1830 was known as "the king of the romance,"[16] Édouard Bruguière,[17] and Amédée de Beauplan, who was known chiefly for his *chansonnettes*.[18] Between 1830 and 1840 the romances of Loïsa Puget were extremely popular. She imparted to the genre a bourgeois tendency that had already been somewhat noticeable in the songs of

Romagnési, causing one critic to write that "Romagnési tries to depict neither extreme gayety nor strong emotion; he succeeds best at painting the half smile and tempered mood of French *galanterie*."[19] The bourgeois nature of Puget's romances is apparent in her choice of poems (e.g., "La bénédiction d'un père" [A Father's Blessing] and "La mère du matelot" [The Sailor's Mother]).

During the years from 1830 to 1848, corresponding to the reign of Louis Philippe, the fashionable romance is represented by François Masini. Along with his works may be cited those of Frédéric Bérat (romances in popular style), Joseph Concone (dramatic *scènes*), Adolphe Vogel, Théodore Labarre, Louis Clapisson, Joseph Vimeux, Alphonse Thys, and Albert Grisar, who were replaced after 1845 by Paul Henrion, Louis Abadie, and Étienne Arnaud. During the Second Empire of Napoleon III (1851–1870) the romance loses its character as a separate genre, being difficult to distinguish from the chanson and *chansonnette*: "Today little remains of the romance. One cannot continue believing in its stupidities in salons where slang has triumphantly entered with singers from smoke-filled music rooms," wrote one commentator in 1868.[20] And in 1872 Alphonse Daudet wrote of romances as "sentimental mementos yellowing with age in very old cardboard boxes."[21]

The more "serious" composers were usually not interested in the genre. Rossini, Meyerbeer, Auber, Halévy, Adam (who did compose a large number of *chansonnettes*), and Thomas wrote romances that were no better than the average, although the same cannot be said of their *mélodies*, some of which will be discussed later. One journal suggested in 1842 to Adam, whom they recognized "as a clever man," that he "would do well not to waste in single romances the happy ideas that he will always have an opportunity to use much more productively in his operas."[22]

While the works of Romagnési and Duchambge have some artistic value, the production of romances after 1830 degenerated into a matter of mere technical skill. This commercial aspect is described in a pamphlet by Jacques-Auguste Delaire:

A romance ordinarily costs two francs; the average number published in one year is about five hundred. If the number of copies of each sold in one year is put at about the same figure, one would more likely be below than above the real number, for if some do not reach that figure, there are others that exceed it by far. Thus it follows that the annual sale of romances is at least 250,000, earning 500,000 francs.

Delaire also points out that it was a remunerative business for composers as well as publishers:

> On the business side, the romance is a commodity that has a sale when it is launched in drawing rooms under the patronage of a fashionable singer. A phenomenon of which our age should not be proud is that the romance's stock rises in proportion to the lowering of that of quartets, quintets, and other major works that publishers reject as unwanted merchandise and therefore not salable, while they pay five hundred francs for a romance and as much as six thousand for a collection of six romances by a popular composer, who sings them himself or entrusts them to such interpreters as Mlles. d'Hénin or Drouard and MM. Ponchard, Géraldy, Vartel, Boulanger, or Richelmi.[23]

At the end of each year a veritable avalanche of romances appeared in the form of albums that served simultaneously as bonuses for subscribers to musical journals. In *Le ménestrel* of December 13, 1840, a critic successively reviews no less than thirteen albums (by Puget, Labarre, Rubini, Meyerbeer, Herz, Masset, Bérat, Duchambge, Adhémar, Messemaeckers, Latour, Masini, and Clapisson). The same year collections of romances by several composers also appeared (e.g., *Album de La France musicale*, containing works by Pauline Viardot-Garcia, Auber, Halévy, Adam, Monpou, and Thomas). It may be noted in passing that an almost equal number of piano albums were produced by composers who specialized in the writing of quadrilles, waltzes, *galops*, *pots-pourris*, and *variations brillantes*.

During the Empire there had already been periodicals that regularly offered their readers an unpublished romance. After 1815 this musical supplement became the essential part, the journalistic section being restricted to theatrical news, anecdotes concerning famous musicians, and a fashion column. Among the many music journals of that time, only *Le ménestrel* managed to survive, developing over the years into a serious musical periodical; the others (e.g., *La romance*, *Le Protée*, and *La mélodie*) soon disappeared. But the practice of publishing French romances as journal supplements was popular enough to spread beyond the borders of France, to be taken up by similar music journals in other countries (e.g., *Der Minnesänger*, issued in Mainz, and *L'amateur* in Brussels).

As the songs acquired more and more clichés and banalities, publishers tried to attract the public's attention with extravagant titles.

An announcement in *Le ménestrel* shows the excesses to which they succumbed:

> *Homeopathic Romance.* We have thought it apt to designate by this title a pretty work by M. Strunz, of which the words are by Mme. Hahnemann, née d'Hervilly, wife of the famous homeopathic doctor. This romance will appear in our number for next Sunday.[24]

Needless to say, the doctor's wife is not instructing the readers of *Le ménestrel* in her husband's therapeutic functions; her text is only a trivial sentimental poem entitled "La séparation." Nevertheless, her example seems to have been imitated in a "*mélodie épileptique*" entitled "L'étoile du malheur" (The Star of Unhappiness) with words and music by Amédée de Beauplan.[25]

Chansonnette text writers found many varied subjects in daily events and in the fashionable novels of Balzac. In 1837 *Le ménestrel* published a short piece entitled "La femme de trente ans," with words by Isidore Sinard and music by the Chevalier Lagoanère. The *chansonnette* is dedicated to Balzac, whose novel of that title had appeared in 1832. The last lines of the text read:

> À quinze ans, on *veut* plaire,
> À vingt ans on *doit* plaire,
> À quarante ans on *peut* plaire,
> On *sait* plaire à trente ans.[26]

The mercenary character of song production is clearly demonstrated in this review of a concert by Panseron:

> One of the last pieces performed was a new romance, "Je te hais! ... et t'adore" (I hate you! ... and love you). I cite it not because of its worth, which seemed slight even for a romance, but because of a typically French gallantry of M. Panseron. The romance, ornamented with a lithographed vignette and printed on beautiful rose-colored paper, was distributed to the ladies together with the program. This pleasant innovation will surely have a favorable influence on M. Panseron's next concert.[27]

Composers were usually more highly regarded than their text writers. "The preeminence of the musician over the poet is such that the former improvises sketchy melodies to which the poet, after seeking the inherent implications, attempts the task of adapting some words."[28] Poets complained of being underpaid:

When a publisher pays his authors an unequal and assuredly unfair percentage, they accept the conditions, since he is the master of the situation; but when the same publisher pays a much higher sum to a singer for the interpretation, that is to say, for public performance of the manuscript owned by the publisher, that is surely an extreme miscarriage of justice.[29]

To the poets' laments, musicians and publishers replied spitefully:

It is known that these gentlemen work with all speed and that their supply of poems is inexhaustible, like a flower bed strewn with blossoms. But just as some flowers have no perfume, many words convey no ideas ... We know a certain composer to whom a certain author sent one hundred romances and *chansonnettes* at one time; that might be called a fertile sterility.[30]

An incalculable number of amateurs tried their hand at composition. One could "learn" the trade in a short time, thanks to a "Short Treatise on Melodic Composition Applied to Waltzes, Quadrilles, and Romances,"[31] a work containing illustrative examples from both Loïsa Puget and Beethoven!

Clearly, the romance was an object of great demand. Nevertheless, it would be difficult to find a single page of real artistic value in the entire production of a quarter century. The romance marks the triumph of the bourgeoisie during an era that is generally called, with oversimplification, "the Romantic period." Claude Laforêt explores this idea in his excellent little book on "Musical Life During the Romantic Period":

Let us not forget that if this epoch, extending from the middle of the Restoration to the last years of the July Monarchy [ca. 1820 to ca. 1848] is the age of Romanticism, it is also that of the French bourgeois. The disciples of Victor Hugo and the friends of Théophile Gautier heaped such wild abuse on the bourgeois only because he was powerful and therefore a person of consequence. Prosperous wholesale merchants, lawyers, doctors, financiers, and government officials also had their salons where poetry was recited and romances sung. Their families attended the Opéra and the Théâtre des Italiens to applaud Nourrit and Giulia Grisi and also went to the concerts of Liszt, Chopin, and Thalberg. These bourgeois constituted an audience, no doubt less brilliant, but more numerous than the friends of Mme. de Girardin or Mme. Ancelot, and one which neither musicians nor poets could ignore.[32]

Finally, the pictorial aspect of the romance should be mentioned, since almost all editions include illustrations depicting the subjects of the poems. Laforêt judges them no less severely than the poetry and music: "Neapolitan fishermen, Tyrolian herdsmen, Gypsies, or even simple country folk, are shown in pathetic poses attuned to the mediocre poem and commonplace melody they are announcing."[33] It should be observed, however, that such well-known artists as Nanteuil, Devéria, Charlet, Gigoux, and Gavarni produced a large proportion of these illustrations. Célestin Nanteuil alone lithographed no less than 5000 compositions of this type.[34]

The Romantic Romance

Though seemingly a pleonasm, the Romantic romance was actually a contradiction, since the bourgeois character of the genre became dominant about 1830, the so-called "Romantic year." Only two composers, Louis Niedermeyer and Hippolyte Monpou, clearly displayed Romantic qualities, both in their choice of poems and in their compositional style.

Niedermeyer's name is indissolubly linked to "Le lac," the famous poem from Lamartine's *Méditations poétiques*. Although his was not the earliest setting of the poem,[35] Niedermeyer was the first to show real understanding of this type of poetry. His achievement is emphasized by Saint-Saëns in his preface to the Swiss composer's biography:

Niedermeyer was above all a precursor. He was the first to break the mold of the antiquated and insipid French romance; taking his inspiration from the beautiful poems of Lamartine and Victor Hugo, he created a new type of song of a superior artistry, analogous to the German *Lied*. The resounding success of "Le lac" paved the way for Gounod and all those who followed this path.[36]

But Niedermeyer cannot accurately be called the creator of the *mélodie*. Basically his songs are still romances, even though distinguished from their dull contemporaries by the superior quality of the text,[37] by structural changes, by a closer relationship between words and music, and by the relative importance of the accompaniment.

The composer's structural innovations may result from the fact that Lamartine's *Méditations* lend themselves poorly to the traditional strophic form. Niedermeyer precedes his romances with an

Louis Niedermeyer in 1853

Title page of an early edition of Niedermeyer's "Le lac"

extended introduction which, considered by itself, has a free structure and is somewhat reminiscent of the *scène*. The romance proper is meant to interpret the essential thought of the poem, a plan that proves quite satisfactory for "Le lac." The introduction embraces the first three stanzas. The romance starts at the words "Un soir, t'en souvient-il?" and follows the customary strophic outlines. The second and third verses are taken from stanzas 13 and 16 of the original poem. By omitting the episode in which Lamartine expresses his fears concerning the swift passage of time, Niedermeyer loses the contrast effect of the peaceful mood at the end, but he attempts to compensate for this by a somewhat heavy depiction of the roaring waves at the end of the introduction (Example 3).

Example 3: Niedermeyer, "Le lac"

The plan described obviously creates a piece more closely allied to the text in its introduction than in its romance section. Although Lamartine's language may be considered contemplative, it is too copious to fall neatly into the traditional strophic form. This limitation is clearly apparent in "L'isolement," where Niedermeyer's attempt to interpret musically the typically Lamartinian exuberant idealism ends in failure. In "L'automne" the composer seems to have tried to remedy this weakness through enlargement of the eight-line stanzas by repetition of the last two lines. The complete structure appears thus:

MUSIC:	Introduction	Romance					
		Strophe I	AB	ACC	Strophe II	AB	ACC
TEXT:	Stanzas I–IV	Stanza	V	VI	Stanza	VII	VIII

This scheme does not prevent the lines:

> Au fond de cette coupe où je buvais la vie,
> Peut-être restait-il une goutte de miel!

from having the same melody and accompaniment as:

> Moi, je meurs; et mon âme, au moment qu'elle expire,
> S'exhale comme un son triste et mélodieux.

As noted above, the relationship between text and music is closer in the introductions. The melancholy impression paradoxically produced at the beginning of "Le lac" by the use of the major mode is typically Romantic (Example 4).

Example 4: Niedermeyer, "Le lac"

The instrumental transition from the introduction to the romance proper also has a personal character; its resemblance to a passage from "Der Nussbaum" by Schumann (who was only a boy of fifteen when Niedermeyer's piece was published) is undoubtedly accidental (Example 5).

Example 5: Niedermeyer, "Le lac"

From the musical point of view, "L'isolement," "L'automne," and "Le soir" are at least equal to "Le lac," even though the connection between text and music is more superficial in those works. In the second strophe of "L'isolement," at the words:

> Ici gronde le fleuve aux vagues écumantes;
> Il serpente, et s'enfonce en un lointain obscur;

the attempt to imitate the waves in the accompaniment results in reminiscences of a Czerny piano étude. Sometimes there is even divergence between text and music, as in the passage given in Example 6, on the following page, which offers incontestable evidence of the composer's power of expression, although it is a flagrant contradiction of the poet's gloomy feelings.

The strong German influences at work on Niedermeyer, here clearly evident, may result from the fact that his musician father was born at Würzburg. Occasional traces of Zumsteeg, Beethoven, or even Schubert (although it is not certain that the composer knew the latter's *Lieder*) may be heard. In summary, Niedermeyer's songs may be considered as a partially successful attempt to infuse new life into the romance, an endeavor characteristic of an era when musicians were gradually becoming aware of the genre's decadence.

Hippolyte Monpou was another composer who was attracted by Romantic poetry. Probably the first to put the verse of Alfred de Musset to music, he also wrote numerous romances on texts of Victor Hugo. Biographical notices found in Fétis, Gautier, and Bachelin reveal that Monpou studied at Choron's school, where his

Example 6: Niedermeyer, "L'isolement"

teachers (among them Fétis) and his fellow students (Wartel, Duprez, and Scudo) considered him a rather mediocre talent. During the "Romantic year" of 1830, Monpou suddenly found himself in the vanguard of the new movement.[38] The publication of "L'Andalouse" (words by Musset) in September of that year immediately made him famous. Several *ballades* and *orientales* of Victor Hugo followed, as well as translations of German poems (e.g., Bürger's "Lenore" and Goethe's "Mignon"). Encouraged by his success in Paris salons, Monpou then tried his hand at opera, but his imperfect knowledge of the craft and his lack of dramatic power betrayed him. Most of his operas are merely a succession of pieces in romance style and their popularity was only short-lived. He died in 1841 at the age of thirty-seven.

Monpou's romances are often set in southern countries, Spain and Italy being equally his favorites. Sometimes the texts evoke the Orient or relate historical or legendary events of the Middle Ages. Not only the scenery but also the characters differ considerably from those of the traditional romance: clowns, bandits, odalisques, and other unusual types made their debut in Paris drawing rooms. At the same time, love was no longer expressed in a coquettish or sentimental manner, but with passion and realism.

Romantic versification posed difficult problems for composers. Monpou's predecessors set their music to isometric verses, using the balanced or "square" phrase, a melodic construction subdivided into groups of two, four, or eight measures. This squareness was altogether ineffective for the poetry of Victor Hugo or Musset, and Monpou was consequently forced to seek new solutions. The rhythmic and metric complexities of Romantic verse confronted him at the opening of Hugo's "Sara la baigneuse," where his setting is far from satisfactory; the musical prosody is questionable and the enjambment awkwardly handled (Example 7).

Example 7: Monpou, "Sara la baigneuse"

Some of Monpou's romances have an irregular structure even when this is not required by the poetic rhythm. The six-syllable lines of Musset's "Le lever" are rendered by a phrase constructed of a

group of three measures and by two groups of two measures each
(Example 8).

Example 8: Monpou, "Le lever"

"Unnecessary" changes of meter also occur frequently, as at the
end of "La chanson de la nourrice," an otherwise quite conventional piece (Example 9).

In the accompaniment Monpou likes to follow a long, uneventful
passage with sudden and rapid changes of harmony. Thus in
"Madrid" (Musset) the tonic chord of D major is sustained for

Example 9: Monpou, "La chanson de la nourrice"

Caricature of Hippolyte Monpou, 1840

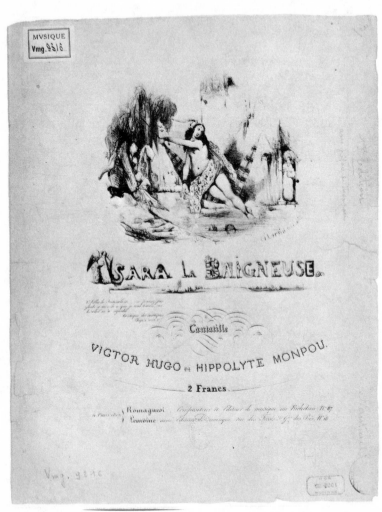

Title page of Monpou's "Sara la baigneuse"

twenty-one measures, then alternates with its dominant chord for ten measures. A passage in C major at measure 32 is followed by rapid modulations returning to the tonic D major. The final measures are again restricted to tonic and dominant harmonies. The harmonic rhythm may be schematically represented as follows:

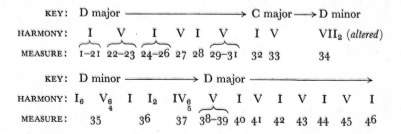

In the schematic:

KEY: D major ——————————→ C major ——→ D minor

HARMONY: I V   I V I V   I V   VII$_2$ (altered)

MEASURE: 1–21 22–23 24–26 27 28 29–31 32 33   34

KEY: D minor ——————→ D major ——————————→

HARMONY: I$_6$ V$_6^4$ I I$_2$ IV$_6^5$ V I V I V I V I

MEASURE: 35   36   37 38–39 40 41 42 43 44 45 46

Monpou's piano preludes sometimes show harmonic instability. In "La Juive" (Hugo) the initial measures suggest the key of G but at the final moment there is a sudden turn toward C major, whose tonic chord falls on a weak beat (Example 10).

Example 10: Monpou, "La Juive"

In "La chanson du fou" (Hugo) the prelude ends on the tonic D minor; the first verse then begins with the submediant B-flat major chord (Example 11).

A just appraisal of Monpou's romances is difficult to arrive at, since there is a temptation to attribute his bizarre inventions to awkwardness or lack of craftsmanship.[39] Nevertheless, there is sufficient evidence to show that the composer intended to break with traditional routines, and sometimes he succeeded. One can easily see,

Example 11: Monpou, "La chanson du fou"

for example, why the chivalrous aspect of "L'Andalouse" (Musset) made such an impression in the salons of 1830, despite the impoverished harmonic background that supports its melodic élan (Example 12).

Unlike Niedermeyer, Monpou valued the strophic form; in this regard he seemed to retreat from change (although he sometimes preceded the stanzas by a recitative, as for example in "Le clocheteur des trépassés"). Furthermore, he became more reactionary as he gradually overcame the technical difficulties of his craft. A piece like "La captive" (Hugo), published in 1841, is only distinguishable from those composed by Puget and Masini in its choice of poem. In a few of his last works Monpou seemed to be influenced by Schubert (e.g., "L'âme du bandit," "À genoux," and "Chanson du Triboulet"). A naïve, ballad-like character, to which the monotony of the accompaniment is well suited, distinguishes other romances (e.g., "Pauvre Hélène").

Among Monpou's friends was Gérard de Nerval, for whose idol,

Example 12: Monpou, "L'Andalouse"

the singer Jenny Colon, the composer wrote the opera *Piquillo*, with libretto by Nerval and the elder Dumas. The latter two, as well as Gautier and the engraver Célestin Nanteuil, were among the many literary and artistic figures who praised Monpou highly. Many musicians, on the other hand, criticized his bizarre inventions. In the musical press, "the Berlioz of the ballad," as he was called by Gautier, was sometimes violently attacked. One critic mocked the extravagance of his title pages:

Here there is a black, horned devil, waving his infernal torch in one hand and in the other carrying through the air a pale woman hanging by her long tresses. Elsewhere there are body-snatchers who violate the graves of the dead by the light of the moon, while a griffon (terrier) of Mephistophelian aspect runs madly through the cemetery's open graves ... the whole accompanied by those letters that are generally called "Hu-gothic," with downstrokes of uneven height, quite reminiscent of the crude characters traced by children's inexperienced hands or of ancient inscriptions half-eroded by the weather.⁴⁰

In spite of his sarcasm, this critic may hardly be considered a member of ultra-conservative circles, since he dares speak out in favor of freer melodic construction and considers Monpou's use of unequal measures to be entirely justified. But a chord of G♯-B-D-F against a D♯ in the vocal part (in a passage at the end of Bürger's *ballade* "Lenore") exceeds the permitted limits and he considers it "neither diabolic, fantastic, terrible, sinister, nor frightening in any way; it is merely deplorable!"

The Word "Mélodie" Designating a Vocal Piece

Dictionaries, encyclopedias, and other musical literature offer little information on the origins of the word *mélodie* as the designation for a type of song. The dictionary of the Académie Française (7th ed., Paris, 1878) still lacks this new meaning of the word. Nor does René Brancour's detailed article in *La grande encyclopédie* (Vol. 23, Paris, [1886–1902]) mention the *mélodie* as a vocal piece, although the author was hardly a musical amateur. The same is true of the Escudier *Dictionnaire de musique*, even in the fifth edition, "revised, corrected, and considerably enlarged" (Paris, 1872). Littré's *Dictionnaire de la langue française* (Paris, 1887) says that the term "is often used, although wrongly, as a synonym for romance, [e.g.] the *mélodies* of Schubert." The same year Bescherelle's *Dictionnaire national ou universel de la langue française* appeared with unreserved acceptance of the term's new connotation, although it added several erroneous comments to the definition:

A title given to several musical works, in which case it is often used in the plural, as in this quotation from Voltaire: "The *mélodies* of Lulli and Rameau are different." ⁴¹ A romance performed by a voice or solo flute, or a sacred choral work sung and accompanied at the unison, are *mélodies*.

Georges Kastner gave a detailed explanation of the term as early as 1866 in his *Parémiologie musicale de la langue française* (pp. 126–127):

In our time the name *mélodie* has been given to the principal part (the expressive and continuous melody) of a composition, to distinguish it from the harmony and accompaniment; but the term also applies to a type of vocal composition of a rather arbitrary outline, which by its style and atmosphere falls midway between the French romance and the German *Lied*. It was under the title of *mélodies* that our publishers issued the type of songs called *Lieder* beyond the Rhine; no doubt the popularity enjoyed about ten years ago in Paris salons by *mélodies* of Dessauer and especially of Schubert, has not been forgotten. Lamartine's *Harmonies* and *Méditations* provided our composers with the opportunity to rival German masters in this genre. How many *mélodies* blossomed from these poetic harmonies, beginning with "Le lac," which had such success with Niedermeyer's music! The poetry of Victor Hugo, Alfred de Musset, Théophile Gautier, and Émile Deschamps likewise served as inspiration for *mélodies* written by more or less famous composers. Such was the favor afforded this vocal form about fifteen years ago, that the shallowest of *chansonnettes* did not hesitate to borrow the title in order to attach some importance to its wretched pretensions.

Charles Soulier (*Nouveau dictionnaire de musique illustré*, Paris, 1855) defined the *mélodie* as "a sort of romance of a cantabile and melodious construction, distinguished by sweet and piquant inflections. Fr. Schubert invented this new type of vocal piece about twenty years ago."

Most twentieth-century writers ignore the problem, while others generally agree that Berlioz was the first composer to call his short vocal pieces *mélodies*. Michel Brenet (*Dictionnaire de musique*, Paris, 1936) insists, however, that the word was introduced at the time Schubert's *Lieder* were first published in France, a few years before Berlioz' use of the term in 1835. Both Schubert and Berlioz undoubtedly contributed to the acceptance of this new musical term; but the more complicated circumstances surrounding the eventual adoption of the name are generally ignored in musical literature and require a more detailed explanation.

In the years between 1808 and 1834 the Irish poet and musician Thomas Moore published a large number of poems adapted to popular Irish airs. The songs appeared in ten numbers and a supplement under the title *A Selection of Irish Melodies, with Symphonies and Accompaniments by Sir John Stevenson, Mus. Doc., and Characteristic Words by Thomas Moore, Esq.* (accompaniments to the ninth and tenth numbers were actually arranged by Henry R. Bishop). Moore's use of the title *Irish Melodies* makes clear his intention that words and music were to be considered a unity. Although the patriotic Irish texts were less than flattering to the English people, the songs were immensely popular all over Great Britain. Moore's own account of his travels to Scotland in 1825 (chiefly to visit Sir Walter Scott) includes a charmingly modest description of the enthusiastic acclaim he and his *Irish Melodies* enjoyed there:

> He [Scott] and I and Thomson went to the theatre, and I could see that Scott anticipated the sort of reception I met with. We went into the front boxes, and the moment we appeared, the whole pit rose, turned towards us, and applauded vehemently. Scott said, "It is you, it is you; you must rise and make your acknowledgement." I hesitated for some time, but on hearing them shout out "Moore, Moore," I rose and bowed my best for two or three minutes. This scene was repeated after the two next acts, and the *Irish Melodies* were played each time by the orchestra.[42]

Moore often sang the melodies himself in a "slight but agreeable voice."[43]

> The manner in which he sang them in London drawing rooms contributed more than a little toward making them admired and applauded by the very persons whom they damned. ... Translated into all the European languages and even into Latin verse by an Englishman, they spread the name and glory of the author everywhere; in French we have two translations.[44]

Moore's memoirs testify also to the international reputation he enjoyed. The entry for January 12, 1825 complains that he was being "pestered with letters from all parts of the world. The other day received four, from New York, Frankfort, Paris, and Birmingham."[45] Outside of Ireland and England, however, the tunes were less well known than the texts.[46] In France several composers set Moore's poems to music, borrowing the title *mélodie* from him. Pauline Duchambge, for example, wrote a "*Mélodie* in Imitation of Thomas Moore"[47] (published about 1829) which is in no way distinguishable from her romances. Berlioz' *Neuf mélodies imitées de l'anglais* are closely related to the romance, except for one of the collection entitled "Élégie." During the last years of the Restoration *mélodies* were written to other types of texts too (e.g., the collection issued by Janet in 1827, called *Mélodies romantiques* and probably containing folk songs).[48]

At this stage of its development *mélodie* had almost the meaning of "air" (signifying a tune) and came close to the German *Weise*.[49] Since "air" had long been used to designate a selection from an opera, oratorio, or cantata, the new name had the advantage of avoiding confusion between the two meanings. Before 1830 the term *mélodie* was often qualified by adjectives indicating regional or other special characteristics. Among the numerous examples of this practice in the musical press of the time are "Mélodie romantique" with words by Breuil, music by Vimeux; *Mélodies polonaises*, a collection of ten romances, *chansonnettes*, and mazurkas with music by Albert Sowinsky; *Mélodies dramatiques* for one to three voices with piano by Antoine Bessems; and "Mélodie hébraïque" with poem by Henri O'Neill and music by Barrault de Saint-André.[50] Like the air of the seventeenth and eighteenth centuries, the *mélodie* also existed as a purely instrumental composition, sometimes called "Song without words" (e.g., "Un soupir, mélodie sans paroles pour le piano" by S. Thalberg, published in *La France musicale*).[51]

At first critics regarded the *mélodie* as no more than a modest little piece. In reviewing Théodore Labarre's *Huit romances, chansonnettes et nocturnes* (1830), an anonymous commentator wrote of one of the songs: "'Le contrabandier' is much more than just a *mélodie*; it is a dramatic *scène*."[52] Another critic, discussing Edmond de Coussemaker's *Six mélodies*, mentions the "unpretentious title" under which the composer offers his "six charming romances."[53] Gustave Carulli affixed the title *Mélodies* to a collection of songs for three equal voices intended for the use of boarding-school students.[54]

Most of these *mélodies* are simple romances; some have a quasi-folklore character (e.g., *ranz des vaches* or *mazureck*). Clearly, the name *mélodie* still bears the same value as *barcarolle, ballade, nocturne, cantatille*, etc., and remains entirely in the domain of the romance. Only after Schubert's *Lieder* were published in France did the *mélodie* develop into an independent genre.

Schubert and the German Lied

The first French translations of German *Lieder* appeared in *Alfred*, the very mediocre adaptation of Goethe's novel *Wilhelm Meisters Lehrjahre* made by Charles-Louis de Sévelinges (1802).[55] Six *Lieder* by Reichardt were added to the novel, the translator explaining that "all the romances found in this work have been translated according to the German rhythm so that they may be sung to the airs composed by the famous Reichardt."[56] The French text is actually rather well adapted to the music, although Sévelinges has occasionally modified the rhythm of the vocal part. But his efforts can only be regarded as a free fantasy rather than as a strict rendering. A caricature such as the following cannot be excused or explained in any other way:

> Bon troubadour, sans nul souci,
>   Peut se mettre en voyage;
> Partout il trouve un doux abri,
>   Partout joyeux visage.
> Le châtelain le fait chanter,
> Fillette accourt pour l'écouter.
>   Que faut-il davantage? [57]

This romance in "troubadour" style is supposed to be a translation of the famous *Ballade* "Der Sänger":

> Was hör ich draussen vor dem Tor,
>   Was auf der Brücke schallen?
> Lass den Gesang vor unserm Ohr
>   Im Saale widerhallen!
> Der König sprach's, der Page lief;
> Der Knabe kam, der König rief:
>   Lasst mir herein den Alten!

Reichardt's "romances" remained virtually unknown in musical circles and no German *Lieder* appear to have been published in France during the Empire and Restoration periods. Several French composers did, however, set poems translated from the German (e.g., Amédée de Beauplan's music to "Marguerite," a rather free adaptation of Goethe's "Gretchen am Spinnrade," from *Faust*).[58]

In the autumn of 1833 Richault published some of Schubert's best-known songs in *Six mélodies célèbres avec paroles françaises par M. Bélanger de Fr. Schubert*.[59] A short time later the same publisher issued "Le roi des aulnes" ("Erlkönig" by Goethe), also translated by Bélanger.[60] In 1834 or 1835 Prilip issued four new Schubert *mélodies* translated by Sivol.[61] A collection of *Six mélodies de Schubert* with French words by Crevel de Charlemagne and Italian words by Di Santo Mango was issued by Schlesinger in 1839 or 1840. Since a copy could not be found, its exact contents are unknown.

After 1840 Schubert *Lieder* were published in large numbers, the principal translators being Émile Deschamps and Bélanger (e.g., *Œuvres musicales de Schubert*, Paris, Schlesinger, 1839–40, containing twelve songs with French words by Deschamps and *Quarante mélodies de Schubert*, Paris, Brandus, 1850, with texts by the same poet).

Richault was among the most active publishers in the field, issuing no less than 367 *mélodies* between the years 1840 and 1850, all translated by Bélanger and some of them also appearing in Italian translation. This enumeration is far from complete.[62] The Bibliothèque Nationale possesses many French versions of Schubert *Lieder*, both printed and manuscript. Many carry no date and few of the translations are signed.

During the same period several of Beethoven's *Lieder* also appeared in French, among them "Le chant de la caille" ("Der Wachtelschlag" by Sauter)[63] and the cycle *À la bien-aimée absente* (*An die ferne Geliebte* by Jeitteles).[64] Alfred de Musset's "Rappelle-toi," based on an anonymous German poem entitled "Vergiss mein nicht," was published "with words set to Mozart's music" in a collection called *Voyage où il vous plaira, par Tony Johannot, A. de Musset, etc., avec musique* (Paris, Hetzel, 1843). The music to "Rappelle-toi" was, of course, falsely attributed to Mozart, having since been established as the work of Georg Lorenz Schneider.[65]

The French were interested in contemporary German music as well as in earlier works. In 1840 several of Heinrich Proch's *Lieder* appeared with adaptations by Castil-Blaze and Bélanger. Proch was highly esteemed by his contemporaries and even considered by the Paris press to be the equal of Schubert. The most famous of his songs was "Le cor des Alpes" ("Von der Alpe tönt das Horn"). Another favorite composer was Joseph Dessauer, whose collection *Chant de voyages*, set to Ludwig Uhland's poetry, evoked some discussion in 1835.[66] During his long stay in Paris Dessauer also wrote *Lieder* and romances to original French texts (by Émile Barateau, Maurice Bourges, Victor Hugo, and others).[67] These songs were characterized by a combination of technical features derived from several sources: the strophic form came from the French romance, the extensive epilogues and rich harmony from Germany, and the embellishments in the vocal part were incontestably of Italian origin. Ferdinand Hiller and Friedrich Kücken also composed *mélodies* to French words during their sojourns in Paris.[68] Three collections by Mendelssohn appeared in Paris in 1846, 1848, and 1849.[69] Schumann's songs were not known in France until the Second Empire, when the singer Stockhausen introduced them on March 26, 1855.

The fame of Schubert's songs spread rapidly in France, in large part due to the publicity given them by Adolphe Nourrit, the greatest singer of the Romantic period. Nourrit's interest in the

Lieder was first awakened during a performance of "Erlkönig" by Liszt (the *Lieder* were often arranged for piano solo and were actually even better known in France than Schubert's original piano music). The great manifestation is vividly described by Nourrit's biographer Quicherat:

I am happy to have gathered this unknown information from one of my friends who was present at the first revelation of Schubert's songs to Nourrit, at the home of M. Dessauer, a Hungarian banker who was a friend of Liszt. The latter was at the piano playing "Erlkönig" when Nourrit entered. All the more reason to continue. Nourrit was all ears. As he became aware of this dramatic music, he showed deep emotion and his face lit up. When the piece ended, he requested that it be played again, but Liszt replied that it would be better if he sang it. Nourrit excused himself on the grounds that he did not know German. When Liszt explained the text to him, the singer agreed to merely vocalize the melody, which he did with the expressiveness of an inspired interpreter; *longumque bibebat amorem*. From that day on, he was taken with an intense passion for those songs; at his request a certain number were translated and he became their indefatigable propagator.[70]

In January 1835, as part of a program at the Société des Concerts du Conservatoire that also included Beethoven's Third Symphony, Nourrit sang "La jeune religieuse" ("Die junge Nonne" by Craigher) with orchestral accompaniment. Although Nourrit had performed the "Ave Maria" at Loïsa Puget's concert the previous month,[71] this was probably the first opportunity for a large Paris audience to hear a Schubert *Lied* and Fétis' review reports that "this piece produced an intense effect on the audience."[72] Several performances followed, but Nourrit was temporarily too occupied with the stage to devote as much time as he would have liked to his chosen mission. After his rupture with the Paris Opéra he expressed a desire to dedicate himself entirely to the *Lied*. In a letter to Ferdinand Hiller dated October 26, 1836, he explained that he was "leaving the Opéra and giving up the theater. ... After that, I shall retire into my shell and sing for my pleasure Schubert, Hiller, in short all my Germans whom I love."[73] He took advantage of his freedom to make Schubert known to the provinces. One of the high points of his tour was the concert in the large theater of Lyons, where, accompanied by Liszt, the singer performed "Le roi des aulnes" ("Erlkönig" by Goethe), "Les astres" ("Die Sterne" by Fellinger), and "Sois toujours mes seuls amours" ("Sei mir gegrüsst" by Rückert). The

Frontispiece illustration by Célestin Nanteuil for Clapisson's "Le jugement du Diable"

Adolphe Nourrit

local press sang Nourrit's praises, avowing that he aroused even stronger emotions than opera could awaken.[74] During their stay in Lyons the two artists performed together daily at the home of a mutual friend and Liszt himself reported of Nourrit that "he declaimed Schubert's *Lieder* with so much power that he projected us into outbursts of enthusiasm that were gradually communicated to our intimate audience."[75]

In Marseilles similar feelings prevailed:

A *mélodie* entitled "Les astres," which we had never heard before, produced such an effect that it was immediately requested again. There was such an elevated emotion in the singer's voice and in the soul of the piece, that we remained dumbfounded and as we write Nourrit's powerful voice is still vibrating in our ears. ... It makes one believe in God.[76]

Nourrit considered certain *Lieder* (e.g., "Abschied" by Rellstab, "Geheimes" by Goethe, "Ständchen" by Rellstab, and "Auf dem Wasser zu singen" by Stolberg) too intimate for performance in large halls. Until the end of his tragic life, the singer found consolation in Schubert. According to several of his contemporaries, Nourrit's interest in Schubert's *Lieder* extended to their texts.[77] Dissatisfied with Bélanger's translations, he constantly modified them, sometimes even going so far as to translate directly from the original words of a *Lied* (e.g., "La jeune religieuse," in a manuscript at the Bibliothèque Nationale dated 1835 and signed "Ad. N."). The explanation of how a man who knew no German could perform such an astonishing feat is furnished by a letter Nourrit wrote in 1835:

I have procured some of Schubert's new songs, which are magnificent. The [prose] translations which you gave me have served me well and I have succeeded in arranging them in verse under the music, which is beautiful enough to do without beautiful poetry. How happy you must be to know German! Because if you knew how to sing you could unite the poetry of Goethe with the inspirations of Schubert. Teach me German and I shall teach you how to sing. That's a bargain.[78]

French adaptations of German *Lieder* are often severely criticized and not without cause, since even the cleverest versifier cannot always surmount the particular problems raised by translations intended for singing. Of primary importance is the necessity of adhering strictly to the succession of ideas and poetic descriptions, in order to retain the close relationship between text and music. Secondly, musical prosody requires that the rhythm and number of syllables be identical with those of the original lines. Finally, the physiological aspects of singing must be considered (e.g., acute vowels should not be placed on high pitches).

Such musical considerations are more important than purely literary values. A strict rendering of the poem's contents is of secondary importance and often the translator is not even capable of one. The many *Lieder* chosen for translation were generally selected with an eye for the music only, the beauty of the text having little influence. Although Paris salons were captivated by Schubert's music, they undoubtedly received a false impression of the verse. This may explain why France's discovery of the *Lied* failed to stimulate interest in German poetry. The true literary value of the *Lied* was revealed some years later in the translations of Nerval, Xavier Marmier, and Henri Blaze.

The two most important translators of Schubert texts each represented a distinct style: Bélanger the clever librettist, and Deschamps the often inspired poet. The former proceeded in the manner described above, serving the music first, although sometimes to the detriment of literary considerations, as in Goethe's "Rastlose Liebe," where the original:

> Dem Schnee, dem Regen,
> Dem Wind entgegen,
> Im Dampf der Klüfte
> Durch Nebeldüfte,
> Immer zu! Immer zu!
> Ohne Rast und ohne Ruh!

became, by Bélanger's hand, under the title "Toujours":

> Charmante amie,
> A toi ma vie,
> Ma foi chérie,
> Jamais trahie;
> Tu seras mes amours,
> Mes amours toujours!

Almost nothing remains of the impetuosity of the original text, even though Goethe's rhythm is scrupulously imitated. Bélanger obviously attaches extreme importance to the rhyme, a relatively unimportant element in adaptations for singing. While the rhyme has an important auditory function in recited poetry, its value, unless reinforced by a musical rhyme, is much more restricted in music, which is all sonority. For this reason later translators often rendered German texts in blank verse.

Diametrically opposed to Bélanger's concepts were those held by the "theoretician" of Romanticism, Émile Deschamps, who forcefully proclaimed that "the time for imitating is past; one must either create or translate."[79] He closely followed the German text, sometimes added a detail, but rarely omitted one. He further aimed at writing verses that were purely French, i.e., that satisfied the requirements of the language's prosody.[80] These claims forced him either to make numerous rhythmic modifications in the melodic line or to allow musical accents to fall on weak syllables. An example of the latter procedure appears in his translation of "Die Forelle," which otherwise, from a purely literary point of view, is admirable (Example 13).

Example 13: Schubert, "Die Forelle" ("La truite," translated by Deschamps)

The efforts of Bélanger and Deschamps were judged by their contemporaries in quite divergent ways. One critic expressed tempered admiration for Deschamps' translations and inveighed against Bélanger without actually naming him:

Thanks to M. Émile Deschamps, the melodious bard of "Le roi des aulnes," "Marguerite au rouet," and "La belle meunière" is going to strip away the ridiculous tawdry finery in which the lyric poets [i.e., the translators] have dressed him. It is really impossible to imagine anything more surprising than the inventions to which Schubert's music has given inspiration. Never before has poetry been so misused by music publishers. And to be sure, one might wonder how they managed it, translating Schubert into such rhymes! The same Schubert who only composed his music when inspired by Goethe, Schiller, Schlegel, Rückert, or Wilhelm Müller, which, incidentally, is sufficient response to those who claim that beautiful poetry cannot be allied with beautiful music.[81]

It is easy to criticize. The author of this article does not grasp the delicate problems inherent in translation intended for singing. Blaze de Bury makes a similar error, unfairly comparing Deschamps' adaptations of Schubert's *Lieder* with the purely literary translations that the poet had published earlier in his collection *Études françaises et étrangères*, naturally arriving at the conclusion that the latter are of much higher quality.[82]

The Parisian public of 1835 seems not to have agreed with today's assessment of Schubert as a composer endowed primarily with an unequaled power of melodic invention. In his review of the memorable concert in which Nourrit sang "La jeune religieuse," Fétis expressed this opinion of the *Lied*:

It is certainly not without merit; however, its weakest feature seems to me to be its melody. All the composer's attention is focused on the portrayal of the storm by the orchestra, and the voice appears only as a sort of recitative with little effectiveness. A song-like phrase that ends each strophe of the romance is practically the sole melody to be found and even this phrase is more remarkable for its expressiveness than for the novelty of its form.[83]

As a judge of contemporary music Fétis certainly did not equal his role as a historian, but in this opinion he did not stand alone. Berlioz was another who did not consider Schubert a master of melody, although he valued him all the more highly for this very reason.[84] In the domain of melodic writing, Rossini's style was generally considered as the norm and this prejudice was difficult to combat. Some critics did recognize Schubert's melodic talent, but considered the new and surprising element of his songs to be the relatively important role of the instrumental accompaniment: its harmonic richness, its close relationship with the vocal part, and the characteristic motivic rhythm. These attributes are continually mentioned, while references to the pure beauty of the melodic line are relatively rare. Legouvé rhapsodized:

He has introduced science into the romance. ... See "La religieuse" ..., "La truite," "La barcarolle!" How intimately the accompaniment is joined with the melody! How they form a unity together! How the accompaniment joins forces with the voice to make the poet's thoughts fly straight to their goal![85]

Another critic writes:

Reichardt was the first to give this type of music that variety, that richness of harmony in the accompaniment, that distinguish it from the French romance. ... The great merit of Schubert's work resides in the profoundly poetic conception of the words, the originality of the melodies, the novelty and beauty of the harmonies, and above all, in the close relationship between the song and its accompaniment. The many to whom the latter quality is only a fault claim that a melody written for a solo voice should even be able to do without an accompaniment. This principle appears to us to be entirely false. We are far from believing, however, that the accompaniment must render the meaning of each word, that a tremolo is absolutely required for the word "thunder," that "river bank" cannot properly be presented without an undulating movement, and that the word "trumpet" must never be encountered without imitation of that instrument; it is far from our intention to transform the *Lied* into descriptive music and thus materialize the art. But we must defend the principle that is the basis for Schubert's accompaniments: that a summary of the poem, its character, its various feelings, in a single word, the *color* of the poetic thought, must be rendered as much by the accompaniment as by the voice. Schubert's *mélodies* are dramatic; they are not at all songs intended to be sung by *grisettes* or in the guardroom, to which they are as unsuited as Lamartine's beautiful poems would be.[86]

This quotation shows clearly that Schubert's *Lieder* were considered to have a dramatic rather than a lyric character. Fétis spoke of "Die junge Nonne" as "a dramatic romance" and Joseph d'Ortigue deplored the neglect accorded Schubert's operas, insisting that "with such melodic ability, capable of such strong expressiveness, it is impossible that Schubert would not have written masterpieces for the stage."[87]

The Mélodie after Schubert

The development of the French *mélodie* was naturally affected by the concept of Schubert's *Lieder* that was prevalent in France. The composer's influence on French song may be said to have had both negative and positive aspects, for while the prestige of the romance was undermined at its very foundations, the genre of the *mélodie* simultaneously acquired definite rights of French citizenship. The "revolution in drawing-room music"[88] created by Schubert's songs could neither be ignored nor denied. Partisans of the romance, among them the critic Henri Blanchard, who had composed many romances in his youth, tried vainly to protect their favorite from the baneful foreign influence:

What is happening to the romance? What will become of it? Will it be transformed into a *Lied*? Will it grow longer, acquire more modulations? Or will it remain simple, naïve, and as characteristic as it has always been of our national taste, just as the bolero is the expression of Spanish music?[89]

Elsewhere Blanchard wrote sadly of the romance:

It is with regret that we see it distorted, losing its freshness, its melodic and especially its harmonic simplicity, and finally going somewhat out of fashion, after having shone for so long with a radiant brilliance in Parisian salons.[90]

Legouvé said unequivocally of Schubert that "he has killed the French romance. ... After you have feasted on this bountiful and satisfying music, try if you can to fall back on the twittering of Mlle. Puget; it is impossible."[91] This judgment was undoubtedly somewhat premature, since the romance still had many partisans. In *La France musicale*, which became their organ of protest, one writer argued unconvincingly that "the *mélodie* will not kill our romance because the French romance also has its value."[92]

Blanchard's enduring faith in the national genre was noted above; but his basic objectivity on the sensitive subject is clearly apparent from his humorous remarks on "the revolution in the salons," published in the New Year's Eve number of the *Revue et Gazette musicale* of 1840. The personified musical types, Mr. Requiem, Lady Symphony, The Lied, etc., are holding a heated discussion, each complaining of the other to "Mr. Eighteen Forty-One":

THE ROMANCE: I am eminently French and I beg you to protect me, to take my side.

1841: Against whom?

THE LIED: Mein Gott! Against me, who haf replaced her. I am as light-headed as she, ant more so; I am fresher dan she. I haf peen Schubert's faforite chilt ant now I am de same von Proch ant von Dessauer.

1841: Enough, enough. Despite your accent, we grant you civil rights here until you become naturalized.

THE LIED: I ton't vant to be naturalizet; I vant to remain Cherman.

1841: Well then, remain German.

THE LIED: But I vant to lif in Paris, zing in Paris, enchant Paris.

1841: Then live in Paris, sing in Paris, and enchant Paris.

THE LIED: Put I ton't vant de romance to tell me dat she gafe me birt, dat I come von 'er.

1841: Oh, what a stubborn head! Settle it between you. Get married; from your union only something lovely could result.

THE LIED: She iss too olt.[93]

Yet this aged romance prolonged its existence for another twenty years. The title "romance" soon disappeared, but among the *mélodies* published during the Second Empire are many old-style pieces, dressed up with the new name solely for commercial purposes.

The positive aspect of Schubert's influence is more important. The choice of the name *mélodies* for Schubert's *Lieder* (by Richault?) carried this designation to a higher level. After 1835 the "air" type of *mélodie* disappeared and there arose a new kind of *mélodie* which may be characterized by four features:

I. THE STRUCTURE. Strophic form is no longer obligatory, many *mélodies* having a free structure or schematic form. A *mélodie* by Adolphe Vogel for two voices, entitled "Le souvenir,"[94] offers an example of the latter type, in which the construction follows this plan:

STRUCTURE:	A	B	C	A¹	B¹ (extremely varied)
TONALITY:	E minor	E major	A minor (modulating)	E minor	E major

In instances where composers still use the strophic form, the musical strophes are extended to include several stanzas of the poem.

II. THE VOCAL PART. The square phrase is not always respected; sometimes the vocal part is treated like recitative. In the *mélodie* "Sisca l'Albanaise" (published in the *Album 1841 de La France musicale*), Halévy combines the principle of the square phrase with a vocal part in recitative style (Example 14).

Example 14: Halévy, "Sisca l'Albanaise"

III. THE ACCOMPANIMENT. The piano assumes a more important role in the musical interpretation of the text and sometimes even takes the lead in this respect (e.g., Halévy's "Sisca l'Albanaise," above). Orchestral effects are frequently used, since the art of writing an expressive accompaniment adapted to the character of the piano was not yet very advanced. The rhythmic motifs so characteristic of Schubert's accompaniments appear only in the songs of Clapisson, who, aside from numerous insignificant romances and *chansonnettes*, wrote some *mélodies* of a much higher quality. Among the latter, "Le vieux Robin Gray" (words by Florian)[95] has an initial motif that dominates the entire piece. The triplet figure gives this *ballade* a pastoral coloring and an artless character that suits the genre better than the theatrical pathos displayed by Concone, Vogel, and many others (Example 15).

Example 15: Clapisson, "Le vieux Robin Gray"

IV. THE TEXTS. Interest in verse of high literary value is continually increasing. Composers begin to set poems of Victor Hugo, Lamartine, and Gautier, whose free structures, run-on lines, and broken meters required the abandonment of the square-phrase principle. Romantic poetry also forced them to emphasize the accompaniment, in order to allow it to suggest musically what remains unexpressed in the poem. Among the first composers to be attracted to Romantic poems was Edmond de Coussemaker, who, as early as his *Six mélodies* (1834), included two *orientales* of Hugo along with poems by Paul de Kock. Coussemaker's *Huit mélodies* (1838), containing texts by Hugo, Lamartine, and Marceline Desbordes-Valmore, were severely criticized by Blanchard for the composer's nonchalant attitude toward musical prosody.[96] In spite of this shortcoming, the erudite musicologist may be said to have actively fostered this reform in his youth.

Not all *mélodies* written during the July Monarchy conform to the above description, since the romance and even more, the dramatic or expressive *scène*, continued to exert some influence. Donizetti's *Rêveries napolitaines* (1838), for example, are written entirely in the style of the *scène*, while his collection of *Matinées musicales* (1842) contains several romances.[97] Adolphe Vogel's "Satan" appeared in the *Album 1842 de La France musicale* carrying the rather startling generic subtitle of "Blasphème." It also possesses some characteristics belonging to the *scène*, in spite of its strophic form. But whereas Donizetti's accompaniments play only a secondary role, those of Vogel contribute significantly to the expression. This minor Romantic composer has a predilection for experiments in the harmonic domain. The way in which he juxtaposed chords that are the interval of a third apart from each other (*Terzverwandschaft*) is quite audacious (Example 16).

Unlike Donizetti's dramatic and expressive *scènes*, the French *mélodies* of his compatriot Rossini have rather the character of the Italian *canzonetta*. In "Nizza" and "Beppa la Napolitaine," both on texts by Émile Deschamps, the sustaining function of the accompaniment is reduced to a minimum. The vocal part is richly melodic and heavily embellished. The same is true of "La séparation" (words by Méry), although this piece is called a *mélodie dramatique*. On the whole Rossini's contribution to the development of the French *mélodie* was minor.

Je jet-te mon blasphè _ _ _ me à ta di.vi.ni.té

Example 16: Vogel, "Satan"

Besides Halévy's "Sisca l'Albanaise," cited above, the *Album 1841 de La France musicale* contains two other remarkable pieces, "Viens" by Ambroise Thomas, and "L'hirondelle et le prisonnier" by Pauline Garcia. "Viens" is divided into identical long stanzas (of seventy-two measures each) followed by a coda. Since the poetic lines are not all of the same length, the composer attempts to balance the musical phrases by repeating parts of them and by prolonging some notes. Elsewhere he destroys this balance by instrumental interruptions and long interludes. Since the result exceeds the compass of a romance, it may be considered a *mélodie* even though it is not designated as such. The same is true of Pauline Garcia's song, but for other reasons. This *mélodie* is schematically constructed of six-line stanzas, each containing twelve measures and ending with a double bar. From a musical point of view, the stanzas differ greatly from each other, only an elemental waltz rhythm tying them together.

In spite of their attempts at reform, the composers discussed played only a modest role in the history of the French *mélodie*. More important because of the intrinsic value of their work and for their influence on the masters who followed them are Berlioz, Meyerbeer, and Liszt. The works of these eminent representatives of music in the Romantic era will be discussed in a later chapter, after the consideration of several musico-literary questions which now follows.

CHAPTER II

Some Observations Concerning the Literary Aspects of the Mélodie

HISTORICAL SKETCH OF THE THEORY OF PROSODY[98]

> *Car notre idiome, à nous, rauque et sans prosodie,*
> *Fausse toute musique; et la note hardie,*
> *Contre quelque mot dur se heurtant dans son vol,*
> *Brise ses ailes d'or et tombe sur le sol.*
>
> T. GAUTIER, "La diva"

NO LANGUAGE OF WESTERN EUROPE PRESENTS MORE DIFFICULT problems in the rhythmic relationship between words and music than French. Since the middle of the sixteenth century musicographers have been formulating contradictory theories on the subject. Composers, however, have generally had little to say about problems of musical prosody, with the exception of Grétry, Saint-Saëns, and d'Indy. Consequently the historical summary presented here is based chiefly on the theories of writers who were not primarily creative musicians. The procedures followed by composers in actual practice will be discussed in the course of the analysis of their works.

41

The Burden of Syllabic Quantity Imposed on Song

When the polyphonic chanson gave way to the air de cour toward the end of the sixteenth century, musical prosody was still under the influence of the humanistic movement. Antoine de Baïf's metrical principles were transferred to music by Claude Le Jeune, Eustache du Caurroy, and Jacques Mauduit, whose chansons mesurées à l'antique are among the major achievements of French humanism. Their feat is all the more remarkable because Baïf, who started with little accurate historical knowledge of linguistics, believed that French verse, in imitation of the metrics of antiquity, was composed of alternating long and short syllables. French, however, was not born from the language of Virgil, Ovid, or Horace, as he believed, but derives instead from the Latin of the decadence, in which the tonic accent played a very important role and verse possessed almost the same laws that later governed French poetry (i.e., syllable-counting and rhyme).

Some contempories of Baïf and of his disciples sensed intuitively that the recommended division into measured syllables could not be adapted to the spirit of the French language. Although the principle of quantity was not condemned a priori, those who analyzed humanistic poetry objectively were forced to admit that the distinction between long and short was very vague. But this criticism is no longer valid when poems are sung; since tempo is determined in advance, music has the power of giving an absolute duration to syllables and thereby establishing their quantity. Departing from a principle that is inexact from a linguistic point of view, one arrives, thanks to music, at an esthetically satisfying result. In this connection, Masson rightly concluded that "the copy is more accurate than the original."[99]

In the relationship between poetry and music may be found another paradox, that measured verse destroys musical meter. Only in a free rhythm, not submitted to the regular alternation of strong and weak beats, may a melody succeed in representing the true quantity of syllables. In such a case music no longer possesses independent meter, the latter having become the slave of the ruling word, even in cases where the bar suggested by the time signature includes the entire line of verse. For example, in the fragment from an air (dating from 1615) by Pierre Guédron[100] shown in Example 17, each line is rendered by a total value of nine quarter notes:

Example 17: Guédron, "Cette Anne si belle"

The time signature $\frac{9}{4}$ would be incorrect in this instance since it would imply a constant division of three times $\frac{3}{4}$, in which case the "mute" *e* of "Anne" would fall on a strong beat, while the note G on the word "si" would take on the character of a syncopation. In reality the subdivision is dependent on the words:

WORDS	Cette	An – ne	si	bel – le
MELODY	C	G A	G	E D
SUBDIVISION OF THE MEASURE	2/4	2/4	2/4	3/4

In the second strophe, however, the subdivision has been regularized:

WORDS	Son Lou –	ys sou –	pi – re
MELODY	C G	A G	E D
SUBDIVISION OF THE MEASURE	3/4	3/4	3/4

In the early stages of their development, the *airs de cour* and related types still show clear traces of the *chanson mesurée à l'antique*. Verse was set to music according to humanistic principles even when the poetry was not based on supposed antique meter. The above-quoted air by Guédron, of which the words are by Malherbe, is such a case. Not until the first half of the seventeenth century did music slowly regain its rights under the influence of the dance, so that the so-called "quantity" no longer exists except in theory.

The influence that humanism still exercised in the seventeenth century is revealed in a treatise of the Dutch scholar Isaac Vossius, *De poematum cantu et viribus rythmi*, which appeared anonymously in 1673. Taking a very conservative position with regard to the question of prosody, Vossius goes so far as to defend the thesis that music must use only two types of values, half notes and quarter notes, in order to attain the classic unity of melody and verse:

All those notes of which music is comprised today, *maximae, longae, breves, semibreves, minimae, semiminimae, fusae,* and *semifusae,* are useless contrivances as barbarous as their names. If we wish song to be beautiful and pleasant, we must be quite careful that each syllable be expressed by its own note. Since there exist only short and long syllables, and since, as has often been said, the short syllable consists of one beat and the long of two, it is thus improper to use either more or less than two types of notes, corresponding approximately to the so-called *minimae* and *semiminimae.* Besides, who has ever conceived of syllables of eight, sixteen, or thirty-two beats, or of syllables so short that no one can pronounce them? Who would not laugh at hearing a syllable sung on a note so prolonged that one could easily recite two or three epic verses while it lasts? Let us then eliminate these signs of degeneracy and if music still holds our affection, let us follow the example of the ancients in this domain as in others. Indeed, if we succeed in restoring rhythm and the clear diction which inevitably accompanies it, so that the pristine form and beauty of music return, all the wretched rubbish of today's music—ornaments, warbling or trills(?), fugues, syncopations, and other contemptible artifices—will vanish like shadows and mist at the rising of the sun.[101]

Vossius is lost in sterile academicism. The *maxima* and *longa* of which he speaks had not been used for centuries. Moreover, he fails to take into account the fact that notes do not have an absolute duration but depend on the tempo indicated. He was undoubtedly thinking of the *tactus* of mensural notation, which indicated a "standard" tempo by its integral value. In trying to reform the music of his day with the aid of obsolete principles of the fifteenth and sixteenth centuries, the famous scholar merely demonstrated that he was more familiar with earlier treatises than with current musical practice.

During the eighteenth century the principle of quantity was still the point of departure for research into the relationship between words and music.[102] However, some attention was also paid to grammatical accent, although with admittedly negative results at the start. Jean-Jacques Rousseau denied the existence of the accent with the claim that it is not manifest in the rising pitch of the voice:

We believe our language has accents, but it has none. Our so-called accents are only vowels or signs of quantity; they do not mark any change in pitch. The proof lies in the fact that these accents are all expressed either by uneven meters or by modifications of the lips, tongue, or palate that distinguish one sound from another, but not by modifying the glottis, which provides the various pitches. Thus, if our circumflex is not simply a sound, it indicates a long syllable or it has no meaning at all.[103]

Rousseau then shows that the Greek language *did* possess a melodic accent, referring to the writings of Dionysius of Halicarnassus.

In the above quotation the words "or it has no meaning at all" must not be overlooked. Rousseau's doubts concerning the real existence of syllabic quantity in the French language, added to his categorical denial of accent, lead him to conclude that French is the antimusical language *par excellence*. But he also denies the existence of the accent in other European languages, even Italian: "Like French, Italian is in itself not at all a musical language. The difference is only that the latter lends itself to music, whereas the former does not."[104]

Elsewhere Rousseau attempts to explain why the French language cannot be united with music. He emphasizes the deficiencies in the sound of vowels: a muffled tongue produces a shrieking music.[105] Furthermore, the large number of consonants impedes the flow of the melody: "If you try to hurry the tempo a bit, its movement resembles that of a hard and angular body rolling over the pavement."[106]

·A point not mentioned by Rousseau is that these inconveniences, to which may be added the endings -*an*, -*on*, -*en*, and -*in*, as well as the notorious mute *e*, become advantages when put to the service of the most characteristic quality of the French language, its clarity. When he mercilessly criticizes the monologue from Lully's *Armide* in order to confirm his theories, he omits any mention of the composer's prosody, which is generally very precise. Instead, Rousseau violently attacks the static nature of this recitative, and especially the pompous cadences that are so uncharacteristic of Armide's state of mind. The philosopher claimed to be attacking French music, but in reality his barbs were aimed at the musical esthetics of Lully's time.

Rousseau's *Lettre sur la musique françoise* (1753), and particularly his astonishing conclusion that "the French have no music," caused an enormous stir. Among the many pamphlets discussing the philosopher's radical musical ideas, few have any value, since the authors were merely reacting to wounded national pride or motivated by personal malice. Nevertheless, Rousseau's attacks served to stimulate investigation into the relationship between words and music and during the second half of the eighteenth century several treatises on prosody appeared, of which a few merit brief examination.

During Rousseau's lifetime the esthetician Michel-Paul de Chabanon published a "Letter on the Musical Properties of the French Language," [107] in which he suggests that public opinion shares three different views on this subject:

1. The French language is musical, but Lully created the only music possible with it.
2. Although this language lends itself to the flexibility of modern singing (i.e., the Italian style), it is unsuited to the dignity of the Opéra.
3. No good music can please the French and they are condemned never to sing.

Chabanon himself believed in none of the three concepts, but considered music as more independent than was generally supposed, an autonomous and universal language that cannot be influenced by any national speech patterns:

In the act of pronunciation, the most prosodic or accented language possesses only a few measurable intervals. In music, however, all intervals may be measured and must be; all its notes are subservient to the laws of harmony and melody. How, then, can one make that which is always singing submit to that which never sings?

Thus, in principle Chabanon denies the existence of a melodic relationship between language and music. In only one respect does he admit the dependence of the melody on the words, namely in the domain of prosody. Still using quantity as his point of departure, he asserts that composers are too often unaware of its importance, and gives several examples. In the *Stabat Mater* of an unnamed composer (undoubtedly Pergolesi), the phrase "cujus animam gementem" is rendered by a series of syncopations:

$$\cup - \cup - \cup - \cup \cup$$
Cujus animam gementem
$$\cup - \cup - \cup - \cup \cup$$
Contristatam ac dolentem
$$\cup - \cup - - \cup -$$
Pertransivit gladius.

Chabanon sensed the contradiction present here between linguistic and musical prosody, but its true cause escaped him. Obsessed by the notion of quantity, he believed that the lines of the *Stabat Mater* were composed of classical trochees and that Pergolesi had mistakenly set them to music as iambs. Of course there is no question of short or long in this medieval poem; the syllables are alternately accentuated or unstressed and Pergolesi's error lay in making the syncopations accent the unstressed syllables too often.

Le devin du village is similarly criticized, Rousseau's rendering of the lines "J'ai perdu mon serviteur" and "Si les galans de la ville" by a series of notes of equal value being considered a condemnable leveling of syllabic quantity. Chabanon adds: "M. Rousseau, that ardent defender of the privilege of language, must have realized that music also has its privileges, since he disregards the quantities of a language that he speaks and writes so well." Chabanon's conclusion is curious:

> The observance of quantity is, for music, an impediment from which it attempts to free itself as far as possible. But this obstacle would disappear if there existed a language whose vague, indefinite, flexible, and changing prosody would lend itself to the composer's needs. The words of such a language would have no fixed or actual value. Its longs would be more or less long, its shorts more or less short; many syllables would be neither long nor short, they would resemble the syllables *ut, re, mi, fa, sol, la,* and *si,* which Italian, French, or German musicians pronounce long or short according to the requirements of the melody.

In spite of his being basically too attached to academic traditions to abandon the principle of quantity, Chabanon must have unconsciously felt the need for such a step since he projects his ideal onto an imaginary language in which quantity no longer plays a role. He continued to explore the ideas expressed in his letter, the investigations culminating some years later in a more detailed work entitled *Music Considered for Its Own Sake and in Its Relationships with Speech, Languages, Poetry, and the Theater.*[108] In addition to the problems previously considered, Chabanon discusses the "square" phrase, which was to exert so strong an influence on the prosody of the nineteenth century:

> In the phrasing of songs it is generally agreed that cadences, especially in opening phrases, should be placed at regular intervals, and that each phrase should contain an even number of measures. ... The regularity of

our mechanical bodily movements may perhaps be the cause for this feeling, which makes us sense the meter, just as the symmetry of the human structure is the secret principle behind our desire for all order and symmetrical arrangements.

Unlike some later theoreticians, and in spite of his acknowledgment that reasoning is based on such regular physiological phenomena as the heartbeat, Chabanon is still somewhat doubtful about the validity of the principle of the square phrase: "I do not know what to think about this principle; the ear has such a strong tendency to follow it that one might consider it a natural intuition. And yet, it permits such happy exceptions that one is tempted to refuse it the power of a law." Among the "thousands" of exceptions he knows, Chabanon cites the reprise of the air "Je suis Lindor," by Dezède, which ends with a five-measure phrase.[109]

André Grétry's observations on prosody are based in part on the precepts of the Abbé Batteux. In his well-known work *The Fine Arts Reduced to a Single Principle* (1746), the latter had recognized only two kinds of music, of which one paints (e.g., a storm, a brook, or a zephyr) and the other reproduces the intonations of the human voice.[110] Although Grétry agreed with this dichotomy, he strove in his own music for a melodic line imitating spoken language, preferring this to such physical effects as "rain, wind, a hailstorm, the song of birds, earthquakes, etc."[111] At the same time, Grétry was too much a musician to tie himself to the word. He approved of the "square" phrase, meaning phrases made up of four measures or multiples thereof, believing that "symmetry of phrases is necessary to make [instrumental] music suggest dancing. In vocal music it is no less useful to the melody to square the phrases as often as possible."[112]

Scattered throughout the composer's *Mémoires* are remarks on the esthetic and technical aspects of prosody. Grétry believes that syllabic quantity is not a sufficient norm for the composer:

The rhythm of French verse is not very perceptible; the poet must derive movement from the meaning of the words, for unless he has paid the utmost attention, the longs and shorts of one line will not correspond at all with those of the next line. And even if the poem were to establish a consistent rhythm, it would be a hindrance to be compelled to follow it, because I believe that in the course of time continuation of the same movement would cause unbearable monotony.[113]

Like Chabanon, Grétry cites the beginning of Rousseau's air "J'ai perdu mon serviteur" as an example of a poor rendering of text rhythm, but he adds that it would be impossible to change the phrase without harming the song.[114] In his first French opera, *Isabelle et Gertrude* (Geneva, 1767), written to a libretto by Favart, Grétry elides the mute *e* in several places so as to imitate spoken

Example 18: Grétry, *Isabelle et Gertrude*

language more closely (Example 18). The procedure had been recommended to him by Voltaire,[115] but in his later works Grétry no longer followed the philosopher's advice.

The opinions expressed in the *Mémoires* are generally sounder than those found in other sources of the time. Since he was above all a craftsman, Grétry did not burden himself with sterile formulae and unmanageable theories. Unfortunately, his thoughts were noted down in an improvisatory fashion, so that they lack logical coherence.

About 1800 a treatise entitled *La prosodie musicale* was published by a certain Lamouroux. A detailed description of the work, which appeared soon afterward in the proceedings of a scientific society, gives a broad view of the author's theories.[116] Lamouroux still mentions quantity, but solely from the linguistic point of view. Syllabic quantity is to be rendered by strong and weak beats:

Musical prosody consists of the agreement of melody with words, that is, of the correspondence of the strong or weak musical beats with the value of the syllables of each word. ... Thus, for the musician, understanding of the syllabic quantity consists, in general, of merely placing the strong beats on long syllables and the weak on short syllables.

This point of departure is still acceptable to a musician, but in later passages Lamouroux reaches an impasse by exaggerated simplification and over-elaborate schematization. He defends a thesis according to which musical beats are always alternately strong or weak, deriving this theory, like Chabanon, from our physical organization:

The movements of the lungs, the heart, and the arteries of the animal organization must long ago have given man the feeling of musical rhythm. The latter movement appeared to him in both song and dance, always divided into two beats, the down and the up. He then became convinced that since the up beat is only the suspension of the down, the latter is much more marked, much more accentuated than the other. Thus arose the alternate strong and weak beats, and musical rhythm.

The reader of this specimen of naïve reasoning is inclined to ask how this principle of alternation would be applied to the ternary measure of a minuet, for example, but apparently Lamouroux does not answer this question. His error becomes even graver when he extends the thesis to versification, which he also places under the rule of alternation:

In all regions, the art of versification has reflected differences or variations in peoples' customs; but if it were possible to make a musical trip around the world in all the different ages, I am sure one would conclude that alternation is a principle of nature and that the prosodic accent of all languages has been obliged to conform to it. Being unable to procure examples for comparison, we have restricted ourselves to our own language, and having actually found that its prosodic principle is alternation, we have come to the logical and correct conclusion that our poetry is essentially iambic.

Lamouroux tries to demonstrate the presence of alternation in French *verse* by scanning several *words*:

$$\overset{-\quad\cup\quad-}{\text{ap – pe – ler}} \qquad \overset{\cup\quad-\quad\cup}{\text{j'ap – pel – le}}$$

$$\overset{-\quad\cup\quad-}{\text{pro – me – ner}} \qquad \overset{\cup\quad-\quad\cup}{\text{pro – mè – ne}}$$

$$\overset{-\quad\cup\quad-}{\text{chan – ce – lier}} \qquad \overset{\cup\quad-\quad\cup\quad-\quad\cup}{\text{chan – cel – le – ri – e}}$$

He fails to consider the fact that in a line of verse, two or three unstressed syllables ("shorts") could easily follow each other, as in a sequence of monosyllabic words like: "Je ne le dis qu'à vous." Lamouroux scans the line in this manner:

$$\overset{\cup\quad-}{\text{Je ne}} \mid \overset{\cup\quad-}{\text{le dis}} \mid \overset{\cup\quad-}{\text{qu'à vous}}$$

His error lies in designating the quality of a *word* by a term belonging to versification (i.e., saying that a verse is iambic when it is formed of "iambic words"). The examples intended to prove the truth of this strange theory are, moreover, badly chosen:

HEXAMETER: Grand Dieu, | tes ju – | ge – ments || sont rem – | plis d'é – | qui – té

PENTAMETER: Je suis | Lin – dor, | ma nais – | san-ce est | com – mu – || ne

QUADRIMETER: Ah! que | je fus | bien in – | spi – ré – || e

TRIMETER: Je ne | le dis | qu'à vous

DIMETER: Dans no – | tre a – si – || le.

Only in the last-quoted example (dimeter) do the strong and weak syllables happen to fit the iambic scheme. Lamouroux' theory is *a priori* inapplicable to uneven meters. He resolves this difficulty in a radical manner by arbitrarily designating the first syllable as long and making it precede the first foot. He also offers the possibility of entering the initial syllable in the first foot, which then takes the name of "amphimacer" (−∪−), the inversion of amphibrach (∪−∪).

The only syllables that Lamouroux considers as incontestably long are monosyllabic nouns and syllables with circumflex accents (e.g., *fête, gîte, tâcher, prêter*). The penultimate of three-syllable words is the only one that is always short, on condition that it consist of a consonant followed by a vowel, by preference a mute *e*. All other syllables are doubtful, that is, the composer may place them on a weak beat, according to what is suggested by the "oratory" accent. The real existence of the language imagined by Chabanon is demonstrated here. In spite of serious objections to Lamouroux' theories, which seem entirely outmoded and even illogical, he should be acknowledged as the first theoretician to recognize the vagueness of the notion of quantity in French verse and accept its consequences. With the tonic accent clearly in mind, he preserved the name of quantity while strongly undermining its importance. His unfortunate failure was caused by submitting the accent to a fictitious alternation.

Theories of Scoppa and Castil-Blaze; the "Square" Phrase

The growing doubt concerning the existence of a syllabic quantity was bound to result in the complete negation of the principle.

Probably the first to replace the concept of quantity with that of intensity was Scoppa, who in 1803 presented a work with the long explanatory title of *Treatise on Italian Poetry in Relation to French Poetry, in Which Is Shown the Perfect Analogy Between these Two Languages and the Similarity of Their Versification: In It One Discovers that the Prosodic Accent Is the Source of the Harmony of French Verse; and the French Language Is Defended Against All the Unjust Accusations Made by J.-J. Rousseau in His Letter on French Music.* Scoppa bases his discussion primarily on the Italian language, in which he distinguishes three types of words: *tronco, piano,* and *sdrucciolo,* meaning words accented on the final, penultimate, and antepenultimate syllables, respectively.[117] He insists, however, that French does not contain words of the *sdrucciolo* type, although it does have the other two. He therefore advises composers to be aware of this:

> One may distinguish *piano, tronco,* and *sdrucciolo* types of measure in music, just as one finds them in all verse; recognition of this helps one to understand the errors of some poor musician, who, taking some piece of Italian music set to pretty *sdrucciolo* verses, tries to apply it to French poetry also. He tires, frets, and being unable to attain the impossible, gives vent to slanderous abuse against his art, instead of laying the blame on his own ignorance; for he is unaware of the fact that this *sdrucciolo* music can only fall on *sdrucciolo* words, of which the French language is absolutely devoid.[118]

Although the broad outlines of Scoppa's theory lent a solid basis to musical prosody, serious difficulties were still encountered in practice. To begin with, the tonic accent of French words is quite weak, so that it may be deplaced to an atonic syllable under the influence of the "oratory" or emphatic accent. In a word like "jamais," *tronco* according to Scoppa, the accent often falls on the first syllable instead of on the last. Thus the prosody in the excerpt from a French folk song given in Example 19 is quite correct:

Ja. mais je ne t'ou. blie.rai

Example 19: "Le rossignol" (folk song)

The tonic accent may also be deplaced to avoid a collision, as in the case of "C'est joLI" and "JOli bois." Furthermore, a difference in intensity exists between two accents of a single word or of a group of words. Often the accent on the last syllable is weaker than on the antepenultimate, as in "MERveilleux," "MÈne-moi," or "SOM-bres lieux." Later theoreticians like Castil-Blaze and Louis Roger[119] mistakenly concluded from this that the French language does contain *sdrucciolo* words, not realizing that in such cases the tonic accent depends on the "oratory" or emphatic accent and that the examples cited by them do not fall into the same category as the Italian words "NApoli," "diMENtico," and "sorRIdere." The instability of the tonic accent was probably the reason why the fictitious quantity had dominated the theory of literary and musical prosody for two centuries and a half and why, even after Scoppa had rejected quantity, detailed guide lines for the relationship between music and poetry could not be established.

The greatest obstacle to correct prosody, however, arose from a purely musical precept, that of the "square phrase" mentioned above in connection with Grétry. The periodic structure of phrases occupies an important place in the musical esthetics of the first half of the nineteenth century. Fétis, for example, considers the square phrase an indispensable condition for the creation of a good melody:

> The ear is struck by an impression of the number of measures, without actually counting. Out of this arises the ear's need for repetition and if it is satisfied in this respect, a new type of rhythm, based on the symmetry of the phrase, becomes apparent to the ear. This rhythm constitutes the *phraseology*, which in music is designated as "squareness of phrases." ... The more similar the arrangement of the rhythmic elements of each measure, the more satisfying the new rhythm is to the ear.[120]

Phrases and half phrases need not always contain an even number of measures; a ternary rhythm of phrases, analogous to triple meter, may be used. But a group of five measures is considered less pleasing, this rhythm being "the least simple and consequently the weakest for the ear." The regularity of the phraseological rhythm should not be broken; an isolated three- or five-measure phrase in the midst of other regular phrases will always be "shocking to the delicate ear." In summary, Fétis requires of a melody that it fulfill three conditions: "Tonal agreement, rhythmic symmetry, and numerical symmetry."[121]

On the surface, the square phrase appears entirely consistent with French poetry; indeed, theoretically the symmetry of the number of measures corresponds approximately with the constant number of syllables that is the main feature of French verse. Example 20, taken from a romance of Méhul, shows clearly, however, that a continual displacement of accents breaks the balance between the verse and the musical phrase:

Example 20: Méhul, "L'infortunée Lyonnaise"

In the first stanza, the sixth syllable of the first line (Âme) has a tonic accent, as does the seventh syllable of the second line (éPOUX). Consequently Méhul has placed them both on strong beats. The corresponding syllables of the second stanza are, however, atonic (l'aVEnir and EST) and are thus abusively accented by the musical rhythm at the expense of the syllables avenIR and CRIme. Clearly, strict strophic form cannot coexist with correct prosody.[122] If the rhythm of the poem determined the musical rhythm of the *chanson mesurée* of the sixteenth century, their roles are now reversed, for the rhythm of the melody here destroys the poetic rhythm.

Many romance composers attempted to avoid this difficulty by changing the musical rhythm of each stanza so that accents would fall on strong beats. Although successful in itself, this solution could not please the theoreticians, among whom Castil-Blaze was most notably preoccupied with problems of prosody. His translation of Da Ponte's libretto for Mozart's *Le nozze di Figaro* and his study *De l'opéra en France*[123] provided him with the opportunity to submit sung poetry to both practical and critical examination. Toward the end of his life he summarized his ideas in two voluminous treatises, *L'art des vers lyriques* (1857) and *Molière musicien* (1852). In the latter work he quotes a pertinent passage from *Le bourgeois gentilhomme* (Act I, Scene 2):

M. JOURDAIN: This song seems somewhat gloomy to me; it puts me to sleep and I wish you could liven it up a little here and there.

MUSIC MASTER: It is absolutely necessary, Monsieur, that the tune be adapted to the words.

Using this quotation as a springboard, Castil-Blaze examines prosodic problems:

There are two ways of making the text agree with the melody. The first concerns the feeling of the images and the emotions that they indicate and announce, and which the composer must express and paint by the powerful means of his art. The second consists in making the words move along steadily and freely under the vocal line, while observing the rules of punctuation with sufficient exactitude so that the grammatical sense is not changed. The first of these conditions is almost always fulfilled by our musicians. They can give a brisk and brilliant pace to airs written to lively words and can darken their colors or retard the movement of their compositions if the literary work serving as theme for the melody is sad or melancholy in nature. Our composers would fulfil the second condition more easily if there existed verses that move freely and continuously. Instead, our poets too often give them rhymed prose, without rhythm, cadence, or meter.

How, then, is one to follow Molière's precept? Consider an air whose smallest fragments are drawn with all gracious regularity of rhythm and meter. How can we possibly adjust an air of such elegant symmetry to the insipid jumble, the lifeless and unpolished prose, the mess produced by our librettists? Such elements are incompatible with all regular melody; the composer sees it immediately and, despairing of making them agree with his songs, he breaks, tortures, massacres those rebellious words, and spreads their deplorable shreds over the music.[124]

Castil-Blaze considers the choruses from Racine's *Athalie* (set by many composers, including Servaas de Konink, Moreau, Schultz, Gossec, and Boieldieu) entirely unsuited to music; in the unrhymed prose of the Psalms he finds analogous qualities, "the same sublimity of thought, the same poetic turn; but you would search in vain for meter, rhythm, cadence, exquisite symmetry, sectional identity, exact repeat, and the obligatory accents that are the essentials of true verse, the verse that is appropriate for music."[125] In the chanson and romance of his day he sees the same unfortunate conditions:

The French, who for so many centuries have produced such a quantity of songs, so many thousands of charming pieces and verses both happy and

melancholy; the French, who consider themselves the creators of this type
of poetry—are they devoid of feeling for rhythm and meter? They have a
marvelous capacity for writing chanson texts but are unable to render them
singable. Instead of adjusting the lines to measured verse, they write in
rhymed prose. Not one of their romances or chansons can be performed
without either the melody or the text being mangled.[126]

The charging of blame to the poet alone in the conflict between
music and words is indicative of music's domination during the
epoch of Meyerbeer, Auber, and Halévy. In the directly opposite
eighteenth-century attitude, the composer had generally been
blamed. After his examination of the negative characteristics of
poetic texts, Castil-Blaze presents his own suggestions for the writing
of good lyric verse:

Accent is what defines the lyric poem. The first line is always good, but if
those that follow are to be equally good, if the ear is not to suffer from those
sudden movements of "prose," the accents must be placed squarely in the
places indicated and marked in the first line, where the patterns are chosen
by care or by the happy chance of inspiration. Once adopted, this pattern
must continue with unvarying conformity. The least license or divergence
ends in the vernacular, in stammering prose; all poetic energy disappears;
you creep, limp, flounder like our lyric poets Racine, Quinault, J.-B.
Rousseau, etc. etc. ... [Music] demands complete symmetry of meter, which
I grant her. No equivalents, always exact duplicates; always three pennies,
never six halfpennies. Melody does not permit additions in order to make a
balance; it insists on a series of small amounts, round, square, oval, or tri-
angular, that must be symmetrically arranged on the page. The music of a
stanza thus arranged takes form in the composer's eye.[127]

Finally, Castil-Blaze refers again to the notorious mute *e*. He
quotes Voltaire's comments to Grétry (see p. 49 above) expressing
his dislike for pronunciation of the mute *e* as *eu* and questioning its
use in music: "Will it sound better in music than in simple speech,
where it is never heard?" This is Castil-Blaze's answer:

Unquestionably no, my kind and quite unmusical Voltaire. But this mute
e, this *eu* which distresses you, and many others also, this *e* which is the object of your contempt, is very valuable to the librettist. If this mute *e* did
not exist in French, it would have to be invented for [vocal] music. This
very precious *e* is the treasure of our lyric poets, even their anchor, alas, their
sole salvation. We have only the mute *e* for the semi-cadences and these,
with respect to full cadences, appear regularly in the proportion of three to

one. For this reason three feminine rhymes should almost always, or at least very often, precede the masculine rhyme in poetry intended for music. What makes both Provençal and Italian so lovely is that these most poetic and musical languages possess four mute vowels: *a*, *e*, *i*, and *o*. These sounds give a wonderful variety to word endings in feminine rhymes.[128]

What Castil-Blaze mistakenly sees as mute vowels are simply unstressed syllables, for neither Provençal nor Italian has mute vowels. The following stanza is among the several examples he gives of lines that illustrate his precepts:

> Séchez vos larmes,
> Loin des alarmes,
> Goûtez les charmes
> D'un sort plus doux.
> Comptez sans cesse
> Sur la promesse,
> Sur la tendresse
> De votre époux.[129]

Castil-Blaze believes that instrumental music offers proof of his theory, since "music personified in the voices of its flutes and violins has revealed its will and its laws by expressing itself in measured verse, wonderfully rhythmic and well-sounding, but devoid of words." Along with examples from Haydn and Weber, he cites the opening of the Allegretto movement of Beethoven's Seventh Symphony:[130]

— ∪ ∪	— —
E E E	E E
E E E	E E
E E F♯	G G
G G G	G
G G A	B B
F♯ F♯ G♯	A A
E E E	E E
E F♯ G♯	A

To have Beethoven establish the rules of French versification is certainly pushing the dictatorship of music to the extreme! Here again Castil-Blaze lets himself be carried away, since the periodic phrase used so often by the Viennese masters is not purely musical in origin, but derives from the dance.

The theories of Castil-Blaze enjoyed little success, neither poets nor librettists being willing to forego one of the most attractive elements of French verse, the arbitrary placement of the accents. He did, however, influence other theoreticians, among them the Lyons lawyer J. Lurin, who raised the same objections against the poetic rhythm of verse intended for music, although the solution that he offered was somewhat different. Taking up the humanist theory once more, Lurin recommends the construction of French verses with feet of four syllables instead of the two established in the ancient system.[131]

Ducondut in his *Essay on French Rhythmics* and Fleury in "Concerning Rhythm in Poetry Set to Music"[132] agree entirely with Castil-Blaze. Fleury recommends absolute symmetry of verse rhythm. He disapproves of the practice (followed by romance composers) of adapting musical rhythm to the displaced tonic accents of the various stanzas. Since the fault in such cases lies entirely with the poet, the composer should not submit to him. Fleury, however, was solely concerned with the *cantique*, a type of music which, in view of its religious purpose, must be simple and synoptic.[133]

The experiments of André van Hasselt, described in 1863 by Fétis,[134] were more interesting. While still conserving rhythmic symmetry, this Belgian amateur endeavored to break the monotony of poetry by employing not one, but several caesuras. But this attempt came too late, since the square phrase was no longer used with such strictness in the second half of the century.

Imperfect Prosody at Mid-Century; Sterility of Musical Rhythm

The conflict between words and music became very acute about 1850. Several writers testify to the degeneration of prosody and singers' abominable diction. Gilbert Duprez' opera *Jeanne d'Arc*, first performed in 1865, contains an astonishing number of prosodic errors. Louis Roger's review of the *première* sharply criticizes the vocal instruction offered by Duprez, a former rival of Nourrit:

I have been present on several occasions at lessons given by Monsieur G. Duprez in the rue Turgot. Once in a while I would notice very bad mistakes among the examples he gave his students. I am not speaking about breaking prosodic rules, but those of simple usage. ... For example, he allowed only a single syllable to the word *rouer*, which always has two, according to all our poets and rhyming dictionaries.[135]

In a pamphlet intended as a "Guide to French Musical Prosody for the Singer," Charles Beauchemin accuses certain singers of transforming the mute *e* into the *o* or *eu* sound. This ridiculous practice, he says, enriches the French language with such words as *patrio* and *amio* or *patrieu* and *amieu*.[136]

Saint-Saëns regarded operetta as the cause of the degeneration of prosody, especially since Jacques Offenbach, the great master of this genre, was of foreign origin. As an example of Offenbach's misusage, Saint-Saëns quotes a phrase from *La belle Hélène*:

> Et VOI-là comme
> Un GA-lant homme
> Évite tout désagrément.[137]

Even conceding that operetta exercised a baneful influence on the romance and the chanson, another culprit must be sought for the *mélodie*. Fétis' precepts were acceptable in principle so long as a composer limited himself to Classic and pre-Romantic poetry; but these theories no longer answered the needs created by the rhythmic innovations of Victor Hugo and his followers, because the square phrase cannot be made to fit the run-on line and the arbitrary caesura. The romance of earlier days was intended for singing, the poet making allowances for the needs of the composer, or at least being presumed to do so. The poetry of the Romantics, on the other hand, was purely literary. Even in his *Chansons à mettre en musique* (Songs to be Set to Music), Alfred de Musset makes no concessions in the avoidance of technical difficulties for the composer's sake, as shown in this example of enjambment:

> Beaux cheveux qu'on rassemble
> Les matins, et qu'ensemble
> Nous défaisons les soirs!
> MUSSET, "Le lever"

Beauchemin, like Roger, tried to combat the boredom of poor prosody by establishing more flexible rules, but he seems to have been unaware of the fact that only liberation of the phraseological rhythm could resolve the problem.

On this essential point it was Maurice Bourges who placed the emphasis where it belonged. In his excellent article describing "The Present Melodic Situation," he underlines the dangers of rhythmic sterility:

The principles underlying melodic writing lead us aimlessly in the same circle. ... If the variety of movements, the nuances of expression, and the resources of the accompaniment were not more subtly exploited here than in other countries, we would already be sadly satiated with this excessively prolonged reign of the phrase that is divided only by two or four, always marching in coupled pairs. Most certainly this procedure has some merit in itself when it is not abused; it is lucid, distinct, intelligible at first approach, and logically arranged. But is this really the only way to interpret the doctrine of squareness? Is it not possible to extend the range of this principle in order to break down the terrible monotony of melodies of sixteen or twenty-four measures each, further subdivided into groups of two or four, all of equal meter? In bestowing the periodic *cabalette* on us, Italy gave us a fine present, but the gift is poisoned; opium is just as charming and dangerous for the Chinese.

To improve the situation Bourges believes that musical rhythm must necessarily be developed in an analogous manner to that of poetry:

Rhythmically free strophes, with their lines of varying meters, like those conceived by Ronsard, du Bellay, and Rémy Belleau, have been revived today by Victor Hugo and his school, so rich in skilled versifiers. The dynasty of alexandrines, endlessly following each other two by two, falling with perpetual uniformity, no longer wields the poetic sceptre alone. Ears that were numbed by this continual resonance are beginning to awaken to new kinds of rhythm. So great was the ear's need to steep itself at all costs in the unexpected, that the enjambment, that notorious run-on line, that was the cause of so much ink and bitterness being wasted, has acquired passionate defenders for some time now. There is no doubt that musical fatigue regarding the current system of regular phrases is such that a similar phenomenon must infallibly recur, according to an imperious law of reaction, if in fact it has not already manifested itself in several eccentric works that unfortunately are examples of sterile license, rather than of productive freedom.

Bourges advises composers to study folk tunes like the cachucha of Andalusia or the mazurka of Poland, since these will lead to the discovery of novel rhythms. He calls rhythm "a still unexplored region where there are enormous discoveries to be made" and he praises Hippolyte Monpou in this regard:

Some parts of his operas and especially of his ballades and romances provide ample evidence that he was trying to regenerate the musical sentence without, however, depriving it of an indispensable regularity. Starting as a pioneer in a domain needing to be conquered, Monpou fell before his time; no one can estimate what he might have done, but the tendency remains indicated.[138]

Bourges' ideas were not likely to find an immediate echo among his contemporaries, since his article appeared in 1846, at a time when few were aware of the crisis besetting French music. (In this connection Berlioz, a stranger in his own country, may legitimately be considered irrelevant.) Some seven years later even the formerly conservative Henri Blanchard took up Bourges' suggestions:

The intellectual servility of Italy's *signor poeta* must cease, for monotonous verse and rhythm necessarily produce melodic monotony. ... Composers, tell your writers: "Poets, surrender to your genius if you have any, to your imagination, to the Romantic caprice that interrupts the rhythm and the pauses, and marks arbitrary punctuation, just so long as your sentiments are sincere and passionate, whether in love or in religion."[139]

Restoration of Prosody; Purism toward 1900

The developing interest in rhythm was reflected in the *Traité de l'expression musicale* (1874) by the Swiss Mathis Lussy, who spent almost sixty years of his long life in Paris. This well-known treatise is devoted in large part to rhythmical problems. Prosody is discussed in a separate chapter that includes a description of so-called rhythmic inversion, in which a masculine line is rendered by a feminine rhythm, the last syllable falling on a weak beat. The contrary is also possible, with the "mute" ending of a feminine line falling on a strong beat. Lussy illustrates this procedure in the excerpt given here in Example 21.[140]

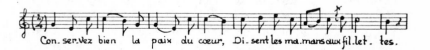

Con. ser. vez bien   la   paix du cœur,   Di. sent les ma. mans aux fil. let. tes.

Example 21: Inverted rhythms (Gaveaux) from Lussy

As a matter of fact, composers had already been permitting themselves such rhythmic license for a long time. In this example, however, there is a question whether a rhythmic inversion is really produced in the last two measures. If the fragment is regarded *metrically*, the last syllable of the word "fillette" falls on a strong beat. But from the viewpoint of *rhythm*, the long half note of the preceding measure destroys the force of the note B so that, in fact, the musical rhythm here is feminine, like the rhythm of the verse. The strength of the first beat of the last measure has only a purely optical value. The musical rhythm is actually more clearly delineated by fusing the two measures (Example 22).

Example 22: Alteration of the previous example

The disappearance of the balanced phrase as the fundamental principle of musical structure and the development of rhythm exerted a favorable influence on prosody, enabling Brancour to state that after Gounod practically all composers respect the rhythm of their texts.[141] The problems that had occupied French estheticians and theoreticians for three centuries appear to have been resolved to a large degree by the end of the nineteenth century.

Nevertheless, the development of prosodic theory was not entirely arrested. Under the influence of the Wagnerian principles of *Sprechgesang* and *unendliche Melodie*, several French writers and theoreticians, particularly Schuré, Combarieu, and d'Indy, attempted to formulate a theory that would unite poetic and musical expression. Combarieu's concepts were still rather timid, recognizing the autonomy of poetic as well as of musical rhythm. He criticized in principle both the complete servility of music with regard to the words (as in recitative, or continuous melody) and the composer's absolute arbitrariness in relation to his texts (as in Mozart's or Rossini's airs), admitting no compromise between these two extremes. To avoid this impasse, he developed a technical procedure in which the functions of voice and orchestra (or piano) are essentially distinct:

The conflict disappears thanks to a combination of which there is an example in the first scene of [Berlioz'] *Damnation*: only the vocal part—without ceasing to be a melody—sacrifices itself, that is, agrees to follow the text faithfully and model itself on it. The orchestra, among its other functions, retains those of restoring to music its liberty and offering it a field large enough for its rhythmic combinations.[142]

D'Indy goes farther in pushing to its extreme consequences the dependence of music on language. His point of view is illustrated in some excerpts from his textbook of musical composition:[143]

Musical notation serves to represent graphically the *language* of sounds, for the same reason and in the same way that writing represents the language of words. ... Accent is the point of departure for melody. ... In all ages the meaning of words has been associated with musical accent. The Greeks and Romans declaimed lyric poetry as a sort of song in which the voice of the orator was sustained by means of a rudimentary instrument that controlled its intonation. During the Middle Ages musical accent was once more associated with word accent in psalmody, the collective recitation of prayer on a single note (*chorda*), with simultaneous inflection of the voices on the last accent of each phrase. Both musical and spoken language are actually ruled in an identical manner by the laws of accent. Rhythmic patterns are the musical image of syllables, whose succession produces words and phrases. ... Our contemporary [dramatic] music has for its starting point the rhythm of the words as they are spoken and as they are sung. ...

When a cadential formula is repeated at the ends of two corresponding phrases, either on the same or on differing notes, the result is a sort of musical rhyme, comparable in every way to poetic rhyme. Two rhyming periods may be consecutive (regular rhymes), or may be separated by an intermediary period (alternating rhymes) or even by two (tercets), etc.[144]

Such concepts as these of d'Indy led to exaggerated purism of prosodic theory, as exemplified in Henry Woollett's brief work on *Prosody for the Use of the Composer*.[145] The author presents an axiom with sixteen corollaries, from which the following are extracted:

The axiom: Strong syllables on strong beats, weak syllables on weak beats or on weak parts of beats.

Corollaries:

   1. Mute *e* on weak beats (or on half-weak beats in fast tempos).
   2. Mute *e* on values shorter than the preceding strong syllable, or equal

if the value is short and the strong syllable falls on the strong part of the beat.

3. Mute *e* on notes lower in pitch than the preceding strong syllable, or equal in pitch to that syllable.

4. Never place a mute *e* on an appoggiatura (and especially not on a vocalized passage).

6. Where a mute *e* is preceded by a vowel (as in "vie," "loue," "joue," or "haie"), the two syllables must be placed on two similar tied notes.

8. It is possible not to assign a beat to the mute syllable only in the ending -*aient* of the imperfect and conditional tenses. The same is true of the mute *e* appearing after a vowel within words like "loueront" and "paieront."

9. The appoggiatura should be used sparingly and only on strong open syllables.

10. Vocalises are a misconstruction. They may be permitted only as an element of local color in folk-song style, or as a means of musical depiction.

15. Proper names should be given prosodic treatment according to their pronunciation in their country of origin.

16. Repetition of words not suggested by the librettist is forbidden. The composer must always respect his text.

The composer who respects poetic rhythm but wishes at the same time to retain his musical liberty may accept these rules if he applies them in a flexible manner. Woollett, however, demands strict submission to his precepts. In the course of the treatise he points out "errors" in works of Gounod, Fauré, Charpentier, and Debussy, all of them composers known for the correctness of their prosody. In Example 23 from *Roméo et Juliette*, for instance, Woollett accuses Gounod of wrongly placing the mute syllable of *convie* on a strong beat:

Example 23: Gounod, *Roméo et Juliette*

In the analogous case of Example 21, Gaveaux appeared to respect the feminine rhythm by prolonging the penultimate syllable. In this Gounod example there is even more evidence in the composer's favor, since the mute *e* is sung on the same pitch and therefore is hardly noticeable. Vincent d'Indy is another victim of Woollett's dogmatism (Example 24).

Example 24: d'Indy, *Fervaal*

Here the descending interval in both instances makes the mute *e* sound weaker than the preceding syllable. Woollett's rules for the musical realization of feminine rhythm may be summarized in one word: relaxation. The various ways in which a composer may achieve this relaxation (without adhering to *all* the rules) are not even mentioned by Woollett. In the examples from *Fervaal* the desired effect is obtained because the rhythmic tension (the mute syllables falling on strong beats) is completely destroyed by the relaxation of the melody (descending intervals). In Example 25, a fragment from Berlioz' song "L'absence," relaxation exists in the harmony if not in the melody (at the point where the dominant resolves to the tonic chord), even though Berlioz disobeys rules 1 and 3:

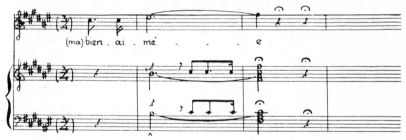

Example 25: Berlioz, "L'absence"

Even though most composers about 1900 did not share Woollett's purism, they still had such respect for poetic rhythm that they hesitated to set regular verse to music. A number of poets, dramatists, and composers made their opinions known in response to an inquiry organized by the journal *Musica*. The question submitted for consideration was "What should be set to music—beautiful poetry, poor poetry, free verse, or prose?"[146]

The poets Henry Bataille, Henri de Régnier, and Edmond Haraucourt preferred not to have their verse set to music: "I detest music" (Haraucourt); "From the poetic point of view, I prefer being recited to being sung" (Bataille). The Comtesse de Noailles' conservatism led her to the opposing opinion: "Poetry may be set to music; for this purpose, regular verses are the most beautiful." Composers answered at greater length. Ravel preferred free verse and prose to the regularity of Classic poetry:

> The latter, however, may permit very beautiful results, provided the composer is willing to efface himself completely behind the poet and agrees to follow his rhythms step by step, cadence by cadence, never displacing an accent or even an inflection. In a word, if the composer wishes to set regular verse, his music has to simply underline and sustain the poem, but not explain it or add anything to it.
>
> I believe it is better, if the composer is ever to express feeling or imagination, to set free verse. It actually seems criminal to me to "spoil" Classic poetry. ... Prose is sometimes very gratifying to set to music and there are some circumstances in which it is wonderfully appropriate to the subject. Thus, I have used several of Jules Renard's *Histoires naturelles*; they are delicate and rhythmic, but rhythmic in quite a different way from Classic verse.

Debussy also preferred prose, because "Classic poetry has its own life, an 'interior dynamism,' to quote the Germans, that does not serve our purpose at all. With rhythmic prose one is more at ease, one has more freedom in every way." Dukas believed that only prose was suitable for theater music, and considered the fusion of poetry and music as a fiction:

> Do not fool yourself, *poems cannot be set to music*. An accompaniment may be given to words, but that is quite a different thing. The first idea suggests a *fusion*, the second states a *parallelism*. ... Poetry and music do not mix; they never merge. ... I practice what I preach and never, never, have I adapted a melody to a single poem.

The responses indicate that free verse and rhythmic prose are generally preferred. Such an attitude is easily understood if one considers that at the precise instant when the composer is straining toward a perfected prosody, he destroys the regularity of the verse. If he maintains the poetic structure, his melody becomes too monotonous, too cadenced. If, on the other hand, he considers only the tonic accent and the syntactic structure, then he destroys the lines and makes prose of them. The logical conclusion is therefore that only heterometric verses and rhythmic prose lend themselves to musical rendition.

If Saint-Saëns had contributed to the *Musica* inquiry, his response undoubtedly would have differed from those of the other composers. In his correspondence with the poet Pierre Aguétant, several of whose poems he had set, the composer expresses his aversion to modern license in versification:

> Monsieur P ... finds -*ée* and -*é* to be the same thing, but that is not French and does not take account of the subtleties of the French language. They are the same in prose but not in verse, unless one adopts a system of reading verse like prose, which is barbarous. ...
>
> You are not careful enough with your rhymes. ... I would never permit the placing of a word astride a caesura, even when the accent falls on the fourth and eighth foot. ... My principle is quite simple: What is verse? Language submitted to certain rules. If the rules are suppressed, there is no longer verse.[147]

Saint-Saëns had such an intense interest in regular verse that he advised young composers to submit their musical rhythm to ancient and modern literary meters. The point of departure for this "entirely new art" is found in two poorly versified lines from an operetta by Charles Lecocq:

> C'est un mari qui se sauve avec sa femme,
> Une femme qui fuit avec son mari.

By means of music, Lecocq gives rhythmic profile to the lines and also makes of them a distich of four feet:

> $\cup$ $\cup$ $\cup$$\cup$ $\cup$ $\cup$ $\cup$ $\cup$ $\quad$ — — $\quad$ — $\quad$ $\cup$
> C'est un mari / qui se sauve a- / vec sa / femme,
> $\cup$$\cup$ $\cup$ $\cup$ $\cup$ $\cup$ $\cup$$\cup$ $\quad$ — — $\quad$ —
> Une femme / qui fuit avec / son ma / ri.[148]

The ideas of humanistic poets and composers reappear here in a new light.

Saint-Saëns' divergent point of view resulted from his personal concept of art. As a craftsman in the best sense of the term, he was more interested in versification than in poetry. The technical aspect of the relationship between words and music fascinated him, while young composers were more interested in the impression, that subtle echo of the poet's thought. They preferred to set prose, but their music was "poetic." Saint-Saëns defended the use of verse, but many of his *mélodies* are too "prosaic."

FOUR ROMANTIC POETS; RELATION OF THEIR POETIC EXPRESSION TO MUSIC

The literary aspect of the *mélodie* has many facets. Even though texts for *mélodies* composed during the period extending from Berlioz to Duparc were furnished by practically all the great lyric poets from Charles d'Orléans to Verlaine, they are exceeded in number by a multitude of versifiers who hardly merit the name of poet. Viewed as a whole, the body of poetry set to music is so heterogeneous that critical examination is difficult. For this reason the discussion here is restricted to the most important poets of Romanticism: Lamartine, Hugo, and Musset. The fourth great lyric poet, Alfred de Vigny, is omitted because he played no role in the history of the French *mélodie*. His place is taken by Théophile Gautier, who, although generally considered a precursor of the Parnassian school of poetry, may be grouped with the other three as a writer of *mélodie* texts, since it was his early Romantic poems (*Poésies* of 1830, 1832, and 1845 and *La comédie de la mort*, 1838) that provided song texts, rather than his later and more famous *Émaux et camées* (first edition 1852).

An assessment of the role played by the "poets of 1830" in the birth and development of the *mélodie* should consider first their general attitude toward music, a subject approached by many literary historians, of whom few, however, show evidence of sound judgment.

A tenacious and unjustified tradition maintains that most of the Romantic poets and novelists were absolutely insensitive to music. This misconception was already expressed by contemporaries of Hugo, Lamartine, and Balzac. In 1838, for example, an article on "Poets and Musicians" claimed that "Almost all poets have an anti-musical ear. For them music is an unknown language, a dead letter." The victims of this malicious journalist included Chateaubriand, Madame de Staël, Byron, Scott, and Dumas, but Lamartine and Hugo were his favorite targets:

Monsieur de Lamartine has extolled in beautiful verses all the harmonies of heaven and earth. He is familiar with David's harp and Sappho's lyre.

He hears distinctly the music of the spheres, the plaintive and mysterious voices that re-echo on the shores of the ocean. He knows the song of the nightingale, the warbler, and the owl. He understands the whistling of the north wind in the cracks of an old wall. M. de Lamartine is the man of political harmonies, of social harmonies, of religious harmonies. There is only one harmony that he does not comprehend, that of the Conservatory orchestra. ...

Monsieur Victor Hugo spends his life inventing poetic rhythms. ... No other poet is as familiar with the riches and harmony of our language ... but his best friends affirm that neither the prettiest tune nor the most beautiful symphony gives him the slightest emotion; that his ears are equipped with triple armor. A drum and fife or the Opéra orchestra are absolutely the same thing to M. Victor Hugo.[149]

Such outbursts seem to have convinced contemporaries of the great Romantics' musical insensitivity, a misunderstanding seemingly confirmed by various statements made by Gautier and Lamartine.

Théophile Gautier

The most obvious aspect of Gautier's relation with music is undoubtedly his journalistic work. For thirty-five years, from 1837 until his death in 1872, he held a position as music critic. Unusual as it may seem today for a man of letters to formulate critical opinions concerning an art in which he himself is hardly more than an illiterate, such a phenomenon was considered normal during the nineteenth century. Nerval, Heine, Musset, Jules Janin (known as "the Prince of Criticism"), and Ernest Legouvé filled newspapers and journals with articles on musical topics, perhaps assuming the right to do so from a misinterpreted statement of Rousseau's: "It is the poet's right to create poetry and the musician's to create music, but only the philosopher may rightly speak of both of them."[150] The fact that financial necessity forced Gautier to write reviews does not necessarily imply that he wrote without conviction. His articles on Cimarosa and Rossini, as well as his reviews of works by Berlioz and Wagner, reveal an enthusiasm that seems as sincere as his distaste for Offenbach.

Two of Gautier's remarks are often cited as proof of his alleged musical deafness: "Music is the most disagreeable and the most expensive of noises" and "I admit that the squeaking of a saw and that of the fourth string of the most able violinist have exactly the same effect on me."[151] Gautier's daughter Judith has conclusively demonstrated that in the first sentence the poet was not expressing his own opinion, but quoting "the words of a geometrician *who is no music lover, surely*" at a noisy and tasteless performance in London of Donizetti's *La favorite*.[152] As for the second statement, the passage immediately following it shows it to have been an unpremeditated outburst (against virtuosos?), one of the many that the brilliant but rash Gautier wrote in his youth:

Music must be relegated to its proper position. It is often regarded as poetry itself, although one appeals more especially to the senses, and the other to the imagination, which is quite different. Music makes an impression on animals; there are melomanic hunting dogs who have spasms when they hear the swell-organ being played and poodles who follow strolling players and howl in the most harmonious and intelligent manner. ... Read them the most magnificent poetry in the world and they will be insensible to it.

Gautier's musical capacities, on the other hand, must not be overestimated. Judith speaks of her father's habit of spending some time each morning on a varied repertoire of chansons and tunes, "to stave off hunger." She also related that he could play the famous waltz from *Der Freischütz* on the piano, "all the way through and in a fast tempo" and naïvely adds, "not with just one finger, but with good fingering and with the bass."[153]

These are entertaining anecdotes, no more. Nor should undue importance be attached to Gautier's use of technical terms in his musical reviews. He expostulates at length, for example, on the manner in which Berlioz, in his *Roméo et Juliette*, employs for the first time [!] an upper or "inverted" pedal corresponding to the usual bass pedal point, a technique that the composer had quite probably explained to him beforehand.[154] Moreover, Gautier apparently was not always so well instructed, since he speaks of "fugues and canons" in the Overture to *Tannhäuser*! Even after long years of criticism, Gautier possessed only a modicum of musical knowledge and his love for music was quite temperate compared with his passion for the plastic arts. To be entirely fair to the poet, however, the question must be viewed from another angle.

Gautier's most characteristic qualities were his refined taste (although tinged with sensuality) and his exceptionally objective and intelligent views on the intellectual currents of his time. With this equipment he threw himself into the struggle against bourgeois tastelessness, virtuosos' desire to shine, and the custom of pleasing a conservative public, in short, against all that constituted an obstacle to the realization of his ideal of beauty. He never compromised, although the possibility was often open to him in his position of critic. For his journalistic work he received only about 6500 francs yearly, leading Émile de Girardin to remark cynically: "Gautier is a fool. I put a fortune into his hands. His articles should have brought him 30,000 or 40,000 francs a year. There is not a theater director who would not have provided him with an income in return for having him as a spokesman." [155]

In music more than in other areas, Gautier's objectivity and intuition helped to compensate for his lack of talent and knowledge. Evans is correct in saying that Gautier expected from the theater "orgies of light and color, feasts for the eyes as well as for the ears," [156] but along with this predilection he possessed a marvelously refined sensitivity to the interrelationship of the arts. In this respect he shows his affinity with Baudelaire.

In Berlioz Gautier saw a partisan and for this reason defended the composer against the "philistines," probably without understanding his music. His tastes were eclectic; he was an Italianist at heart, but more moderately than Musset, Balzac, or Stendhal. In "Le nid des rossignols," an exquisite short story Gautier wrote at the age of twenty-two, the sisters Fleurette and Isabeau sing their motets, madrigals, and villanelles with embellishments *à la Rossini*! [157] But Gautier also appreciated *Tannhäuser*, which he heard for the first time at Wiesbaden in 1857; he was sufficiently moved by the event to spontaneously write an article on Wagner for *Le moniteur*, even though at the time he was not attached to that journal as music critic. Four years later, after the notorious row at the Paris Opéra, Gautier said with considerable pride: "I, who am considered only an ass in music, did not make a fuss and simply found *Tannhäuser* very beautiful." [158]

The question of how Gautier reacted to musical settings of his own verse is difficult to answer, since he is silent on the subject. Several of his poems were written expressly for composers. He wrote "Villanelle rythmique" for Xavier Boisselot, who, in 1837, published a romance on the text. [159] Gautier sent two *orientales* entitled "Ghazel" and "Dans un soupir" to Félicien David, who set them to music and included them in the collection *Les perles d'Orient*.[160] "L'esclave" was written for Charles le Boigne.[161] No doubt "Lamento" ("Chanson du pêcheur") and "Les matelots," set to music respectively by Monpou and Bazin, were also intended for music, since these composers received the texts in manuscript.[162]

Curzon believes that the poet must have liked several of these songs, "because some of them are so charming,"[163] but this argument is hardly convincing. One might wonder whether Gautier could have been satisfied with Berlioz' dramatic rendering of a mannered poem like "Le spectre de la rose." The poet's silence with regard to his "musicked verse" is probably significant.

Alfred de Musset

Reviewing Pauline Garcia's first appearance, Alfred de Musset wrote: "I do not pretend to report in detail on the concert given at the Théâtre de la Rennaissance; I shall not tell you if Mlle. Garcia goes from G to E and from F to D, nor if her voice is mezzo-soprano or contralto, for the very good reason that I am no expert in that sort of thing and should probably be mistaken. I am no musician and can say, almost in the manner of M. de Maistre, 'I call on Heaven as witness, and on all those who have heard me play the piano.'"[164]

In spite of this admission, the poet, who was the most spontaneous lyricist of the Romantic school, possessed a well-developed musical sensitivity. Certain evidence even suggests that Musset was at times obsessed by music. Léon Séché says that the poet would forget an errand if upon leaving his house he heard a tune on the piano.[165] Musset's brother Paul tells how, upon returning unhappily after his parting from George Sand in Venice, Alfred could find rest and comfort only by listening to the playing of his sister Hermine, a pupil of Liszt:

Our young sister, although almost a child, already played the piano very well. We noticed that Hummel's beautiful Concerto in B minor had the power to bring the patient out of his seclusion. After several minutes we would hear the doors of the room open and Alfred would come and seat himself in a corner of the salon, where, once the piece was finished, we would often succeed in keeping him by speaking of music.[166]

But let the poet express the same thought himself:

> Quand on perd, par triste occurrence,
> Son espérance
> Et sa gaieté,
> Le remède au mélancolique,
> C'est la musique
> Et la beauté!
>
> MUSSET, "Chanson," date unknown [1837?]

The *Contes* and the *Nouvelles* abound in personal recollections containing numerous allusions to the power of sound. Almost all the characters sing or play an instrument. Emmeline, who represents an unknown mistress of Musset (and not George Sand, as Evans believed), listens "with all her soul" to the Masked Trio from *Don Giovanni*, sung by Henriette Sontag, Sabine Heinefetter, and Rubini; or in playing Beethoven's "Le désir," "her favorite tune," she puts the most passionate expression into her playing.[167] Javotte says that "great music, serious music" was the pursuit of his entire life. Madame de Parnes plays the *Invitation to the Waltz* and "the first mistress" constantly sings a Tyrolian romance, "Altra vota gieri belle." The characters that represent the poet himself are equally under the influence of music. Tizianello sings "an ancient air composed to a Petrarch sonnet" while accompanying himself upon the mandolin; Octave's reaction while listening to the Tyrolian romance[168] is somewhat reminiscent of Heine's *Lyrisches Intermezzo* (no. 41):

> Hör ich das Liedchen klingen,
> Das einst die Liebste sang,
> So will mir die Brust zerspringen
> Vor wildem Schmerzensdrang.

But it is Gilbert in *Emmeline* who reacts the most violently. Seated beside his "Ninon" in a box at the Théâtre des Italiens, he listens with her to the Masked Trio:

His whole soul was on Mlle. Sontag's lips and someone who did not understand would have believed him madly in love with this charming singer. The young man's eyes shone. His rather pale face, shaded by long black hair, reflected the pleasure he was experiencing; his lips were half open and his trembling hand beat the time lightly on the velvet of the railing.

In Musset's dramas, comedies, and "proverbs," chansons and romances are sung by numerous characters, among them the Abbé

Desiderio, Silvio and Nino, Césario and Grémio, Fantasio, Giomo of Hungary, Barberine and Rosemberg, Fortunio, Van Buck, the Marquis of Valberg, Minuccio, and Bettine.[169]

Several of Musset's poems ("Rappelle-toi," "À la Malibran," the Prelude to "La nuit de juin," and the three chansons "Bonjour Suzon," "Non Suzon, pas encore," and "Adieu Suzon") were conceived under the immediate influence of music.[170] Fragments of other poems (including "Rolla," V, lines 8–19, "Jamais," and "Le saule") sing of music's power:

> La poésie,
> Voyez-vous, c'est bien. — Mais la musique c'est mieux,
> Pardieu! voilà deux airs qui sont délicieux;
> La langue sans gosier n'est rien. — Voyez le Dante;
> Son Séraphin doré ne parle pas, — il chante!
> C'est la musique, moi, qui m'a fait croire en Dieu.
> MUSSET, "Les marrons du feu," Scene V

And music is of divine origin:

> Fille de la douleur, harmonie! harmonie!
> Langue que pour l'amour inventa le génie!
> Qui nous vint d'Italie, et qui lui vint des cieux!
> MUSSET, "Lucie"[171]

Of course the word "harmonie" here has the figurative meaning of music itself. In any case Musset would not have used it thus in the technical sense, since he considered melody rather than harmony to be the essence of music. He detested the "learned" style of music, including in this category not only Berlioz' works, but also the operas of Halévy and Meyerbeer, of which he intemperately wrote:

The composer adds forty trumpets to the orchestra so that his opera can make more of a racket than the preceding one. ... The orchestra tries to make as much noise as possible in order to be heard; the singer, trying to rise above the din of the orchestra, shrieks at the top of his voice ... and in the midst of all this, not a single honest person wonders if once there did not exist something that could be called music.[172]

It is melody pure and simple that moves Musset. Although he preferred Italian music, he did not object to hearing Schubert (see his poem "Jamais"), Mozart, Weber, or Beethoven. If he had not spent most of his life in a drawing-room atmosphere, Musset would probably have been strongly subject, like Nerval and George Sand, to the influence of folk music. "Mimi Pinson," a short story dating from 1845, contains a poem which is already strongly oriented in that direction:

> Mimi Pinson est une blonde,
> Une blonde que l'on connaît.
> Elle n'a qu'une robe au monde,
>   Landerirette
>   Et qu'un bonnet.

Did Musset prefer music to poetry? He admits that the rational word cannot explain the power of music and says further that "no words will ever equal the tenderness of such a language" (in "Emmeline"). His defense of music's autonomy is remarkable for a poet:

Do not be deceived. They [the two Muses] cannot always be united. On this subject, I believe Diderot in *Rameau's Nephew* was the first to state an idea that seems completely false to me. He claims that music is only exaggerated declamation, so that if one compared declamation to a straight line, presumably like a staff, music would twine around it, enveloping it almost like a branch of a vine or ivy. This is an ingenious absurdity. Declamation is speech and music pure thought.[173]

Like Gautier, Musset never expressed his opinion of the songs to which his poems were set. The best of these (by Gounod, Delibes, and Lalo) were not composed until the end of his life or after his death. It certainly seems likely that a poet who could write *Chansons à mettre en musique* would be sympathetic in principle to the work of the *mélodistes*. Musset considered the word insufficient as a means of rational expression in lyric poetry, and saw music as coming to the poet's aid:

In the best verse of a true poet there is always two or three times more than what is actually said; it is up to the reader to supply the remainder according to his ideas, his drive, and his tastes. ... Let us speak of melody. Everyone feels it, from the boxes at La Scala, where the women are poised under the chandeliers, to the hills of Beauce, where the cattle stop when they hear a herdsman blow. It is essentially in melody that the poet's passion lies. Poetry is so inherently musical that there is no beautiful thought before which a poet would not hesitate if there were no melody in it; thus by dint of practice, he arrives at the point of having not merely words, but rather musical thoughts.[174]

Alphonse de Lamartine

Julien Tiersot says flatly that Lamartine was hostile to music,[175] basing his statement on the poet's own commentary to "Le lac":

A thousand attempts have been made to add the plaintive melody of music to the wailing of these verses. Only once has it succeeded, when Niedermeyer movingly translated this ode into notes. I have heard this romance sung and seen the tears it produces. Nevertheless, I have always believed that music and poetry detract from each other when they are associated. Each is an art complete in itself: music contains its own feeling and beautiful poetry its own melody.[176]

These words prove nothing more than Lamartine's disapproval of the combination of words and music. Tiersot was probably unaware of the poem in which the poet speaks of "those sounds more powerful than the cold word,"[177] and of his article on Mozart,[178] which claims that music equals poetry and sometimes even goes beyond it, "for music expresses above all the inexpressible." Music is defined as "the literature of the senses and of the heart," having no need of words. Like Musset, Lamartine does not consider music as a special form of declamation; but while the former willingly exchanges the rhythm of poetry and the clarity of diction for musical feeling, the latter is hostile to all compromise: "Declamation is not made to be sung; music is not made to be declaimed. Each has its own sphere."[179] Thus Lamartine's partiality to instrumental music follows logically. He believed the musician "more eloquent and moving in the sublime nudity of his notes than in the heterogeneous alliance of his notes with poetry, drama, declamation, stage decoration, and cheap finery." Liturgical music, with its "impersonal" texts, also attracted him, Mozart's *Requiem* being a special favorite.

But since Lamartine's true domain was the world of nature, he was uncomfortable in a concert hall or drawing room. Only under the skies could his auditory sensitivity clearly manifest itself. The *Méditations* and *Harmonies* are full of "melodious voices" and "mysterious sounds." He finds a meaning for every one of nature's sounds, describing the "sad chords" of the brook[180] and the bird singing of "his sorrows."[181] All nature is filled with divine voices:

> Adore ici l'écho qu'adorait Pythagore,
> Prête avec lui l'oreille aux célestes concerts.
>
> LAMARTINE, "Le vallon," from *Premières méditations*

Man also has a place here. His "rustic church bell" spreads "a religious sound."[182] The fisherman welcomes the day with a song.[183] Human music is harmoniously blended with the whisper of the evening wind:

> Elle chante; et sa voix par intervalle expire,
> Et, des accords du luth plus faiblement frappés,
> Les échos assoupis ne livrent au zéphire
> Que des soupirs mourants, de silence coupés.
>
> LAMARTINE, "Ischia," from *Nouvelles méditations*

Seen in this light, Lamartine's musical sensitivity is no less strong than that of Musset, although it reveals itself in an entirely different milieu. Nevertheless, the moment arrives when the paths of the two poets separate. For Musset, music constitutes a means of restoring and strengthening his inspiration, but excludes rational thought. Lamartine, on the other hand, believes it his duty as a poet to regulate his emotions according to his reason. After having effected this synthesis in himself, he can, as a thinking man, sing of the harmony of nature. Music then becomes an instrument to explain the human soul:

> Comment l'air modulé par la fibre sonore
> Peut-il créer en nous ces sublimes transports?
> Pourquoi le cœur suit-il un son qui s'évapore?
> Ah! c'est qu'il est une âme au fond de ces accords,
>   C'est que cette âme répandue
> Dans chacun des accents par ta voix modulés
> Par la voix de nos cœurs est soudain répondue
> Avant que le doux son soit encore écoulé,
> Et que, semblable au son qui dans un temple éveille
> Mille échos assoupis qui parlent à la fois,
> Ton âme, dont l'écho vibre dans chaque oreille,
>   Va créer une âme pareille
> Partout où retentit ta voix.[184]
>
> LAMARTINE, "La voix humaine," from *Harmonies poétiques*

And not only man, but the whole universe is animated by this melodious being:

> Loi sainte et mystérieuse!
> Une âme mélodieuse
> Anime tout l'univers;
> Chaque être a son harmonie,
> Chaque étoile son génie,
> Chaque élément ses concerts.
>
> "Désir," in *Harmonies poétiques*

Perhaps Lamartine's true greatness resides in the fact that he brought his emotions and his intelligence into harmony, without attenuating the intensity or purity of either.

Victor Hugo

Victor Hugo was a victim of his imperfect knowledge of musical history. This deficiency is particularly apparent in one stanza of the poem "Que la musique date du seizième siècle" (from *Les rayons et les ombres*), that has evoked virulent criticism from many musicians:

> Puissant Palestrina, vieux maître, vieux génie,
> Je vous salue ici, père de l'harmonie,
> Car, ainsi qu'un grand fleuve où boivent les humains,
> Toute cette musique a coulé de vos mains!
> Car Gluck et Beethoven, rameaux sous qui l'on rêve,
> Sont nés de votre souche et faits de votre sève!
> Car Mozart, votre fils, a pris sur vos autels
> Cette nouvelle lyre inconnue aux mortels,
> Plus tremblante que l'herbe au souffle des aurores,
> Née au seizième siècle entre vos doigts sonores!
> Car, maître! c'est à vous que tous nos soupirs vont
> Sitôt qu'une voix chante et qu'une âme répond!

The historical errors contained in these admirable lines need not be examined here, since Henry Expert has already described them clearly.[185] Hugo's unfortunate compulsion to speak of matters in which he lacked technical and historical knowledge has been shared by other "universal" geniuses. But to deny the poet any taste in music solely on the basis of this quotation is absurd. Nor does the fact that in his enormous production Hugo only rarely speaks of music define his attitude toward the art.

Hugo was seldom seen in the concert hall. His attendance at a Berlioz concert where the *Symphonie fantastique* was performed[186] cannot be considered important in itself; the composer had taken an active part in the "battle of *Hernani*," and Hugo's presence at this concert may perhaps have been nothing more than a friendly repayment. Besides Hugo, Berlioz numbered many other Romantic writers among his friends: Vigny, Gautier, Eugène Sue, Legouvé, Jules Janin, Balzac, and George Sand were all sympathetic toward the artistic tendencies of his work but few among them enjoyed his music.

Hugo's preference for German music is revealed in his essay entitled *William Shakespeare*:

Music is the speech of Germany. The German people, so repressed as a nation, so emancipated as thinkers, sings with a somber love. Singing resembles a freeing from bonds. Music expresses that which can neither be said nor suppressed. Therefore, all Germany is music while it waits for its liberation. ... Singing is the means by which it breathes and conspires. The note being the syllable of a sort of vague universal language, Germany's true communication with humanity is made through harmony, which is the ideal first step toward unity. ... Germany's greatest poets are her musicians.[187]

For Hugo, Beethoven and Weber are the true representatives of the German nation. He considers one of the choruses from *Euryanthe* as "perhaps the most beautiful piece in all music."[188] Beethoven is "the great German" as Dante is "the great Italian" and Shakespeare "the great Englishman."[189] In another work Hugo speaks of Mozart as "a fountainhead" and Gluck as "a forest."[190] In his taste for German music he is truly conspicuous among the Romantics, most of whom were fervent Italianists.

Although Hugo is capable of describing an orchestra with poetic virtuosity and in a suggestive manner,[191] his true sense of music is not revealed in the concert hall. A quite different impression of his auditory sensations emerges from the pages of *Notre-Dame de Paris*. In describing the procession of the "Pope of Fools," he characterizes music as "a magnificent *cacophony*"; in the interior of Gondelaurier's dwelling is heard "a *noise* of music"; the chimes of Paris *blend* in a magnificent concert" and this "*mass* of sonorous vibrations," and that "*sea* of harmony" extend well beyond the horizon "the *deafening* circle of its oscillations."[192] Hugo appears to sense music rather as an impressive noise than as a harmonious ensemble of sonorous nuances. Probably he hears in the organ, here "exploding like a hundred trumpets," elsewhere "murmuring here on earth some beginning of infinite things,"[193] no more than the mass of sounds and not the distinct parts.

Hugo's notebooks contain a definition of music as "the nebula of art."[194] Vigny, Lamartine, Musset, Deschamps, and other Romantics are known to have held similar opinions, but with this difference. The other poets also feel that music, unlike the precise word, expresses vague feelings, but they are still capable of distinguishing the various sounds, of mentally capturing the melodic design, of humming the tunes. Hugo, on the other hand, submits to music without analysis, without even hearing it actively. For him the nebulosity applies not only to the irrational character of music, but also to the physical sound that impinges on his consciousness in a compact mass.

If Hugo, like Gautier, was chiefly visual in nature, his auditory impressions nevertheless contributed to his imaginative powers. Sounds awaken visions (the poet says "the ear also has its sight"[195]) and conversely, visionary imagination can create a rich and unknown music. This seems to be true for the ode to Palestrina, whose music Hugo probably never heard.

Hugo's dramas contain several songs intended to be sung, but in general the poet was not very receptive toward musicians who destroyed his powerful rhythmic suggestions. He seems to have even formally forbidden them "to place music alongside the verses."[196]

Poetic Qualities of Musical Interest

What qualities should a poem possess, what requirements should it fulfill in order to awaken the composer's interest and permit him to reinforce the expressiveness of the words by means of his notes? The first broad requirement is that the poem must be lyrical, but beyond that, the special qualities that orient the composer's choice are difficult to determine. Many factors, some of them with only a very distant relationship to music and poetry, may play a role here. An unknown young composer, for example, may choose the verses of a famous poet in the hope of awakening the interest of publishers and public. Another may consider the composition of a *mélodie* as a purely technical task, in which case the artistic value of the text will hardly interest him. A third will investigate the topicality of a poem, choosing his text according to whether shepherds and shepherdesses, languorous elegies, or *orientales* are in style at the moment. Aside from these, composers with more substantial requirements for the *mélodie*, those who "made" the history of the genre, chose according to the quality of the poetry. Three elements determine the nature of this quality:

1. The exterior atmosphere, i.e., the concrete objects described by the poet and the surroundings onto which he projects his ideas.
2. The interior atmosphere, i.e., what the poet does not express, but only suggests.
3. The "music" of the verse.

For the lyric poet, the exterior atmosphere is usually secondary and may remain extremely vague without weakening the intensity of expression. For the composer, however, it has immeasurable value, since he possesses the power of suggestive imitation. A word such as "rain" remains an *idea* that must be perceived through the reason; deprived of its meaning, it is an abstract sound that expresses nothing. The musician, however, can express the phenomenon of rain more directly, by imitation or suggestion. Many composers are naturally tempted to exploit this faculty and they consequently have a certain predilection for texts that permit them to do so.

During the period of French Romanticism the exterior atmosphere had extraordinary significance for musicians; there was a strong preference for the exotic milieu, especially the Orient (including Spain). Orientalism had become fashionable during the war for Greek independence (1821–1833) and fascinated not only Hugo and Gautier, but also many Romantics of secondary stature. Their interest was probably due less to artistic convictions than to their desire to succeed in society. But by 1831 Balzac already dared to say in the preface to his novel *La peau de chagrin* that the public was sated with the Orient and the following year sultans, slaves, opium, and other Levantine attributes were blithely mocked by Musset in "Namouna, an Oriental Tale."

Many *orientales*, the most important of them by Hugo and Gautier,[197] were set to music by *mélodie* composers. If it was the exotic atmosphere that attracted them, they took surprisingly little advantage of its inherent possibilities. Even Félicien David is less Oriental in his *mélodies* than in his famous symphony-ode *Le désert*. Not until Bizet, Saint-Saëns, and Delibes appeared was the element of local color offered by the poet successfully translated into music.

The depiction of exterior atmosphere becomes more effective when it simultaneously accents a psychic state. The humming of the spinning wheel in Schubert's "Gretchen am Spinnrade" becomes the symbol of the heroine's anxiety, and Fauré, in his imitation of falling rain, conveys something of Verlaine's "spleen" in the song of that title. But it is only the great masters who are able to achieve such unity between exterior and interior elements; the others usually stop at imitation of guitars, exotic rhythms, and natural phenomena, a technique that may accentuate the effects of word and music if used with moderation and taste. But if the composer exaggerates, his painting may absorb the essence of the poem. Such artists as Duparc and Fauré deliberately avoid the picturesque in their *mélodies*, unless it offers the possibility of symbolism charged with meaning.

This symbolism brings us to the domain of interior atmosphere. One might even say that in a lyric poem it is the irrational expression that constitutes the essential value. This element was rarely present in French literature of the seventeenth and eighteenth centuries, and consequently the period lacked a truly lyric poetry (except perhaps for André Chénier, whose work was unknown until the Romantic era). A few pre-Romantic authors show something resembling interior atmosphere (e.g., Chateaubriand and Marceline Desbordes-Valmore) but most of the poets of the Revolution and the Empire are much closer to the literature of the *ancien régime* in their images and choice of words. While they do reserve an important place for feeling, they consider it as an *object* rather than as a means of expression. Not until Lamartine does the poet's psychic state become the point of departure for lyric verse. With subjectivism, the vague and indefinable make their entry into the rational world of French poetry.

This evolution is closely related to the French discovery of German literature, the *Lied* in particular strongly influencing poets.[198] The two most important characteristics of the literary *Lied*—*Empfindung* and *Volkstümlichkeit*—were almost completely alien to French tradition, so that the terms are even difficult to translate into French. Among other somewhat secondary, although still important aspects of the *Lied*, are a predilection for the fantastic, a certain pantheistic feeling, and an affinity for music. From these qualities derives the irrational character of the *Lied*; its value is defined by its interior atmosphere.

While being subjected to the influence of the German *Lied*, French poets were impressing their own spirit on it. In the process, *Emp-findung* became *sensibilité*, a slightly different phenomenon, best observed in Musset, the most spontaneous and non-cerebral among the great Romantic poets. Gautier is often mistakenly considered to be lacking in true sensitivity, but in fact he wrote many emotional and sensitive poems in his youth.

Volkstümlichkeit clashes with the centralized urban cultural life of France, in which poets have lost almost all ties with nature.[199] Even Nerval, the untiring propagandist for folk song, is not truly *volks-tümlich* in his poetry. Only Auguste Brizeux, a minor poet from Brittany, comes close to writing folk poetry.

The fantastic element that plays such an important role in the German *Ballade* found a less favorable terrain in France, for its civilization and the heritage of rationalism acted as moderating factors. The poems of Hugo and Gautier do occasionally feature fairies, sylphs, gnomes, and water-sprites that seem to be imported from Germany, but in French poetry the fantastic element generally surrenders its place to the exotic atmosphere of which we have already spoken.

Pantheism was so prevalent a feature of German literature that Henri Blaze described it as being "in the air, there."[200] In France this element of the Romantic conception is clearest in the work of Hugo and Lamartine.

The role of *music* in poetry will be discussed below.

Irrational expression was widely accepted by the French Romantics as the basis of lyric poetry. Hugo suggested that the poet "does not need to write with the tools used earlier, but with his soul and with his heart" and he characterizes his *Feuilles d'automne* as "verse from within the soul."[201] Musset wrote his first works "almost unconsciously"[202] and Lamartine called poetry "interior song."[203] Eighteenth-century estheticians had been seeking the meaning of vocal music in the imitation of nature (Batteux) or in declamation (Diderot and Grétry), an attitude that was understandable with a poetry that offered no other possibility. Now, during the Romantic period, poetry becomes predominantly irrational and the interior atmosphere acquires great importance for the composer, since Lamartine, Hugo, Musset, and Gautier put at his disposal verse that makes strong demands on his genius. The manner in which he accomplishes his task touches on the most profound secret of art and evades all rational analysis. Nevertheless, the composer's contribution is of considerable importance, for only music possesses the faculty of expressing the inexpressible and thus realizing interior atmosphere.

At the beginning few composers were capable of thus expanding the contents of a poem and many *mélodies* dating from the period between Berlioz and Duparc do little to intensify the text, although paradoxically composers are most often attracted by poetry in which the interior atmosphere dominates. Gertrud Sattler provides proof of this in her list of French literary *Lieder*; most of the favorite texts of mid-century composers, set to music over and over, appear there.

The *musical* qualities of French verse are determined chiefly by the three elements usually designated by the words "harmony," "melody," and "rhythm." The last-named has already been discussed in the first section of this chapter in its relation to musical prosody. Opinions differ greatly as to the significance of the other two terms. Among the clearest and most logical definitions are those offered by the linguist Trannoy, according to which harmony is "the phenomenon by which the sounds of one or several lines adapt to and harmonize with each other or with a preconceived idea." Harmony reveals itself in alliteration and assonance. Trannoy describes melody as "the element of variation introduced into verse by the different timbres of successive vowels."[204] Uniformity is thus the essential character of harmony, diversity that of melody.

This differentiation of the musical properties of French verse did not capture the attention of theoreticians until the end of the nineteenth century. Before that time the role of sounds was considered only from the narrow viewpoint of imitative harmony, i.e., "imitation of sounds by sounds, speed by speed, slowness by slowness."[205] Becq de Fouquières was the first to enlarge the concept of "music" in a significant way, even going so far as to consider sonority the essential quality of poetry: "A verse is a sonorous conception, representative of a mental conception." His theory leads him to extend the concept of imitation to that of suggestion, so that "the word that generates the idea becomes the generator of the sound of the verse."[206] He quotes many illustrative examples (not all of them convincing), among which are these two lines from Racine:

> Je mourrai, mais au moins ma mort me vengera   (*Andromaque*, V, 2)
> Tout m'afflige et me nuit et conspire à me nuire   (*Phèdre*, I, 3)

In the first line *mourrai* is the sound-generator and this word, by its initial consonant, causes a quintuple resonance; in the second line the word *afflige* brings into subjection precisely those syllables that carry the tonic accent.

These theories found a rabid adversary in Jules Combarieu,[207] who demonstrated that Becq de Fouquières was sometimes blinded by his imagination, as in his interpretation of the famous lines from *Phèdre* in which Ariadne's death from her unhappy love is mourned by her sister:

> Ariane, ma sœur, de quel amour blessée,
> Vous mourûtes aux bords où vous fûtes laissée!

When Becq de Fouquières describes the "muffled moaning" (*mou-*, *vous*) and the "wail" that "exhales on a sharp note" [!] (*-rû-*, *fû-*), it is he and not Racine who is projecting Phèdre's feelings onto the sound of the words. One cannot deny that the four assonant vowels create a very musical impression, but their sonorous effects are still not susceptible of detailed interpretation.

Nevertheless, Combarieu goes too far in qualifying Becq de Fouquières' theory as "the most eloquent argument in favor of imitative harmony," since the latter often omits an interpretation, seeming to feel that a poet may also aspire toward an "absolute" sonority, distinct from his poetic thought. Combarieu's curious belief that the music of poetry is based on a fiction, or that at least it constitutes a handicap to the beauty of the verse, is indefensible, as the quoted lines from *Phèdre* convincingly prove. Yet Combarieu even claims that Racine wrote poor verse whenever he wrote lines that were musical! The concept of "music" in verse obviously had very limited significance for Combarieu, for he claimed that to achieve a good style one has to avoid music, not invent it. He attempts to demonstrate the correctness of this thesis by an analysis of the first stanza of Lamartine's famous "Le lac":

> Ainsi, toujours poussés vers de nouveaux rivages,
> Dans la nuit éternelle emportés sans retour,
> Ne pourrons-nous jamais sur l'océan des âges
> Jeter l'ancre un seul jour?

This strophe is characterized by considerable sonorous variety and consequently possesses a beautiful melodic contour. According to

Trannoy's table of vowels, the melody of the second line may be visually represented in this manner:[208]

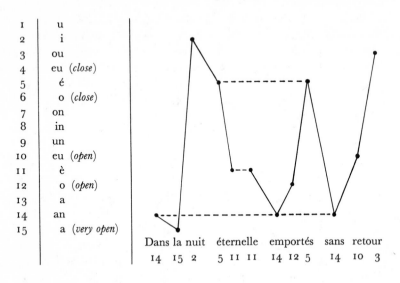

1	u
2	i
3	ou
4	eu (*close*)
5	é
6	o (*close*)
7	on
8	in
9	un
10	eu (*open*)
11	è
12	o (*open*)
13	a
14	an
15	a (*very open*)

Dans la nuit   éternelle   emportés   sans   retour
14   15   2   5   11   11   14   12   5   14   10   3

The graph also suggests that melody and harmony (the latter indicated by the dotted lines) are not mutually exclusive, but on the contrary, together determine the musical value of a line of verse. That Combarieu, after his precise and intelligent analysis of the stanza, can still speak of "the opposite of something musical" is incomprehensible.

Finally, Combarieu concludes that poetry's force of expression is limited to the intelligence. This art can express itself only with the aid of arbitrary and conventional symbols and its domain is constituted by the *imitation of ideas*. In this way the musicologist places himself diametrically opposite Becq de Fouquières, who considers *sonorous representation* to be the very essence of poetry. Although still arguable, neither theory can be accepted today because of the extremes to which they have been forced by the two writers, both of them victims of an exaggerated tendency toward schematization.

The French Romantic writers' use of interior atmosphere was not their only gift to poetry; they also effectively improved the sonority of their language. Of the four poets discussed here, Lamartine is especially remarkable in this respect. Musset's verse became increasingly musical after the early work *Contes d'Espagne et d'Italie*

(1830). Opinions regarding Hugo's poetry vary widely. While his language certainly lacks the fluidity found in Lamartine, the suggestive sonority of a poem like "La captive" (*Les Orientales* IX) is striking. Gautier's language presents fewer musical characteristics than that of the other three poets.

What remains of the sonorous abundance of the Romantics when their poems fall into the hands of composers? It would be foolish to deny that musical sounds erase poetic sounds. Even the most scrupulous musician cannot possibly make allowances for the poetic "melody" without entirely renouncing his liberty of invention, nor can he apply his attention to the "harmony" of the verse. Musical transposition of assonance and alliteration are a rare exception. A curious example of the latter is found in Hugo Wolf's *Lied* written to a poem by Eduard Mörike, demonstrating how alliteration may be rendered in music; all the *l*'s are placed on B-flats falling on initial beats of measures (Example 26).

Example 26: Wolf, "Verborgenheit"

The true significance of "music" in poetry is found, however, in its stimulative action. By nature extremely sensitive to sound, the composer usually bases his choice of text principally on the relative sonorous properties of poems. The popularity of *Les méditations* as musical settings, despite their protracted length, may be largely explained by the attractive musical suavity of Lamartine's verse. The same characterization holds true for some of the chansons and *orientales* of Musset and Hugo.

Neglected Poets

In closing this chapter, a few words are due the great poets who played only a minor role in the history of the French *mélodie*. The verses of Alfred de Vigny were understandably uninspiring to musicians; a poet who customarily masks his feelings, and who is philosopher rather than bard, does not, moreover, feel the need for music. The plastic and impersonal idiom of the Parnassians was also unattractive to composers,[209] even leading Fauré to admit that "I have never been able to set the pure Parnassians to music because their form, so elegant, pretty, and sonorous, resides entirely in the word—and because the word does not hide a single true thought." The composer confesses to having great difficulty with the poems of Leconte de Lisle:

> His verse is too full, too rich, too complete for music to be effectively adapted to it. Attributive adjectives take on enormous importance. Thus "Helen with the white feet" is charming to say; it provides an image. If one adds notes to it and tries to sing it, those feet become gigantic, entirely disproportionate. It would be absurd and ridiculous, impossible not to smile at.[210]

Among poets overlooked by the masters of the *mélodie*, the neglect of Gérard de Nerval is particularly surprising. His profound feeling for music was matched by a real understanding of its principles. His interest in rehabilitating folk song is generally recognized, but his clear judgment and progressive taste in other areas of music is less well known. Nerval's language, characterized by his biographer Aristide Marie as "emotive" and "intimately musical,"[211] comes very close to the German literary *Lied* and is already oriented toward symbolism. The poet himself composed an air for one of his *odelettes*, "Les Cydalises":

> Où sont nos amoureuses?
> Elles sont au tombeau:
> Elles sont plus heureuses
> Dans un séjour plus beau!
>
> Elles sont près des anges,
> Dans le fond du ciel bleu,
> Et chantent des louanges
> De la mère de Dieu.
>
> O blanche fiancée!
> O jeune vierge en fleur,
> Amante délaissée,
> Que flétrit la douleur!

L'éternité profonde
Souriait dans vos yeux ...
Flambeaux éteints du monde,
Rallumez-vous aux cieux!

Nerval explains that this poem "came to me as a song in spite of myself; I conceived both verse and melody at the same time. The latter, which has been judged indeed quite suitable to the words, I was obliged to have noted down. ... I am convinced that every poet would easily write music to his verse if he had some knowledge of notation."[212]

Although this poem seems to beg for musical commentary, none of the great masters of the nineteenth century embellished its lines, nor any other of Nerval's poems.

CHAPTER III

The Mélodie During the Romantic Era

In the domain of music the word "Romanticism" may be interpreted in diverse ways. If every composition that aroused and upset the Paris public of 1830 is categorized as Romantic, then Rossini, Auber, Halévy, and Meyerbeer are Romantics for the same reason as Berlioz. René Dumesnil appears to favor this concept, since all the famous composers of the Louis-Philippe period are included in his *La musique romantique française* (1944). But closer examination of his study reveals that he correctly recognizes only Berlioz as a truly Romantic composer. Berlioz remains no less Romantic when his music is stripped of all its symbols, when its programs, its literary texts, and even the man himself are disregarded. The works of the other composers would not sustain such a dissection, for the musical characteristics of Romanticism (e.g., amplitude of melodic line, bold modulation, unusual resolution of dissonance, and clashing of ornamental notes with chordal tones) are used by Meyerbeer or Halévy only as special procedures or effects, whereas true Romantics use these techniques as an integral part of their idiom.

However interesting the ecstatic comments of Gambara and Massimilla Doni may be from the historical point of view, they teach us nothing about the *musical* qualities of *Robert le diable* and *Mosè in Egitto*.[213] These attributes can be determined only by careful scrutiny of the score, a procedure that leads to the conclusion that the Romanticism of Meyerbeer and Rossini existed on an entirely different level from that of Berlioz, Chopin, and the German Romantics. The same judgment is valid for the *mélodie*. Neither the exuberant title-pages and lithographs nor the bombastic pronouncements of the musical press present an accurate delineation. The sole decisive factor, the musical text, reveals that relatively few *mélodies* are purely Romantic. The description may justly be applied to only a few pieces by Berlioz and Liszt, insufficient in number to constitute a genre. Their other vocal works may be either Romantic or *mélodies*, but not both; in the first case they are *scènes*, in the second romances or chansons. Significantly for the art of song in this epoch, composers were always drawn into the dramatic current when they turned away from the bourgeois atmosphere; profound emotion and intimacy of expression were apparently incompatible at the time. Thus, the works to be examined here hardly present a unified picture. They nevertheless include several compositions of high artistic value, quite unjustly neglected.

Hector Berlioz (1803–1869)

"It is indeed a rare genius who can create works whose simplicity is in direct proportion to their size. Unfortunately, I am not one of them; I need ample resources to produce any effect."[214] Berlioz made this admission when Liszt played some of Schumann's short pieces for him. Certain passages of *L'enfance du Christ* and *Les Troyens* prove that Berlioz was entirely capable of expressing deep emotion with simple means but he never felt comfortable in the intimate genres and this was undoubtedly the reason why he wrote relatively few *mélodies*. His lack of self-confidence in this area is demonstrated by his frequent dissatisfaction with the original conception. Many of the songs appeared in two or three versions, the changes always being in the direction of expanded resources. The ballade "Hélène," originally a simple duet with piano accompaniment, was arranged for chorus and orchestra. "La captive," first a strophic romance, received a violoncello part within two years; still not satisfied, in 1848 the composer recast the piece as a "symphonic *mélodie*" for contralto and orchestra. "La mort d'Ophélie" exists in both solo and choral versions. More than half of his songs were orchestrated and in the course of this process Berlioz considerably modified the original

Title page of *La mélodie, Album de chant,* supplement to the periodical *Le monde musical,* 1845

Hector Berlioz in 1845

versions. Several of the pieces were inserted in large compositions (e.g., the *Symphonie fantastique,* its sequel *Lélio, Roméo et Juliette,* and the opera *Benvenuto Cellini*).

Viewed as a whole, Berlioz' vocal music is very heterogeneous. But since a composer of his genius cannot touch even the simplest form of musical expression without leaving his mark on it, he evinced surprising originality even in this limited domain.

The *mélodies* may be grouped in three chronological periods:

1. The youthful romances and the *Mélodies irlandaises,* in which the composer is already trying to free himself from established procedures.
2. The separate pieces written between 1830 and 1838, and the collection *Les nuits d'été,* composed about 1840. The evolution from romance to *mélodie* occurred during this time.
3. The last songs, composed from 1841 to 1850, and of unequal value.

Berlioz' first vivid musical impression, dating from 1816, was of a romance from Dalayrac's *Nina,* "naïvely adapted to some sacred words and sung in a religious ceremony," i.e., his first Communion.[215] An album containing hand-copied romances by Dezède, Martini, Boieldieu, and Berton dates from a few years later. Their accompaniments, arranged for guitar, are apparently the work of the young Hector. Since the romance played a significant role in his early musical experiences, it may be assumed that some of his own compositions in this genre were already written during the early years at La Côte-Saint-André. Among these first works, "L'Arabe jaloux," "L'invocation à l'amitié," and "Le dépit de la bergère" show considerable harmonic ineptness, containing chord progressions likely to have disturbed the equanimity of even the most liberal music teacher. These negative signs are hardly worthy of note but it *is* important to ascertain that the young Berlioz began trying to destroy the uniformity of the strophic structure very early in his career. The first three stanzas of "Le dépit de la bergère" are identical, but the fourth is modified and considerably amplified, an enlargement perfectly justified from the esthetic point of view. A minor structural liberty in "L'Arabe jaloux" is even more remarkable. Comparison of a section from the first stanza with the corresponding phrase of the second indicates that Berlioz is already aspiring to faithful rendition of the text, even in his very first works (Example 27).

a)

b)

Example 27: Berlioz, "L'Arabe jaloux"

The slightly more mature style of "Toi qui l'aimas, verse des pleurs," "Canon libre à la quinte," and "Pleure, pauvre Colette" suggests that they were written somewhat later. In spite of some inexcusable harmonic transgressions, the musical expression is stronger and more varied. But the most important of the youthful works is "Le montagnard exilé," a vocal duet. The text of this romance contains no less than fourteen quatrains, which Berlioz joins two by two to make seven (dissimilar) musical sections. The piece is based on two contrasting ideas, a twice-varied A, and an unchanging B section:

LITERARY STANZAS:	1–2	3–4	5–6	7–8	9–10	11–12	13–14
MUSICAL SECTIONS:	A	A′	B	B	B	B	A″
METER:	¢	¢	6/8	6/8	6/8	6/8	¢

The harmony makes its contribution to the musical expression, chromatic and altered notes serving to underline the text (Example 28).

Example 28: Berlioz, "Le montagnard exilé"

The influence stemming from the romances of the type composed by Adrien *l'aîné* and Méhul may be recognized in the pathetic accents at the end of section B (Example 29).

Example 29: Berlioz, "Le montagnard exilé"

Despite these examples of Romantic exaltation, Berlioz' early works are still dominated by the spirit of the *ancien régime*. Easily visible traces of Dalayrac, Dezède, and Martini reside in the choice of texts (among eight romances, five are *bergerettes*) and in the various harmonic and melodic formulae. Even in "Le montagnard exilé," undoubtedly the most progressive of these youthful compositions, the end of section A is strongly reminiscent of the eighteenth century (Example 30). The passage has a rather curious resemblance to part of a Haydn song (Example 31).[216]

Besides the seven songs already mentioned, Berlioz' early vocal

Example 30: Berlioz, "Le montagnard exilé"

Example 31: Haydn, "Der erste Kuss"

works also include a romance on the poem "Je vais donc quitter pour jamais" from Florian's *Estelle et Némorin*. The music is lost, but the composer confides that he literally borrowed the melodic line of this adolescent essay for the introduction to his *Symphonie fantastique*: "It is the melody sung by the first violins at the beginning of the Largo in the first movement of the work, entitled 'Rêveries, Passions.' I have changed nothing."[217] With the aid of the score Julien Tiersot has attempted a reconstruction of the original vocal line (Example 32).[218]

Apart from a few large intervals, the melody possesses an excellent cantabile quality, certainly sufficient for Berlioz to have respected it enough to use it again. Nevertheless, it seems unlikely that the original version was identical with the passage of the symphony. The young Berlioz of 1820 would hardly have been capable of creating such an accomplished melodic contour, since his first compositions display little of the exceptional precocity present in the youthful works of Schubert and Mendelssohn.

Terminating the first group of Berlioz' vocal compositions are the *Neuf mélodies imitées de l'anglais*, with words by Thomas Gounet after Thomas Moore. Generally known under the name *Mélodies irlandaises*, they were reprinted in 1850 with the title *Irlande*. The composer's choice of Moore's poems is of course related to the Irish

Example 32: Berlioz, romance from *Estelle et Némorin* (according to Tiersot)

revolt, which had such passionate echoes on the Continent. These verses were a natural source of inspiration for the young Romantic who so ardently adored the Irish actress Harriet Smithson. In spite of the evidence presented above to show that the term *mélodie* derives from Moore's usage and does not yet constitute a new genre (see above, p. 24), certain of Berlioz' *Neuf mélodies* do circumvent the limitations of the romance.

"Hélène" and "La belle voyageuse" are the simplest of the set of nine. The first is a duet composed of six identical strophes separated by *ritornelli*. The only remarkable feature of this *mélodie* is the use of unaccented syncopations in the vocal line, for which the composer provides the stipulation that they be performed without being felt as such. Aside from this, neither the voice part nor the accompaniment is particularly interesting and the work gives a general impression of conventionality. "La belle voyageuse" possesses a much more personal charm. While its melody and accompaniment are also extremely simple, its harmonic aspect is quite unusual. The traditional modulation toward the dominant (E major) is replaced by one to the subdominant key (D major); the tonic chord of D becomes in turn the dominant of G major, the key in which the first phrase is repeated (Example 33).

Example 33: Berlioz, "La belle voyageuse" (measures 5–16)

A contemporary critic called attention to this "very special effect produced by the harmonic progression. ... It is nothing but the key of G following the key of D, and yet this succession has such an effect that even practiced singers experience the greatest difficulty in attacking the D of the thirteenth measure."[219] The transposed repetition gives the piece an archaic flavor, an impression later reinforced by the progression dominant–subdominant (Example 34).

In "La belle voyageuse" Berlioz escapes the insipidity of the romance while still conserving the poem's artlessness; this quality is unfortunately lacking in the orchestral version of 1834.

"L'origine de la harpe" and "Adieu Bessy" offer less of interest. The only noteworthy point is the juxtaposition in the latter piece of major and minor versions of the same motif, a typically Romantic procedure often used by Schubert (Example 35).

Example 34: Berlioz, "La belle voyageuse"

"Le coucher du soleil" is the most poetic of the *Mélodies irlandaises*. The strophic form is still retained, but the length of the stanzas gives the composer sufficient leisure to allow his fantasy free play. Each strophe contains forty-two measures. Berlioz obtains this length by joining two quatrains, by repetition of several textual passages, and by occasional melismatic treatment of the voice part. The descending chromatic line of the prelude effectively symbolizes the setting sun (Example 36).

The soaring flight described in the last lines of the first stanza also permits musical painting (Example 37).

As in "La belle voyageuse," the modulatory designs are quite unconventional. By the equivocal function of the first inversion of A-flat major, changing from tonic chord to Neapolitan sixth, the tonality of G major is rapidly reached. The original key is then regained by means of stepwise chromatic descent (Example 38).

Example 35: Berlioz, "Adieu Bessy" (1st version)

Example 36: Berlioz, "Le coucher du soleil"

In France about 1830 such a harmonic succession was considered extremely audacious. The same is true for the amplitude of melodic line, a feature not found in a single romance of the period. The second stanza, no more than a literal repetition of the first, is less attractive. The lack of agreement between music and text caused Boschot to remark that "the smell of the romance is too strong

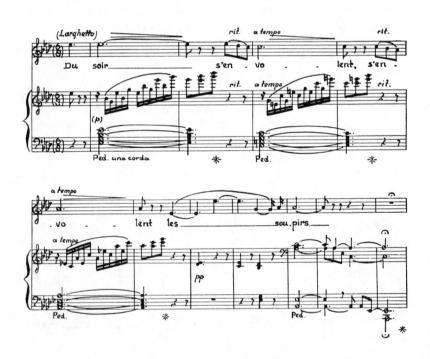

Example 37: Berlioz, "Le coucher du soleil"

Example 38: Berlioz, "Le coucher du soleil"

here."[220] In summary, "Le coucher du soleil" may justly be called
Berlioz' first true *mélodie*, since it bears not only the name, but more
important, the essential characteristics of the new genre.

The *Mélodies irlandaises* were moderately praised by Paris critics:

> M. Berlioz deserves nothing but congratulations for employing a much
> more pleasing melodic scheme in this work than in his other compositions.
> This collection of *mélodies* has charm and it is clear from them that to follow
> the right path, the only one leading to lasting success, M. Berlioz has only
> to desire it.[221]

The detailed review of François Stoepel also included some flattering remarks. Speaking of "La belle voyageuse," this critic noted
its grace and the "witchery in the melody." He referred to "Le
coucher du soleil" as "a pleasant and poetic composition" but he
objected to its lack of phraseological symmetry:

> Such regularity is lacking from these compositions and in spite of all the
> beauty and truthfulness of the melody, in spite of all the originality in the
> harmony and in other features of the piece, the defect mentioned surely pre-
> vents our complete satisfaction.[222]

When compared with the cantatas written for the Prix de Rome
competition, the eight scenes from *Faust,* and other large works composed prior to 1830, the *Mélodies irlandaises* do not convey an impression of progress. Boschot even described them as "a halt, if not
a step backward."[223] But if considered as successors to the first
romances, they represent a considerable advance; they display a
generally more competent technique and the accompaniment in

particular shows less frequent awkwardness. Some rhythmic and harmonic extravagances found in "Adieu Bessy" and "L'origine de la harpe" cannot be attributed to youthful lack of knowledge, since the composer deliberately permitted them to remain in the revised edition of 1850.

Berlioz' own opinion of this song collection is difficult to determine, since he rarely mentions it in his memoirs and letters. One reference in the *Mémoires* describes how in Rome, "stretched out on a sofa," he had sung them in "a bored voice" for Mendelssohn and experienced a feeling of some resentment that the latter, who always disliked his overtures and symphonies, found pleasure only in these songs.[224] Thus it appears that later in life Berlioz considered the *Mélodies irlandaises* a work of minor importance.

In January 1830 Berlioz composed the song called "Élégie," which was added at the last moment to the collection of Irish *mélodies*. Moore's poem depicts the last farewells of Robert Emmet, the condemned Irish hero;[225] it was conceived by the impassioned composer as his own farewell to Harriet Smithson, to whom it was dedicated.[226] Berlioz describes its conception in the following manner:

> Returning home from one of those trips in apparent search of my soul, I found open upon my table the volume of Thomas Moore's *Irish Melodies*; my eyes lighted on the one that begins with the words "When he who adores thee." I picked up my pen and at one sitting wrote the music for the heart-rending farewell which, under the title "Élégie," serves as the final piece for my collection *Irlande*. This is the only time I have been able to depict such emotion while still under its active and immediate influence. But I believe that I have seldom been able to achieve such poignant truth as in its melodic accents, submerged in such a storm of sinister harmonies.[227]

"Élégie" is an important document in the life of Berlioz. Investigations made by Boschot, Prod'homme, and Tiersot show that the "lightning-struck" composer almost never wrote spontaneously and that his operas and symphonic works contain many passages derived from previous works. "Élégie," however, bears all the characteristics of feverish inspiration; it actually does possess "a poignant truth in its melodic accents" and its daring harmonic combinations unquestionably resounded in 1830 as "a sinister storm." The work's technical deficiencies nevertheless make it unsuccessful from the musical point of view and Berlioz' own comment

IRLANDE

9 Mélodies pour une et deux voix avec Chœur.

PAROLES DE THOMAS GOUNET,
MUSIQUE DE

HECTOR BERLIOZ

N°

Paris, chez Richault, Editeur Boul! Poissonnière 26 au 1er

Title page of Berlioz' song cycle *Irlande*

Title page of an early edition of Berlioz' "La captive"

that "this piece is immensely difficult to sing and accompany" is a vain attempt to cover such defects as forced tension in the voice part and especially the ineffective accompaniment; these elements make satisfactory realization of the composer's intentions virtually impossible. The piano part is written almost entirely in tremolo, with the unpianistic motif shown in Example 39 being repeated no less than twenty-one times:

Example 39: Berlioz, "Élégie"

Berlioz never completed his attempted orchestration of the piece, rationalizing that "such compositions are not intended for the broad concert public and since it would be a profanation to expose it to its indifference, I suspended my work and burned what I had already put into score."[228]

Nevertheless, the faults of this *mélodie* should not blind us to its esthetic innovations. The disturbance of Emmet-Berlioz is translated in a striking manner by the unusual placement of rests and the insertion of exclamatory words (Example 40).

Example 40: Berlioz, "Élégie"

When Emmet invokes the testimony of Heaven, the melodic design makes way for a declamatory passage in which a phrase is again cut by rests (Example 41).

Example 41: Berlioz, "Élégie"

In this inflated hyper-Romantic composition Berlioz uses a pre-Wagnerian style that opened a new perspective for the French *mélodie*. But his audacities fell on deaf ears; not until forty years later did a link with this technique appear in the songs of Duparc.

Contemporary reviews of "Élégie" clearly show the critics' lack of understanding. Stoepel cleverly avoids committing himself to a concrete judgment, although the end of his article contains a hint of malice:

> We never considered an attempt to explain this work of M. Berlioz in words, since he has departed in this instance from all the usual methods of composition and we know of no precedent, no point of comparison, that might serve as the basis of our criticisms. ... It can only be comprehensible to those who share with M. Berlioz the privilege of allowing themselves to be dominated by the influence of a poetic idea, to the point of passing successively from ecstasy to bitter grief and from tears to violent despair.[229]

At Subiaco in 1832 Berlioz set "La captive" (one of Hugo's *orientales*), which became one of his best-known songs.[230] The original version of this *mélodie* has a strophic form and at first sight resembles a romance, but closer examination of its expressive vocal line reveals that the piece is far superior to the platitudes of the time in depth of expression and modulatory flexibility (Example 42).

After his return to Paris Berlioz added a violoncello part to the song. The arrangement for contralto and orchestra dating from 1848 constituted a much more radical alteration and resulted in a virtually new composition. Although the form became freer, the music

Example 42: Berlioz, "La captive" (1st version)

still reflects the poetic structure (from which Berlioz omitted stanzas
IV–VII):

LITERARY STANZAS		MUSICAL STRUCTURE
I	A	(*almost identical with the first version*)
II	A'	(*free variant, stretto of the vocal part*)
III	A''	(*slightly varied*)
VIII	B	(*new theme in the voice; the text is sung twice; the accompaniment has bolero rhythm; counterpoint in the violoncellos uses theme A*)
IX	A'''	(*rhythmic variant*)
I (lines 1–2)	Coda	(*beginning of theme A*)

Sections A and B are especially interesting for their structure and
technique. The stretto of A' imparts an entirely new character to the
original theme (Example 43).

Example 43: Berlioz, "La captive" (3rd version, measures 25–34)

Berlioz' constructive dexterity is demonstrated in section B, where
a capricious vocal melody and a piquant accompaniment illustrate
these playful words:

> J'aime en un lit de mousses
> Dire un air espagnol

The lofty singing theme of the violoncellos (theme A) adds a mean-
ingful contrast to the section, while conserving not only the musical,
but also the poetic unity.

Despite the evident beauties of this last version, the deep and varied expression, the careful prosody, and the richness of the orchestral accompaniment, "La captive" in its simple strophic form with only piano accompaniment is preferable as a work of art; the "symphonic *mélodie*" of 1848 robs this spontaneous inspiration of its intimate atmosphere, so fully in harmony with the poem.

The vogue this work enjoyed in Rome is reflected in the words of Horace Vernet, director of the Villa Médicis:

> Your "Captive" is beginning to make it quite disagreeable to stay in the villa. One cannot take a step in the palace, in the garden, in the woods, on the terrace, or in the corridors, without hearing sung, hummed, or grunted, "Le long du mur sombre ... le sabre du Spahis ... je ne suis pas Tartare ... l'eunuque noir, etc." It's enough to drive a man crazy. Tomorrow I am firing one of my servants and I shall take a new one only on condition that he not sing "La captive."[231]

In Paris the song awakened less interest. The reviewer of a concert in which it was sung by Marie Falcon wrote:

> M. Berlioz is less successful with vocal music than with symphony. In spite of our most diligent attention, we could not understand what he was attempting in his *orientale*; we found it only an interminable and soporific lament.[232]

"Le jeune pâtre breton," with words by Brizeux, underwent virtually the same transformation as "La captive." The first version was written about 1833 for voice and piano, the second in 1834 for voice, horn, and piano, and the third in the same year for voice and orchestra. In this instance also the first version is the best, reflecting the rustic simplicity of the poem. Several other vocal pieces of this period (e.g., "Le pêcheur" by Goethe, "Premiers transports" by Émile Deschamps, and "Chant du bonheur" with words by the composer), however, show their best side in the symphonic version and were very likely conceived in that form. "Le pêcheur" and "Chant du bonheur" were used in *Lélio*, while "Premiers transports" reappeared in *Roméo et Juliette*. Along with many interesting details the songs include passages of a bombastic or banal character.

Pressed by the need for money, Berlioz wrote two romances in 1834 for musical journals: "Les champs" (Béranger) for *La romance* and "Je crois en vous" (Léon Guérin) for *Le Protée*. Boschot accurately characterizes these songs as "halfway between Berlioz and the romance," and indicates that the composer himself was well aware that he could no longer satisfy the simple taste of amateurs, for when asked shortly after for another "sparkling trifle," he replied that he "was unable to do so." [233] "Je crois en vous" fortunately survived in its later version as Arlequin's arietta in the second act of *Benvenuto Cellini*. By means of several modifications and an exquisite orchestration, this *mélodie* of little intrinsic interest acquired a surprising charm. The other piece, "Les champs," was also preserved in a second version made in 1850. While more interesting than the original, it never reaches the level of "La captive."

In 1841 appeared Berlioz' most important work in the domain of the *mélodie*, six songs on poems from Gautier's *La comédie de la mort* (1838) gathered under the title of *Les nuits d'été*. The dates of composition of five pieces of the collection are not known; an autograph of the first song bears the date 1840.[234] In this first *mélodie*, entitled "Villanelle," a new Berlioz may be seen at first glance. The lively and agile tune is supported by sprightly chords full of surprising harmonic turns but without the least trace of eccentricity. Some imitations develop naturally out of the melodic line and weld the accompaniment to the vocal part (Example 44). The strictness of the strophic form is softened by slight melodic alterations. "Villanelle" may be considered the most accomplished of all Berlioz' songs.

Example 44: Berlioz, "Villanelle"

"L'île inconnue," whose text (like that of "Villanelle") expresses a sort of *invitation au voyage*, is less brilliant but more imposing in concept and more profound in expression. In place of the rising melodic line of the first piece, a descending hexachord plays a major role in both melody and accompaniment. In typically Romantic fashion, the music is impregnated with a melancholy atmosphere entirely lacking in the poem. This conflict between words and music is even sharper in "Le spectre de la rose," where a rose wilts after being pressed to the bosom of a young beauty. In the evening the ghost of the flower returns to her bedside, telling her:

> O toi qui de ma mort fus cause,
> Sans que tu puisses le chasser,
> Toute la nuit mon spectre rose
> À ton chevet viendra danser,
> Mais ne crains rien, je ne réclame
> Ni messe, ni *De Profundis*;
> Ce léger parfum est mon âme,
> Et j'arrive du paradis.

The somewhat precious subject and its mannered treatment add nothing to Gautier's glory. But Berlioz found inspiration in this poem for the composition of a tragic scene. The emotional atmosphere of the prelude (Example 45) and the progression of diminished seventh

Example 45: Berlioz: "Le spectre de la rose" (2nd version)

chords, descending by semitones and modulating from C-sharp minor to B major (Example 46), show to what extent the composer "dramatized" the text.

"Absence," the best-known piece of *Les nuits d'été*, is by contrast

Example 46: Berlioz, "Le spectre de la rose" (2nd version)

quite simple in conception. Its noble and poetic melody, cast in the classic rondo form (A B A C A), succeeded in charming even the public of 1840.

The two laments entitled "Sur les lagunes" and "Au cimetière" are, if not the most beautiful, certainly the most interesting of these *mélodies.* Both pieces are based on a short germinal motif constructed of a minor second interval that dominates the vocal part as well as the accompaniment (Example 47).

Example 47: Berlioz, "Sur les lagunes"

The motif appears in many variant forms (Example 48).

Example 48: Berlioz, "Sur les lagunes"

Used as embellishment of a minor third, it produces a diminished fourth that evokes an impression of anguish (Example 49).

Example 49: Berlioz, "Sur les lagunes"

In the other lament the minor second reappears as an appoggiatura (Example 50). The motif later provokes some extraordinary harmonic frictions that persist until the final chord, which has the minor sixth added (Example 51). Significantly enough, no less than four versions of this final measure are known.

Such exceptional audacity is not unusual in *Les nuits d'été*, a collection which abounds in original harmonic combinations. The phraseological constructions are also very daring, to the extent that one can hardly speak of musical phrases in the usual sense of the term. The requirements of prosody break the periodic regularity and sometimes the vocal line seems to sprout from the harmonic

Example 50: Berlioz, "Au cimetière" (1st version)

tensions. Elsewhere Berlioz uses the declamatory style already mentioned in connection with "Élégie" (Example 52; compare Example 41).

In the composition of *Les nuits d'été* Berlioz displayed the kind of artistic devotion usually reserved for operas or symphonies. All ties with the dying romance are broken; the *mélodie* has become a serious genre.

The last period (1840–1850) brings little of novelty. "La belle Isabeau" is characterized by a heavy Romanticism perhaps already

Example 51: Berlioz, "Au cimetière" (1st version)

Example 52: Berlioz, "Au cimetière" (1st version)

obsolete when it was composed in 1844. "Le chasseur danois" is an insignificant piece attracting attention only by its unusual instrumentation for 18 strings (5-5-3-2-3), 2 flutes, 2 oboes, 2 clarinets, 4 bassoons, 4 horns, *no* trumpets, 3 trombones, and 2 timpani. In the bolero "Zaïde" Berlioz makes an attempt at local color; this piece, as well as the piquant scherzo "Le trébuchet," is of a higher level. In "Le matin" and "Petit oiseau," two *mélodies* written to the same text, the composer returns to the stylistic simplicity of "La belle voyageuse." These last two pieces offer some charming details but at the same time show how close to the romance Berlioz could still come.

The only song of this period truly worthy of Berlioz is "La mort d'Ophélie," a *ballade* with words by Ernest Legouvé. Returning from his travels to Russia, the composer had been present at a performance of *Hamlet* in Riga. He was once more fascinated by Shakespeare in finding his Ophelia of old, his Harriet. But the state of exaltation did not return and the *mélodie* resulting from this renewed confrontation reveals an atmosphere of weariness and melancholy. The twilight of Romanticism has descended. The accompaniment is much simpler than in the preceding works; unlike the spiced harmonies of *Les nuits d'été*, chromatic chords are relatively rare in this piece. All the expression resides in the melodic line, sometimes confided to the voice, sometimes to the right hand of the piano part, and most often to the two simultaneously. The rendering of Ophelia's voice is exceptionally moving (Example 53).

Here the music is so powerfully lyric that the epic character of the text is forgotten. "La mort d'Ophélie" already presages Berlioz' last style, that of *L'enfance du Christ*.

The texts of Berlioz' *mélodies* often illustrate certain phases of his intimate life, the allusions being too clear to be deemed purely accidental. The "Romance d'Estelle" reflects the young Hector's admiration for Estelle Dubœuf. "Élégie" sings of his passionate love for Harriet Smithson. "La captive" is Berlioz himself, "imprisoned" in Italy thanks to the Prix de Rome, obtained with so much

Example 53: Berlioz, "La mort d'Ophélie"

difficulty. The lithograph illustrating the first printing of "Les champs" shows an elegant young man, "A Romantic lion." Perhaps it is the composer himself, inviting his Harriet to leave Paris to set up house in Montmartre, at that time still just a rustic village:[235]

> Cherchons loin du bruit de la ville
> Pour le bonheur un doux asile.

The lack of homogeneity in Berlioz' *mélodies* was mentioned at the beginning of this chapter. Certain of the pieces (e.g., "L'origine de la harpe," "Le chasseur danois," and "La belle Isabeau") are of little value; others attain an artistic level surpassing by far the taste of the time and could only be appreciated by later generations. From the beginning Berlioz' songs reveal a struggle to escape the insipidity of the romance.[236] His attempts resulted in two different types of songs. The first maintains the external characteristics of the romance, i.e., the strophic form and the subordinate piano part. But the pieces of this type (e.g., "La belle voyageuse," "Le jeune paysan [later "pâtre"] breton," "Petit oiseau," and "Le matin") are distinguished from the stereotypes of the time by the originality of their melodic line and their harmony. In the other, more Romantic type, the text to some extent determines the musical structure and interior form; that is, the phraseological construction is also subject to the rhythm of the words. In a similar manner, their accompaniment is closely tied to the text. The harmonies are entirely unconventional and sometimes very complicated. Examples of this type may be found in *Les nuits d'été* (except "Villanelle" and "Absence") and in some detached pieces ("Élégie" and the third version of "La captive"). As might be expected, Berlioz orchestrated most of these latter works, an operation that must have been almost mechanical, since orchestral characteristics were already present in the piano parts.

At first Berlioz' influence on the young generation of *mélodie* writers was very slight. Much later Duparc's songs show a link with the style of *Les nuits d'été*, and also development of the constructive procedures used in "Sur les lagunes" and "Au cimetière." Gounod, Bizet, Saint-Saëns, and Massenet rejected Berlioz' esthetic innovations. The low level of public taste was not the only factor that barred a just appreciation of the composer's songs. His mishandling of the piano parts resulted in ineffective accompaniments that are particularly surprising from the author of a *Treatise on Instrumentation*. The tremolos and anti-pianistic batteries of "Élégie" and "Sur les lagunes" explain why even today these *mélodies* appear only rarely on concert programs.

Berlioz' manner of resolving problems of prosody merits a closing comment. His early romances are full of erroneous accents, as demonstrated in this phrase from "Le dépit de la bergère":

> Au-TRE-fois infidèle
> Faisait dire AUX échos
> Que J'É-tais la plus belle.

Such glaring errors no longer appear in "Le montagnard exilé" and the *Mélodies irlandaises*. But since Berlioz is no purist, in spite of the complete liberty permitted him by the prose text of "Élégie," he places the mute syllable of the word "noircissent" on a strong beat. The following phrase:

> Et CES as-TRES sans nombre

remains unchanged in the third version of "La captive," a condition that can hardly be attributed to the composer's nonchalance. He was clearly unwilling to sacrifice the perfect melodic line of 1832 to the rhythmic requirements of the verse. Nevertheless, these examples of incorrect prosody are exceptional; tonic accents generally fall on strong beats.

Giacomo Meyerbeer (1791–1864)

Berlioz' painful attempts to rejuvenate the romance and develop a genre equal to the German *Lied* were simultaneous with Meyerbeer's great success in the domain of the *mélodie*, obtained almost effortlessly. In 1835 a critic referred to his "Rachel à Nephtali" and "Le moine" as "true innovations in the romance genre" and thirty-two years later the German composer was still called "the initiator of the *mélodie*."[237] Berlioz himself saw Meyerbeer as an ally in his struggle against the inanity of the romance. Writing a review of "Le moine," Berlioz suggested that:

> In spite of the innate French preference for the vaudeville style, three or four compositions of the type of this one would probably suffice to cause the miserable products of the romance industry to disappear. While making us the laughing stock of musicians of all nations, they have at the same time stopped the advance of the art here at home more than all the material obstacles that are daily opposed to such progress.[238]

Today most of Meyerbeer's *mélodies* seem obsolete to us. Even his biographers Dauriac and Curzon have had to recognize that they display few of his great qualities and that the song environment was uncomfortable for Meyerbeer.[239] The enormous success of his operas *Robert le diable* and *Les Huguenots* naturally stimulated the vogue for his small vocal works, but it would be unjust to claim that the favor transferred to his songs was only a consequence of snobbism and the large public's lack of discrimination. Certain characteristics of style that offend today's esthetic feelings were admired by music lovers of 1830. Even Berlioz praised passages in various pieces (e.g., "Le moine," "Le vœu pendant l'orage," "Le ranz-des-vaches d'Appenzell," and "Ballade de Marguerite de Valois") that to present-day ears seem to lack naturalness and to abound in exaggerated pathos.[240] Thus the historic importance of Meyerbeer's work, indisputably surpassing its artistic value, justifies an examination within the framework of this study.

Meyerbeer wrote most of his songs before the *première* of *Les Huguenots* in 1836. A collection of forty pieces published in 1849 gives a clear picture of the various types he united under the name of *mélodie*: dramatic and lyric *scènes* ("Le moine," "Le poète mourant," "Le vœu pendant l'orage," and "Rachel à Nephtali"); *chansonnettes* and *canzonette* ("Mère grand," "La chanson du Maître Floh," "Fantaisie," "Nella," "Canzona," and "Le ricordanze"); "salon" hymns and true religious songs ("Le baptême," "Sonntagslied," "Luft von Morgen," and "Cantique du Trappiste"); pieces imitating folk songs ("Lied des venezianischen Gondoliers" and "Chant des moissonneurs vendéens"); and finally

Giacomo Meyerbeer in 1836

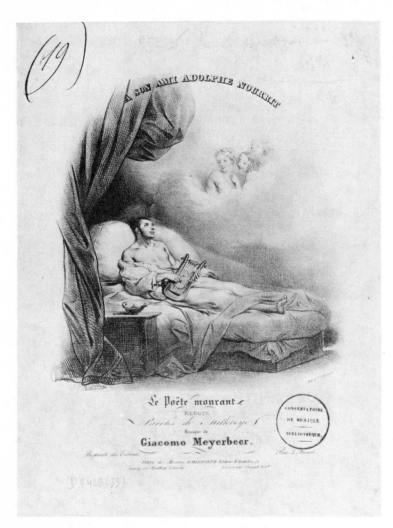

Title page of Meyerbeer's "Le poète mourant"

some *mélodies* that are close to the German *Lied* in style ("Suleika," "La marguerite du poète," "Hör ich das Liedchen klingen," "Die Rose, die Lilie, die Taube," and "Komm").

Meyerbeer's work is as cosmopolitan as the man. Besides the many French *mélodies*, he wrote some songs to German and Italian words, most of them also appearing in French versions. The translations by Henri Blaze, Émile Deschamps, Maurice Bourges, and others were supervised by the composer and he was furious when an adaptation appeared without his prior knowledge, as shown by this fragment of a letter to his publisher, Maurice Schlesinger: "I have never written a *Lied* entitled 'Le pénitent' nor any with a title resembling it even slightly. A translation could therefore only be a deformity. I am alerting you not to publish it, as I must decline to accept it."[241]

The three nationalities are reflected in both the choice of texts and in the music. The vocal part is usually in Italian style, containing embellishments, *portamento*, and even cadenzas, whether the pieces are Italian, French, or German. An example taken from a *nocturne* for vocal duet indicates the importance of *bel canto* (Example 54).

Example 54: Meyerbeer, "Mère grand"

In "Le ricordanze" and "Canzona" even the piano part is impregnated with Italianism. But more typically Meyerbeer plays his German cards in the accompaniment. His musical language does not attain the profundity of most German composers, but he does retain some of the national characteristics. The prelude to "Sici-lienne" shows Schubert's influence (Example 55).

Example 55: Meyerbeer, "Sicilienne"

Some pieces written to texts by Goethe, Heine, and Rückert come very close to the *Lied* and even one of the French *mélodies*, "La marguerite du poète," may claim this designation. Inspired by the Germanophile Henri Blaze, Meyerbeer adds German harmonies to a tune suggestive of *opéra-comique* (Example 56).

The last two examples show how ably Meyerbeer could handle lively and light poems. In pieces with lyric texts (e.g., those of Goethe and Heine), however, he vainly seeks for the essence of the *Lied*; the master of grand opera lacks the true *Empfindung*, an atmosphere more aptly depicted not only by Schubert, but even by second-rank com-posers like Hiller and Proch.[242]

The richness of Meyerbeer's harmony is specifically German. With his "learned" combinations, the composer had no difficulty in surprising the French, accustomed at that period to the banalities of hundreds of romances. The modulating passage of Example 57, for instance, is in no way extravagant when examined in the light of the styles of Beethoven, Weber, or Schubert. Nonetheless, to French ears it seemed extremely original. Even today Meyerbeer can sometimes astonish by his boldness. In the *mélodie* "Sur le balcon" dominant

Example 56: Meyerbeer, "La marguerite du poète"

Example 57: Meyerbeer, "Sicilienne" (harmonic scheme of measures 26–37)

seventh chords progress by parallel movement; yet the fragment remains entirely in the key of E-flat major, the chords in the second measure functioning merely as passing chords (Example 58).

Example 58: Meyerbeer, "Sur le balcon"

The relatively rare appearance of purely French characteristics in Meyerbeer's vocal works may be explained by the still nascent state of the *mélodie* genre, as contrasted with the maturity already attained by the German *Lied* or the Italian *canzonetta*. This makes even more curious a page of "Chant des moissonneurs vendéens" that already presages Bizet and Delibes (Example 59).

Meyerbeer indulges in few structural liberties, generally using the strophic or schematic forms. Monotony is avoided by the opposition of contrasting motifs, instrumental interruptions, and lengthy stanzas. By these means he is able to construct a large dramatic *scène* like "Le moine," for example, with the structural scheme A B C A B C A' C. Another work of the same type, "Rachel à Nephtali," even has the identical strophes so typical of the romance's simple structure.

One of the most important characteristics of Meyerbeer's *mélodies* is the close tie between voice and accompaniment, the vocal line sometimes even growing out of the piano part in an entirely natural way. Thus the prelude to "Chant de mai" is dominated by an anapaestic motif finally taken up by the singer (Example 60).

The same piece offers a vivid demonstration of the important role of harmony in the interpretation of the text, by the underlining of

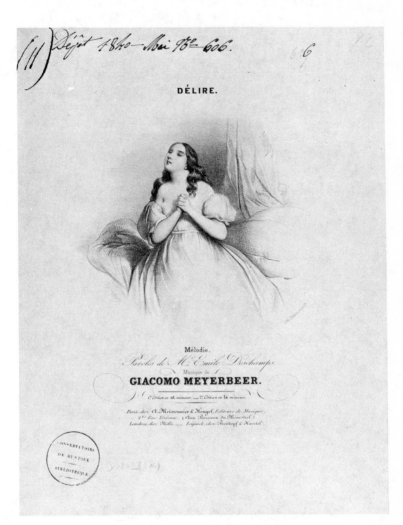

Title page of Meyerbeer's "Délire"

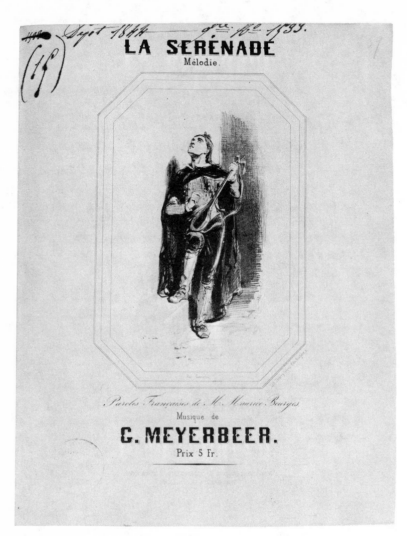

Title page of Meyerbeer's "La sérénade"

Example 59: Meyerbeer, "Chant des moissonneurs vendéens"

the word "amour" with a sudden modulation from F to G-flat major (Example 61).

Unity of words and music is manifested just as clearly in "Sicilienne," where the contents of the three preceding stanzas appear to be summed up at the end:

> Fleurs qu'adore la beauté,
> Ciel que dore la gaîté,
> C'est l'été;   } résumé of 1st stanza

> Lune pleine, mer qui luit,
> Tiède haleine qui la suit,
> C'est la nuit;   } résumé of 2nd stanza

> Feu qui dore tout séjour
> Et dévore chaque jour,
> C'est l'amour.   } résumé of 3rd stanza
>   MÉRY, "Sicilienne"

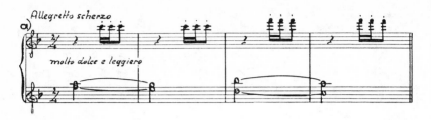

Example 60: Meyerbeer, "Chant de mai" (measures 1–4 and 19–22)

In modulating from B-flat to D-flat major the music keeps pace with the words (Example 62). "The composer changes his tonality as the orator modulates the inflections of his voice when progressing to a new order of ideas."[243]

In addition to symbolic interpretation, Meyerbeer offers many examples of musical painting (e.g., in "Le poète mourant," "La fille

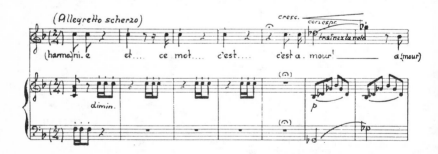

Example 61: Meyerbeer, "Chant de mai"

Example 62: Meyerbeer, "Sicilienne"

de l'air," "Le vœu pendant l'orage," and "La chanson du Maître Floh").

In Meyerbeer's operas the prosody is often deplorable. The instance of contradiction between musical and poetic rhythms shown in Example 63 is not at all unusual.

Example 63: Meyerbeer, *Le prophète* (4th Act)

These errors and signs of carelessness are usually attributed to the composer's German origin and to his lack of respect for versification. But Meyerbeer was well aware of the hazard of allowing himself the same liberties in the salon as on the stage. The prosody of the songs, although not perfect, is much more careful than that of his opera airs. Correspondence with his publisher shows that he even tried to control his translators in this respect: "I am now making it a formal condition that you send me the French lines after Émile Deschamps has written them, so that I can make changes in the prosody before printing."[244] Further proof of Meyerbeer's concern for poetry appears in a sentence from another letter to Schlesinger: "On artistic grounds I cannot allow the publication of the romances without the [original] German text."[245]

The twentieth century regards Meyerbeer as the representative of an age, hardly considering his compositions any more as living music. The question of whether his operas are unjustly neglected has been discussed in Lionel Dauriac's excellent biography, where the problem is clearly formulated:

> Meyerbeer's faults remain in his works. The good qualities have re-appeared in those of his successors ... in an improved state, so that no one looks for them at their source. Thus it is that one hundred years after his birth, nothing remains of a once great and illustrious name but a shadow: *magni nominis umbra.*[246]

The shorter works just examined suffer equally from the same condition. Gounod would probably not have succeeded in creating the true French *mélodie* if he had not been acquainted with these pieces and yet almost nothing of his predecessor appears in his "Venise" or "Chanson du printemps."

A few of Meyerbeer's *mélodies* (e.g., "La marguerite du poète," "Sicilienne," and "Sur le balcon") can still charm today. But the pathos of "Le moine" and the lachrymose language of "Le poète mourant" are no longer moving;[247] only their technical adroitness arouses admiration. Meyerbeer tried to compensate for his lack of lyrical feeling by the use of theatrical procedures belonging neither to the *Lied* nor to the *mélodie*. His "cries" and "explosions" (as in "La barque légère" and "Rachel à Nephtali") exceed the limits of the genre and may even have misled younger composers like Bizet and Delibes. But these weaknesses should not cause his more admirable qualities to be forgotten. The importance of his accompaniment was recognized by all contemporary critics, most notably by Fétis (who remarked also that "in his *mélodies*, Meyerbeer is entirely German").[248]

Franz Liszt *(1811–1886)*

The French *mélodies* of Franz Liszt occupy an entirely special place in the history of the genre. Published between 1840 and 1850 (except for "Tristesse," which was composed at Weimar in 1872), they remained virtually unnoticed until the end of the nineteenth century. The contemporary press ignored them almost completely and even German biographical and critical studies mention them only in passing.[249] This negligence cannot be attributed to the fact that Liszt published these songs in Berlin and Mainz, for Henri Schlesinger was represented in Paris by his brother Maurice, while the firm of Schott entrusted its French interests to Bernard-Latte. A more significant obstacle to the popularization of his *mélodies* in Parisian salons was the extreme difficulty of the voice parts, although even this explanation does not account for the indifference of the French press.

The complete edition of Liszt's musical works published in Leipzig after the First World War by Breitkopf & Härtel contains only ten songs written to French words.[250] Another piece, entitled "Élégie," with words by Étienne Monnier, found in the course of research done at the Bibliothèque Nationale, appears at the end of this book (Appendix II) with a brief technical analysis. Two unpublished French songs since found by Humphrey Searle ("Le Juif errant" [Béranger] and "Oh pourquoi donc" [Mme. Pavlov]) have been added to Appendix VI.

Although Liszt was as much of a cosmopolite as Meyerbeer, he does not display the same multifarious character. His songs to words of Victor Hugo, Musset, or Alexandre Dumas reveal no essentially

French traits, just as his pieces set to Petrarch's sonnets show none that are typically Italian. The point of departure for Liszt was the German *Lied*; his best vocal works follow in the tradition of Beethoven, Schubert, and Schumann, whose songs he had long known and many of which (along with those of Dessauer and Mendelssohn) he had arranged for piano solo before the composition of his own songs.

Liszt's *mélodies* nevertheless agree perfectly with their French words and this may be explained by his choice of texts. The Hugo poems set by Liszt are almost all true literary *Lieder*, to which the German style could easily be adapted. When Liszt chose a dramatic text, he introduced, according to the custom of the day, elements of the *scène*. Such is the case in "Jeanne d'Arc au bûcher" (Dumas), in spite of the somewhat misleading subtitle *romance dramatique*. The piece actually confirms the composer's preference for the German tradition since it is truly a dramatic *Lied*. Neither a strophic romance

Example 64: Liszt, "Jeanne d'Arc au bûcher" (1st version)

nor a free *scène*, its structure rather resembles the medieval *Gesätz* (*Bar*), a form also found in several of Schumann's *Lieder* (e.g., "Mondnacht" and "Abschied von der Welt"). In Liszt's "Jeanne d'Arc" two almost identical *Stollen* (A) are followed by an *Abgesang* (B); a common refrain (R) appears after each section (the last time in extended form) and functions as a connecting element among the three parts: A R A′ R B R′. Stanza A has a *Lied* character, its phrases being constructed in periods (Example 64).

The refrain, on the other hand, is closer to a *scène* (Example 65).

Example 65: Liszt, "Jeanne d'Arc au bûcher" (1st version)

In the last stanza Liszt turns away from the *Lied* style, seemingly led by the pathos of Dumas' language to Meyerbeer's grandiloquence. The perfect synthesis of *Lied* and dramatic *scène* achieved in Schubert's "Die junge Nonne" is, however, lacking here. The later orchestral version could not save the composition, since both music and text had greatly aged in the thirty years separating the original from the score of 1876. Liszt himself considered "Jeanne d'Arc" as one of his weakest compositions, derisively calling it "my poor little monody" in a letter to Karl Rieder.[251] "Le vagabond" (Béranger) shows the same stylistic clash between *Lied* and *scène*. "Il m'aimait tant" (Delphine Gay) is in strophic form; although less dramatic in concept, the music still contradicts the simplicity of the poem.

The songs which may more properly be called *French Lieder* (with words by Hugo) are on a much higher level. The most Germanic of these, "S'il est un charmant gazon," is distinguished from the *mélodies* written to the same text by Reber, Franck, Saint-Saëns, and Fauré by a tenderness very close to the *Innigkeit* that is so typically German. The simple strophic form is in perfect harmony with the text. At the end of each stanza the composer interrupts the undulating movement of sixteenth notes by a lyric and graceful utterance in the voice part that underlines the poetic thought in a happy fashion (Example 66).

Example 66: Liszt, "S'il est un charmant gazon" (2nd version)

"Oh! quand je dors" is more complicated in both structure and harmony. The motif adapted to the initial words (Example 67)

Example 67: Liszt, "Oh! quand je dors" (2nd version)

dominates the entire piece. Sometimes it appears in modified form (Example 68).

Example 68: Liszt, "Oh! quand je dors" (2nd version)

As with Meyerbeer, harmonic progressions contribute to the interpretation of the text. The composer reinforces the suggestive assonance of the doleful lines

> Sur mon front morne où peut-être s'achève
> Un songe noir qui trop longtemps dura,

by employing the first motif in the lower registers. But in the lines

> Que ton regard comme un astre se lève ...—
> Soudain mon rêve
> Rayonnera!

the horizon opens out in music as well as poem. By means of the enharmonic of the dominant seventh, the key of F major is attained, producing such an impression of deliverance that the first somber motif, taken up by the voice, seems to have been transformed in character (Example 69).

Example 69: Liszt, "Oh! quand je dors" (2nd version)

The piece's closing harmony is also worth noting. The final cadence:

$$\text{I II}_6 \text{ VI}_{6\sharp\atop 4}\underline{\text{—}6\natural}\text{ I}$$

marks Liszt's preference for plagal progressions. In this particular case such a harmonic procedure is entirely justified, since an authentic cadence would have provoked too "realistic" an impression, thus breaking the poetic atmosphere.

The vocal line is broader than in the preceding piece. Inspired by the poet's sublime thought, the melody takes off in flight (Example 70).

Example 70: Liszt, "Oh! quand je dors" (2nd version)

Such amplitude requires great respiratory effort. Sometimes Liszt goes too far in this direction, as when he writes "et soudain" instead of "soudain" with the obvious intention of eliding the last mute syllable of the preceding line in order to avoid an interruption in the musical phrase. Such a procedure may be criticized because it breaks the rules of versification by destroying the syllabic equilibrium and because it creates difficulties, even for the very experienced singer, by requiring an inordinate length of breath (Example 71). On the question of elision Liszt might be defended on the grounds that composers apply its rules more flexibly than do poets, especially when treating the text as prose; but his decision to elide the mute syllable of a feminine line, particularly in a situation in which the enjambment is not clearly indicated by the poet, still seems unjustified. In this case Hugo certainly appears to have visualized a syntactic separation between the two lines (note the punctuation "… —" after the word "lève").

This minor prosodic lapse is overshadowed by the respect that Liszt otherwise demonstrates for the words. His almost impeccable prosody is even more careful than that of Berlioz. The rendering of the line

Pose un baiser, et d'ange deviens femme …—

Example 71: Liszt, "Oh! quand je dors" (2nd version)

shows, to what extent the composer has penetrated the subtleties of
poetic thought. Liszt appears to have made the change from the corresponding phrase of the first stanza ("Et qu'en passant") in order
to reinforce the suggestion of the poetic image; he accomplishes this
with an alteration in rhythm, advancing the G-sharp of the last beat
of the previous measure in order to prolong the word "pose"
(Example 72).

Example 72: Liszt, "Oh! quand je dors" (2nd version)

"Oh! quand je dors" is certainly the masterpiece of Liszt's French
songs and may even be described as one of the most beautiful
mélodies written before Duparc. Hugo's language, so rich in imagery,
has only rarely found such a worthy musical equivalent.

This profound unity is lacking in "Enfant, si j'étais roi," a piece
that otherwise contains many fine details; but the poetic richness is
precisely what trips up the composer in his rendering of the lines

> Et le profond chaos aux entrailles fécondes,
> L'éternité, l'espace, et les cieux, et les mondes,

by ascending and descending tremolos in the left hand. This exterior painting of chaos is only a feeble reflection of the poet's
visionary language and results in a rather tasteless effect that
demonstrates the truth of Fauré's above-quoted statement: Verse
that is too rich and complete in itself cannot profitably be adapted
to music.

Of the two *mélodies* set to "Spanish" poems by Hugo, "Gasti-

Franz Liszt

Richard Wagner in Paris, 1842

belza" emphasizes the Southern atmosphere by the use of bolero rhythm, but is quite weak in other respects. The second, entitled "Comment, disaient-ils," is by contrast an exquisite composition whose particular charm distinguishes it from all Liszt's other songs. In spite of the indication *quasi chitarra*, exterior effects are secondary in this work, the sounds of the guitar being suggested rather than imitated. The poem's structure is carried over to the music in an ingenious fashion. The young men ask their questions in a *parlando* voice sustained by staccato notes in the piano, always in the key of G-sharp minor (Example 73).

Example 73: Liszt, "Comment, disaient-ils" (2nd version)

The girls answer in a more cantabile and varied manner. Their different suggestions "Ramez ... dormez ... aimez," are sung successively in B, F, and A-flat major, leading to striking modulations in which the leading tone of F becomes the sixth of G-sharp (Example 74).

Example 74: Liszt, "Comment, disaient-ils" (2nd version)

In this way Liszt not only subtly fixes the psychological relationships between questions and answers, but also gives a purely musical form to the piece, that of a rondo in miniature:

MUSICAL STRUCTURE	Ritornello	1st stanza	Ritornello	2nd stanza	Ritornello	3rd stanza	Coda (*ritornello and stanza combined*)	
TONALITY	G-sharp minor	B major	G-sharp minor	F major	G-sharp minor	A-flat major	A-flat major *and*	G-sharp minor
TEXT	Question	Answer	Question	Answer	Question	Answer	Summary of Answers	

This lively piece ends with a striking effect probably unique in song history. The voice, at first sustained by arpeggiated chords, finishes entirely alone:

Example 75: Liszt, "Comment, disaient-ils" (2nd version)

Liszt's last *mélodie*, written in 1872 to Musset's poem "Tristesse," is of a different type from those already examined, demonstrating how the master's style gradually evolved into the declamatory type of *Lied*. The vocal line has become almost recitative, following the most subtle nuances of the words. Several passages are unaccompanied and some lack bar lines. The tragic destiny revealed by the poet's moving confession is painted by heart-rending chords recalling Wagner's idiom in *Tristan* (Example 76).

Example 76: Liszt, "Tristesse"

The harmony is as unstable as the structure of the vocal part; even the final chord fails to resolve the tension (Example 77).

Example 77: Liszt, "Tristesse" (close)

This piece endowed with features of unusual beauty is no longer either a *mélodie* or a *Lied*; it is a musically declaimed poem sustained by chords almost no longer obeying musical laws.

Unlike Meyerbeer's vocal works, Liszt's French *mélodies* had little historical impact, having remained unknown for too long a period to have had much in influence in France. Their intrinsic value, however, is great. The best inspirations (e.g., "S'il est un charmant gazon," "Oh! quand je dors," and "Comment, disaient-ils") surpass the *mélodies* of Berlioz in technical prefection and those of Meyerbeer in poetic sensitivity. By using his great German predecessors as models and by succumbing to the spirit of French poetry, the master of Weimar united the Romantic souls of two nations in an admirable manner.

Richard Wagner (1813–1883)

The genius who so disturbed European culture in the second half of the nineteenth century made a very modest contribution to the history of the *mélodie*. Richard Wagner wrote only six French songs; all of them were composed during the winter of 1839–40, while he was staying in Paris under the most uncomfortable circumstances.[252] In order to earn money he tried to adapt to the current taste, but none of the pieces appears to have been sung in public and publishers' interest in them seems also to have been lacking.

Wagner's choice of texts does him honor. Rather than set the insipid doggerel heard daily in Paris salons, he chose poems of Hugo, Ronsard, Béranger, and Heine. But since his position forced him into concessions, he was unable to use the original text of the "Two Grenadiers," choosing instead a French translation that is certainly inferior, even though it had been approved by Heine.

Wagner's failure to make a name for himself in Parisian musical circles by means of his French *mélodies* was due in great part to the character of the music itself. Although he tried to conform to the drawing-room level, the songs were somewhat too difficult for the amateurs for whom they were intended. This fact alone would have been sufficient cause for the pieces to be put aside and forgotten. To make matters worse, he practically eliminated all chance of success by allowing himself occasional extravagances. An instance of this is found at the beginning of "Mignonne" (Ronsard), where the singer intones the poem in the middle of a musical phrase (Example 78).

Despite this passage, Wagner leans in this *mélodie* toward the traditional rómance style and the music has a French flavor. The lullaby "Dors, mon enfant" (anon.) is by contrast particularly German in nature. It is a *Lied* divided into three identical sections whose exquisite tenderness already presages the *Siegfried-Idyll*. Again in this work the construction of the vocal phrases does not coincide with that of the accompaniment (Example 79).[253]

Example 78: Wagner, "Mignonne"

Three other songs merit only passing mention: "Attente," a quite insignificant *mélodie* on words of Hugo; "Tout n'est qu'images fugitives" (Reboul), somewhere between a *Lied* and a *scène*; and "Les adieux de Marie Stuart" (Béranger), whose vocal style is too reminiscent of Meyerbeer's procedures. Unlike these three, "Les deux grenadiers" has much to offer and in addition poses the irresistible temptation for comparison with the music that Schumann set to Heine's original text. The conceptions of the two masters display a basic difference. In Schumann's artless and spontaneously senstitive composition the accent is placed not on the narrative aspect of the poem, but on the *Stimmung*, the heroic atmosphere. Since he evidently considered this ambiance more important than a mere recital of events, Schumann felt free to give the piece the purely musical structure of a rondo. Wagner, on the other hand, behaves

Example 79: Wagner, "Dors, mon enfant"

like a dramatic composer, following the text step by step and giving his version a more varied character, but also a weaker structure from the musical point of view. His piece comes close to a *scène*, while Schumann's is a true *Lied*. The difference between the two concepts emerges clearly in the excerpts given in Example 80.

Example 80: Wagner, "Les deux grenadiers," and Schumann, "Die beiden Grenadiere"

Wagner aspires to a realistic representation of the situation. His wounded warrior speaks with such difficulty that his mental and physical suffering are felt by the listener. Schumann's phrase expresses nothing in particular and could be adapted to almost any text. For him the musical idea prevails over that of the words. This is not to say that Schumann's *Lied* is completely detached from the poem; his music takes its inspiration from Heine's *Ballade*, but in the course of development the composer follows the laws of musical logic without attention to small literary details. These observations remain valid even if one concedes that the French translation conveys a more theatrical impression than the original words.

Both composers interpolate "La Marseillaise" at the end of their pieces, having arrived independently at the thought (Schumann's *Lied* was written a few months after Wagner's *mélodie*). Their differing methods of realizing the idea are again typical of their contrasting esthetic views. Wagner acts logically, putting Rouget de Lisle's song in the piano part to illustrate the vision of the dying grenadier. Schumann has the soldier himself attack the patriotic hymn in a powerful voice, a procedure justified for purely musical reasons, since "La Marseillaise" replaces the reprise of the rondo theme (Example 81).[254]

Wagner's esthetic conception is theoretically more correct than that of Schumann. But the latter's composition is unquestionably superior, a fact which may be explained by the specifically subjective character of the German *Ballade* and *Romanze*. Although such poems of Goethe, Uhland, Heine, and Mörike certainly belong to the epic genre, fundamentally they remain lyric poetry, very close to the

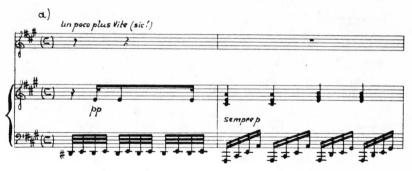

Example 81: Wagner, "Les deux grenadiers," and Schumann, "Die beiden Grenadiere"

literary *Lied*. Consequently, musical adaptations that place the emphasis on the atmosphere, like Schubert's "Erlkönig" and Schumann's "Die beiden Grenadiere," surpass the epic and dramatic compositions of Carl Loewe and Wagner.

In summary one may conclude that Wagner's French songs have more biographical than artistic interest, being "curiosities" in the work of a great artist. Wagner most certainly rises above the level of the romance, but he clearly did not feel at home in the French musical climate. Since he was unable to exploit fully the verses of Hugo and Ronsard, his musical translations of these poets are somewhat dull. The difficulties of handling a foreign language also created errors of prosody. Thus the inflated praise of Wagner's German biographers, who sacrificed even Schumann to their hero, is entirely unjustified.[255]

Félicien David (1810–1876)

After the brilliant success of his "ode-symphonie" *Le désert* in 1844, Félicien David was immediately labelled a "Romantic symphonist." Paris critics and music lovers placed him with Berlioz at the opposite pole from composers of "classical" symphonies (e.g., Georges Onslow and Henri Reber). While history has confirmed the fundamental difference between the two esthetic movements represented by program music and absolute music, the assumption of an artistic relationship between David and Berlioz cannot be accepted without reservation. If David is considered a "satellite" of Berlioz, the concept is somewhat reasonable for the symphonies, much less so for his dramatic works, and not at all for his songs.[256]

Most of David's *mélodies*, which number sixty, barely depart from the romance formula. Their forms, melodic turnings, and modulations are quite conventional although much above average in quality, having neither the melodic tediousness nor the defective accompaniment typical of most romances. They testify to a cultivated taste which, without seeking originality, avoids the platitudes of the Puget type of song.

To achieve this, David often calls upon German music for assistance. Yet truly Romantic *Lieder* attracted him less than those exuding a Biedermeier atmosphere. It should not be forgotten that many of Schubert's songs also belong to the latter type. Thus Schubert's influence shows in many of David's *mélodies* (Example 82).

Example 82: David, "Les hirondelles"

The upper pedal on the dominant, the sonority of the sixths, and the soothing rhythm of the slow waltz are all incontestably of Viennese origin. "Les hirondelles" had an enormous vogue; the poet Théodore de Banville even deigned in 1847 to write a "Couplet sur

l'air des Hirondelles" which appears in his *Odes funambulesques* (1857).
The Parisian public proved the amelioration of its taste by preferring
the natural simplicity of David's style to the pretentious dullness of
the productions of Loïsa Puget, Paul Henrion, and so many others.

"Plainte amoureuse" displays other facets of Schubert's style
(e.g., the *Wanderrhythmus* and the use of double pedal; Example 83).

Example 83: David, "Plainte amoureuse"

Among romances and conventional *mélodies*, several are still ap-
pealing (e.g., "Une plainte," "Le vieillard et les roses," "La vengeance des fleurs," and "La pluie"); others have faded with time.
Only rarely (as in "Le Rhin allemand") does David fall prey to
triviality.

A few of his songs have real historical value and show less conventional qualities. These are the *mélodies* written to the poems
called *orientales*. David's language generally does not contain exotic
formulae. Even in *Le désert* he evokes the East rather than actually
painting it. But the composer is clearly more inspired and daring
when he is treating an Oriental subject. "Le Bédouin" (words
"adapted from the Arabic" by J. Cognat)[257] and "Sultan
Mahmoud" (text by Gautier) show quite original touches. The
latter piece especially reveals a truly spontaneous animation. If the
composer translates nothing of Gautier's mocking spirit, at least he
avoids the slightly pallid sentimentality of some of his "Occidental"
mélodies (Example 84).

The best songs of this type appear in the collection *Les perles
d'Orient*, published late in 1845. Some of its pieces are unimportant
(e.g., "Reviens! reviens!," whose music is decidedly inferior to that
which Berlioz set to the same text (i.e., "Absence"); "L'océan," a
piece in *scène* style; and "Bonheur d'aimer," a pleasant work, but
too reminiscent of the romance. Besides these, the collection contains
two charming songs, "Amour pour amour" (Gautier) and "Mon

Caricature of Félicien David

Title page of David's "Le Bédouin"

Example 84: David, "Sultan Mahmoud"

almée" (Marc-Constantin), which in spite of their exotic subjects show David more than ever under Schubert's influence. Every note of the first piece could have issued from Schubert's pen, as is shown by the passage, chosen at random, illustrated in Example 85.

The stylistic affinity with Schubert also shows in the other *mélodie*, particularly in the rhythm and harmony. The lowering of the third in the tonic chord, transforming it into the subdominant of the new key, is a typically Schubertian procedure (Example 86).

The melody of this piece suggests that the Oriental dancer has been replaced by Lorelei, the German siren immortalized by Heine, so closely does its contour resemble the famous air composed by Friedrich Silcher to Heine's words (Example 87).

But the "pearl" of the collection is the piece entitled "Tristesse de l'odalisque," set to words written expressly for David by Gautier. The opening of this *mélodie* exhales an atmosphere of classical calm that is already almost Fauréan.[258] Nothing in David's vocal writing

Example 85: David, "Amour pour amour"

is more exquisite than this melodic line supported by an imaginary
'cello (Example 88).

The simple chords added to the words "The evening wind
laments to the ancient cypress trees" give an impression of noble

Example 86: David, "Mon almée"

Example 87: David, "Mon almée," and Silcher, "Lorelei"

sadness in a passage that could have been written by one of the great masters (Example 89).

In 1837 the composer wrote to his friend Sylvain Saint-Étienne:

> I am entirely occupied with quite a serious undertaking that demands all my attention. I am setting to music Lamartine's *Harmonies*. You see that the subject is very inspirational, but it is very difficult to handle.

Several months later he announced that he had written "three vocal pieces, among them Lamartine's 'La pensée des morts,' for baritone."[259] David's setting of the latter work (entitled "Le jour des morts") stands apart from the rest of his songs. Since the *Harmonies poétiques*, needless to say, could not be properly rendered in romance style, contemporary composers usually treated such a subject as a *scène*, a form to which Lamartine's contemplative poetry was ill-suited. David handled the matter differently. He enlarged the strict outlines of the romance and in this manner arrived at the *mélodie* naturally.

Example 88: David, "Tristesse de l'odalisque"

Example 89: David, "Tristesse de l'odalisque"

Lamartine's original poem contains no less than 234 lines grouped in nineteen ten-line stanzas and eleven quatrains. From these David selected stanzas I, V, VIII, XV, and XVIII, arranging them according to the scheme A A A B C. The conformity of the first three stanzas recalls the romance, but the sober atmosphere of the instrumental prelude gives an immediate impression of a more serious type of composition (Example 90).

Example 90: David, "Le jour des morts"

The descending scale of the prelude reappears in the course of stanza A and in the interludes, where a counterpoint is added (Example 91).

Example 91: David, "Le jour des morts"

The voice intones the initial phrase on the dominant harmony and the tonic is not reached until the latter half of the second measure (Example 92).

Example 92: David, "Le jour des morts"

After the third stanza the appearance of the major mode intensifies the expression of melancholy.[260] The key of F-sharp minor is not regained until the end of the phrase (Example 93).

It is curious that a musician with such a poetic talent showed carelessness in handling the versification.[261] The prosody of this *mélodie*, as of some others, is defective. Furthermore, the repetition of the last line of section A is unjustified, particularly in the third stanza. The meaning of "Je dis: 'N'es-tu pas leur voix?'" (I say,

Example 93: David, "Le jour des morts"

are you not their voice?) cannot be understood without reference to an earlier strophe (VI) in which the poet wonders "'Où sont ceux que ton cœur aime?'" (Where are those dear to your heart?). But this is one of the stanzas omitted from David's *mélodie*.

In spite of these shortcomings, "Le jour des morts" may be

counted among the most remarkable French songs of the Romantic era. Today the evolution that transformed the banal romance into the expressive *mélodie* seems quite natural to us, but in David's time many attempts to bring new life to the art of song failed because of the harmful influence of both *scène* and opera. In the light of these conditions, the piece just examined takes on added importance. It also places in evidence the stimulating role of Romantic poetry in the birth of the *mélodie*. While Gautier's *orientales* forced the composer to depart from conventionality, Lamartine's contemplative verse gave depth to his style and intensified his expressiveness. If David had appealed more frequently to the great poets of his age, he might have conquered the timidity that prevented the flourishing of his talents. A composer who could write "Le jour des morts" and "Tristesse de l'odalisque" was preeminently suited to song composition, for he possessed both a penchant for the intimate and a sympathetic understanding of poetry.

Henri Reber (1807–1880)

Henri Reber also made an important contribution to the birth of the *mélodie*. Like David, he started from the romance, but an important difference separates the two musicians. Reber was less strongly attracted by expressive poetry than David, generally preferring texts in which feeling and *esprit* are more evenly balanced. A number of his *mélodies* bear the title of chanson, a designation that aptly expresses the nature of these pieces. They are not, of course, the "patter" chanson of the *caveau* but in spirit rather resemble the lyric chansons of the sixteenth and seventeenth centuries. Before discussing Reber's works, a few remarks should be made about this relatively unknown composer's place in nineteenth-century music history.

Reber's music is certainly not notable for its originality. Under the conscious influence of the Viennese Classics (Mozart and Beethoven were his preferred masters) he did not seek new paths and in a certain sense, had no need to do so, since the fertile terrain on which he built his work provided perfectly for his artistic needs. Thus Reber may not be described as a neo-Classicist (like Mendelssohn, for example, whose balanced structures nearly always enclosed Romantic ideas), but rather as a modest continuator of the Viennese Classic style. The Romantic fervor of Berlioz and Schumann never struck him in any form. Saint-Saëns evokes this vivid image of Reber:

Although there was never the slightest affectation in his conversation or person, his mind readily turned toward the past and the exquisite urbanity of his manners awakened thoughts of vanished days. His white locks seemed powdered, his frock-coat took on the airs of a garment *à la française*. It seemed as though, lost by the eighteenth century in the nineteenth, he was strolling about there like a contemporary of Mozart's, astonished and somewhat shocked by our music and manners.[262]

Reber's thorough knowledge and deep love for the craft of composition also testify to his preference for the old masters. He was an extremely expert musician and as such exercised a beneficial influence on young composers during a period when the salons were inundated with the products of dilettantism. The admiration of Saint-Saëns, himself a consummate craftsman, is thus understandable. Reber's handling of his material within the restrained framework of standards voluntarily imposed is worthy of admiration. He seems to be the exception to the often stated (but never really proven) claim that harmony teachers write only dry music. Although his style is customarily conventional, it may nonetheless charm with melodic and harmonic details that are present for those who seek them.

Reber also possessed a real feeling for poetry, a property sometimes lacking in the Viennese masters. His musical imagery is neither ecstatic, clever, passionate, nor even stirring; these qualitites must be sought in Berlioz, Liszt, or Schumann. But Reber's ingenuity in falling in with his poets confers on his music a certain simplicity that conveys their thoughts quite accurately.

His interest in the past included its poetry as well as its music. He used texts by Thibaut de Champagne, Charles d'Orléans, Marot, Malherbe, Quinault, Corneille, and Florian. Some of his *mélodies* are tinged with an archaism that occasionally makes them oppressively heavy. An example of this appears in "Mortel, ouvre les yeux" (Corneille), whose accompaniment resembles a piano reduction of a concerto grosso (Example 94).

The same objection applies to "Stances de Malherbe." The true lyric chansons (e.g., "Chanson de Thibaut," "Chanson du Duc Charles d'Orléans," "Le départ" [Malherbe], and "Les hirondelles" [Florian]) are handled with more skill. The retrospective character of these works resides in the poetic atmosphere rather than in the use of particular procedures. Simplicity, balance, discrimination, and precision are the notable qualities of this group of songs, among which "L'ermite" (Marot) is certainly the most successful.

Example 94: Reber, "Mortel, ouvre les yeux"

In the lively and angular rhythm of the opening (Example 95) the spirit of Jannequin, Costeley, or Sermisy seems to return to life under Reber's pen. The freshness of this musical adaptation of old French poetry will not be surpassed by either Gounod or Delibes.

A place somewhat apart is held by "Regrets," of which the poem by Mary Stuart leads the composer to an imitation of the first stages of seventeenth-century monody; the evocation of an *air de cour* of the time of Guédron and Boësset shows how deeply Reber had imbibed the spirit of that period (Example 96).

Reber's interest in poetry was not restricted to that of the *ancien régime*, but included the verse of his own day. Among his works written to contemporary poetry are "Hai luli" (Xavier de Maistre), "Bergeronnette" (Dovalle), "Chanson du pays" and "Toi et moi" (anon.), "Rosette" and "Le voile de la châtelaine" (the Abbé de l'Écluse), and "Le prisonnier" (Béranger). Some of these

Example 95: Reber, "L'ermite"

exquisite chansons were written long before 1840, at the height of the Romantic era, but they already resemble the type of *mélodie* to be discussed in the next chapter. Indeed, Reber's work contains neither the positive qualitites of the "Romantic" *mélodie* (original-

Example 96: Reber, "Regrets"

ity, refinement, and depth), not its negative ones (theatrical pathos and excessive sentimentality); it does exhibit the intimate atmosphere, the graceful forms, and the French sensitivity that will characterize the best *mélodies* of the Second Empire. Some of these traits are displayed in the passages given in Example 97.

Sometimes the composer's guileless simplicity brings him close to folk song (Example 98).

With the exception of "Regrets," all the above-cited songs may be termed "lyric chansons." Reber also wrote a number of true romances (e.g., "Le serment" [Marceline Desbordes-Valmore] and "L'amour" [Louise Bertin]) and a French *Lied*, "Au bord du ruisseau" (Quinault) that show some slight Schubertian influence.

Victor Hugo takes first place among the poets chosen, being the author of no less than fourteen of Reber's *mélodie* texts. The composer was not one of those who permit their inspirations to smother the verse, replacing poetic refinement with musical riches. On the contrary, Reber effaces himself before the poet and leaves the

Example 97: Reber, "Bergeronnette," "Le voile de la châtelaine" (prelude), and "Rosette"

Example 98: Reber, "Chanson du pays"

structure of the text intact, in the Hugo songs even more than in his
other vocal works. This attitude explains his lack of psychological refinement, brilliance, and rich fantasy, qualities found, for example,
in Liszt's songs (Reber was apparently well aware that his true
vocation was not to be found in the Romantic domain, a judgment
confirmed, moreover, by the failure of more complicated pieces like
"Les proscrits" and "À un passant"). His adaptation of Hugo's
"Guitare" is much simpler than Liszt's (entitled "Comment,
disaient-ils"; see Example 73) but it is delicate, distinguished, and
pleasant (Example 99).

"Si mes vers avaient des ailes" is imprinted with a delicately
poetic feeling; its rhythm harmonizes very well with the élan of
Hugo's verse (Example 100).

A few technical aspects remain to be discussed. Reber's use of the
balanced phrase is perfectly justified in the context of his sober style.
Where such treatment is ruled out by the poem's structure, the composer re-establishes equilibrium by prolonging the musical phrase
(Example 101).

Example 99: Reber, "Guitare"

Example 100: Reber, "Si mes vers avaient des ailes"

Order and regularity, however, are not synonymous; raised in the traditions of French Classicism, Reber understands very well that *perfect* symmetry can paralyze and for this reason breaks the square-ness from time to time, even when this is not required by the text (Example 102).

In the repeat of a stanza the accompaniment is sometimes varied, often by utilizing the most primitive method, the ornamental variation. This procedure contributes in large part to the charm of "Chanson de Thibaut" and "Rosette" but it is less successful in "La captive," where the atmosphere of weariness and sensual pleasure is lost after the first stanza because the variations create an effect of digression.

On the problem of prosody Reber takes a moderate position. Sometimes he sacrifices the rhythm of the words to the musical logic, although his liberties are never excessive. Here too, this true musician shows his respect for the poet's efforts.

Example 101: Reber, "Le papillon et la fleur"

Example 102: Reber, "Bergeronnette"

The contemporary musical press was generally favorable toward Reber's *mélodies* and a feeling of sincere liking may be discerned in the criticisms.[263] Even today Reber merits our admiration, not only because he cultivated the best musical and literary traditions of his country, but especially because, gifted with a modest talent, he extracted the maximum profit from his good qualities, providing a worthy model for the younger generation.

CHAPTER IV

The Bourgeois Mélodie

ABOUT 1850 THE MÉLODIE ENTERS A NEW PHASE, DEVELOPING INTO AN independent, specifically French genre, able to maintain its position opposite the German *Lied*. Needless to say, the superiority of German composers will have to be recognized for several decades, but aside from Germany, France is the first country where a school arises, supported by almost all its leading composers. Various types of song related to the *mélodie*, which up to this time had impeded its natural flowering, either became extinct (e.g., the romance and the *scène*) or else developed quite independently (e.g., the *chansonnette*). German *Lieder* still exercise some influence, but can no longer overshadow the indigenous characteristics of the *mélodie*. If the *Lied* will later strongly affect the style of Édouard Lalo and Alexis de Castillon, these exceptions will not be able to alter the historical picture of French song.

The *mélodie*'s position in society is also clarified. The best pieces of Berlioz and Liszt had been intended for the professional singer and not the amateur, who would have faced insurmountable difficulty, even if he had been aware of the songs' artistic value. Now public taste slowly improves, while the composer on his side makes allowances for the limited abilities of the music-loving amateur. Especially in bourgeois circles the *mélodie* replaces the former romance. While surely an improved state of affairs, the new situation contains elements of danger for the composer, who, adapting to the technical level of the dilettante, is disposed toward artistic concessions. Too often texts of the great Romantic poets give way to mediocre doggerel and the music sometimes degenerates into an adroit succession of clichés. Thus the *mélodie* is menaced by industrialization in the same way as the romance had been earlier. Fortunately Lalo, Fauré, and the school of César Franck prevent such a development, even though some others (e.g., Gounod, Massé, and Massenet), after having enriched the repertory with some exquisite songs, become in the course of time the victims of their indulgence of the average taste.

The vocal pieces of David and Reber already foreshadow the character of the pieces we shall call "bourgeois" *mélodies*. Among these one seeks in vain for such high points as Berlioz' *Nuits d'été* or Liszt's "Oh! quand je dors," but the production as a whole has a more homogeneous character and the mean level is higher than that of the *mélodie* during the Romantic period. Although their artistic pretensions were reduced, composers of the Second Empire nevertheless wrote many charming songs that do not merit the oblivion into which they have fallen.

Charles Gounod (1818–1893)

> "*The true founder of the* mélodie *in France was Charles Gounod.*"
>
> MAURICE RAVEL
>
> "*... the somewhat tasteless confections of Gounod.*"
>
> TRISTAN KLINGSOR[264]

The "problem" of Gounod is enclosed within the apparent contradiction of these two quotations. Each contains a basic element of truth, although jointly they do not lead to the conclusion that sweetened tastelessness is the essential characteristic of the French *mélodie*. Ravel is alluding to the artist, the composer of some twenty accomplished pieces full of a particular charm; Klingsor is blaming the routinist, the musician who wastes his talent ceding to public taste and the solicitations of his publisher. A disciple of Fauré,

Ravel honors in Gounod his musical ancestor; Klingsor is shocked by the many facile pieces that became popular while the profound inspirations of Duparc, Chausson, and Debussy were neglected.

The curious circumstance of Gounod's becoming in the course of time his own epigonus may provisionally be passed over; the positive aspect of his work, the foundation of the true French *mélodie*, is more interesting. An exact description of its native characteristics is difficult, even when approached from the viewpoint of its contrast with the German *Lied*. The psychological differences between French and German poetry (i.e., *sensibilité* vs. *Empfindung*) and the contrast between the saturated atmosphere of a highly sophisticated, centralized civilization and the *Volkstümlichkeit* of German culture have already been discussed (in Chapter II, above). The distinctions are equally valid for *mélodie* and *Lied*, but refer to subjective and relatively vague qualities that are difficult to describe and unsuitable as tools for musical analysis. Georges Servières even denies the presence of purely French elements in Gounod's *mélodies*:

> If one extracts from Gounod's talent what is essentially German, and especially the harmonic and rhythmic formulae borrowed from Mendelssohn and Schumann, what remains is the craftsmanship of a constructor of catechistic hymns or *scènes* for bass voice, just like those that had been produced before him and that were still being produced in his time by Niedermeyer and Auguste Morel.[265]

Without agreeing entirely with Servières, one must admit that minute analysis of Gounod's songs leads to the disappointing conclusion that this is one of the instances where art refuses to divulge all its secrets. Nevertheless, Gounod's musical procedures (i.e., his structure, prosody, melodic line, accompaniment, and harmony) are sufficiently interesting to warrant a few remarks concerning their nature before going on to a survey of his total song production.

STRUCTURE. In this regard the composer follows established paths; he has a marked preference for the strophic form, although major structural differences exist between the Romagnési type of romance and Gounod's *mélodies*. Gounod's stanzas are considerably longer than those of his predecessors, twelve-line strophes being not at all exceptional (as in "Venise," "Chanson du printemps," and "Le soir"); the *mélodie* "Chant d'automne" even has strophes of sixteen eight-syllable lines, two of which are repeated. On the other hand, the pieces in which the number of stanzas is reduced to two (e.g., "Chant d'automne" and "Le soir") can no longer be called strophic at all. In these cases it would be more accurate to speak of a *Lied* form (according to the terminology employed by Vincent d'Indy) in two parts. These are sometimes subdivided into two sub-sections written in different modes (e.g., "Le vallon," "Medjé," and "Solitude"). Short strophes are employed only in cases where the text does not permit the joining of literary stanzas. Such an instance occurs in "La chanson de la glu" (set to a ballad from Jean Richepin's drama), where each strophe marks a phase of the story. Gounod achieves variety by means of precise directions concerning the tempo and the musical expression:

STANZA	TEXT (*condensed*)	TRANSLATION OF TEXT	DIRECTIONS
1	Y avait un' fois un pauv' gars Qu'aimait cell' qui n'l'aimait pas	(A poor boy once loved a girl who did not love him)	Moderato quasi allegretto; piano
2	Ell' lui dit: apport' moi, d'main, L'cœur de ta mèr' pour mon chien!	(She told him: to-morrow bring me your mother's heart for my dog)	Same tempo; forte; "cruelly," then "ferocious-ly"
3	Va chez sa mère et la tue! … Lui prit le cœur et s'en courut! …	(Went to his mother's and killed her, took her heart and ran away)	Same tempo; pia-nissimo; then fast and forte
4	Comm' il courait, il tomba! … Et par terr' le cœur roula! …	(He fell as he ran, and the heart fell to earth)	Moderato quasi allegretto; piano
5	Et pendant que l'cœur roulait, Entendit l'cœur qui parlait;	(And as the heart rolled he heard it speak)	Same tempo; piano then mf; "with terror"
6	Et l'cœur disait en pleurant, T'es-tu fait mal, mon enfant? …	(And crying, the heart said: Did you hurt yourself, my child?)	Slower; pianis-simo; "like a ghost," then "with tenderness and concern"

Another means employed by Gounod to avoid tedium is ampli-fication of the instrumental introductions and epilogues. Several piano preludes occupy a whole page (as in "La chanson du pâtre" and "Tombez, mes ailes"). Extended introductions also appear in free-form pieces (e.g., "Le Juif errant," "À une jeune fille," and "La

Henri Reber

à sa table de travail reflété par
le papier à musique éclairé par la
lampe à gaz —
Essayant un passage au clavier
après avoir écrit.

Charles Gounod

fleur du foyer"). In "Le vallon" a short instrumental introduction is followed by a vocal prologue in a recitative-like style which, changing imperceptibly to an arioso, leads to the *mélodie* proper. Already known to composers of the Empire period,[266] this procedure undoubtedly originated in opera. Gounod often prolongs the last musical phrase also, to emphasize the effect of conclusion.

In spite of these devices intended to soften the strictness of the strophic form, the hazard of monotony is not always overcome. Curiously enough, Gounod's best *mélodies* are precisely those that suffer from this weakness (e.g., "Venise" and "Chanson du printemps"). While this failing may easily be neutralized in performance by the omission of one or more strophes, such a procedure was not, of course, within the composer's intention.

The songs composed before 1870 are almost all in strophic form, only the duets and *scènes* of that period enjoying a freer structure. Gounod's break with the principle of uniformity during his visit to England in 1870 resulted in a less rigid type of *mélodie*. But during the same time he became a victim of routine, with all its unfavorable consequences. His technical mastery went hand in hand with a growing lack of artistic self-criticism, creating a paradoxical situation in which the essential value of his songs decreased proportionately as his feeling for a more refined architecture increased.

PROSODY AND MELODIC LINE. The crisis that occurred in musical prosody about 1850 is described by Saint-Saëns in his already-quoted article on the relationship between poetry and music:

Disdain for poetry and prosody was born in the mid-century school. Not only musicians, but also poets thought that the musical accent could be placed at will, believing that no syllable has an accent, aside from the caesura and the [masculine] ending of the line. In putting words to a known air, poets would follow this principle, resulting in a horrible gibberish to which people have become accustomed, even though they notice in listening to a piece that they are unable to understand the words.

Although Saint-Saëns is speaking principally of opera, the sad consequences of this prosodic anarchy applied equally well to the *mélodie*. Among the factors responsible for the decline, two may be cited. The first was the influence of certain composers who enjoyed tremendous popularity while exhibiting complete indifference to poetic rhythm; the chief offenders were musicians of foreign origin, like Jacques Offenbach and Friedrich von Flotow, who were able to affect the *mélodie* even though in their mature periods they had little actual contact with the genre. Secondly, many of the chansons and *chansonnettes* sung in the *café-concerts* of the period contained deliberately false rhythms that may have encouraged disrespect for the principles of correct prosody.

Gounod's early preoccupation with this problem led Saint-Saëns to consider him the savior of French prosody: "Not the least of his merits is that he guided us toward the great tradition of the past, basing his vocal music on correctness of declamation."[267] A strong feeling for prosody is already apparent in Gounod's first works. The balance between poetic and musical accents is very carefully handled in them; only rarely is the rhythm of the verse sacrificed to musical demands. Gounod was not, however, a purist. He entirely avoids esthetic theories like those of d'Indy and Woollett, which led poetry to become prose and song to become almost spoken recitation. With Gounod the structure of the lines is almost integrally retained while at the same time the melodic line has a purely musical physiognomy. The many instrumental arrangements of his songs (especially of "Sérénade" and of the air adapted to the first Bach prelude) show that when deprived of words Gounod's *mélodies* may still charm the public. But even in passages where the poet has a character speak, the composer succeeds in combining speech with a beautiful melodic line (Example 103).

Example 103: Gounod, "Boire à l'ombre"

Gounod attains his synthesis of musical and poetic rhythms by the varied use of different accents. Most theoreticians of his time sought an easy solution of the problem by advising composers simply to make tonic accents fall on strong beats. Such a procedure suggests that only the *metric* musical accent may serve prosody. But of course the composer's resources for emphasizing tonic syllables also include the dynamic accent, the melodic accent, and the accent of duration. The application of these means considerably increases his liberty and makes it possible for him to render musically the emphatic and oratory accents of the spoken language. The opening of "Boire à l'ombre," cited above, offers an example of the melodic combined with the metric accent. The second syllable of the word "merci" carries a tonic accent, but since it is also an exclamation, the initial syllable carries an emphatic accent. Gounod gives both syllables equal stress: the tonic syllable falling on a strong beat bears the metric accent, while the emphatic accent of the first syllable *mer-* is rendered by a note on a higher pitch, creating a melodic accent.

Sometimes the melodic accent replaces the metric accent, as in "L'absent," where the word "voix," while falling on a weak beat, still overshadows the preceding word (Example 104).

Example 104: Gounod, "L'absent"

The most interesting aspect of Gounod's prosody lies in his use of the durational accent. If an atonic (or unstressed) syllable happens to fall on a strong beat the composer neutralizes this license by prolonging the following tonic syllable. The result is a fluid syncopation that imparts special charm to the melodic line, as shown by the random instances given in Example 105.

This procedure, born of the conflict between the rhythm of the words and that of the music, may be considered specifically French and was later adopted by many younger composers (Example 106).

While these rhythmic formulae are employed by almost all French composers even without prosodic necessity, very few instances are found in the German *Lied*. In his songs set to poems of Mörike and Goethe, Hugo Wolf ties weak beats to strong, but the syncopations that result from his particular prosody have rather the character of anticipations. The expressive force of Wolf's melodic declamation is so strong that it might be said to subjugate the musical meter, creating syncopations that are hardly felt as such. In Example 107, the anticipation of the high F alters the rhythmic physiognomy of the phrase.

The fluidity of Gounod's melodic sweep is unanimously praised by his biographers; illustrative examples may be found in practically

a)

b)

c)

d)

Example 105: Gounod, "Chant d'automne," "L'absent," "Medjé," and "Au rossignol"

every song. This suppleness may result from Gounod's study of Italian music. His use of melismatic passages probably stems from the same source; the embellishments in the famous "Sérénade," however, have a type of refinement that is characteristically French (Example 108).

From the features of Gounod's vocal style described above, one may conclude that it contains elements of an inherently French nature that were lacking in the music of his predecessors.[268]

ACCOMPANIMENT AND HARMONY. The piano is almost always subordinated to the voice. The style of accompaniment is generally simple, graceful, and well adapted to the instrument. A single melodic or rhythmic motif often dominates the entire piece. In many songs the figure is composed of arpeggiated, broken, or repeated

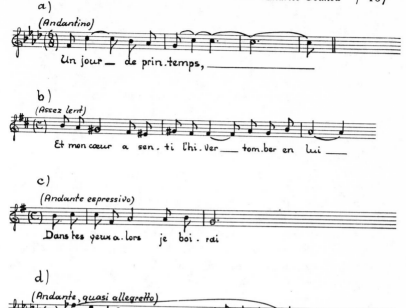

Example 106: Bizet, "Pastorale"; Massenet, "Les marronniers" (*Poème d'octobre*, no. 2); Saint-Saëns, "Chanson triste"; Fauré, "Nell"; and Duparc, "La vie antérieure"

chords which may create a calm and poetic atmosphere (as in "Au rossignol" and "Crépuscule"), although at faster tempos they have a tendency to degenerate into a type of drum roll (as in "Noël" and "À Cécile").

Two aspects of Gounod's harmony merit particular attention. The first is the pedal, which the composer uses in a special manner, repeating the pedal note against each chord in such a way as to

Example 107: Wolf, "Karwoche"

reinforce the momentum and especially the effect of the dissonance (Example 109).

The second procedure is the repetition of chords against each harmonic note (Example 110).

The last example shows a combination of the two procedures. Both issue from the same principle, the friction of dissonant against chordal notes. Only the distribution of roles is different, sometimes the dissonant note (i.e., the pedal) being repeated against the moving chords, sometimes the harmony remaining stable while the dissonant notes in turn move along.

Example 108: Gounod, "Sérénade"

Example 109: Gounod, "À Cécile"

Such harmonic procedures had the obvious advantage of offering the composer a means of extending the possible sonorous combinations without shocking the conservative public. Gounod's contemporaries considered him a learned harmonist. Even professional musicians sometimes wondered how they could possibly enjoy his harmonic complications. Indeed, very strong dissonances occasionally resulted from the imposition of non-harmonic on chordal tones (Example 111). But even in this case, the removal of the dissonant notes shows the harmonic design to be entirely clear and Gounod's texture is revealed as relatively simple. Such an explanation did not, of course, occur to most nineteenth-century writers; but in 1938, a respected author like Servières still speaks of chords of the eleventh and thirteenth in a surprisingly naïve fashion.

Gounod's harmonies exercised a strong influence on the younger generation. Bizet, Massenet, Delibes, Saint-Saëns, Fauré, and many minor composers applied and developed his procedures, which may consequently be called typically French, even though they are of foreign origin. In the same 1938 article Georges Servières aptly speaks of Gounod's "acclimatizing" in French music the traits he borrowed from Schubert, Mendelssohn, and Chopin.[269]

GENERAL VIEW OF THE SONGS. Gounod's total song production consists of some two hundred *mélodies*, most of them composed after 1870. But the songs written before the Franco-Prussian War (published chiefly in Choudens' collections) are more important both historically and intrinsically.

The first song, "Où voulez-vous aller?" (Gautier), appeared in 1839 and displays a weakness of concept that lacks any suggestion of

Example 110: Gounod, "Medjé" (2 excerpts)

Gounod's individual style. In spite of this, the composition seems to
have achieved a much greater popularity than Berlioz' *mélodie* set to
the same words (*Les nuits d'été*, no. 6).[270]

During his stay in Italy as a Prix de Rome laureate in 1839,

Example 111: Gounod, "Dernières volontés" (prelude)

Gounod arrived at a much more personal style. The years 1840 to 1842 mark the composition of "La chanson du pêcheur" (Gautier), "Le vallon" and "Le soir" (Lamartine), "Venise" (Musset), and perhaps also the latter's "Le lever." Later followed "Chant d'automne" (anon.), "Sérénade" and "Aubade" (Hugo), "Le premier jour de mai" (Passerat), "Ô ma belle rebelle" (Baïf), "L'âme d'un ange" (Banville), "Chanson du printemps" (Tourneux), and the *mélodie* based on the first prelude from Bach's *Well-Tempered Clavier*. These pieces show considerable stylistic diversity and most of them are vastly superior to the average song of the period.

The *mélodies* written to Lamartine's words form a separate group. Since both poet and composer are notable for fluidity of expression, Gounod was bound to confer musical prominence on Lamartine's verse. When the young musician became acquainted with the *Méditations* and the *Harmonies poétiques* during his stay in Rome,[271] he was inspired to set two of the most famous poems ("Le vallon" and "Le soir") to music. Animated by a high artistic ideal, he found the musical industry that flourished in the salons a disgusting phenomenon, as indicated by this letter to his friend Louis Besozzi:

The *Romance Puget, L'Album musical* has, in a word, reached its highest level of brutalizing influence. It pleases me little, as you may imagine. Although such epidemics are insufficient to kill art, they still destroy too many ears that might perhaps be destined to hear "the good voice." How unfortunate that one cannot prevent weeds from growing.[272]

Niedermeyer's interpretation of Lamartine as a combination of *scène* and romance did not attract Gounod; he understood that such a solution was unsuitable for the poet's contemplative lyricism. Instead he took the German *Lied* for his point of departure, sensing its

perfect suitability to this type of poetry. Schubert's influence is
clearly recognizable in both "Le vallon" and "Le soir," sometimes
in a quite specific manner (Example 112).

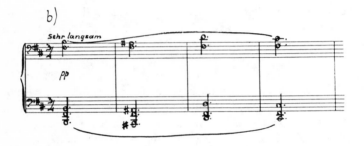

Example 112: Gounod, "Le vallon," and Schubert, "Der
Doppelgänger"

But other influences also brought the German *Lied* close. In 1840
Mendelssohn's works had been played for the young boarders at the
Villa Médicis in Rome. Their lasting impression on Gounod[273] is
revealed in many passages (Example 113).

Both pieces are moving in their expressive sincerity but somehow
the effect wears thin with time. Furthermore, Gounod's inability to
avoid the harmful influence of the *scène* is evidenced by a cadenza,
completely out of place, at the end of the introduction to "Le vallon"
(Example 114).

Under the title "Seul," Gounod wrote music to a section of
Lamartine's "La pensée des morts," already set by David. The latter's unwise choice of stanzas (as noted above) impaired the meaning
of the poet's thoughts by omitting some essential lines. Gounod tried

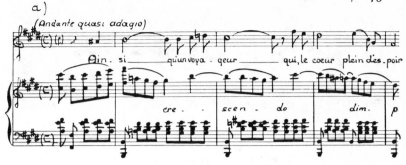

Example 113: Gounod, "Le vallon" and "Le soir"

another approach, renouncing in advance any attempt to depict the complete contents of the poem. From the varied subject matter he chose the atmosphere of solitude and tried to make a closed unity of it. He succeeded by selecting stanzas I and IV (containing a

Example 114: Gounod, "Le vallon"

melancholy picture of autumn) and stanza VI, which carries in its
lines the essential thought of solitude already present in youth:

> Quoique jeune sur la terre,
> Je suis déjà solitaire

and in which the poet asks "Where are those dear to your heart?"

Even though it ends with a question the song leaves an impression
of cohesiveness because of its sober and controlled style. The linear
nature of the accompaniment, particularly the stepwise bass and the
steady quarter-note rhythm throughout, convey a feeling of profound composure entirely in harmony with the words. The prelude,
whose last seven measures also serve as interlude, prepares the atmosphere (Example 115).

This *mélodie* is less poetic than the preceding two and lacks their
exuberant lyricism; but its classical outlines and its depth of expression have better preserved it from the destructiveness of time.

The relationship between "Seul" and another *mélodie* entitled
"Solitude" resides only in their titles. The music of the latter cannot
support a comparison. The accompaniment is especially disappointing, being dry and reminiscent of a piano étude. But it must be
recognized that in this case Lamartine's text is also far from the level
of his "Pensée des morts."

Gounod achieves synthesis of expressive depth and lyricism in "Au
rossignol," a piece that seems to have escaped the attention of his
admirers, being rarely heard at concerts. Although its subject in-
vites musical painting, the composer does not yield to the temptation.
The melody is admirably modeled over calm and sonorous chords,
leaving the fine poem intact (Example 116).

The piece's harmonic structure and the limpidity of its vocal line

Example 115: Gounod, "Seul"

Example 116: Gounod, "Au rossignol"

represent a truer French style than do the other *mélodies* set to Lamartine's poems; it is indeed one of Gounod's most inspired songs.

In addition to the five poems already mentioned, Gounod made use of another Lamartine text (taken from the *Recueillements poétiques*) bearing the title "Vers sur un album":

> Le livre de la vie est le livre suprême
> Qu'on ne peut ni fermer ni rouvrir à son choix;
> Le passage attachant ne s'y lit pas deux fois,
> Mais le feuillet fatal se tourne de lui-même:
> On voudrait revenir à la page où l'on aime,
> Et la page où l'on meurt est déjà sous nos doigts!

These pessimistically fatalistic words served as text for the melody that Gounod added to Bach's first prelude. Later he replaced the poem with the "Ave Maria" and in this form the piece attained its none too flattering fame. The fact that Lamartine provided the original inspiration seems to have been completely forgotten.

Two *mélodies* written to anonymous words breathe the same serene and poetic atmosphere as those adapted to Lamartine's lines. "Crépuscule" reveals Schubert's influence in its rhythmic and harmonic structure, while "Chant d'automne" possesses a chiaroscuro quality produced by the alternation of major and minor modes, a procedure undoubtedly also borrowed from Schubert.

Another side of Gounod's art is displayed in a second group of *mélodies*, whose atmosphere is impregnated with a typically French grace. Some of them are notable for their freshness and simplicity, some display a certain refined voluptuosity, and still others have an archaic outline. In all, however, Gounod proves his perfect craftmanship and his stylistic elegance. The poets include some great names (e.g., Passerat, Baïf, Hugo, Musset, and Gautier) along with many lesser talents.

"Chanson du printemps" (Tourneux) shows clearly to what extent the composer had assimilated the German style. Although Mendelssohn's influence is obvious, the piece's clarity and transparency plainly mark its French origin. Gounod appears to have been particularly responsive to the theme of springtime, since two other poems of similar content ("Au printemps" by Jules Barbier and "Primavera" by Gautier) also inspired him with charming results.

The style of "Venise" (Musset) and "Sérénade" (Hugo) is more delicate. These two pieces are among Gounod's best-known *mélodies* and offer perfect examples of the originality of his musical language. The introduction of "Venise" alternates chords on the first and third degrees in such a way as to suggestively paint the softly voluptuous atmosphere of the lagoons (Example 117).

Example 117: Gounod, "Venise"

At the end of the stanzas the same procedure is employed in the major mode and with considerable harmonic enrichment; the melodic line in the right hand covers the two harmonies and unites them (Example 118). The piece is full of supple modulations (Example 119).

This admirable composition was written when Gounod was barely twenty-four years of age, showing how much natural talent he had for song writing. Unfortunately, pieces of this level are rare among his works.

The distinguishing characteristics of "Sérénade" are rather of melodic essence. An extremely graceful and attractive melody is modeled over a lulling and sensuous rhythm filled out in the accompaniment with an elegant sixteenth-note motif (Example 120).

However French the nature of the impression left by this masterpiece of salon music, it nevertheless retains a reminiscence of Mendelssohn (Example 121).

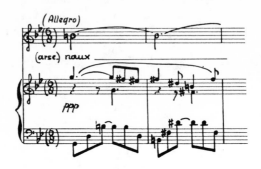

Example 118: Gounod, "Venise"

"Sérénade" has its antipode in "Aubade," where Hugo's lines concerning the lover who sings, but also cries, render the atmosphere more melancholic and veiled. While its harmonies are more forced, this *mélodie* generally resembles "Sérénade" closely and is in no way inferior to it, although it has not attained the latter's vogue.

The two pieces written to sixteenth-century poetry ("Le premier jour de mai" by Passerat and "Ô ma belle rebelle" by Baïf) form a separate category. The German influence is entirely absent from them; instead Gounod follows in the footsteps of Reber, whose songs he surely knew and admired. In the first of these *mélodies* the voice

Example 119: Gounod, "Venise"

Example 120: Gounod, "Sérénade"

often moves in parallel motion with the right hand, occupying
sometimes the lower, sometimes the upper third (Example 122).

This practice, as well as the effective interruptions in the piano
illustrated in Example 123, was often used by Reber. In this example
the emphatic stresses (rendered by melodic accents) on the syllable
gra- and the word *de* clearly imitate natural speech.

In "Ô ma belle rebelle" the accompaniment, tinged with archaism, hides a number of exquisite harmonic combinations in
which the secondary chords (II, III, and VI) play an important
role. The general aspect of the harmony is diatonic and yet piquant
dissonance is sometimes present. As in the preceding piece, the
rhythm of the voice part is very simple but some unusual syncopations may nevertheless be found (Example 124).

Example 121: Gounod, "Sérénade"

Example 122: Gounod, "Le premier jour de mai"

The comments made above concerning Reber's best *mélodies* are even more valid for these two Gounod songs. Their freshness and charm clearly separate them from the more usual sentimental products of the period and surely place them among the composer's

Example 123: Gounod, "Le premier jour de mai"

Example 124: Gounod, "Ô ma belle rebelle"

most beautiful inspirations in the domain of intimate vocal music. Unfortunately, the same cannot be said of another *mélodie* set to Renaissance poetry, "Heureux sera le jour" (Ronsard). Although certainly not without merit, this song written about 1871 betrays the promise of the two earlier works just discussed.

Gounod's *scènes* and *cantiques* have little importance for the history of the *mélodie*. The doubtful character and the esthetic objections inherent in the *scène* have already been discussed in various connections. Gounod's inability to escape these drawbacks is apparent in the turgid and obsolete style of such pieces as "Le Juif errant," "Prière d'Abraham," and "The Worker." More successful are "Départ" and "Boire à l'ombre," which are a compromise between the *mélodie* and the *scène*.

The *cantiques* and religious *mélodies* add little to the composer's glory. The procedures that contributed to the formation of his secular style are completely out of place in his sacred music, where "percussion sections" ("Noël"), arpeggios ("Le ciel a visité la terre"), tremolos ("Invocation"), and even a waltz rhythm ("Jésus de Nazareth") produce either sickly sentimentality or inflated grandiloquence. In strict fairness to Gounod it must be admitted that French musical language of the Second Empire was not really suited to religious texts and that the weaknesses of his sacred works are the faults of the epoch, appearing also in several compositions of Bizet and Saint-Saëns, and even in the liturgical music of César Franck (e.g., the unjustly celebrated "Panis angelicus"). When the melody Gounod added to the Bach Prelude is heard with Lamartine's original words the ingenious sacrilege is much less shocking than when it is sung to the sacred text of "Ave Maria." As for the *cantiques* themselves, their words generally lacked even the slightest literary value and could not be expected to inspire any composer. When Gounod set religious poems of superior quality (e.g., "D'un cœur qui t'aime," from the third act of Racine's *Athalie*) he rose above the level of mediocrity, although still unable to convey the psychological power of Racine's language; the result is a pleasant work but nothing more.

In 1870 Gounod took refuge in England, for which the German journals either ridiculed him or tried to adopt him:

It has been announced that Gounod has written a new song called "À la frontière" that General Trochu can now sing to the Germans at the proper time and place. We fervently hope that Gounod's "Harlequin" operas become outdated as easily as his war songs. We shall see how long this superficial elegance will last.

The same journal wrote several months later that "Gounod deeply deplores the war, of which he disapproved from the first day. He claims that his own artistic vocation was chiefly derived from the German spirit and German art."[274]

The French were irritated with him, particularly when he deferred his permanent return until 1874. But his crossing of the Channel had much more serious artistic consequences. In Mrs. Weldon's circle he was blindly idolized "for the weakening of his musical faculties."[275] The quality of the abundant production of those years was only a pale reflection of the fresh and poetic compositions of his youth. Eighty years earlier an Englishwoman had inspired Joseph Haydn to some of his finest works, but history was not repeated in 1870; Georgina Weldon was no Mrs. Schroeter and as for Gounod himself, he lacked Haydn's artistic conscience.

Some aspects of the work postdating the Franco-Prussian War nevertheless merit attention. The many songs set to English words correspond completely to the mawkishness of Victorian taste, an atmosphere from which Gounod was only rarely able to escape, as in "Maid of Athens."[276] He *was* able to retain his fine sense of prosody in the English *mélodies*, the handling of a foreign language apparently causing him no difficulty.

The Italian *canzonette* are generally superior to the English pieces, revealing a less conventional taste and sometimes even a certain spirituality (notably in the cycle *Biondina* and in "Quanti mai").

Gounod also wrote a number of chansons more or less in the manner of Reber and Massé. Some of these have a certain charm (e.g., "La fauvette," "Chanson d'avril," and "Viens, les gazons sont verts"). A song mentioned earlier with regard to its structure, "La chanson de la glu," is also interesting from the harmonic point of view. The use of the minor second and seventh confers a special complexion and offers a rare example of Gounod's use of "harmonic color" (Example 125).

The inverted double pedal is also characteristic of Gounod's chansons (Example 126). The same type of inverse double pedal is also used in "Vincenette," a "*chanson provençale*," and in the duet "Sous le feuillage."

While Gounod's chansons are certainly artistically inferior to those of Reber and Delibes, they are still superior to many of the banal *mélodies* he composed after 1870. Comparison of the uninteresting "Réponse de Medjé" with the lovely "Medjé" of 1865 suggests the decline in quality. Choudens' third and fourth

Example 125: Gounod, "La chanson de la glu"

Example 126: Gounod, "La chanson de la brise" (duet)

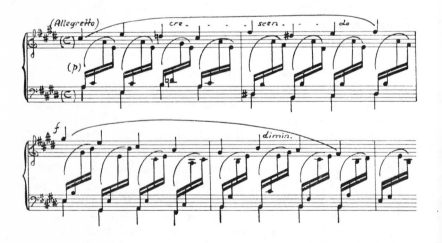

Example 127: Gounod, "Le temps des roses"

Example 128: Gounod, "L'absent"

collections, as well as those issued by Lemoine, contain many of these false pearls, hardly worthy of notice. The compositions showing Schumann's influence (inherited through Massenet) may be excepted from this judgment, although the Schumann who appears in them is considerably sweetened (Example 127).

Two of the *mélodies* postdating 1870 have real artistic value and recall Gounod's earlier days. The composer had set the poem "Ma belle amie est morte" (Gautier's "Lamento") for the first time in Rome under the title "La chanson du pêcheur," but the entirely new composition he wrote in 1872 is decidedly superior. The voice part, sustained by an undulating barcarolle rhythm, has none of the expected sentimentality, but is expressive, sincere, convincing, and marvelously adapted to the atmosphere of the well-known poem. Although his piece is less original than Berlioz' "Lamento," Gounod surpasses the latter in careful and balanced writing.

The second piece, "L'absent," is set to words written by Gounod himself:

> Ô silence des nuits dont la voix seule est douce
> Quand je n'ai plus sa voix,
> Mystérieux rayons qui glissez sur la mousse
> Dans l'ombre de ces bois,
> Dites-moi si ses yeux, à l'heure où tout sommeille
> Se rouvrent doucement
> Et si ma bien-aimée, alors que moi je veille,
> Se souvient de l'absent.

To these lines, which could only have been written by a true poet, Gounod adds music of equivalent value, whose melodic sweep is a model of his fluid and expressive style. The arpeggios in the accompaniment suggest the silence evoked by the words. A few measures from this admirable composition suitably conclude this discussion of Gounod's songs (Example 128).

Victor Massé (1822–1884)

The press of the period often mentions Victor Massé's *mélodies* in connection with those of Reber, probably because both composers showed particular interest in Renaissance poetry. This identity of literary tastes did not, however, result in agreement of their musical styles, the two composers approaching the *mélodie* genre from entirely disparate bases. Reber was primarily an instrumental composer, a "pure" musician, while Massé's preference was for comic opera. In his choice of song texts, however, he tried from the very beginning of his career to avoid the vapid Puget type. He wrote a total of about 120 songs, many of them appearing in three collections each having a particular theme: *Chants d'autrefois* (1849–

1850), *Chants du soir* (1850–1854), and *Chants bretons* (1853). After 1854 he wrote only separate *mélodies*.

The series *Chants d'autrefois* begins happily with the famous "Mignonne" of Ronsard. An animated and piquant melody softened by occasional passages in the minor mode faithfully translates the poet's spirit. The structural scheme (strophic variations) is also well chosen for the text, as illustrated in the corresponding passages of Example 129.

Example 129: Massé, "Mignonne" (1st verse, 2nd verse, and 3rd verse)

The other pieces of the collection are far below this level. Some are true romances (e.g., "Félicité passée" by Jean Bertaut), some *chansonnettes* (e.g., "L'aubespin" by Ronsard), and others are written in the form of a *scène* (e.g., "Icare" and "Une fontaine" by Desportes and "Consolation" by Malherbe). Several suffer from an exaggerated simplicity, with musical ideas lacking in development (e.g., the adaptation of Ronsard's "Épicurienne," which resembles a children's song). On the other hand, the lines from a simple pastoral poem by Boileau

> Voici les lieux charmans
> Où mon âme ravie
> Passait à contempler Sylvie,

are introduced in a style of misplaced pathos (Example 130).

Example 130: Massé, "Souvenirs"

Massé's contemporaries disagreed in judgments of his *Chants d'autrefois.* An anonymous critic praised the composer's respect for the rhythmic structure of the lines,[277] while Maurice Bourges denied the suitability of early poetry as texts for music:

> Our singers, no matter how clearly they enunciate, already have enough difficulty in properly pronouncing today's language, without further complicating the problem by adding a dialect overcharged with obsolete words, inversions, and Latinisms unfamiliar to the large majority of listeners.

Bourges' statement is, of course, vastly exaggerated, since the texts chosen by Massé are easily understood in spite of their inversions and Latinisms. But the writer's objections to the composer's prosody are more solidly founded:

He should have more rigidly avoided the abusive use of prosodic license, as for example, the unpleasant rhythmic accentuation of mute syllables in numerous passages, especially in the first number. Words are not set to music in order to alter their natural scansion and thus prevent comprehension of their meaning.[278]

Massé's preference for old poetry was rarely matched by an understanding of its spirit. Unlike Reber, he was too much a child of his time to revive the Renaissance. The simple texts of Brizeux which, together with some folk poetry form the contents of the collection of *Chants bretons*, were more suited to the composer's talents. The set includes several charming pieces (e.g., "La chanson de la Loïc," "La chaumière," and "La chanson de Marie"). The voice parts contain vocalized passages, while in the accompaniments Massé aspires toward a deliberate primitivism. His use of pedal differs from Gounod's, suggesting rather the character of a musette

Example 131: Massé, "Le sonneur de Cornouaille"

bass instead of producing smooth and resounding dissonances (Example 131).

Despite these modest efforts to create local color, the *Chants bretons* are not at all true folk songs. In the bourgeois atmosphere of Paris Massé was too far removed from the surroundings of his native landscape to faithfully render Brizeux' unsophisticated characters. He presents them rather like *opéra-comique* peasants (Example 132).

Example 132: Massé, "La chaumière"

This lack of naturalness may explain why the *Chants bretons* were not imitated by other composers. The French *mélodie* was essentially a fruit of civilization and could never be "popular."

The title of the third collection, *Chants du soir* (Evening Songs), is only partially justified by two serenades, "Ninon" (Musset) and "Mandoline" (Jules Barbier). The remainder of the set includes pieces of uneven value without a unifying relationship. "Ninon" (from *À quoi rêvent les jeunes filles*) is by far the best of the pieces. Its

Victor Massé

Title page of Massé's "Mignonne"

Title page of Massé's "Le baiser donné"

Ernest Reyer

ample and complex structure resembles an operatic aria more than a *mélodie*:

SCHEME	A	B	C	D	A′
TEMPO	Andante sostenuto	Allegretto moderato	Largement	Moderato, then Récitatif	Tempo primo
METER	6 8	2 4	3 4	4 4	6 8
KEY	G minor	B-flat major	D major	G major	G minor

The recapitulation of the first part (A′) has a particular beauty. The voice becomes very tender and expressive as the accompaniment suggests string instruments sustaining the harmonies while a flute and oboe seem to play elegiac motifs. Musset's lines may be credited with having inspired one of the most beautiful pages in Massé's work (Example 133).

The pieces published outside these three collections bring nothing new. Occasionally the composer has a felicitous inspiration but for the most part the work is routine and was already outdated by the end of the century. Massé lacked Gounod's harmonic refinement and delicacy of style. His accompaniments are very full and too suggestive of the orchestra. In summary, Massé's songs, with a few exceptions, may be considered to have limited artistic value; nevertheless, a place in the historical development of the French *mélodie* should not be denied him.

Ernest Reyer (1823–1909)

"He had only genius, no talent." Reyer was characterized in this way by "a malicious composer." The remark (probably made by Saint-Saëns) was quoted by Henri de Curzon, who added no less maliciously, "It is true. While so many others display such a fine talent for hiding their lack of genius, he [Reyer] lacked even enough talent to make the most of the genius that welled up in his soul."[279]

Reyer was indeed a poor artisan. This weakness is apparent in even a modest genre like the *mélodie*, so that his output of about thirty songs teems with awkwardness. What is worse, the genius mentioned above is unfortunately wanting too. None of the *mélodies* exhibit the originality of his opera *Sigurd* or even the unpretentious

Example 133: Massé, "Ninon"

freshness of the comic opera *Maître Wolfram*. The thirteen opera airs inserted in the two song collections published by Choudens are incontestably superior to the original *mélodies*. Reyer appears to have been capable of producing a lyric style only on the stage; the drawing room was not his natural milieu.

The composer made various attempts to free himself from the conventional romances of the time. Besides some developed romances (e.g., "Voguons!" and "Sous les tilleuls") his work includes "*Lieder*" ("Sommeil" and "Les gouttes de pluie"), chansons ("Adieu Suzon" and "Vieille chanson du jeune temps"), exotic songs ("Pantoum," "Hiamina," and "Le comte Belfégor"), Parnassian sonnets ("Le chant des sirènes" and "Hylas"), and one song on a Renaissance text ("Pourquoi ne m'aimez-vous"). Some of these pieces offer intriguing details but the composer does not really succeed in creating a homogeneous language. This shortcoming is exemplified in the sonnet "Hylas." The piece opens in a sober style with refined declamation (Example 134), but later is lost in tremolos and common rhythms.

Example 134: Reyer, "Hylas"

The exotic *mélodies*, especially the *orientales*, lack harmonic color, so that the rhythmic monotony quickly becomes tedious. The pleasant tunes added to Hugo's "Vieille chanson du jeune temps" and Musset's "Adieu Suzon" are spoiled by heavy and awkward accompaniments. The "*Lieder*" are written in a more transparent style but they are wanting in intimate warmth and leave an impression of dryness.

Reyer's melodic line reveals certain positive qualities, among them careful prosody, declamation that is often ingenious and subtle, and restrained use of the square phrase. But the accompaniments show his weaknesses: unpianistic writing and the right hand often moving in unison with the voice, attenuating the strength of expression; this is a true theatrical procedure, ineffective in the drawing room. Finally, the structure becomes rather disordered, particularly when the composer tries to avoid the strophic form. One must conclude that Reyer's songs are more important for what they attempted than for their actual results, which have only minor importance for the history of the *mélodie*. Nature endowed him for the stage more than for this genre.

Georges Bizet (1838–1875)

Most of Bizet's *mélodies* are contained in three collections: one of twenty pieces, another of sixteen posthumous songs (both published by Choudens in volumes also containing the usual opera airs),[280] and a collection of six *mélodies* issued by Heugel under the title *Feuilles d'album*. Several separate pieces (of which six remain in manuscript) bring Bizet's total number of songs to forty-eight.

The composer appears to have had little real interest in the genre. His published correspondence refers only once to the composition of *mélodies*; he evidently considered the task as an interruption in his operatic and symphonic work, mentioning the songs in the same breath with some tedious orchestrations he was forced to do by financial necessity. He appears nevertheless to have been satisfied with the results:

> I am working very hard, having just finished at top speed six *mélodies* for Heugel. I believe you will not be unhappy with them. I have chosen the words carefully: Alfred de Musset's "Adieux à Suzon" and "À une fleur," Lamartine's "Le grillon," an admirable sonnet of Ronsard, a graceful affectation of Millevoye, and an exuberant "Guitare" by Hugo. I have not omitted a single stanza, using all. A musician has no right to mutilate the poets.[281]

Although conceived at one time, the six pieces that make up the *Feuilles d'album* are uneven in quality, a judgment that is equally true of Bizet's other *mélodies*. His capacity for self-criticism is shown, however, by the fact that he refused to publish a number of mediocre songs that are found among the posthumous works released by his heirs and those still in manuscript. To judge the composer by those *mélodies* would be manifestly unfair.

Bizet generally moves in the path of Gounod, whose influence is often noticeable (as in "Ma vie a son secret," "Absence," "Douce mer," "À une fleur," "La nuit," "Voyage," "Chant d'amour," etc.) Gounod's formulae are revealed in the accompaniment more frequently than elsewhere. Certain fundamental differences in the styles of the two composers, however, are worth examining. In the first place, Bizet adapted less easily to the salon atmosphere in which French song had been flourishing for so long. When handling a modest genre like the *mélodie* he was unable to forget the stage entirely. This handicap is apparent in the frequent instances where he is led astray by theatrical procedures inherited from Meyerbeer. Simple chansons are swollen to pretentiousness, as in Hugo's charming "La coccinelle," which begins with a recitative that leads to a banal waltz, and ends in a pompous style that is quite contradictory to the poet's tenderly witty ending:

> — Fils, apprends comme on me nomme,
> Dit l'insecte du ciel bleu,
> Les bêtes sont au bon Dieu,
> Mais la bêtise est à l'homme.

To this stanza he adds superfluous exclamations not in the original and renders Hugo's short poem as heavy as lead by swelling it to three pages.

On the positive side it may be argued that Bizet's sense of theater conferred a certain suppleness to his structures. His *mélodies* submit to the strophic form less rigorously than do Gounod's, departing frequently from exact phraseological symmetry. Furthermore, the dramatic quality of Bizet's songs sometimes conveys a striking sincerity of expression that contrasts favorably with the false and sickly-sweet sentimentality of so many *mélodies* of the era.

Bizet also differs from Gounod in his treatment of the human voice. Since his father was a vocal teacher, he was initiated into the mysteries of the voice at a tender age. The fruits of these childhood studies may be seen in two pieces entitled "Vocalise" and "Barcarolle" that were written at the age of eleven and are now in the manuscript collection of the Paris Bibliothèque Nationale. The early technical experience is apparent in the many *mélodies* sprinkled with vocalized and melismatic passages not always justified by the text. Sometimes the vocal formulae do underline the words in a graceful manner. Most composers would depict such words as "fauvette" (warbler) and "papillon" (butterfly) in the accompaniment, but Bizet renders them in the vocal part (Example 135).

Example 135: Bizet, "Vieille chanson" (2 excerpts) and "Tarantelle"

Elsewhere, Lamartine's lament to the gentle sea:

> Murmure autour de ma nacelle,
> Douce mer dont les flots chéris,
> Ainsi qu'une amante fidèle,
> Jettent une plainte éternelle
> Sur ses poétiques débris

is symbolized by several vocalized measures (Example 136).

Example 136: Bizet, "Douce mer"

Bizet leans toward brilliance in the accompaniment as well as in the voice. A consummate pianist himself, he required more from the accompanist than his contemporaries generally did, so that several of the songs seem to be intended for none but professional musicians.

In his *mélodies* Bizet's widely recognized originality in the harmonic domain is manifested in some unusual progressions. Gounod's practices, mentioned at the beginning of this chapter, appear in his works with increased audacity. In a G minor section of "Tarantelle," for example, the Neapolitan chord (Ab-C-Eb), alternating with its own dominant (Eb-G-Bb), is maintained for five measures over a

pedal on the dominant of the actual tonality. The dissonances provoked by this daring combination are carried even further by
embellishments and passing notes (Example 137).

Example 137: Bizet, "Tarantelle"

Besides upper and lower pedals, Bizet also uses the pedal in an
intermediate voice, i.e., in the right hand of the piano part (as in
"La sirène").

In spite of these examples, Bizet's originality does not usually
reside in an accumulation of dissonant notes. He often creates
surprising sonority with extremely simple means. The opening of
"Berceuse sur un vieil air" shows his use of the tonic chord with
added sixth (Example 138).

Example 138: Bizet, "Berceuse sur un vieil air"

This may perhaps mark the origin of a procedure whose invention
is often attributed to the impressionists and which today is a frequent jazz idiom. Finally, a passage of a posthumous work,
"N'oublions pas!," is worthy of mention. Here the triads G-B-D

and G♭-B♭-D♭ must be interpreted as complex embellishments of the tonic chord (Example 139).

Bizet's stylistic excellence shows to best advantage when he leaves the French climate for foreign atmosphere; he was the first *mélodie* composer to cultivate true local color. Some of the boleros, *orientales*, and pseudo-popular chansons of Monpou, Berlioz, David, Massé, and Reyer are certainly picturesque pieces, but with those composers

Example 139: Bizet, "N'oublions pas!"

exoticism is suggested only by special rhythms. Bizet goes much farther, utilizing *all* the elements of musical technique, harmony and melody as well as rhythm, in the depiction of exotic atmosphere (Example 140).

The rhythm is that of a bolero; the four sixteenth notes on the first beat of measures four and eight are characteristic of Spanish song. The strongly melismatic vocal line is also borrowed from Iberian folk song. Finally, the harmony reveals a deliberate primitivism: the daring heterophony of the third and fourth measures, which results in consecutive fifths and octaves; and the lowered seventh in the eighth measure. In the latter instance the triad G-B♭-D might be interpreted theoretically as the third step of the key of E-flat major, but the ear does not perceive the modulation to E-flat until the following bar.

This piece is curiously different from Reber's bland *mélodie* and Liszt's delicately animated composition, both written to the same words. In the letter quoted above Bizet speaks of an "exuberant 'Guitare'" and he actually set these tender lines, full of humor and depth, as if they expressed extremely passionate feelings. The

Example 140: Bizet, "Guitare"

painting of the exotic atmosphere was obviously more important to Bizet than the poetic ambiance.

"Pastorale," written to a charming poem by Jean-François Regnard, is less spectacular. Like *L'Arlésienne*, whose famous chorus in F-sharp minor it resembles somewhat,[282] it evokes Provence. The lowered seventh reappears (Example 141).

As in "Guitare," the added phonetic interjections are perfectly

Example 141: Bizet, "Pastorale"

justified as an unsophisticated expression of pleasure in pure song (Example 142).

But the most remarkable of Bizet's "foreign" compositions is his "Adieux de l'hôtesse arabe" (from Hugo's *Orientales*), written in 1866. Musical orientalism has finally attained full bloom and is expressed with extreme subtlety.[283] All technical resources are put to

Example 142: Bizet, "Pastorale"

the service of exotic painting. The augmented second, symbol of conflict in *Carmen*, here evokes languid sadness. The Gounod-like use of
the lower pedal provokes voluptuous dissonances and creates an
atmosphere of monotony and lassitude (Example 143).

Example 143: Bizet, "Adieux de l'hôtesse arabe"

The mélismas of the epilogue do not seem strained but rather express graphically the resignation and sadness of the forsaken woman.
The initial motif of the accompaniment resounds like a faraway
echo (Example 144).

Because Bizet painted the Orient as it was seen by the Parisian of
the Second Empire, his composition enjoyed enormous popularity.
Today we find it difficult to accept this cardboard Orient; in spite of
their obvious beauties, Bizet's music as well as Hugo's verse now
seem too closely identified with the period of their creation.

One *mélodie* that has retained its freshness is "Sonnet" (Ronsard).
Like the exquisite compositions of Reber, Gounod, and Massé, it is

Example 144: Bizet, "Adieux de l'hôtesse arabe"

another masterpiece inspired by sixteenth-century poetry. The literary form of the sonnet, difficult to translate into music, is handled here with much suppleness. The song's free structure is dominated by one fundamental thought (Example 145).

The graceful sicilienne rhythm recalls the episode in C-sharp minor of the "carillon" from *L'Arlésienne* (Example 146).

Example 145: Bizet, "Sonnet"

Georges Bizet

Léo Delibes

Example 146: Bizet, "Sonnet"

The voice does not try to shine but waits until the end to take a graceful turn (Example 147) reminiscent of the old *air de cour* (Gounod had already used a similar formula in "Le premier jour de mai").

Example 147: Bizet, "Sonnet"

"Sonnet" surpasses all Bizet's *mélodies* in charm. Its sole fault is defective prosody, a point on which the composer did not emulate Gounod.

Even if Bizet's songs do not realize the fullest potential of his genius, they must be conceded some merit, above all for their expression of local color; they excel also in dramatic intuition, originality of harmonic combinations, and brilliant vocal writing. Since almost all of Bizet's works were conceived in the shadow of the theater, his qualities naturally show themselves to best advantage there. Nevertheless, his innovations also had great importance for the *mélodie* genre, as the works of Léo Delibes will show.

Léo Delibes (1836–1892)

The composers already studied prefer the romance as the point of departure for their songs; Léo Delibes derives his style from another genre, the *chansonnette*. Romagnési had described the principal characteristic of this song type as "gracious gayety" but thought it quite different from the "chanson comique,"[284] especially in its subject matter. The latter is quite frankly farcical while the *chansonnette* is inoffensively good-natured. The style of performance varies too, the verses of the chanson being almost spoken, while the *chansonnette* is intended for normal singing. But the *chansonnette* is also different from the romance, the two genres each representing an aspect of bourgeois taste, one sentimentality and the other innocent gayety. Being less sensitive to foreign influences than the romance was to the German *Lied*, for example, the *chansonnette* was able to survive as an independent genre for a longer time.

Among Delibes' youthful works are a number of comic chansons and *chansonnettes* (e.g., "Les animaux de Granville," "Le code fashionable," and "La taxe sur la viande"). They appeared between 1850 and 1860 in various journals such as *Paris Magazine* and *Le journal des dames et des demoiselles*. Written with facility, they do not yet reveal the delicate and refined style of the composer of *Coppélia*. All the same, they indicate his artistic development. Just as his operas and ballets show vestiges of his early operettas, so the piquant tone and charm of Delibes' serious *mélodies* may be traced to his *chansonnettes* dating from the Second Empire.

Because of this charm his songs seem the most French of all those already studied. Italian and German influences cannot be discerned except those filtered through the intervening work of Gounod and Bizet. Starting with the *chansonnette*, Delibes arrives at a new style that reacts against the maudlin productions of the Romantic era. If, as Ravel has suggested, Gounod was the founder of the *mélodie* in France, it is Delibes who divested it of its hallowed sentimentality. Paradoxically, this inherently French *mélodie* often leaves its native soil. Exploring the two collections published by Heugel, one makes the grand tour of Europe and the Middle East. Two pieces sing of Spain: "Les filles de Cadix" (Musset) and "Sérénade de Ruy Blas" (Hugo); Italy is represented by "Sérénade à Ninon" (Musset); the Orient by "Chant de l'almée" (Philippe Gille); the Danube countries furnish two *mélodies*: "Chanson de Barberine" (Musset) and "Chanson hongroise" (François Coppée, after Petőfi), to which may be added two Bohemian pieces taken from the opera *Kassya* and added at the end of the second collection: "Chanson slave" and "Dumka"; finally, there is a choral work for female voices entitled "Les norvégiennes." The total impression made by these compositions is not at all eclectic; they are written in a homogeneous style that does not exclude the use of varied means.

Example 148: Delibes, "Les filles de Cadix," "Chant de l'almée," and "Chanson hongroise"

Thus Delibes follows the path indicated by Bizet and becomes the master of local color. The passages in Example 148 offer convincing evidence of this skill.

Delibes' methods of realizing local color are virtually the same as Bizet's. Rhythm, as well as melody and harmony, contains folk-music elements of various regions. The innovations of Gounod and Bizet are developed by Delibes chiefly in the harmonic domain. Pedal points appear in almost every one of his pieces. In" Chanson de l'oiseleur" the pedal begins without preparation, i.e., as a dissonant note from the beginning of the phrase (Example 149).

Example 149: Delibes, "Chanson de l'oiseleur"

"Chrysanthème" demonstrates the constant use of the upper pedal: the high G-sharp continues for twenty-one measures, combined from time to time with the lower pedal (Example 150).

Example 150: Delibes, "Chrysanthème"

The minor seventh ceases to be unusual; like Bizet (in "Guitare"), Delibes applies it in a bolero (Example 151).

Another procedure dear to Delibes is the employment of the sub-

dominant chord as harmonic embellishment of the tonic chord (Example 152).

Example 151: Delibes, "Les filles de Cadix"

The same piece has a variant of this unusual combination (I-II₇-I over a double pedal; Example 153).

This is only a modest selection from among the numerous examples of harmonic refinement. In structure Delibes generally con-

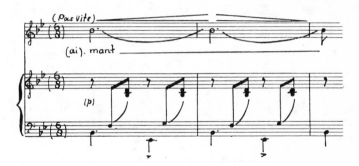

Example 152: Delibes, "Que l'heure est donc brève!"

fines himself to such clear and schematic designs as variants of the rondo or *Lied* forms, thus avoiding the monotony of the strophic romance as well as the pretentious complexity of the *scène*. The melodic line is equally simple and graceful, but its amplitude

Example 153: Delibes, "Que l'heure est donc brève!"

is rather limited. The prosody is treated less skillfully, sometimes being sacrificed to an elegant turn of melody or else handled with a certain nonchalance.

Several songs merit separate mention. "Avril," an exquisite *mélodie* on the famous poem of Rémy Belleau, demonstrates once more the inspirational strength of older French poetry. Here Delibes achieves a rare stylistic perfection. Its clarity, grace, and balance define "Avril" as one of the most innately French compositions of the *mélodie* repertoire. Even its structure is based on the "national" form, the rondeau of Couperin's time: R A R B R'. Curiously enough, this *mélodie* is not an original work, having been written in 1866 for *a cappella* chorus and later arranged by the composer himself for solo voice with piano accompaniment. The slightly archaic style and four-part writing recall the original version (Example 154).

Example 154: Delibes, "Avril"

Nevertheless, the instrumental introduction added to the rondo theme has an elegance entirely natural to the *mélodie* genre as the composer conceived it, so that the work should not be considered as an arrangement in the conventional sense, but rather as a new version written with extreme care (Example 155).

"Chanson de l'oiseleur" is somewhat akin to "Avril"; although it does not attain the latter's perfection, it possesses many interesting details and strongly suggests Bizet's influence (Example 156).

For Delibes the *scène* is no longer a fragment in operatic style transferred to the drawing room, as it had been in Meyerbeer's time. In spite of its dramatic character, "Départ" (Émile Augier) is written as a true *mélodie*, being distinguished from the others only by its length. The *chansonnette* was also forced to give up its individuality.

Example 155: Delibes, "Avril"

Even though Musset's gay lines suggest a facile kind of composition, "Bonjour Suzon" is conceived on a more serious level, only the initial measures recalling somewhat the geniality of the *petit bourgeois*.

Delibes composed four songs for plays by Hugo and Musset performed at the Comédie Française: "Sérénade à Ninon," "Sérénade de Ruy Blas," "Vieille chanson," and "Chanson de Barberine." These pieces were all inserted in the second collection of his *mélodies*, but they do not show to advantage there, mainly because the piano is inadequate as a replacement for the original instrumentation (mandolin, harp, tambourine, etc.). Only the reduction of "Chanson de Barberine" is at all effective.

The *mélodie* "Myrto" should be mentioned because of the originality of its accompaniment, which is practically a separate piano piece. The song's charm is destroyed, however, by an inflated ending that recalls Meyerbeer's worst pages. The same weakness occurs at the end of "Arioso," the text of which is also by Silvestre. The attempts

Example 156: Delibes, "Chanson de l'oiseleur"

at brilliant vocal writing in "Chant de l'almée" and "Le rossignol" result in platitudes unworthy of Delibes' talent.

Examination of Delibes' total vocal writing nevertheless results in a generally favorable impression. His creative power is admittedly somewhat limited, being incapable of expressing emotions that are either passionate or profound; but in spite of this, many of his pieces retain their freshness and charm because of their careful and graceful style. Delibes may also be credited with having reinforced the French character of the *mélodie* by divesting it of its foreign elements.

Jules Massenet (1842–1912)

Even more than Bizet or Delibes, Jules Massenet must be considered Gounod's true successor in the province of the *mélodie*. The essence of his style is not the picturesque, exotic painting, or local color, but the expression of a delicate sentimentality realized with extreme refinement. He was the idol of the cultivated bourgeois of his time, those Reynaldo Hahn called the "intellects of a relatively high level ..., able to understand, or at least to perceive the thought, the intention, and the talent of a poet and a musician."[285] Thus his *mélodies* "in suède gloves"[286] were the daily bread of every Mademoiselle Dax.[287] Xavier Aublet's painting "Autour d'une partition de Massenet" depicts the composer at the piano surrounded by a group of intent auditors, all visibly captivated by a new *mélodie* that the master has performed for them.[288] This faithful representation of the epoch reflects the quite astounding success enjoyed by Massenet's songs. His manuscripts were published almost while the ink was still wet, sometimes even appearing in five different keys. He wrote about 260 songs, approximately the same number as Schumann or Wolf, but surpassing the number produced by all other French masters, even Gounod.

A body of works that was so fashionable during the life of its author must necessarily lose its luster today. Jean d'Udine's passionate defense in 1931[289] could not retard the neglect of a music that had earlier been a high point of French civilization. Today the affected listlessness, the "blue" mood so vulgarized and exploited, can no longer be accepted. Camille Bellaigue, who can hardly be called a progressive critic, wrote as early as 1919 that composers had abused the feelings of melancholy, sadness, and despair, and suggested that after the triumphant ending of the war, with a new age

"Autour d'une partition de Massenet" by Aublet

Jules Massenet

dawning, the time had come for "the smile, perhaps even the laugh, to return to the musical lips of the nation."[290] Massenet's *mélodie* is so indissolubly linked to the now-vanished *fin-de-siècle* salon ambiance that its revival is highly unlikely.

In fairness to the composer, however, his work should be examined in its technical aspect, where his musical craftsmanship manifests itself. This quality alone makes his contribution to the development of the genre far from negligible.

First Massenet must be credited with having finally delivered the *mélodie* from the yoke of the square phrase. He sacrifices the line as a structural element to the poetic content and introduces into the genre a sort of musical prose, capable of conveying all the nuances of the literary text. Of course, the periodic phrase does not vanish completely; it appears quite often in his *mélodies-chansons* (e.g., "Madrigal" and "Nuit d'Espagne") and elsewhere alternates with free passages. In general, however, Massenet's *mélodie* tends toward the "poem in prose," more or less analogous to the free verse written by poets of the period.

Such a concept of song requires considerable competence in vocal writing in order to prevent degeneration into recitative. In this sphere Massenet demonstrates his great mastery; he understands perfectly that the voice's role in the drawing room is not the same as at the theater. Unlike Bizet, he rarely allows himself to be tempted by brilliant writing; his melodic line is generally simple, limpid, and very fluid. The vocal part is no longer an air to be hummed, because Massenet often uses the piano for completion of his musical thought. Sometimes the instrument ends a vocal line by itself or else, under the final note of the melody, it intones a new phrase that the voice picks up only after two measures (Example 157).

Sometimes the piano connects two unaccompanied phrases (Example 158).

Often the theme proper appears in the instrument while the voice "declaims" the words (Example 159).

These procedures are alternately applied in such a manner that voice and piano form an indivisible whole. The tendency toward unity is also manifested in another innovation. Massenet was the first in France to write a true song cycle. No longer is a series of pieces united under a more or less vague title (e.g., Berlioz' *Nuits d'été* or Massé's *Chants bretons*) but instead a set of *mélodies* grows out of a definite subject, preceded by a prelude whose motifs reappear at

Example 157: Massenet, "Lève-toi" (*Poème du souvenir*, no. 1)

Example 158: Massenet, "Que l'heure est donc brève" (*Poème d'avril*, no. 6)

Example 159: Massenet, "Prélude" (*Poème d'octobre*)

the end. In such a cyclic work, to which the composer gave the title *poème*, his style shows at its best.

Poème d'avril (1866; words by Armand Silvestre) begins with three recited stanzas ("Prélude") between which the piano announces some motifs of the next pieces. Two songs, "Sonnet matinal" and "Voici que les grands lys," are then followed by another recited poem ("Riez-vous?"), this time without any musical interruptions. The piano replies with a short romance without words that is linked with the following *mélodie*, "Vous aimerez demain." The cycle ends with three vocal pieces, of which the last is again preceded by a recited poem. Although the work gives an impression of spontaneous improvisation, the roles of voice, recitation, and piano are almost methodically distributed and the forms reveal a perfect balance.

Two years later Massenet wrote the *Poème du souvenir*, also on verses by Silvestre. This time the composer omitted the recitation with the exception of an epigraph which, however, may be intended for reading rather than for declamation. The *mélodies* here are less closely connected, although at the end the piano echoes the initial theme (see Example 157). The same procedure is used again in *Poème pastoral* (1872), which begins and ends with a chorus of female voices. The words are by Florian, but Massenet has added two interludes to texts by his favorite author, Armand Silvestre. The remaining cycles, *Poème d'octobre*, *Poème d'amour*, *Poème d'hiver*, *Poème d'un soir*, and *Poème des fleurs*, are almost all written on the model of *Poème du souvenir*.

Massenet's vocal writing shows the strong influence of Schumann. The latter's *Lieder* were not introduced into France until 1855, a time when the climate was more receptive than it had been for Schubert's works during the Romantic era. Particular characteristics of Schumann's style may be easily recognized in the procedures just described: the important role of the piano; the interdependence of voice and instrument; the original quasi-improvised forms; and the vocal cycle (especially *Frauenliebe und Leben*, which seems to have served as model for Massenet's *Poèmes*). Schumann's influence betrays itself not only in the technical aspects described, but also in the general style, as the passage in Example 160 demonstrates. Another striking example of Schumann's impact is the beginning of "L'air du soir" (from *Poème du souvenir*), which recalls the famous "Lotusblume."

It must be admitted, however, that Massenet acclimatized

Example 160: Massenet, "Vous aimerez demain" (*Poème d'avril*, no. 5)

Schumann to French music, just as twenty years earlier Gounod had transferred Mendelssohn's techniques. Massenet's cycles reveal many pages of a very personal style, such as the second interlude from the *Poème pastoral*, which still retains all its freshness (Example 161).

Example 161: Massenet, "Crépuscule" (*Poème pastoral*, no. 5)

In his turn Massenet influenced young composers and certainly not the least talented. Several pieces in Fauré's first two collections are impregnated with an atmosphere that is pure Massenet. As to Claude Debussy, the germ of his particular type of *mélodie* finds most of its origins at the same source. At various times both of these great masters expressed their frank admiration of this predecessor.

In addition to the cyclic *Poèmes*, Massenet wrote an innumerable quantity of separate *mélodies*, 160 of which were collected in eight albums by the publisher Heugel. Since they add nothing essential to the observations already made they may be passed over. The volumes do include several charming pieces of some artistic value, but in general the technical superiority does not compensate for the saccharine sentimentality and the lack of real inspiration. Like Gounod, Massenet became a victim of routine and of his own competence.

A single work of great originality remains to be noted, even though it is beyond the limits imposed on the subject matter of this book. The collection *Expressions lyriques* (1913) contains ten pieces in which sung passages alternate with declaimed sections. In most of these pieces Massenet makes use of rhythmic declamation, a difficult feat for performers. The texts are chosen with care, not according to their poetic value but for their structural qualities, which offer the composer opportunities for contrasting the two means of expression. Thus a single person may suggest a dialogue by singing the questions and declaiming the answers (Example 162).

The procedure appears much more effective when the dialogue is relatively fast, the questions and answers succeeding each other after each phrase (Example 163).

In "Battements d'ailes," a neo-Lamartinian poem by Jeanne Dortzal, the first, contemplative, part is declaimed, while the final stanza, more rapturous, requires song:

DECLAIMED: Les soirs d'été si doux, voilés de crêpes bleus,
Où le cœur vient mourir dans un battement d'ailes
Font les arbres légers comme de blonds cheveux
Sur lesquels, en rêvant flotteraient des dentelles.

Le lac a revêtu ses tons de camaïeux
Et reflète en son eau, du ciel l'unique étoile …
Regardons-nous, veux-tu, tout au fond de nos yeux
Afin que notre amour hisse sa blanche voile.

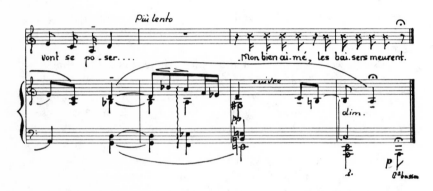

Example 162: Massenet, "Dialogue" (*Expressions lyriques*, no. 1)

SUNG: Ah! Laissons-nous bercer par le divin hasard …
       Quel bonheur de s'aimer au cœur même des choses,
       De jeter sur la vie un doux et long regard,
       De jeter sur la vie, à pleines mains, des roses! …

"La dernière lettre de Werther à Charlotte" (Gontaut Biron), of which the even more obsolete words could have served as the text of a romance of the Napoleonic era, shows the same process handled in a more subtle way:

SUNG: "Il faut nous séparer …
DECLAIMED: Au bord de cet abîme,
          L'heure a sonné pour nous de l'éternel adieu;
          Et j'irai, s'il est vrai que l'amour est un crime
          En demander pardon à Dieu.

Example 163: Massenet, "En voyage" (*Expressions lyriques*, no. 3)

SUNG: C'est fini! pour toujours! J'entreprends un voyage,
    Dont pour vous retrouver, je ne reviendrai pas;
    Mais, en mon cœur brisé j'emporte votre image,
        Afin d'enchanter mon trépas!

Jusqu'au moment suprême, enivré par vos charmes,
    Mon cœur n'aura battu dans l'ombre que pour vous,
    Et mon dernier baiser, et mes dernières larmes,
        Je les dépose à vos genoux.

Je vous fais mes adieux de la petite chambre
    D'où je ne sortirai plus que dans mons linceul;
    Et, pour me consoler en ce jour de décembre,
        Personne! je suis seul!

DECLAIMED: D'ailleurs, il se fait tard; d'ici quelques minutes,
    À partir pour là-bas je vais me préparer ...
    Noël! j'entends au loin des airs gais sur des flûtes ...

SUNG: Charlotte! ... Je t'aime! ... Adieu! Il faut nous séparer!
(Charlotte ...
DECLAIMED: Adieu ... Adieu!) "291

However interesting these experiments may be, they cannot be said to have succeeded in establishing a new type of *mélodie*. Declaimed poetry needs highly colored surroundings, i.e., an orchestra or instrumental ensemble, and lacks warmth when sustained by a lone piano. Furthermore, the transition from song to declamation is always disturbing. Even in the instances where Massenet attempts to eliminate the difficulty of transition by terminating the vocal phrase as softly as possible in the lowest register, the result remains unsatisfactory.

CHAPTER V

Toward the Apogee of French Song

THE MÉLODIE INFLUENCED BY INSTRUMENTAL MUSIC

THE MÉLODIES DISCUSSED IN THE PRECEDING CHAPTER WERE WRITTEN by composers who were by inclination primarily dramatic. Gounod, Massé, Reyer, Bizet, Delibes, and Massenet wrote their principal works for the stage and their songs naturally show its influence. The properties borrowed from opera were not, of course, all favorable to the *mélodie*; the result was especially injurious to the accompaniment, which imitated its theatrical role of a subservient support for the sovereign voice. The creation of a genre equivalent to the German *Lied* was obviously unattainable under such conditions; the *mélodie* had to be liberated from the domination of the theater before a true poem for voice and piano could develop.

The largest contribution to this undertaking was made by Saint-Saëns, Lalo, and Franck, who, as masters of the symphony, sonata, and concerto inaugurated the renaissance of instrumental music in France. Abstract music, earlier condemned as "too learned," could not fail to favorably effect the *mélodie* after 1860. Gounod had already conferred on it a sensitivity that was uniquely French and now the accompanying harmony will give its support to the poetic expression.

Thus these "instrumentalists" raised the *mélodie* to the level of chamber music and paved the way for the great masters Fauré and Duparc. Their best works may be less specifically French than those of Gounod or Massenet, but they are harmonically richer and manifest a sincerity that is more individual and more profound.

Camille Saint-Saëns (1835–1922)

Saint-Saëns wrote his first romances, "Ariel," "La maman," and "Le soir," at the age of six. Some *cantiques* ("Tandis que sur vos ans," "Reçois mes hommages," and "Nous qu'en ces lieux") date from 1844. These childish sketches naturally have little artistic value but are interesting because they explain how Saint-Saëns acquired his

Example 164: Saint-Saëns, "La feuille de peuplier," and Schubert, "Die Krähe"

astonishing compositional facility. The adolescent's discovery of Lamartine is reflected in his setting of "Le golfe de Baya" about 1847; in 1850 and 1851 he put music to several others of the poet's works, including "Le lac" and "Le poète mourant," the latter a typical subject for a youth of fifteen. The quite diffuse style of these songs reveals an emotivity poorly realized, but a work written shortly after (in October 1851) already shows complete mastery. This setting of Hugo's "Rêverie" is almost faultless in style from the purely musical point of view, only the slightly rigid form and the defective prosody betraying the immaturity of its creator. The lyrical atmosphere of the piece merits even more acclaim than its technical aspect; the song expresses feelings of intimate warmth, an *Empfindung* that is entirely German and undoubtedly derives from Schubert and Schumann. Schubert's language is also reflected in many other compositions of this period. A passage from "La feuille de peuplier" (1853), for instance (Example 164), is very similar to Schubert's "Die Krähe":[292]

As for Schumann, Saint-Saëns was familiar with his works when they were still virtually unknown by the Parisian public. Their influence may be clearly seen in the wide intervals of the melodic line of "Rêverie." The same is true of the lovely "Le sommeil des fleurs," of which Example 165 is a characteristic passage. Like Schumann's famous "Mondnacht," this piece is written in "*Bar*" form.

Example 165: Saint-Saëns, "Le sommeil des fleurs"

The Germanic atmosphere culminates in two unpublished songs, very curious and perhaps unique in the French repertory of the nineteenth century. These are set to the original German texts of Ludwig Uhland's "Ruhethal" and "Antwort" and Saint-Saëns' setting of them is in no way distinguishable from *Lieder* originating on the other side of the Rhine. "Ruhethal" is a true *Stimmungslied*, opening with a very simple melody sustained by smooth thirds (Example 166).

Example 166: Saint-Saëns, "Ruhethal"

The movement subsequently is made more animated by means of repeated chords in triplets, somewhat reminiscent of Mendelssohn. The initial atmosphere is regained near the end, the opening motif reappearing, like a melancholy echo, in a slightly different version (Example 167).

The other song, written for contralto, is also very Germanic, but has more personal accents. While an ostinato motif is heard in the

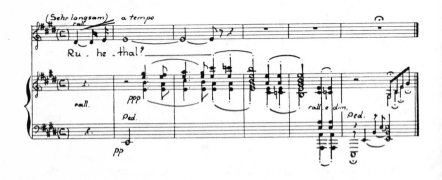

Example 167: Saint-Saëns, "Ruhethal"

bass, the pianist's right hand shares the melodic thought with the voice in alternation (Example 168).

Example 168: Saint-Saëns, "Antwort"

The setting of a phrase expressing the mortal effects of nostalgia has an emotivity that recalls the inspirations of Schubert and Schumann (Example 169).

In the second stanza delicate arabesques float above the dismal ostinato motif of the bass, depicting the spirit of the dead rose; such a passage proves that in his youth Saint-Saëns had a poetic sensitivity of which he is generally thought incapable.

Along with this German lyricism, the youthful works reveal quite a different quality, a sense of the picturesque and humorous. Saint-Saëns had an extraordinary gift for illustration of a somewhat caricaturing type. He needed very little inspiration to draw a vividly spirited picture without any trace of Romanticism or Germanic *Empfindung*, being able to stand apart from his subject and detachedly

Example 169: Saint-Saëns, "Antwort"

observe the persons and events with an amused eye. His superb craftsmanship appears in the compositions of this type even more effectively than in his lyric works. Mobility of rhythm, sonority of harmony, variety of movement, and melody closely tied to the cadence of the words, all contribute to make the game—for basically it is nothing but a game—witty and enthralling.

A subject like "La cigale et la fourmi" seems made for such a conception. Saint-Saëns was not the first to set La Fontaine's fables to music. Offenbach had already published a number of them in 1842, but the volume was roundly jeered by the critics. Bourges' review called it:

... a work of poor taste; or rather, a vulgar, banal taste that has nothing well-planned or individual about it. The initial error was to have imagined that one can make a musical stew of any value by skimming, dismembering, and breaking into pieces the fables of La Fontaine. Ideas of this sort would never have entered a French brain.[293]

However unjust this *a priori* condemnation may be, Offenbach's "La cigale et la fourmi" cannot be judged more than a banality. Its style is somewhat vulgar, especially in the section toward the end where the ant proffers cynical advice to the notes of a trivial waltz (Example 170).

Example 170: Offenbach, "La cigale et la fourmi"

Saint-Saëns' piece is much more personally and artistically conceived. It opens with a concise motif that later effectively underlines the ant's severe question: "And what were you doing in the summertime?" (Example 171).

Among the many humorous apt details is the quasi-tragic appoggiatura on the word "famine" (Example 172).

The ending in particular shows the composer's keen wit. Saint-Saëns' ant gives its malicious advice while the grasshopper's singing of the popular folk tune "J'ai du bon tabac" is suitably depicted in the piano's upper register (Example 173).

"Le pas d'armes du roi Jean" reaches an even higher level. Saint-Saëns dares to introduce the German *Ballade* into French surroundings, but does not concede to the Romantic concept of it as a horrible or fantastic story, seeing it rather as a grandiose and colorful tableau. He is more interested in the characters for the atmosphere they evoke than for themselves, an attitude well suited to the subject of a medieval tournament. Perfectly modeled to Hugo's trisyllabic lines, the principal theme leads immediately to the tilting arena (Example 174).

Example 171: Saint-Saëns, "La cigale et la fourmi" (opening and recall of motif)

All the details are painted with an enormous zest that hides the composer's good-natured smile. More tender ingredients are added at mention of the heroine, the tone becoming very gentle and warlike rhythms giving way to fragile arpeggios at the words

> Là-haut brille
> Sur ce mur,
> Yseult, fille
> Au front pur.

Example 172: Saint-Saëns, "La cigale et la fourmi"

Example 173: Saint-Saëns, "La cigale et la fourmi"

Later the tumultuous action is once more interrupted for the fall of the young page:

> Dans l'orage,
> Lys courbé,
> Un beau page
> Est tombé
> Il se pâme,
> Il rend l'âme;
> Il réclame
> Un abbé.

The sad incident is accompanied by anguished chords that lead to sounds of chanting as the victim dies (Example 175).

The magnificent bravado starts up again and the song ends with the opening theme.

"Le pas d'armes du roi Jean" is unquestionably a masterpiece, not only from the viewpoint of lively and colored expression, but also as a purely musical accomplishment that is almost unbelievable for a young man who was only seventeen at the time of its composition in 1852. The difficult subject is treated with such mastery that the words "Et la guerre / N'est qu'un jeu" (War is only a game) seem to apply to the composer himself; his own game is almost the exact duplication of a Romantic spectacle that he does not really take seriously.

Saint-Saëns was not always so fortunate in his choice of texts. The original version of "Danse macabre," for voice and piano, is not very effective. He arranged it soon afterward for voice and orchestra,

Example 174: Saint-Saëns, "Le pas d'armes du roi Jean"

probably feeling that the piano was too tame an instrument for the creation of the necessary lugubrious atmosphere. In the last metamorphosis he removed the voice entirely and rewrote the piece in the symphonic form in which it is famous.

Example 175: Saint-Saëns, "Le pas d'armes du roi Jean"

Another facet of the composer's talent is shown in "Plainte" and "Tristesse." Noble and majestic in character, they express elevated and serious emotions by very simple means. Despite Madame Tastu's turgid text, the first piece shows extreme sobriety (Example 176).

Example 176: Saint-Saëns, "Plainte"

The repetition of some words is perfectly justified by the refined prosody. The word "jamais," for example, is scanned three different ways in a single passage (Example 177).

With the volume entitled *Mélodies persanes* (1870) Saint-Saëns

Example 177: Saint-Saëns, "Plainte"

paid his tribute to the vogue of Orientalism. His concept of exotic atmosphere is broader than Berlioz ("La captive"), Bizet ("Adieux de l'hôtesse arabe"), or Lalo ("L'esclave"). Instead of languishing women he prefers the impetuous Bedouin ("Sabre en main"), seraglio dancers ("La brise"), meditative wisdom ("Au cimetière"), ardent passion ("La solitaire"), the fantastic and voluptuous dream ("La splendeur vide"), and the exhilaration of opium ("Tournoiement"). His technical procedures are nonetheless those of hallowed Orientalism, including archaic modal practices (as in the first part of "La brise," written in E minor with two sharps), persisting and monotonous rhythms, and melismatic airs. These characteristics are studied more closely in Appendix III.

The songs dating from the Second Empire thus present a varied aspect. After 1873 the production suddenly ceases, the composer being occupied with large compositions (e.g., *Le déluge, Samson et Dalila, Le timbre d'argent,* and *Étienne Marcel*). Between 1873 and 1885 he wrote only three *mélodies*, but in the latter year he turned to the genre once more and songs of the most diverse types came from his pen. Among the second collection published by Durand and the separate pieces of this period are archaic songs ("Chanson à boire"), Spanish-colored works ("Guitares et mandolines" and "El desdichado"), pieces of a typically French gayety ("Suzette et Suzon"), exotic *mélodies* ("Désir de l'Orient"), *pastorales* ("Pourquoi rester seulette?"), and even an abstract composition ("Theme varié"). The strongest of these are the contemplative *mélodies* in which the composer sings of "the stable values of life."[294] A typical instance is the passage at the end of the first stanza of "Aimons-nous" (Banville) in which Saint-Saëns annotates the poet's conclusion that "love is stronger than the gods or death" (Example 178).

Unlike Gounod and Massenet, Saint-Saëns never entirely suc-

Example 178: Saint-Saëns, "Aimons-nous"

Camille Saint-Saëns in 1883

Édouard Lalo

cumbed to routine. But his exceptional talents regrettably were not concentrated in the service of an artistic ideal. Despite the contrary opinion of many French and foreign writers, Servières' judgment that Saint-Saëns possessed a distinct personality[295] still appears sound to me. The composer's mistake lay in voluntarily suppressing it. As his technical faculties were perfected, the inner, poetic sensitivity revealed in his youthful compositions became atrophied. Occasionally it reappeared, as in the exquisite "Chanson triste," unfortunately eclipsed by Duparc's *mélodie* of the same name. Saint-Saëns' choice of texts is in itself a significant indication of his artistic viewpoint. His interest in versification rather than in the poem itself has already been mentioned; this leaning made him more responsive to clever or brilliant poets than to those requiring profound emotion. Even Hugo, his favorite poet, was admired chiefly for his virtuosity, richness of image, and universality of concepts. The poet's inner flame was lost to Saint-Saëns; he was unable to understand it, or at least unable to translate it into music. The talents that led him to become the Victor Hugo of French music proved harmful and finally the artisan stifled the artist.

Édouard Lalo (1832–1892)

"M. Lalo belongs to Schubert's school," said an announcement of the composer's *Six mélodies*, Opus 17.[296] The songs of this musical cosmopolitan are undeniably impregnated with a particularly German kind of lyricism, rather than with the colorful style of his *Symphonie espagnole* or the dramatic accents (strongly suggesting *Lohengrin*) of his *Roi d'Ys*. Lalo's *mélodies* do not merely follow the path of Schubert and Schumann, but sometimes even presage Brahms and Wolf. Many of them are true *Lieder* that betray their French origin only in their language. Lalo cannot justly be described, however, simply as an epigonus. His pieces teem with ingenious harmonic and rhythmic inventions that enchanted even German listeners, much more experienced at that time than their French counterparts. As a matter of fact, Lalo is the only French composer among those studied in this book who succeeded in having his works sung in Germany. His *mélodies* to Hugo's poems had already crossed the frontier when Paris heard them for the first time in 1856.[297]

The properties of Lalo's melodic writing are no less remarkable than the rhythmic and harmonic features. While modeling itself entirely on the literary text, his melody never ceases to sing, creating a kind of semi-recitative or modern arioso. This trait is best observed in "Souvenir," a model of the style. In the matter of form Lalo also shows his sense of balance; most often he introduces slight variations into the strophic form, while in the free forms or through-composed pieces he takes advantage of persistent motifs to guarantee a certain structural equilibrium.

But Lalo's songs are distinguished from those of his contemporaries principally by their profound sense of poetry. Although Gounod, Delibes, and Massenet were capable of charming, their sensitivity remains quite superficial beside the emotivity of Lalo, who could grasp the heart of a poetic thought. Not content with translating words as rational expressions, he adds to them the inexpressible that all essentially lyric poetry contains. Such words as "No doubt we would have suffered badly, but at least we would have

Example 179: Lalo, "Tristesse"

loved," quite ordinary in their literary aspect, take on profound
meaning with the music's support (Example 179).

Similarly, with a simple statement like "My friend has just left,"
an unobtrusive and unexpected modulation reveals the drama
hidden behind those dry words (Example 180).

Example 180: Lalo, "Chant breton" (with oboe)

In translating poetry's interior atmosphere (see Chapter II above)
Lalo introduces an extremely important element, lacking until then,
into French song. Although the total number of his *mélodies* was
small, his range was not limited to the expression of love's sorrows,
as in the examples cited above, but comprises a panorama of human
feelings, from joyous exuberance and capricious humor to tenderness, contemplation, and melancholy.

Of Lalo's first three songs, written in 1848, two are *scènes*. Conceived in the style of the period, these compositions offer nothing
individual. The next year he published (to Béranger's texts) *Six
romances populaires*, gathering under this somewhat contradictory title
authentic romances ("La pauvre femme," "Beaucoup d'amour,"
and "Le suicide"); *chansonnettes* ("Si j'étais petit oiseau" and "Les
petits coups"); and a *scène* in strophic form ("Le vieux vagabond").
Like the previous group, these pieces add nothing to the composer's
glory, although some personal touches may already be noticed:
careful prosody, declaimed song, and strongly profiled rhythms. The
initial phrase of "La pauvre femme" shows how Lalo's "reciting"
style may include a melodic sweep; the supple lines of the bass also

contribute to making the excerpt given in Example 181 less dry than the traditional recitative.

Example 181: Lalo, "La pauvre femme"

The next work, Opus 17, marks a large step forward. In 1855 six Hugo poems inspired Lalo to write this series of songs that places him, with a single effort, among the masters of the genre. Published by Maho under the title of *Six mélodies*, they were then retouched by the composer before inclusion in Hamelle's volume of *mélodies* published in 1894. Although minor in nature, the changes all constitute improvements. But even in the originals, Lalo's choice of Schubert and Schumann as godfathers is obvious in an idiom that is often closely related to that of the German composers. The collection includes "Puisqu'ici-bas toute âme," "L'aube naît," and "Oh! quand je dors," all true *Lieder*; several other pieces ally Germanic harmonies with delicate and lively rhythms of seemingly French or

Spanish origin. Thus, without attaining the psychological refinement
of Liszt's song on the same text, "Guitare" displays a rare perfection
of writing (Example 182).

Example 182: Lalo, "Guitare" (2nd version)

"Dieu qui sourit et qui donne" is similarly delicately rhythmic.
The voice intones the opening phrase in the midst of the harmonic
development begun twelve measures earlier, in which the tonic G
major is carefully avoided (Example 183).

The "*Lieder*" are simpler, being distinguished by their poetic atmosphere, their *Stimmung*. Lalo shows his consummate mastery in
the purity of the sober and clear style of "Puisqu'ici-bas toute âme."
The phraseological structure, corresponding almost exactly with
that of the lines, is worthy of note:

NO. OF SYLLABLES	TEXT	NO. OF MEASURES	
6	Puisqu'ici-bas toute âme	2	½ phrase
4	Donne à quelqu'un	1	complete phrase
6	Sa musique, sa flamme,	2	½ phrase
4	Ou son parfum;	1	

Less contemplative, "L'aube naît" resembles a Schumann *Lied*
(specifically the duet "Unterm Fenster," op. 34, no. 2, which has

Example 183: Lalo, "Dieu qui sourit et qui donne" (2nd version)

almost the same subject). The tone is gay and brisk, although not without a small cloud that Lalo expresses with finesse (Example 184).

While judiciously depicting the details of the text the composer does not neglect the requirements of musical logic. Thus, a rhythmic formula symbolizing knocking at the door serves equally well to render the bird's song (Example 185).

Example 184: Lalo, "L'aube naît"

Example 185: Lalo, "L'aube naît" (2 excerpts)

But the most beautiful of Lalo's "*Lieder*" is "Oh! quand je dors."
Whether he knew the composition that Liszt had written to these
words is difficult to determine, although the opening motif (Example 186) resembles somewhat the one cited above in Example 67.

In pitting himself once more against Liszt, Lalo this time proves
himself the former's equal. Although less imposing in concept and
less refined in its translation of literary details, his composition is
nevertheless very moving precisely because of its sobriety and

Example 186: Lalo, "Oh! quand je dors"

Example 187: Lalo, "Oh! quand je dors"

Example 188: Lalo, "Oh! quand je dors"

intimacy. As in "Puisqu'ici-bas," the fluid movement of the accompaniment gives it a calm and peaceful atmosphere that is entirely in harmony with the nobility of the poetic language (Example 187).

At the beginning of the second stanza (Example 188) Lalo anticipates Brahms, whose first *Lieder* had appeared only two years before, making it highly improbable that Lalo knew them at all.

The last *mélodie* of Opus 17, "Amis, vive, vive l'orgie," was replaced in the second edition by a new piece written on the same words and entitled "Chanson à boire." The first version was marked somewhat too strongly by theatricalism, its exuberance and turbulence carrying it beyond the bounds of the genre. In "Chanson à boire" Lalo omits several of the verses and of the remaining ones makes a musical adaptation that is much more sober and

Example 189: Lalo, "Chanson à boire" and "Amis, vive, vive l'orgie"

homogeneous. He sacrifices, however, the characteristic rhythm of the original version (Example 189).

A reviewer characterized the *Six mélodies* as an interesting, distinguished, and lively harmonic discourse and added:

> They have been for sale just a few days and already the singing world is buying them like mad; not the singing world of New Year albums, bound in calf and gilt-edged, but the intelligent and educated crowd, the artists of wit and taste who have popularized in France the sublime *mélodies* of Schubert and the sweet inspirations of Proch.[298]

This obvious exaggeration may be explained by the fact that the critic (A. Giacomelli) was a friend of the composer, who was in fact almost unknown in the musical world, his fame being confined to an extremely small group of artists.

During the next fifteen years Lalo wrote only two *mélodies*, both of a humorous nature. The "Ballade à la lune," based on Musset's famous poem, is a bold attempt that demonstrates the musician's power when he attacks an original subject. He courageously assaults that moon, which no one had dared to set to music, and makes of it a masterpiece. Now passionate and mock-heroic, now full of tenderness, this *mélodie* is reminiscent of some Hugo Wolf *Lied* on a text of Mörike or Eichendorff. Wolf's musical language is also presaged in the augmented fifths and cadences unexpectedly interrupted (Example 190).

The other piece, "Humoresque," is considerably below this level. These rather dull lines by C. Beauquier contrast sharply with Musset's spirited words:

> Que me fait la politique;
> République,
> Royauté, sont des mots creux!
> Tous les gens qui réfléchissent,
> Ils blanchissent;
> Or, voyez mes noirs cheveux.

Such a sally might have inspired Delibes to compose an amusing *chansonnette*; for Lalo it was a waste of his talent, leading him to write a noisy, quite pretentious kind of music.

About 1870 his wife's beautiful voice inspired Lalo to write some

Example 190: Lalo, "Ballade à la lune"

mélodies for contralto. Three lovely chansons to words of Alfred de Musset are particularly notable for their versatile and unconventional modulations. The beginning of "À une fleur," for example, suggests the key of C-sharp major although the piece is written in A (Example 191).

Example 191: Lalo, "À une fleur"

Similarly, the "Chanson de Barberine" hides its true tonality at the opening. In "La Zuecca" Lalo uses a rhythm typical of Schubert, whose influence is equally felt in the other two pieces.[299] The words of "Souvenir" (Hugo) and "L'esclave" (Gautier) are more suited to the contralto voice even though in the first piece a man is speaking. These dreamy and poetic *mélodies* are conceived and realized with perfect mastery. The same is true of "Chant breton" and "Tristesse," dating from about 1884 and from which some excerpts have already been quoted (see Examples 179 and 180). In all these works Lalo unerringly grasps what we have called the interior atmosphere of the poem while rejecting local color, although the texts of "L'esclave" and "Chant breton" offer ample opportunity for it. And this is the same composer who in the *Symphonie espagnole, Fantaisie norvégienne,* and *Concerto russe* shows such skill in handling musical geography!

Among Lalo's remaining songs, "Marine" had some repute toward the end of the century. It is a thoughtful *mélodie* that contains some pages of great beauty but ends in a grandiloquent and inflated manner. Such a fault shows that vestiges of grand opera's heyday were still in the air in 1883.

To summarize Lalo's contribution to the development of the genre, one may say that no earlier French composer had shown such sensitivity and versatility. He introduced humor and cheerfulness into the *mélodie*, becoming in this way the precursor of Chabrier. Furthermore, in his works sentimentality deepens into sentiment, bringing French song closer to the German *Lied*. Although extremely eclectic, his style nevertheless reflects an artistic personality that often finds originality. Lalo may thus be identified as one of the most important masters of the *mélodie* before Duparc.

César Franck (1822–1890)

Franck's biographers affirm that his literary education was sadly neglected. The texts of *Les Béatitudes* and *Psyché* contain platitudes that would have horrified a more cultured musician; in him they inspired the most elevated musical thoughts. Although he set the verse of some famous poets (e.g., Hugo, Musset, and Sully-Prudhomme), it almost appears as if he chose them by chance, since he showed little respect for the rhythm of their lines. A section of "Ninon" (Musset), for example, is prosodized in this way:

Ninon! Ninon! que fais-tu DE la vie?
L'heu-RE s'enfuit, le jour succède au jour.
Ro-SE ce soir, demain flétrie,
Comment vis-tu, toi qui n'as pas d'amour?

Paradoxically, neither this *mélodie* nor the pieces on texts by Hugo or Sully-Prudhomme count among his best works, whereas the poem "Nocturne" by Louis de Fourcaud inspired the composer toward a noble and profound song, even though it contains some rather indelicate images (e.g., "Mon cœur bouillonne comme une urne" [My heart boils like an urn]).

If Franck was indifferent to the laws of versification and incapable of grasping the value of a poetic image, he did not necessarily lack a sense of poetry. He undoubtedly had such a sense but it lived, so to speak, outside of the poem's words. For him only the subject matter existed. He would transpose it to his own world and from it realize an entirely personal conception. Thus his musical rendering of "Le mariage des roses" (Eugène David) "purifies" a sickly-sweet paraphrase of Ronsard's famous "Mignonne" and makes of it a piece full of charm and freshness, without any trace of sentimentality. No other composer was as capable of improving the spirit of the epoch, of divesting pallid literary productions of their banality; for if he was insensitive to the refinements of poetic language, he was equally untouched by bourgeois hypocrisy and lack of taste.

The romance "Blond Phébus" (1835) is a work of doubtful origin since the manuscript is unsigned.[300] Another youthful composition, not mentioned by any of his biographers and seemingly lost, is a cantata that was performed in 1839 by the sixteen-year-old composer and his thirteen-year-old brother. The event is recorded in *Le ménestrel*:

The concert of the young pianist César-Auguste Franck attracted a goodly crowd last Thursday in the Érard salons. The star and his young brother, a violinist, received many tokens of approval. Ponchard and Mlle. Annette Lebrun performed the vocal parts; one must be especially grateful to them for their willingness to study such a long cantata, whose details require particular care and sustained attention. This cantata (*Notre-Dame des orages*, whose text by M. le Comte de Pastoret was honored at the last competition of the Institut) is the work of M. César Franck. It is a conscientious production, but the piano sometimes overpowers the voice, a common fault of composers.[301]

Between 1840 and 1850 Franck wrote eight *mélodies,* most of them showing a certain immaturity, particularly in their structure. The over-schematic forms do not issue from the musical thought but seem to have been fixed in advance. The same fault has been mentioned in connection with his piano works of the same years, making them all appear to have been poured from the same mold and denoting, according to d'Indy, "a still insufficient study of the art of composition."[302] In the songs of this period the melodic curves are still very timid; they are shortwinded and often marred, as mentioned above, by defective prosody. The harmony, however, does offer something of interest. For example, in "L'Émir de Bengador," otherwise a weak piece, there are already chromatic progressions quite daring for the period (Example 192).

Example 192: Franck, "L'Émir de Bengador"

"Aimer" and "Ninon" are scarcely worth mentioning, since neither is very flattering to the talents of the young composer. A more balanced style appears in "Le sylphe," very much like a romance with accompanying piano and violoncello. The piece "L'ange et l'enfant" has been overestimated by most of Franck's biographers. The spiritual purity of Franck's setting does rise well above the nauseous sweetness of the words, but from the technical point of view the music leaves much to be desired. In spite of some original harmonic combinations in the accompaniment, this drab and monotonous song cannot hold the attention.

Two pieces on "folk" texts are more important. "Souvenance" (Chateaubriand) and "Robin Gray" (Florian) strongly reveal the influence of Schubert, whose four *Lieder* ("Die junge Nonne," "Die

Forelle," "Des Mädchens Klage," and "Das Zügenglöcklein") Franck had transcribed in 1844 for solo piano. Chateaubriand's lovely romance from *Le dernier des Abencérages* had already been set in banal fashion by Choron during the Empire, but Franck's composition is of an entirely different order. An accompanying motif resembling that of "Gretchen am Spinnrade" sustains a vocal part that begins in a hesitating way but blossoms out to express the nostalgia of the exiled mountaineer (Example 193).

Example 193: Franck, "Souvenance" (2 excerpts)

The curiously unbalanced structure of this piece is also note-worthy. The first part is in F-sharp (alternately major and minor); the second begins in B-flat major and modulates toward G, the closing key. The use of different opening and closing keys, a peculiarity also found in Schubert (e.g., "Der Wanderer"), seems unjustified here, where the simplicity of the poem calls for tonal equilibrium.

In "Robin Gray" Schubert's influence is even clearer (Example 194).

Example 194: Franck, "Robin Gray"

This use of the upper pedal leads the composer to analogous combinations that are even more original (Example 195).

The chief weakness of these early compositions is their lack of homogeneity; inspired and personal pages alternate with awkward passages in an almost banal style. While Franck still had much to learn about composing, however, the ingenuity of these *mélodies* removes them from the bourgeois atmosphere and indicates that Franck had already found his spiritual domain.

In the works written during the Second Empire the composer finally attained a balance that had been lacking in the pieces already discussed. Although his genius still had not arrived at complete maturity, from this point on Franck shows his mastery of the compositional craft. His melodic line has gained in fluidity, the architecture is less diffuse, and the awkwardness of the accompaniment

Example 195: Franck, "Robin Gray" (2 excerpts)

has disappeared. His style has become more transparent, more lucid, and in this way more French. Schubert's influence seems to have given way to that of Gounod, although Franck could hardly be said to have embraced Gounod's tendency toward false sentimentality. His works retain their naïve purity, a quality foreign to the spirit of the time.

The two songs "Les trois exilés" and "Le garde d'honneur" show that Franck had no talent for the "heroic" genre and merit no further comment. "Paris," a patriotic ode for voice and orchestra composed during the siege of the capital in 1870, is a more important work but may be passed over since it does not fit into the category of *mélodie*. "Passez, passez toujours" (Hugo), on the other hand, is so weak and clumsily handled that one is tempted to suggest that it must have been composed well before 1872, the date mentioned in d'Indy's catalogue.[303]

Among the more characteristic pieces of this second period are two songs set to Hugo's often encountered "S'il est un charmant gazon." The first, dating from about 1847,[304] is in simple strophic form and shows careful writing, although its emotion is somewhat timid. In the second piece, composed in 1857, Franck also makes use of strophic divisions, but this time handled in a manner recalling Händel's variation technique. While the voice part remains almost unchanged, the movement of the piano part gradually accelerates:

structure	1st stanza	2nd stanza	3rd stanza
movement	8th notes	triplets	16th notes

This procedure, which appears again in "Nocturne" and to some extent in "Le vase brisé," seems to have been a favorite of Franck. The harmony of the second version is much more developed than

Example 196: Franck, "S'il est un charmant gazon" (1st version and 2nd version)

Example 197: Franck, "Lied"

that of the first, as may be seen in the analogous portions shown in Example 196.

The piece entitled "Lied" (Lucien Paté) is unusual for its augmented intervals in both melody and harmony (Example 197).

Example 198: Franck, "Le mariage des roses"

This song, as well as "Roses et papillons" (Hugo), has an entirely French charm. Both are surpassed, however, by "Le mariage des roses" (Eugène David), which counts among Franck's most beautiful *mélodies*. Its simple and natural gracefulness has already been cited but the piece is equally remarkable from a technical point of view. Franck once more applies the procedures used in "Robin Gray" (see Example 195) but in a more subtle way (Example 198). The most admirable feature of this piece is that its harmonic originality does not destroy the ingenuousness of the whole.

The third period, that of the large works, furnishes only a few *mélodies*. The stylistic characteristics of the preceding period do not vanish entirely, reappearing in the *Six duos* for accompanied female choir of 1888, set to artless texts requiring an unaffected style. But Franck's language generally gains in depth, the melodic line is more ample, and the harmonies more complicated. These attributes do not, however, always contribute to the integrity of the style. In "Le vase brisé," for example, the details are more captivating than the whole, which leaves a somewhat tangled impression. Sully-Prud-homme's rich and cerebral language does lend itself badly to music, causing Franck to stumble to his downfall in trying to "dramatize" these lines:

> Son eau fraîche a fui goutte à goutte,
> Le suc des fleurs s'est épuisé;
> Personne encore ne s'en doute,
> N'y touchez pas, il est brisé.

The composer's repetition of the warning "N'y touchez pas" contradicts the contemplative nature of the poem.

Franck is more comfortable with a less intellectual text expressing basic feelings. In "Nocturne" he is able to evoke the majesty of the night. Yet the song's schematic structure seems unsuited to such a poetic concept. The form so well adapted to his settings of the chanson "S'il est un charmant gazon" does not fit this more subtle subject. The chromaticism of the piano part (especially in the introductory section) seems to require a freer architecture.

Such a structure appears in "La procession" (Brizeux), a *mélodie* for voice and orchestra. The first part of the song depicts the solemn parade with its rustic entourage. The accompaniment is constructed of two themes, the first seeming to express the crowd's religious sentiments, the other the eternal Church. The first theme is seen in several

César Franck in 1845

Alexis de Castillon

aspects (Example 199) and even leads to a small fugato (a) while the second theme uses the *Lauda Sion* chant (b):

Example 199: Franck, "La procession" (fugato and second theme)

These two themes no longer appear in the second half of the piece, which is a personal meditation on the picture presented by the procession. The voice, handled as a semi-recitative up to this point, becomes more truly melodic, while the orchestra's role is reduced to that of support. Near the end the two themes reappear with the initial words, "Dieu s'avance à travers les champs" (God advances through the fields). If not the most beautiful of Franck's *mélodies*, "La procession" certainly qualifies as one of the most profound.

Alexis de Castillon (1838–1873)

Castillon's *Six poésies d'Armand Silvestre* resemble a youthful essay more than a work of maturity, even though they were written after the composer's thirtieth year. These six songs that form his entire heritage of *mélodies* show that he never entirely learned his craft. The awkward and unskillfully realized passages are deficiencies that cannot be attributed to poor training, since Castillon had first been a student of Massé before leaving him to take lessons from César Franck. Massé was certainly not the type to encourage audacity in the young Castillon, but at least he could teach him technical principles. As to Franck, it would indeed be superfluous to describe the didactic capacities of the man responsible for the education of Vincent d'Indy, Henri Duparc, Ernest Chausson, and so many other illustrious French composers. Castillon's inability to derive more benefit from the teaching of these two masters is difficult to understand. Disciplined training should have restrained him from writing such nonsense as the passage in Example 200.

Example 200: Castillon, "Le semeur"

Castillon's occasional massacre of word rhythm, as seen in Example 201, may be explained by the fact that neither Massé nor Franck was especially expert in the matter of prosody.

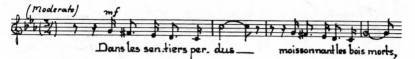

Example 201: Castillon, "Le bûcher"

But the same piece has an unexpected and daring modulation near the end (Example 202).

Example 202: Castillon, "Le bûcher"

Castillon's artistic talent is proved by certain positive stylistic qualities, including many striking details. His *mélodies* even contain hints of genius, in spite of their imperfection. Schumann is often recalled, but Castillon need not be qualified as an epigonus in the pejorative sense of the word. His musical language reflects a strong emotivity that can respond only to its own needs, exactly as Schumann's did. While this emotivity is born of the words, those words soon become embarrassing to the composer and he is able to show his true artistic face only after he has rid himself of the verbal obstacles, generally toward the end of the composition. Thus the instrumental epilogues of "Vendange" and "Renouveau" are the culminating points of Castillon's songs. They resound like the profound echo of a vision only partially realized.

Schumann's influence is revealed even more strongly in "Sonnet mélancolique." A nervous rhythm and appoggiaturas doubled at the octave give the piece a pathetic accent (Example 203).

"La mer," the remaining *mélodie* of the collection, has a majestic expressiveness that is particularly moving.

Example 203: Castillon, "Sonnet mélancolique"

The attraction exercised by German lyricism on both Lalo and Castillon poses the temptation to compare their *mélodies*. Aside from this common bias the two have little in common; the younger man lacked by far the solidity and mastery of Lalo. Full of interior fire, as Paul Landormy so aptly described him,[305] Castillon's artistic conceptions are all too often poorly realized; this explains why his importance resides not so much in his accomplishments as in his ideas. Unfortunately for him, history judges a man for what he has done, not for what he intended to do.

THE FIRST GREAT MASTERS

In this area the ground has already been explored. Unlike the neglected vocal pieces of their predecessors, Gabriel Fauré's *mélodies* and, to a more limited extent, those of Henri Duparc, have been discussed by various writers. In addition to the biographies by Koechlin, Aguettant, Suckling, Fauré-Frémiet, Servières, Oulmont, and Merle,[306] studies by Jankélévitch, Rostand, Northcote, and Schouten have been devoted exclusively to the musical works.[307] Of the authors mentioned, only Koechlin and Suckling are seriously concerned with Fauré's technical procedures, the others treating chiefly such esthetic and psychological questions as Fauré's equanimity, discretion, charm, Italianism, or Hellenism, and Duparc's profound emotivity or his spiritual relationship to Baudelaire. For this reason we have chosen to concentrate on the analysis of the composers' song technique and on the relationship of Fauré's first collection and of Duparc's total *mélodie* production with the masters preceding them.

Gabriel Fauré's First Collection

The *mélodies* of Fauré's first collection (including "Barcarolle," a piece that strayed into the second set, but excluding "Noël," which was composed later) date from about 1865.[308] Several biographers insist that "about 1865" should be interpreted as meaning a spread of some ten years. The first *mélodie*, "Le papillon et la fleur," shows all the symptoms of a very youthful composition and consequently was probably already written by 1860. The latest possible limit is practically dictated by the manuscripts of "Seule" and "Sentiers où l'herbe se balance" (in the Bibliothèque Nationale), which date from 1871. "Seule" was published that year by Hartmann along with "Lydia," "Hymne," and "Mai," while "Sentiers ..." appeared only later under the title "L'absent." Choudens had already issued "Le papillon et la fleur" and "Dans les ruines d'une abbaye" in 1869. The Bibliothèque Nationale also possesses an undated manuscript of "La rançon" and the autograph of an unpublished *mélodie* entitled "L'aurore," a charming piece on a text by Hugo. The latter *mélodie* should not be confused with another of the same title (but without the article) in Fauré's second collection, set to words by Armand Silvestre. Since the unpublished work is generally unknown,[309] a fascimile of the manuscript is included below in Appendix IV.

Apart from the works for solo voice and piano, two duets, "Puisqu'ici-bas toute âme" and "Tarantelle," also date from the same period. This total of twenty-three vocal pieces apparently composed during the period between 1860 and 1871 forms the subject matter of the present discussion.

THE STRUCTURE. The strophic form used in some of the *mélodies* is entirely suited to Fauré's first works, which are characterized by timid lyricism, short phrases, and elementary rhythm. Such pieces as "Le papillon et la fleur" and "Les matelots" manage to avoid monotony by their animated movement, but when the same form is used later in two elegiac *mélodies* the symmetry of this structure shows its limitations: the melancholy atmosphere of "Seule" requires a freer outline and the emotional words of "Tristesse" are unhappily confined in its foursquare frame. "Lydia" and "Barcarolle," on the other hand, carry their strophic form gracefully, the first because of its classic and compact style, the second because of its simplicity.

The second piece of the collection already shows a more complex structure; each of the two stanzas is composed of four different phrases, all derived from the initial motif (Example 204). This structural principle will be used again in several other pieces. Like

Puisque Mai tout en fleurs,

Example 204: Fauré, "Mai"

"Mai," the *mélodies* "Puisqu'ici-bas toute âme" (a duet) and "Aubade" are divided into two almost identical sections. Because of the way in which the stanzas are extended, the formal scheme no longer gives an impression of being strophic.

Other types appear alongside these perfectly symmetrical forms. "L'aurore" is constructed in *Lied* form (A B A), "Dans les ruines d'une abbaye" according to the formula A B A B A, and "Hymne" is based on the scheme A B C A. Fauré is even more successful with the medieval "*Bar*" pattern (A A B), in which the three sections are joined by a refrain (A R A R B). In "Chanson du pêcheur" this plan grows out of the poem, while in "Sylvie" it responds to a purely musical need, since the refrain is sung each time to different words. Other pieces follow this scheme with varying freedom. "Sérénade toscane" is composed of two identical parts followed by a coda; the final verses of "Rêve d'amour" and of "Ici-bas" grow out of the preceding stanzas but seek new paths (as in the phrase of "Mai" cited above in Example 204). In "Après un rêve" the second section already offers a variant, passing almost imperceptibly into the final part, of which only the beginning (the ascending fourth on "Hélas!") still recalls the initial stanza.

Several pieces have an entirely free structure. Although in "La rançon" Fauré seems to be proceeding at random, he generally does not mistake liberty for license. There are usually constitutive elements by which the form retains its balance and is given unity (e.g., the Neapolitan dance rhythm in "Tarantelle" and the suspensions in "L'absent"). The structure of "Chant d'automne" even shows a certain affectation. This piece is based on two motifs (a and b in Example 205). One of them, hidden at first in a banal accompanying formula (Example 205 c), announces these bitter words toward the end of the stanza:

J'aime de vos longs yeux la lumière verdâtre,
Douce beauté, mais tout aujourd'hui m'est amer.

Incapable of grasping Baudelaire's type of "spleen," the young composer gives the words a too rosy interpretation (Example 205 d). The other motif is one of anguish, playing an important role in the first part of the piece and leading to developments that are strongly reminiscent of Schumann (Example 205 e).

Fauré's phraseology within the large outlines described merits some additional observations. His use of heterometric stanzas in several poems engenders difficulties in the construction of musical phrases. He generally tries to reestablish symmetry by prolonging certain notes. In Example 206, for instance, the lines are equalized by the extension of the last syllable of each distich.

The syncopations resulting from these prolongations leave a tedious impression because of their frequency and regularity. The procedure is applied with more success in "Seule," where the octosyllabic feminine lines alternate with the four-syllable masculine lines (Example 207).

In this case the recurrence of the long note at the end of each period is not tiresome. Feminine lines evidently are unable to tolerate systematic prolongation because it pushes the slackness to excess and weakens the strength of expression.

In certain *mélodies* the vocal phrases are unequal, reflecting to some extent the metrics of the words. At the same time Fauré does not repudiate the periodic regularity of four or eight measures, only the subdivisions of the phrases no longer being "square." In "Le papillon et la fleur" the syllabic relationship is 4 to 1 (each alexandrine is followed by a three-syllable line; in the music the proportion is 5 to 3 (cf. Reber's setting of the same lines in Example 101 above). "Au bord de l'eau" offers another and quite original solution of the problem (Example 208).

As in the preceding pieces, the pattern is followed with exact regularity. In writing the songs belonging to the first collection Fauré still had constant need of a relatively restricted framework. Only the subjects of "L'absent" and "Chant d'automne" lead him into a sort of musical prose, but even in those cases the phrases are not entirely divorced from their periodic origin.

Most of the structural procedures discussed above seem to have been borrowed from Gounod. Some more or less personal

Example 205: Fauré, "Chant d'automne"

Example 206: Fauré, "Dans les ruines d'une abbaye"

characteristics may nevertheless be discerned: the use of the form A A B, the technique of developing a single motif in various ways, and the clever handling of heterometric verses.

Example 207: Fauré, "Seule"

MELODIC LINE AND PROSODY. In Fauré's vocal phrase the durational accent (falling on a weak beat and producing a fluid syncopation), mentioned at the beginning of the preceding chapter, appears frequently. It is used abundantly in the first collection, particularly in "Mai," "Les matelots," "Lydia," and "Rêve

Example 208: Fauré, "Au bord de l'eau"

d'amour."[310] In "Seule" the procedure is even applied quite methodically; in each period the syncopation, preceded by a strong beat which is divided into two eighth notes, underscores the feminine ending, while the masculine line is rendered by a rhythm adjusted to the musical metrics (cf. Example 207). The principle underlying the durational accent results from a rhythmic displacement. The anapaestic formula, as it is found in Lully's recitative: ♪♪♩ retreats one beat and becomes ♩♪♪♩. Thus one of the secrets of Fauré's fluid style resides in the weakening of the strong beat, which is divided into the notes of the former anacrusis.

But the composer goes even further. This strong (or relatively strong) beat, divided into two notes, is also produced without having to be followed by a syncopation. The very typically Fauréan theme of "Sérénade toscane" (Example 209) offers a good illustration (see also the left hand of Example 217 below).

Example 209: Fauré, "Sérénade toscane"

The effect of the advanced anacrusis may even be obtained without the division into two eighth notes. By jumping an octave the initial B-flat of the piano part deprives the strong beat of its thesis character.

In general the melodic line appearing in the first collection does not yet have much amplitude, the principal obstacle to its flowering being obviously the balanced phrase. The rhythms, however, are sometimes remarkable. Triplets are employed in a variety of ways: pathetically in "Chanson du pêcheur," gracefully and modestly in "Lydia," and expressively in "Après un rêve." The latter *mélodie*, on a text composed exclusively of feminine lines, is further distinguished by a skillful handling of mute syllables. They fall alternately on strong and weak beats but always retain their character.

With the exception of "Le papillon et la fleur," a juvenile attempt that still reveals the composer's inexperience, the pieces of the first collection are generally lacking in major prosodic errors. "Lydia" and "Au bord de l'eau" have less careful prosody than the other *mélodies*, seeming to have been conceived from the viewpoint of the pianist, with less regard for purity of vocal writing; but even in them Fauré does not exceed the limits of good taste. His liberties, most often caused by his use of the balanced phrase, are nowhere irritating.

Finally, the famous Fauré tritone calls for a few words. It first appears in the third piece of the collection ("Dans les ruines d'une abbaye," measures 23–26 and the bass of the same section); then in "Sérénade toscane" ("Éveille-toi, mon âme, ma pensée"); in "Ici-bas" ("tous les hommes pleurent"); and naturally in "Lydia," where it derives, like its tonality of F, from the title itself. As is so often the case with Fauré, it is impossible to say whether the tritone grows out of the harmonic tensions or whether it is rather of a purely melodic order. This curious melodic-harmonic amalgam, by which Fauré's musical language is so clearly distinguished from that of his contemporaries, will be discussed again later.

THE HARMONY. Fauré's harmonies reveal a character analogous to that of his melodic writing. The softening of contrasts confers on it a special fluidity. The principal chords (I, IV, and V) are often replaced by secondary ones (VI, II, and III), thus forming cadences of moderated tension (Example 210).

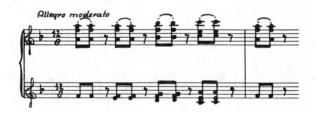

Example 210: Fauré, "Aubade"

The same cadence is later used in a more subtle form at the beginning of "Mandoline," a *mélodie* from the third collection (Example 211).

Elsewhere the dominant seventh chord is preceded by the mediant (Example 212).

Example 211: Fauré, "Mandoline"

The alternation of the tonic chord with the mediant (a progression certainly borrowed from Gounod; cf. Examples 117–118) is already found in "Mai" (Example 213).

The tension between the dominant seventh chord (or that built on the seventh degree) and the tonic is attenuated in various ways. In

Example 212: Fauré, "Après un rêve"

Example 213: Fauré, "Mai"

Example 214: Fauré, "Seule"

"Seule" a delayed note suggests the combination $VII_{4\atop3}$–VI_6 although the chord in question is actually the tonic (Example 214).

In Example 215 the dominant seventh chord progressing to a pseudo-tonic (V_7–VI_6) already presages the characteristic cadence of "Prison" (of the third collection).

Plagal progressions (especially the formulae $II_{6\atop5}$–I and $II_{4\atop3}$–I, so typically Fauréan) are still rare in the pieces of the first collection. "Mai" once more furnishes a sample (Example 216).

Fauré's preference for the secondary chords can hardly be termed audacious. If he made frequent use of mediant harmony at a time when Reber judged it dangerous or even non-existent,[311] more is revealed about the latter's narrow-minded and conservative views (even though he was the author of a treatise on harmony!) than about the boldness of the young composer. The mediant chord was actually very much in use about 1865 and indeed, was even employed by Reber himself (as in his "Chanson de Barberine" and "Mortel, ouvre tes yeux"). As to true harmonic audacities, such as the consecutive sevenths of "Au bord de l'eau" and certain passages in "Tarantelle" and "Après un rêve," the infrequency with which they appear in Fauré's early works testifies to a curious prudence that contrasts with the extreme venturesomeness of Berlioz, Bizet, and Duparc.

And yet Fauré's first harmonic explorations claim attention because they are the basis of his future musical expression. The procedures just noted, of which most were undoubtedly borrowed from Gounod, are found in a more refined and personal form in the later

Example 215: Fauré, "Après un rêve" and "Prison"

collections and in the large cycles, where they no longer recall either Gounod's manner or those of other predecessors, but instead clearly indicate the individual character of Fauré's style.

Example 216: Fauré, "Mai"

MELO-HARMONIC FEATURES. This is undoubtedly the most striking aspect of Fauré's style. Even in the first collection the bass line often rises or descends stepwise (e.g., the end of the stanza in "Les matelots," the refrain in "Chanson du pêcheur," various passages in "Aubade," and measures 7–10 of "Hymne"). But since the notes usually belong to the chords appearing over them, they almost always resolve according to harmonic rules. In the later collections the fundamental line begins to be detached from the actual harmony in order to follow its own purposes. Such an example appears at the beginning of "Arpège" (in the third collection; Example 217).

Example 217: Fauré, "Arpège"

Evidently viewing the question from the traditional harmonic concept, Koechlin describes this passage as an exceptional resolution (the rising bass following the third inversion of the dominant seventh chord).[312] The F-natural appears to me not as a chordal tone but as part of a melodic bass line (E–F–G–C) proceeding practically independently of the chords above it.

In the first collection such configurations are still in the rudimentary stage. The instrumental part of "Aubade" does, however, offer some examples of melodic emancipation within the harmonic body (Example 218).

In this case the succession of chords is dictated to some extent by the movement of the bass, rising from B to G. Similarly, the upper part of the accompaniment may foreshadow the future "melodic" harmonies (Example 219).

Traditional harmonic analysis might describe this as a typically Fauréan cadence in which the subdominant is replaced by a seventh chord on the submediant ($I–VI_4^{}–V_7–I$). But another possible

interpretation is that of a melodic line of four notes (C–D–E–F)

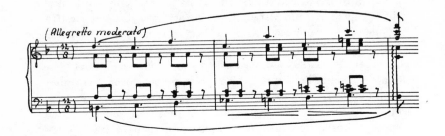

Example 218: Fauré, "Aubade"

superposed on a quite conventional progression (I–I_6–V_7–I), so that the D of the second chord must be considered as a note foreign to the harmony.

In "Sylvie" piano melody and voice proceed by parallel sixths, provoking singular dissonances with the actual harmony (Example 220).

The method of analysis employed for the preceding examples is admittedly open to discussion. Considered separately, these passages could easily be explained in terms of passing notes, embellishments, etc. But such interpretations do not stand when judged within the framework of Fauré's style. The second collection already presents similar procedures that are impossible to explain with the tools of conventional harmony.

Along with this melodic infiltration of the harmony comes the reverse influence of the chords on the vocal line. The first phrase of

Example 219: Fauré, "Aubade"

Example 220: Fauré, "Sylvie"

"Sérénade toscane," for instance (Example 221), seems to be in the tenth plainchant mode (taking account of the final B-flat).

Appearances may be deceiving. The modulation toward D-flat causes the lowering of the leading tone, which becomes the fifth of

Example 221: Fauré, "Sérénade toscane"

the new key. In the next measure the return to the original key is made manifest by an A-natural, proving that instead of a medieval mode Fauré is using modern tonality. In this case the change from A-flat to A-natural in the melody, imitated in the piano, is clearly dictated by the harmony (Example 222).

Sometimes Fauré does employ the old modes without the harmony being involved in their use (as at the opening of "Barcarolle"). But in such a case he is following the example of dozens of analogous or even more daring passages in Bizet, Saint-Saëns, or Delibes.

The close interdependence of the horizontal and the vertical elements in Fauré's music is of extreme importance. Since the appearance of Catel's *Traité d'harmonie* in 1802, counterpoint and harmony had been considered as two entirely distinct entities. The artificial and basically anti-musical separation was justified neither by esthetic necessity nor by historical reasoning. Fauré probably rediscovered the correspondence between the constituent parts of musical technique during his study of sixteenth-century masters

Example 222: Fauré, "Sérénade toscane"

with Niedermeyer, and later succeeded in making the synthesis by which his language, while remaining entirely modern, introduced elements of earlier idioms.

GENERAL VIEW OF THE EARLY MÉLODIES. "The tonality, the chords, the rhythm, and the forms are those that Gabriel Fauré found when he began serving music; in his hands those ordinary things have become precious."[313] The young composer's style should be judged in the light of these words of Nadia Boulanger. The first collection is an exploration in the domain of the *mélodie* and the *Lied* as they had developed by the end of the Second Empire. The very varied musical translations inspired by the diversity of subjects do not arise from an eclectic taste, as was the case with Saint-Saëns and Lalo, but instead reveal a personality in search of its own spirit. Fauré sought his way by trial and error and was not afraid to submit to the influence of his predecessors.

The first genre he tried was the *chansonnette*; the facile and almost banal ritornelle of "Le papillon et la fleur" belongs entirely to this category. While lacking a specifically Fauréan character, this *opus primum* is not entirely devoid of charm, particularly when it is sung at rapid speed. The next pieces ("Mai," "Dans les ruines d'une abbaye," and "Les matelots") are already more lyrical and exhibit some personal qualities. The lively atmosphere of the early *mélodies* is also present in "Aubade," "Sylvie," "Rêve d'amour," and the duet "Puisqu'ici-bas toute âme," which were probably written later, since they evidence a more developed and accomplished style. The expression of melancholy in "Tristesse" poses difficulties for Fauré, making this piece the weakest of the collection. With "Seule" he is more fortunate; here the sober and almost severe writing confers a certain majesty on the mournful atmosphere of the poem. The same style is applied to a dramatic subject in "L'absent." Sully-Prudhomme's two meditative poems, "Ici-bas" and "Au bord de l'eau," are also interpreted in a strongly sober style.

All these *mélodies* remain under Gounod's pervading influence, showing how Fauré gradually enriched the latter's language with his own personality. Some vague traces of Saint-Saëns and Massenet may also be discerned.

The three *mélodies* written to Baudelaire poems present quite a different picture. The young composer's malaise in the spiritual world of the *Fleurs du mal* seems to have deprived him of his self-confidence; perhaps for this reason he tries to interpret the unhappy poet by borrowing from Schumann. But the German composer has no basic kinship with Baudelaire; Schumann's melancholy is full of a warmth that stands out in the music in a spontaneous, sometimes even disorderly fashion, while the poet's unhappiness, harboring the anguish of death, is realized in more elaborated forms. This conflict between poetry and music, in which Fauré actually serves only as an intermediary, is clearly evident at the end of "Chant d'automne" (see Example 205 d), in the banality of "Hymne," and in the dryness of "La rançon," which is created by the music's inability to translate the philosophic thought.

Schumann's influence on Fauré should not be exaggerated. Some critics outside of France (and particularly in Germany) have propagated the thesis that Fauré was deeply in Schumann's debt. This erroneous judgment may stem from the fact that for many years Fauré's early pieces were the only ones known outside the borders of France. With the exception of the Baudelaire pieces just mentioned, the "Schumannesque" characteristics in Fauré's first two collections are all superficial in nature and much less important than those emanating from Gounod. Schumann's nervous spirit, his rapture and his exaltation, are opposed to Fauré's caution, equilibrium, and elegance. The old conflict between Romantic and Classic is once more apparent.

If the Baudelaire songs are disappointing, Fauré compensates with the group of "Italian" *mélodies*. "Sérénade toscane" unites a Southern cantabile with French gracefulness. These very personal pages already presage the songs from *Shylock* and the five *mélodies* "from Venice," although toward the end of the piece the composer lapses into the kind of facility found in Mendelssohn's *Songs Without Words*. More sober and ascetic, "Barcarolle" borrows fluidity from the vocal line, which, while still recalling "Sérénade toscane," is more delicately rhythmic.

The famous "Après un rêve" reveals another facet of the Italian spirit. All the expression seems to be concentrated in the vocal part, the *mélodie* assuming in this way the aspect of a neo-seventeenth-century aria. To this classic *bel canto*, "Chanson du pêcheur" contrasts its folk style that expresses in a very direct manner the elemental grief of the fisherman. Jankélévitch finds the piece "hardly Fauréan" and criticizes its lack of modesty and the freedom with which the voice declaims. He says accusingly that "it takes advantage of the piano's silence, launches into some vocalises [?] and takes us far from the austere recitative that Fauré was already using at that time." But Jankélévitch reserves his severest judgment for "Après un rêve":

> These faults are even more shocking in "Après un rêve," where the voice steals all the song's interest and reduces the accompaniment to impoverished chord repetitions that serve at most to harmonize or furnish bass support. This state of affairs carries us far back, indeed beyond "Chant d'automne," whose bass is far more mobile, varied, and expressive. One is led to think of Robert Schumann and the moving repeated chords of "Stille Tränen" or "Ich grolle nicht." Everyone knows that "Après un rêve" is much appreciated by female singers and understandably, for by definition singers want to sing, and the melody, which pours out brimfull here, is flattering to the well-organized larynx. As long as there will be concerts, and upper-class young girls, then singers will be heard shouting at the top of their lungs "Ô nuit mys-té-ri-eu-se . . ." and roaring out the F-sharp and the thirty-first measure, where the emotion is obviously at its height.[314]

Although his opinions usually testify to admirable clarity of thought, in this instance Jankélévitch is reasoning falsely, since Fauré can hardly be reproached for the poor taste of his interpreters. Nor can the composer be criticized for no longer answering to the image earlier formed of him. "Après un rêve" and "Chanson du pêcheur" ("Lamento") are indeed both Fauréan compositions, not because he is their author, but because they do show his personal characteristics. If the songs lack modesty it is because their texts evoke such a condition, just as that of "Lydia" suggests chastity. Furthermore, the so-called "impoverished chords" of "Après un rêve" constitute a most refined harmonic language, as Jankélévitch himself admits later in the same pages:

> And yet, how French is this solicitude for form that shines forth in the slightest details! Each and every chord of the piano part composes some precious and choice harmony for the voice. So much refinement joined to a melodic effusion so even, powerful, and serene can only presage exquisite works.

As for the lament "Chanson du pêcheur," it is unquestionably the most accomplished piece of the collection, as much from the psychological as from the musical point of view. As the story unfolds, the arpeggios depicting the waves become increasingly fast; this stretto expresses the poorly suppressed misery that finally explodes in the refrain "Que mon sort est amer! / Ah! sans amour s'en aller sur la mer!" (How bitter is my lot, to go to sea without love). The same words had been admirably interpreted by Berlioz and Gounod, but neither attained the appropriateness of expression that Fauré gave them.

"Tarantelle" brings Neapolitan *bel canto*; less expressive than brilliant, this duet is much superior to Bizet's *mélodie* of the same name, whose harmonic audacities it recalls. The piece is seldom heard, evidently because of its technical difficulties.

In summary, the "Italian" *mélodies* may be characterized as having an extraordinary variety. They contain tenderness ("Sérénade toscane"), wild gayety ("Tarantelle"), peacefulness ("Barcarolle"), touching grief ("Chanson du pêcheur"), and deep emotion ("Après un rêve"). For each state of mind Fauré was able to find adequate musical expression.

The remaining song, "Lydia," is aptly qualified by Jankélévitch:

> On what does the pagan gracefulness of this ode depend? One is not quite sure. No more in it than the most chaste intervals: fourths, fifths, and thirds, humble chords that lend their transparency and slenderness to the cantilena. "Lydia" is limpid and divine consonance, a present from the muses.[315]

This song does have an inexpressible quality from which arises a fascination, a charm (in the original sense of the word) that escapes all analysis. Its style does not resemble that of any predecessor, making it an embarrassing work to categorize. Its harmonies and form are of the simplest, suggesting that Nadia Boulanger's words, "in his hands those ordinary things have become precious," are particularly true for this piece. "Lydia" is no longer the language of youthful talent, but of genius. If the "Italian" pieces suggest the future riches of the third collection, this first "Hellenic" composition of Fauré already announces the serene austerity of *Le jardin clos* or "Diane, Séléné."

Henri Duparc (1848–1933)

Duparc left a total of seventeen songs, all written before 1884 and most of them published by 1895.[316] Besides those appearing in the collection published by Rouart et Lerolle in 1911, the composer wrote at least four other vocal pieces. He tried to destroy three of the youthful *Cinq mélodies*, Opus 2 (composed in 1868 and published by Flaxland in 1870) but appears to have succeeded only in considerably reducing the number of prints. Because of their scarcity most musicologists have considered these *mélodies* as lost. The copy in the Bibliothèque Nationale shows that the collection contains the three songs in question ("Le galop," "Sérénade," and "Romance de Mignon")[317] together with "Chanson triste" and "Soupir." Durand reissued "Le galop" in 1948 and hopefully the remaining two will follow.

Besides these youthful pieces, in 1872 Duparc wrote his longest vocal work, a duet for soprano and tenor entitled "La fuite" (Gautier). In spite of its artistic value the work is strangely neglected. Northcote speaks of it as having been destroyed by the composer soon after its composition,[318] but the song was even published by Demets about 1900 (therefore with the composer's authorization) and is still available.

THE FIVE MÉLODIES COMPOSED IN 1868. "Sérénade," reproduced on pages 274–276, is an important document for the study of Duparc's stylistic origins. The suavity of the vocal line, the division of strong beats into two sixteenth notes, the fluid syncopations, and the harmony marked by the use of mediant chords all clearly reveal Gounod as his point of departure. The presence of the same stylistic traits in Fauré brings "Sérénade" very close to certain of Fauré's

Gabriel Fauré

Henri Duparc

mélodies. Yet this similarity does not deny Duparc's personal spirit, which is evident in the amplitude of the arpeggios (extending even to four octaves) and the emphasis of melodic accents on strong beats ("JE me fanerais"; "TE quitter"). Duparc even risks some "forbidden" parallel fifths (measures 1 and 26) that are hardly shocking, and the short "recitative" (measures 39–40) that interrupts the fluid movement of the accompaniment is a happy invention.

The lightly veiled tenderness of this piece takes on an ecstatic character in "Chanson triste." Emphatic accents falling on pronouns, prepositions, articles, and other weak or mute syllables more or less determine the course of the melodic line:

> DANS ton cœur dort un clair de lune,
> UN doux clair de lune d'été
> ET pour fuir la vie importune
> JE me noierai dans ta clarté.
>
> J'OU-blierai LES douleurs passées,
> MON amour, QUAND tu berceras
> Mon triste cœur et mes pensées
> DANS le calme aimant de tes bras.
>
> TU prendras ma tête malade
> OH! quelquefois sur tes genoux,
> ET lui diras une ballade,
>   (U-ne ballade)
> Qui semblera parler de nous,
>
> ET dans tes yeux pleines de tristesses,
> DANS tes yeux alors je boirai
> TANT de baisers et de tendresses
> QUE peut-être JE guérirai ...

This manner of prosodizing, although contrary to the rules, was certainly used deliberately. Duparc also shows his individuality in the development of the accompaniment. The presence of passages that strongly suggest Fauré cannot be denied, but it is the Fauré of the second and third collections who is invoked (Example 223).

The unresolved suspension in Example 224 should also be noted.

In contrast with the truly French compositions, "Sérénade" and "Chanson triste," there are two pieces that evoke a German atmosphere. "Romance de Mignon" (a mediocre adaptation by Victor

SÉRÉNADE.

Paroles de **GABRIEL MARC.**　　　　　　Musique de **H. DUPARC.**

[1-3]

[4-7]

[8-11]

[12-15]

ne me verrais pas, fri _ vo _ _ le, Te quitter pour une au_tre fleur.

[16-19]

[20-23]

Si j'étais la ro _ se charman _ te Que ta main pla_ce sur ton cœur

[24-27]

Si près de toi tou _ te tremblan _ te Je me fanerais

[28-31]

Example 223: Duparc, "Chanson triste" (2 excerpts)

Example 224: Duparc, "Chanson triste"

Wilder of Goethe's poem) reveals the influence of Liszt and Wagner. In 1869 Duparc attended performances of *Tristan* and *Das Rheingold* in Munich and had probably studied some of Wagner's scores before the composition in 1868 of his *Cinq mélodies*. The airy chords of the passage in Example 225 certainly awaken echoes of *Lohengrin*.

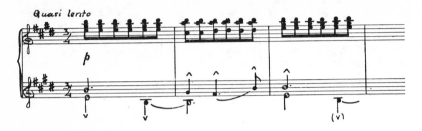

Example 225: Duparc, "Romance de Mignon"

At the beginning of the second stanza, the initial motif anticipating the rhythm of the melody is made up of chromatic notes that reinforce the Wagnerian coloring (Example 226).

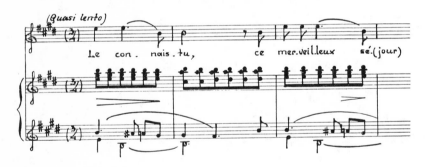

Example 226: Duparc, "Romance de Mignon"

Less flexible from the structural point of view and less fluid also in its harmonic and melodic writing, "Romance de Mignon" does not attain the perfection of the two preceding *mélodies*. But it is entirely superior to the "Mignon" of Reber or of Gounod, to say nothing of the awkward and insipid composition of Monpou.

"Le galop," a dramatic monologue, shows Schubert's influence; the impetuous movement, the repeated chords, and the cadence with

Example 227: Duparc, "Le galop"

suspended fourth quite clearly imitate "Erlkönig." Significantly, the diatonic scales of Schubert's left hand are chromatic here (Example 227).

Some abrupt progressions recall Liszt's style (Example 228).

Example 228: Duparc, "Le galop"

This somewhat disorderly composition is not entirely satisfying, its interest residing more in details than in the whole. But to Duparc's credit it should be noted that the music adds to Sully-Prudhomme's words an element of anguish that reinforces the dramatic expression.

"Soupir" shows the composer already at the height of his genius. Its title is reflected in the chords of the minor ninth on the dominant. This interval, of some importance in Duparc's harmonic writing, will be discussed again later (Example 229).

Example 229: Duparc, "Soupir"

A carefully declaimed vocal line is joined to harmonic combinations which betray the influence of César Franck but also mark the personality of their author (Example 230).

In "Soupir" Duparc's language has achieved an equilibrium. The French tenderness of "Sérénade" is wed here to the German nostaligia of "Romance de Mignon." It is the master's first elegiac *mélodie*, to be followed by "Élégie," "Lamento," and "Testament." The other pieces of the 1868 collection also constitute models to

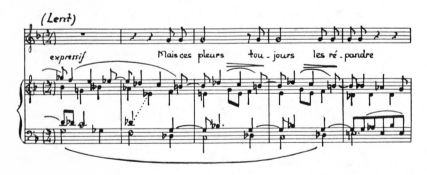

Example 230: Duparc, "Soupir"

which Duparc was to return in the course of his short artistic career. The lyricism of "Chanson triste" will be reborn in "Extase" and "Phidylé"; the nostalgia of "Romance de Mignon" will reappear in "L'invitation au voyage" and "La vie antérieure"; "Sérénade" is succeeded by a single work, "Sérénade florentine," while "Le galop" is followed by four other dramatic compositions: "Au pays où se fait la guerre," "La vague et la cloche," "La fuite," and "Le manoir de Rosemonde."

Thus, at the age of twenty Duparc has already explored his domain and fixed its limits. Far from seeking new spheres, he strives from then on to add depth to his musical language; this depth raises the French *mélodie* to the level of the German *Lied*.

CHARACTERISTICS OF STYLE. Unlike Fauré, whose musical phrases more or less follow the structure of the verse, Duparc most often transforms his texts into prose, perhaps in imitation of Massenet. To compensate for the lack of periodic phrases, this style of writing necessitates an extremely careful prosody, a requirement generally satisfied by Duparc's melodic line. When he does employ a "square" construction, he sometimes sacrifices the cadence of the words to the needs of the musical rhythm (Example 231).

Example 231: Duparc, "Sérénade florentine"

The prolongation of a note falling on a secondary word also demonstrates an abstract musical inventiveness (Example 232).

Example 232: Duparc, "Au pays où se fait la guerre"

But most often Duparc uses the prosodic formulae of his predecessors, especially that of a divided strong beat followed by a fluid syncopation (see Example 106 e). Examples are too numerous to require quotation here, except for two instances of syncopation straddling the bar line (Example 233).

Example 233: Duparc, "La fuite" and "Au pays où se fait la guerre"

The melodic line is generally much more ample than Fauré's, the large intervals conferring an intensity of expression that contrasts with the latter's restraint. Duparc's choice of high voice for most of his songs in contrast to Fauré's preference for medium ranges is also significant. In comparing the vocal writing of the two masters one discovers, in fact, that they followed entirely different, even opposite paths. Only rarely is Duparc intrigued by a Fauréan formula, as in the tritone at the opening of "Phidylé" (Example 234).

Example 234: Duparc, "Phidylé"

Duparc's use of the augmented interval is, however, by no means uncommon, growing quite naturally out of his emotive language (Example 235).

Not all melodic lines display this sweep; sometimes the voice declaims on a single note (as in the refrain of "L'invitation au voyage," certain passages of "La fuite," and the last two pages of "La vie antérieure").

Duparc's musical prose also influences the structure, which in general is based on the poem's contents rather than on time-honored schemes. The early *mélodies* still show some regularity. "Romance de Mignon" is written in strophic form; the same scheme may be recognized in "L'invitation au voyage" but here arpeggios replace the tremolo in the second stanza and the voice part also has

Example 235: Duparc, "L'invitation au voyage" and "Romance de Mignon"

many variants. The structure of "Au pays où se fait la guerre" is modeled somewhat on a rondo form. After 1870 only "Lamento" and "Extase" have schematic structures. In several other *mélodies* of this period the initial phrase does reappear toward the end (e.g., "Testament") but in those cases the repetition is justified by the text. By contrast, in "Le manoir de Rosemonde" the end is fundamentally different from the beginning. This piece shows to what extent Duparc's musical structure is dictated by the words. The voice intones "quite fast and with force" the opening lines expressing the sudden and violent attack of lovesickness:

> De sa dent soudaine et vorace
> Comme un chien l'amour m'a mordu ...

The ending is "slower and pianissimo," translating the nostalgia of the unhappy dying lover:

> J'ai parcouru ce triste monde,
> Et qu'ainsi je m'en fus mourir
> Bien loin, bien loin, sans découvrir
> Le bleu manoir de Rosemonde.

However, Duparc understood quite well that music has its own requirements and for this reason usually departed from a basic musical idea that serves a cohesive function. Constituting the unity of the piece, such an element may be melodic, rhythmic, or harmonic in nature and may even develop into a theme. Example 236 gives several melodic motifs.

Example 236: Duparc, "Sérénade florentine," "Élégie," and "Testament"

"Le manoir de Rosemonde" is built on a rhythmic idea (Example 237).

Example 237: Duparc, "Le manoir de Rosemonde"

In "Lamento" the basic theme is always accompanied by the same chords so that its importance is harmonic as much as melodic (Example 238).

Example 238: Duparc, "Lamento"

Pierre de Bréville has pointed out that these four expressive notes emphasize the metrical structure of the poem by rendering the third and sixth lines of each strophe:[319]

> Connaissez-vous la blanche tombe
> Où flotte avec un son plaintif
> *L'ombre d'un if?*
> Sur l'if une pâle colombe,
> Triste et seule, au soleil couchant
> *Chante son chant.*

In Lalo's "L'esclave" (dating from 1872) the central motif also seems to issue from the words. This procedure derives from Liszt (cf. "Oh! quand je dors," Examples 67–72), while the principle of the generating interval seems to have been Berlioz' invention (cf. *Les nuits d'été*, Examples 47–51).

For Duparc the piano's role is no longer that of an accompaniment, since the instrumental part contributes as much to the poetic expression as the voice. Although only two songs were originally written for voice and orchestra ("La vague et la cloche" and "La vie antérieure"), several others seem equally to have been conceived as symphonic works ("Testament" and "Phidylé") and were later orchestrated by the composer. Among the early *mélodies* there are some, however, which do not tolerate transference to the large concert hall, where the delicately shaded writing is lost and the

Example 239: Duparc, "Le manoir de Rosemonde" (harmonic scheme of measures 38–52)

orchestra cannot compensate for the pianistic subtleties of the original version.

As with the melodic line, Duparc's harmony is essentially different from that of Fauré, replacing the latter's fluidity with unexpected progressions. He juxtaposes dissimilar chords whose mutual kinship can no doubt be explained from a theoretical point of view, but which nevertheless impress the ear as isolated elements. Thus, the last page of "Le manoir de Rosemonde" has the harmonic scheme shown in Example 239.

"La vie antérieure" has even more daring progressions (Example 240).

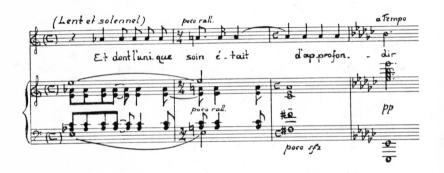

Example 240: Duparc, "La vie antérieure"

The passage in Example 241 is also very characteristic of Duparc. Instead of arriving at the tonic D minor by means of the dominant seventh chord, a progression certainly suggested by the C-sharp of the voice part, the composer prefers to interpolate two chords entirely outside of the harmonic framework.

Duparc often achieves such harmonic surprises in a remarkable way by means of perfect triads and without adding a single dissonant note. The surprise resides solely in the succession of harmonies quite distant from each other. Sometimes he even links two chords separated by the interval of an augmented fourth, thus opposing his "harmonic tritone" to Fauré's melodic tritone. In "Extase" this procedure still answers to a logical design, a modulating sequence based on the formula II_6–V_7 (Neapolitan sixth to dominant seventh) (Example 242).

Example 241: Duparc, "Lamento"

Baudelaire's visionary language in "La vie antérieure" inspires the composer to an even more audacious tritonic progression (Example 243).

Duparc's treatment of dissonance also includes an abundance of embellishments and passing notes. The harmonic color of certain

Example 242: Duparc, "Extase"

pieces ("Extase," "Phidylé," and "Testament") is more or less determined by notes foreign to the chords and which, far from being simple ornaments, contribute greatly to the expression. The composer often uses them with liberty, as for example at the beginning of the refrain of "Phidylé," where passing notes figure between imaginary F's and real A's (Example 244).

Example 243: Duparc, "La vie antérieure"

The appoggiatura is also important. The interval of the minor ninth descending to the octave (or to the fifth if placed on the dominant) pervades entire pieces (e.g., "Soupir," "Élégie," and "Testament"). This procedure is readily attributable to Wagner's

Example 244: Duparc, "Phidylé"

influence, just as the use of the subdominant chord with augmented sixth, passing directly to the tonic, recalls César Franck's harmonic usage (Example 245).

Example 245: Duparc, "Testament"

Apart from these technical features, Duparc sometimes approaches Fauré in other ways; in addition to the passages in "Chanson triste" and "Phidylé" cited above, the latter's influence may be detected in the sober accompaniment of "Sérénade florentine," although here again Duparc outstrips his slightly older contemporary, since this song dating from 1880 is closely akin to certain of Fauré's *mélodies* written about 1900 (e.g., "Le plus doux chemin" and "La fleur qui va sur l'eau"). The parallel fourths and sixths of "Sérénade florentine" (measures 4–5) also appear in "La fuite" (Example 246).

Example 246: Duparc, "La fuite"

In spite of the influences mentioned, Duparc's harmonic style is not at all eclectic. The composer's dominant personality is capable of assimilating traits of his predecessors and contemporaries, and making of them an individual language that, without hiding its origins, from then on belongs only to himself. Herein lies the chief difference between his style and that of Lalo or Castillon, who, even while offering some remarkable inventions, more willingly surrender to their models.

GENERAL VIEW OF THE OTHER MÉLODIES. Among the four pieces that followed "Le galop," only "Au pays où se fait la guerre" and the duet "La fuite" are adapted to true dramatic texts. Strictly speaking, François Coppée's "La vague et la cloche" is a narrative poem, while the words of "Le manoir de Rosemonde" (by Robert de Bonnières) are lyric in essence. But in setting them to music Duparc made true *scènes* of them and without suggesting the theater, they still are somewhat removed from his other songs. While the latter must be sung slowly, the dramatic compositions require quite a lively movement, sometimes even a really rapid one (except for "Au pays où se fait la guerre," where, however, the indication Andante does not mean a really slow tempo). The composer's decision to add an orchestral accompaniment to three of these pieces is also significant. It should be pointed out that in these songs the choice of text is not always fortunate. The forced images of "La vague et la cloche," for instance, mark a low point in poetic quality among the verse set by Duparc. Although sincere in expression, this piece makes one sense the discomfort he experienced in trying to interpret the words. As with "Le galop," the music is interesting more for its details, some of them presenting a grandiose and suggestive beauty, than for the whole, which is hardly satisfying.

The Romantic atmosphere of "Au pays où se fait la guerre" (Gautier) is much more sane and natural. Although this *mélodie* dates originally from 1869, it was recast several times in the course of the next few years, so that the version appearing in the collection of thirteen *mélodies* published by Rouart-Lerolle is apparently later than "La vague et la cloche." Several passages still bear signs of immaturity, but they are largely compensated for by the intensity of melodic expression and the harmonic richness. It is Duparc's last youthful work. He is still able to depict burning grief without psychic complications and without any trace of *fin-de-siècle*. After 1870 he would no longer choose such an elementary subject.

The duet "La fuite," with text also by Gautier, constitutes another advance. The furious movement, as well as the touching and nervous harmonies, are reminiscent of "Le galop" but the style is more homogeneous and the composition as a whole is more balanced. The rapidly changing harmonies are strongly enhanced by appoggiaturas and passing notes (Example 247).

In "Le manoir de Rosemonde" Duparc achieves the perfect synthesis of dramatic and lyric. The ardent and vigorous declamation of the vocal line, interrupted by rests, recalls the older *scène*, although the recognized faults of that form have disappeared. The traditional anti-pianistic and theatrical accompaniment is replaced by an instrumental part whose efficacy results from sobriety itself.

"Sérénade florentine" may be called a "Parnassian" composition. The tender language of the earlier "Sérénade" is here expressed more objectively. The limpid piano part in which the right hand almost systematically avoids the strong beats of measures, as well as the Mixolydian harmonic coloring, are, as already noted, of a clearly

Example 247: Duparc, "La fuite"

Fauréan essence. The interplay of major and minor chords also reappears (cf. "Sérénade," measures 20–21 and "Sérénade florentine," measures 21–24). In a contradiction typical of Duparc, the somewhat sad atmosphere of this little *mélodie* is not at all justified by the words.

The same may be said for "Phidylé," set to words by Leconte de Lisle. The song has been described as having been composed in imitation of Fauré's "Lydia,"[320] but if this is true it constitutes an obvious proof of the two masters' spiritual diversity. Except for the first page, which is probably consciously modeled after Fauré, Duparc's composition is characterized by a veiled tenderness, even a melancholy, that strongly contrasts with the simple clarity of the earlier work. The similar atmosphere revealed in "Extase" suggests that the chiaroscuro of these two compositions has replaced the lyric emphasis of the juvenile "Chanson triste."

In the *mélodies* "Élégie," "Testament," and "Lamento," the

expression of sadness issues directly from the words, as the titles themselves indicate. "Élégie" appears to have been conceived in imitation of the *Lied* entitled "Träume" that Wagner composed as preparation for *Tristan*. "Phidylé" and "Extase" also betray a leaning toward the Wagnerian style, although in those *mélodies* Duparc is able to impose his own personality. In "Élégie," however, the assimilative process is not yet complete and while also showing French characteristics, the piece too closely resembles its German model. "Testament" displays a more original handling of Wagnerian procedures. Although very rarely sung, it is among Duparc's most remarkable inventions. The third elegiac *mélodie*, "Lamento," owes less to Wagner than to Berlioz and Liszt, but the influence of these two Romantics, being of a purely technical order, is dissolved in Duparc's personal language.

His individuality unfurls most freely in the two nostalgic *mélodies* set to Baudelaire's verse that followed "Romance de Mignon." Duparc seems to have been especially attracted by the poet's Romantic aspect as expressed in the desire for (or recollection of) exotic countries that contrast strongly with the banal surroundings of daily life. The three appearances of the theme of nostalgic yearning, evoking respectively Italy, the Netherlands, and southern Africa (?), present a remarkable affinity (Example 248).

And yet each of these nostalgic *mélodies* presents a different psychic state. In "Romance de Mignon" the mood is more sad than melancholy and lacks the ecstatic outburst found in the second *mélodie*. In "L'invitation au voyage" the composer effectively translates Romantic yearning but his youthful spirit is not ready to be abandoned to it and near the end of the piece he is entirely lost within his delicious imagination. "La vie antérieure" is sung by an old man dreaming of his past; the wild joy of youth awakens in him again but this time he is unable to conquer the feelings of sadness whose echoes die away majestically in a long epilogue.

Duparc had no suspicion, as he wrote these last pages of "La vie antérieure," that he was terminating his musical career. He was still full of ideas for vast projects, including the composition of an opera, *Roussalka*, already begun. Its first act was destroyed, rewritten, then destroyed again. A short waltz composed in 1887 suffered the same fate. Nothing remains of a planned musical setting for Molière's *Amphitryon*, and the composer may never even have begun it.

The exact nature of the nervous disease that condemned Duparc to silence has remained obscure; research conducted by one medical investigator has led only to vague conclusions.[321] Whether medical clarification of Duparc's tragic fate would have been musically beneficial is doubtful. Without even considering the re-

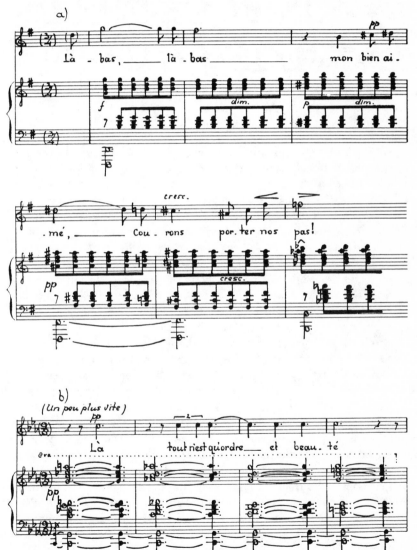

Example 248: Duparc, "Romance de Mignon," "L'invitation au voyage," and "La vie antérieure"

volting indiscretion of publicly analyzing a man's suffering, it seems doubtful that such explanations would contribute meaningfully to knowledge of the man or his music. On the other hand, some characteristics evident in his music (e.g., total absence of cheerfulness, penchant for nostalgic sentiments, and the "obscurity" of his accompaniments) might well have proved diagnostically useful for medical purposes.

Ravel has referred to Duparc's *mélodies* as "imperfect, but works of genius."[322] Blind admiration should not prevent us from admitting that the composer sometimes allows passages unworthy of his genius to escape from his pen. Astonishingly banal measures occasionally occur (e.g., in "La vie antérieure," the arpeggiated dominant seventh chord preceding the line "C'est là que j'ai vécu dans les voluptés calmes"). Elsewhere Duparc makes indulgent use of theatrical procedures (as in "Au pays où se fait la guerre," measures 95–108); nor is the structure always entirely satisfying. These imperfections led Reynaldo Hahn to make some contemptuous remarks which reflect on their author instead of injuring Duparc.[323] Obviously, a purist cannot judge Duparc's style as impeccable. But the perfection of Hahn's *Rondels* or *Les feuilles blessées* is worth little in comparison with the emotivity of "Phidylé" or "La vie antérieure." Those songs display Duparc's chief merit: that he is not satisfied to make words sing, but translates the poet's very thought and feelings. His genius inaugurates the epoch when the *mélodie* becomes a preferred medium for the greatest French composers, who confide to it their most intimate and most profound inspirations.

POSTSCRIPT TO THE

SECOND EDITION

IN HIS EXTENSIVE AND PENETRATING REVIEW OF THE FIRST EDITION of this book,[324] Alexander Ringer asked whether my identification of two distinct types of romance (i.e., expressive and abstract) may not be equally valid for the *mélodie* during the period from Berlioz to Duparc. The idea is suggestive. Several of the composers discussed in Chapters III–V seem to fit quite well into one or the other category. Berlioz, Liszt, Lalo, Castillon and Duparc wrote expressive *mélodies*, while the vocal pieces of Reber, Massé, Gounod, Delibes, Massenet, Saint-Saëns, and Fauré belong to the abstract type.

The former type is characteristic of Romanticism (and post-Romanticism, including *fin-de-siècle*), where the composer's attitude is strongly individualistic and he is rather indifferent to the performer as well as to the social function of his work. The orchestration of piano accompaniments lifted song from its "natural" atmosphere and carried it to the concert hall, where in spite of its complicated harmonic language, it had difficulty competing with concertos and symphonies. This type of song was considered by its contemporaries to be characteristic of the German school.

Those who wrote *mélodies* of the abstract type, on the other hand, represent a social attitude toward song writing. Their pieces remain within the spiritual climate of bourgeois circles and are generally adapted to the limited compass of the more accomplished amateur performer. During the nineteenth century these songs were usually considered as typically French.

Although admittedly a broad generalization, this division does elucidate some aspects of the complex history of French song; but like every schematization, it tells only part of the truth and is contradicted when seen from other angles. To Gounod's abstract style Schubert, Schumann, and Mendelssohn contributed as much, if not more, than the French romance, whereas Berlioz' expressive songs present little affinity with the German *Lied*. One is strongly tempted to explain the character of the Fauréan *mélodie* as having developed from the Boieldieu romance and Duparc's type of song as deriving from Wagner and Liszt, but this would be a gross oversimplification. Fauré was a social, not an artistic conformist. His *mélodies* may suggest the drawing room, but its climate never curtailed his freedom of individual expression. Nor is there reason to assume that Fauré applied a lower standard to the musical interpretation of a poem than did the composers of the so-called expressive group. As for Duparc, among his most mature works we find a song like "Sérénade florentine," conceived with pure classical restraint and lacking any trace of German influence.

The conclusion is inescapable that schematic divisions bring with them the risk of losing contact with reality. The history of French song *may* be represented by a network of clean, straight lines, but the many contradictions within that history make its *true* image an essentially amorphous one that defies every frame, including the one used for this study.

But if history is by nature a continuity, a book must have not only a beginning but an end. The arbitrary limit of 1880 has been crossed several times in the course of the last two chapters and this compulsive inconsistency clearly testifies against the absolute value of divisions in history. The period Berlioz–Duparc belongs only to this book; outside its covers the entity scarcely has rights of existence.

Appendixes

Hippolyte Monpou
and His Romanticism

MONPOU'S PERSONALITY IS UNQUESTIONABLY MORE INTERESTING THAN his music. Gautier paints a highly colored description of the composer's acceptance as a member of the "Cénacle" group, showing him as the prototype of the Romantic artist:[325]

It was a joy to see him arrive at one of the painters' studios that at that time served as a salon for the literati, following Horace's precept, *ut pictura poesis*; everyone would offer him a cigarette, which he would discard half-smoked in order to seat himself at the piano. ... We still remember hearing Monpou sing "Avez-vous vu dans Barcelone ..." with frenzied verve and the poses and gestures that Hoffmann gives to his imaginary musicians. Kreisler would have appeared cold by comparison. He sought originality and often found it. Never did a composer have a more furious, more enthusiastic love for his art; none ever spared himself less. When he was at the piano and felt himself understood, after singing a romance he would say, "And how did you like that?" And to our great pleasure, he would continue until the candles would reach their end and make the candle holders blaze. Like us, he believed in serenades, in Spanish bailiffs, in mantillas, in guitars, in castanets, and in all that somewhat conventional Italy and Spain

made fashionable by [Musset] the author of "Don Paez," "Portia," and the
"Marquesa d'Amaegui." To these stanzas, uproarious, flighty, and im-
pudent as a cock-sparrow, he set a sparkling and extravagant music, full of
bizarre cries and Andalusian portamentos, that greatly pleased us.

Gautier then recounts how the composer was esteemed in bourgeois circles:

For a long time Hippolyte Monpou, as well as all the poets whose verses
he set, was regarded by bourgeois constituents and eligibles as a scatter-
brain, a madman who should not be let out without a muzzle. When he sat
at the piano, eyes blazing, mustache bristling, a circle of respectful awe
would form around him; at the first line of "L'Andalouse" mothers would
send their daughters to bed and with an air of chaste embarrassment hide
their faces, blushing with modesty, in their flowers. The melody was as
frightening as the words! Little by little, however, they became accustomed
to it; except that they substituted "bronzed *teint*" for "bronzed *sein*" and
said "C'est ma maîtresse qu'on me donne" instead of "C'est ma maîtresse,
ma lionne," which, at that time, seemed much too bestial and monstrous.

Not astonishingly, strange stories circulated about this little
Berlioz. One of them is quoted by Bachelin from an obituary of the
composer:

M. Hippolyte Monpou, whose death we mourn today, composed according to the rules of the heart's poetry, while looking at the blue sky, the golden
sunset, or the calyx of the May rose. . . . Why be surprised, then, at the
gracefulness of his works! In winter, being unable to enjoy the stars and
the sun, M. Monpou spread perfume in his study. In the midst of the room's
perfume, "Le voile blanc," the last and one of the sweetest flowers of his imagination, blossomed.[326]

Georges Grand's long article quoting passages from some of
Monpou's letters corrects Bachelin's claim that Monpou was badly
paid for his romances: "I recommend my last song, 'Si j'étais
ange,' to you. I believe it is destined for success. I sold it for eight
hundred francs, an unheard-of sum! That is a far cry from
'L'Andalouse,' which I let go for fifty francs four years ago."[327]

Grand's article also contains many interesting details about
Monpou and his artistic conceptions and includes this physical
description of him:

In the strict sense of the word Monpou was ugly; eyes too small, mouth
too large, too-prominent cheek-bones, a flattened nose; a cracked voice

completed the not very graceful ensemble, to which a first glance was hardly favorable! But when he sat down at the piano and tossed back his long brown hair (without pretension, for that he never had), suddenly the cracked voice became likeable and warm, his eyes lit up, and the artist transfigured the man.[328]

In a long letter addressed to an unnamed friend[329] Monpou defends himself against the reproaches of the musical press. His arguments are interesting enough to reproduce here *in extenso*:

You know, my friend, that I have made it a rule for myself never to answer the critics, not because I scorn them, but because it would waste too much time, and in a matter of feeling, it is steering the wrong course to try to reason. M. .... tells us things known for a long time; one no longer dares to speak of Classic or Romantic or one is branded as a provincial; however, at the impassioned tone of his criticism, at the two or three insults he tosses at my head, I see that you would be happy to answer him with good reasons. Let us try, then, to give him some.

And first, these words: "He calls himself a reformer, no more nor less," I formally deny. I have always had only one intention, that is to be myself, good or bad. You may have read the device on my seal: "Not better, but different." A thousand times already, I have refused to take students, I have such a horror of forming what they call a "school." I believe that Victor Hugo's theories and his prefaces have made him more enemies than his works. I do not wish, then, to lay down principles. Besides, I might be hard put to it to find some. The business of us artists is a sort of revelation; we go our way, we produce, the theoreticians follow after. They vainly discuss the bad things we have done. And thus art passes away and becomes a school. Our greatest enemies are our imitators; it is almost always they who kill us. Auber and Caraffa shortened Rossini's life by ten years.

What is Romanticism in music? I, who am called Romantic, don't know. Hugo has said that in literature it is liberalism. I wish it were liberalism in music! Once more, I am not at all a man of principles; I shall tell the facts. A Classical composer (that doesn't mean anything, but one must use words that others understand) writes an opera. Here is what he must do:

First, an introduction; there will be village maidens who come to celebrate the birthday of their lord. — A chorus. — The village maidens leave, the lord remains with the girl. — A duet. — Andante and allegro. — The girl leaves, the lord remains. — An aria. — Recitative, andante, allegro, if he is a good singer. A short rondo with three repeats if he is a singer like Thénard. The valet arrives with the soubrette. She sings a romance about shallow love, with a slightly smutty joke at the end to amuse the pit! This has three stanzas, in 3/4 time, the usual formula. Six years ago this was replaced by a rondo in 6/8. This is progress, but still convention. The villain arrives, for Classical opera still has villains; he is a baritone. He must sing a lively and declamatory allegro. Always according to convention. The situation becomes involved, the intrigue begins to grow and leads to a finale, a chorus, not too fast; something must be saved for the end, an adagio for six, seven, or eight voices, then the terrifying surge that ends the act! If this is not the first act of every "Classical" opera, I agree to set to music ... whatever you want!

Classical is conventional; to the man who asks "Why?" they proudly answer, "Because." The Classical in music is the art (take heed) of expressing ideas by notes. Ideas! You hear, ideas! I say that music should be the art of expressing "feelings" by notes! That's what it is for me! For them it is the head, for me the heart, the soul. What is the note to me? I see a father who mourns for his daughter, a lover going to his death when he has just been united with the woman he loves, a jealous husband ready to kill the woman who has betrayed him; I see Triboulet, Hernani, Othello; I feel them, I am they and my soul burns!

— But you shout and do not sing!

— Since when does Othello have to produce a steady stream of sound, chatterbox! He has other things to do.

— But your phrases aren't "square"; there are two measures, one after the other, in duple and triple time!

— Who told you that?

— I saw it in the score!

— Is music made for the eyes or for the ears? Do you think it would have been very difficult for me to make that phrase "square?" If I didn't do it, it's because I didn't wish to! It is because I felt it that way, long or short, no matter, but with inspiration, with truth, all of a sudden. If I spin it out, it loses its force; if I cut it, it is not complete! Moreover, what you are asking me for is a piece of work, and it is the head that performs work, not the soul; there is no inspiration left. ...

... That "Madonna col Bambino" that M. ... deigns to find tolerable is pretty, he says, because it is regular. Is that so? Not really. It is in triple meter and in the middle is a measure in quadruple time! And it ends on the second beat of the measure! After all, my kindly critic undoubtedly overlooked these faults because he only *heard* the "Madonna" and did not *read* it!

As to that "Tour de Nesles," he calls it plainsong and upon my word, he is right. Since he is so well informed on thirteenth-century music, he can understand how that chanson [with text] taken from *L'écolier de Cluny* applies it quite properly and how I sought to come as close as possible to song as it was used at that time. What is more, it is as regular as Reicha's counterpoint, so what is there to criticize?

But why does he not speak of "Les résurrectionistes," of "Marine," of

"Le lever," or of "L'Andalouse"? It has sold 4,000 copies, while Beauplan's sold only three hundred. Above all, why not speak of "Lénore," my most complete and important work?[330] That would have been a fair fight: to understand a system perfectly, one must know what the system produced; without this, one has done only a quarter of the task. ...

Monpou's portrait would be incomplete without some reference to his private correspondence (now in the Bibliothèque Nationale), in which some unexpected traits of this "scatterbrained Romantic" are brought to light. One letter shows him as the self-satisfied and watchful father of a family, confirming, not without vanity, that his wife is bored during his absence: "And how are you, my pet? ... Poor woman who must need me! I am proud. Do you have a maid? Are you very bored?" His qualms about his daily expenses are quite un-Romantic: "We are at the best hotel, spending three francs for dinner, two francs for lunch, one for the room. I think that's fine."

Our concept of Monpou's Romanticism is shaken even further by his correspondence with Mélanie Waldor, who played an important role in literary and musical circles: she was a friend of Victor Hugo, but also of Adolphe Adam! For Monpou Madame Waldor was preparing an opera libretto in which all his famous romances would find a place. In one of his letters the composer cites the text of some successful numbers (among others, "L'Andalouse" and "Le lever") and closes with these words: "I still have many others that could do. This way we shall have a quite original work, with tested airs that are sure of success!" A pot-pourri of romances crowded together in an opera surely does not conform to Cénacle esthetics!

Curiously enough, before 1830 Monpou composed a large number of extremely conventional *cantiques* for several voices with organ accompaniment.[331] A comparison of these with Berlioz' earliest romances, dating from the Restoration and already demonstrating undeniable originality, shows the Romanticism of his satellite to be superficial indeed. Hippolyte Monpou appears today as a mixture of artistic temerity, bourgeois sentimentality, and forced extravagance.

A P P E N D I X   I I

"Élégie," an Unknown Mélodie
of Franz Liszt

The printed copy reproduced here was deposited at the Paris Bibliothèque Nationale (call number Vm⁷ 75122) in 1845. The cover reads:

ELEGIE / Paroles d'Etienne Monnier / Musique de / F. Liszt / A. V. / Prix: 4ᶠ, 50 / Publiée à Paris par Bernard Latte / Boulevᵗ des Italiens, 2 / [signed] BERNARD LATTE [stamped]³³²

"Élégie" is not among the vocal works edited by Peter Raabe for the complete edition of Liszt's *Musikalische Werke* (Leipzig, Breitkopf & Hartel, 1907–1934). Although an announcement of its publication appeared in *Le monde musical* of September 19, 1844, the song is mentioned neither by Liszt's biographers nor in the various catalogues of his works. The reasons for the piece having remained hidden for over a century are difficult to determine, although the limited size of the edition appears to have been one factor. As for the neglect of "Élégie" by Paris critics, this was a fate shared by Liszt's other *mélodies*, as mentioned in the discussion of his songs in Chapter III.

ELÉGIE

PAR

F. LISZT.

POÉSIE D'ETIENNE MONNIER

Étienne Monnier, the author of the text of "Élégie," also furnished lines for the romances of some other composers, among them Donizetti and Gabussi.[333] He seems to have been an amateur poet whose verse was of the type established by current usage; this makes "Élégie" the weakest by far of all the French texts set by Liszt. The composer himself further reduced the poem's effectiveness by dwelling endlessly on the last lines.

The musical aspect of "Élégie" offers much more of interest. Since the poem does not permit the opportunity for a delicate and refined interpretation (as in "Oh! quand je dors"), Liszt operates here more like an "abstract" composer. The piano repeats a vocal phrase without any apparent textual reason (measures 26–28); elsewhere the accompaniment doubles the voice (measures 67–75). In other regards also, Liszt appears to have fewer scruples with respect to the words than was his usual habit. In the optional version of the vocal part at the end of the song there are intervals that are quite unsuited for the voice (measures 76–77 and 80–81). Liszt's prosody, although generally very careful, is not always correct here (see measure 20, where the word "que" falls on a strong beat and a high note that produces an operatic effect).

From the melodic point of view the composition is entirely dominated by the initial phrase (measures 4–8), which sets the elegiac atmosphere. When the poet speaks of the memory of his love the phrase appears in the major mode. This technique strikingly resembles that employed in Liszt's most famous piano piece, the *Liebestraum* No. 3, composed much later.

But the most interesting aspect of "Élégie" is its harmonic audacity. The progression from the tonic chord to its altered submediant constitutes a kind of germinating cell of the piece, appearing several times in this form, A–C–E to F–A♭–C (measures 1–2, 5–6, 9–10; then in the major mode in measures 43–44). The tonic followed by its unchanged submediant appears in measures 39–40, 47–48, and 51–52. Near the end the composer augments the effect by opposing the two modes: the altered submediant of A minor succeeds the tonic chord of A major (A–C♯–E to F–A♭–C; see measures 75–76, 79–80, 88–92). Similar harmonic progressions appear on other degrees of the scale: the subdominant followed by its upper mediant (measures 22 and 26) and the alternation of two dominant seventh chords (measures 33–37; see also measures 77–78 and 81–82).

This juxtaposition of chords that are the interval of a third apart (known as *Terzverwandtschaft*) is a procedure of which Liszt was very fond. He may even have abused it at times, although in this piece its effect is quite original.

Some other harmonic combinations are worth noting. An ingenious modulation leads from B major to the dominant of A major:

	B major	B major	B major | Eb minor	Eb minor | A major	A major
KEY STEP	I	VI	III | I	V | II (lowered)	V₇
CHORD	B major	G♯ minor	D♯ minor Eb minor	Bb major	E major (7)
MEASURE	51	52	53	54–58	59

Pedal points are used on the dominant in measures 59–66 and on the tonic in measures 67–75. But the most daring passage appears in measures 30 and 32, where Liszt uses the chord on the lowered second step (Neapolitan sixth) in a special way, preceding it by its own dominant (the chord on the sixth step, with a minor seventh) and following it by the seventh chord on the raised subdominant, which finally resolves by rising to the dominant. In addition, several notes are altered. The total harmony, although quite original, would not be surprising in itself. The impression of extraordinary boldness is produced by the dominant pedal on which all these chords have been superimposed and which provokes strong dissonances.

While "Élégie" may not be one of Liszt's best *mélodies*, it nevertheless provides vivid proof of the composer's originality in the harmonic province.

Orientalism in the Mélodie

ALTHOUGH ORIENTALISM WAS ONLY AN EPHEMERAL FASHION IN THE literature of 1830, the movement left its mark on the history of the *mélodie*. Real musical Orientalism did not appear during the Romantic era but only began to be exploited by Bizet, Delibes, and especially Saint-Saëns. Hugo's "La captive" as set by Berlioz and Reber lacks any exotic coloring; the voluptuous atmosphere of the Levant is merely suggested somewhat in the undulating movement of their accompaniments. Reyer applies the monotonous rhythm (e.g., the double pedal of "Pantoum") rather clumsily, while David simply ignored the so-called Oriental procedures.

Of what does this exotic language consist? Henri Quittard claims that true imitation of Arabic music is illusory, since the Western octave is divided into twelve approximately equal semitones, while the Oriental scale has seventeen dissimilar intervals. Thus the various modes drawn from these intervals do not agree with any of ours and cannot even be correctly transcribed in our notational system. Furthermore, since Oriental music is melodic while ours is harmonic, a composer borrowing an Oriental theme or trying to imitate it is obliged to fit it into our configuration of simultaneous sounds.

But the question is actually more subtle than one of transcription or imitation. The composer is really trying, by whatever means are available, to remove the Western music lover from his habitual surroundings, to give him the sensation of something new. The title and words suggest Arabic music and from there on a slight fraud is called for; the hearer, generally quite unknowledgeable in the matter of musical ethnology, allows himself to be easily duped. Thus the so-called Oriental *mélodie* is generally constructed on the medieval modes, chiefly the first, seventh, and ninth (Example 249).

The augmented second, forbidden in strict counterpoint, may similarly suggest exoticism (see Example 143, Bizet's "Adieux de l'hôtesse arabe").

Rhythmic monotony has only a psychological significance, since

Example 249: Saint-Saëns, "La brise" (*Mélodies persanes*, no. 1; parts a and c of example) and "La splendeur vide" (*Mélodies persanes*, no. 2; part b)

the question of whether Oriental music is truly monotonous still remains to be determined. Western ears certainly receive such an impression, but this may derive from their incapacity to perceive the tonal proportions of Oriental scales. The apparent monotony may be merely a subjective sensory phenomenon caused by mental laziness. This phenomenon, furthermore, is reciprocal, since our tonal system often provokes the same response among Oriental peoples.

Quittard admits that rhythmic imitation may be attempted by means of bass patterns unceasingly repeated during long periods. Such repetitions are a simplified musical translation of "rhythmic harmony," an indispensable element of Oriental ensembles. Melismatic vocal passages are also often imitations of the type of melismas found in Arabic song (Example 250).

J'ai mis à mon cheval sa bri . . . . . . de, sa bride et sa selle d'or;_____

Example 250: Saint-Saëns, "Sabre en main" (*Mélodies persanes*, no. 4)

Harmonic imitation, however, is entirely unrealizable, since Oriental music has no real harmony. As in the case of the melodic line, the composer must resort to the unexpected. He puts unusual chords to the melody, invents harmonic combinations that are quasi-independent of the melody, and uses the double pedal to suggest both the monotony and the "emptiness" of Oriental music.

On the strength of these observations Quittard concludes that "Orientalism in European music can only be a witticism, no doubt amusing, even charming, but necessarily superficial."[334] These practices may not have resulted in a true imitation of the Arabic idiom, but they did contribute to the development of French music in the second half of the nineteenth century.

"L'aurore" by Gabriel Fauré

The manuscript of "L'aurore" is in the Bibliothèque Nationale (number Ms 419c).[335] The words are drawn from Hugo's *Chants du crépuscule*, which also furnished other texts for the composer ("Le papillon et la fleur," "Mai," and "Rêve d'amour"). Saint-Saëns' *mélodie* "Le matin" also uses the same poem.

"L'aurore" clearly dates from the same period as the first collection. The short and regular phrases creating rather doubtful prosody (e.g., "L'om-BRE É-paisse ... Vont OÙ va la nuit ... Tout RE-prend son âme ..."), the simple structure and harmony, and the choice of text point unequivocally to the early years. Nevertheless, the composition is quite remarkable for its fluid and accomplished style of writing. Several traits already presage the mature Fauréan style: the rhythm of the voice part (♪♪♪♪♪|♪♪) maintained throughout the entire piece, the linear construction of the accompaniment, and the tritone in the melodic line (A♭–D in measures 14–15). "L'aurore" occupies the middle ground between "Après un rêve" and "Lydia." Like the latter song, it seems to be conceived in terms of the piano, which may be an additional reason for its prosodic faults. These deficiencies may have been the reason for the composer's refusal to allow publication of the song.

But in this instance Fauré was wrong, since "L'aurore" is superior

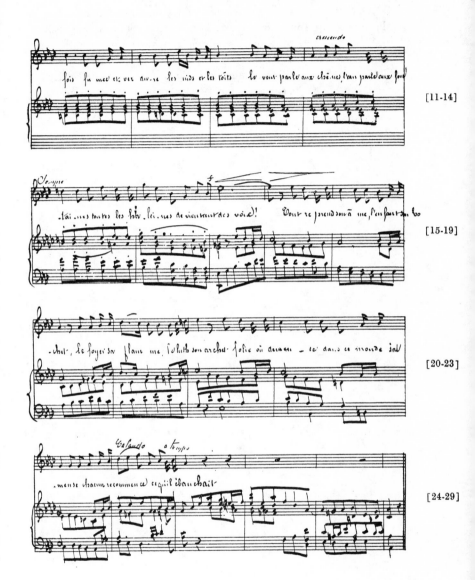

[11-14]

[15-19]

[20-23]

[24-29]

to some of the pieces in the first collection. Composers are not always able to evaluate their own works, as proved by Schumann's dislike of his *Carnaval* and Beethoven's opinion that his piano variations in C minor should never have been published. This song of Fauré's youth is therefore offered unhesitatingly, not only for its intrinsic charm, but also because it clearly foreshadows the composer's greatness.

APPENDIX V

Prose Rendering of Poetic Quotations

p. 10: Sinard, "La femme de trente ans," last stanza (Lagoanère)

> At fifteen, one *wishes* to please. At twenty, one *must* please. At forty, one *may* please. One *knows how* to please at thirty.

p. 14: Lamartine, "L'automne" (Niedermeyer)

> At the bottom of that cup from which I tasted life, perhaps there remained a drop of honey.

> I die and my soul, at the moment when it expires, breathes forth like a sad and melodious sound.

p. 15: Lamartine, "L'isolement," 2d stanza (Niedermeyer)

> Here the river roars with foaming waves. It winds and disappears in a faraway darkness.

p. 26: from Sévelinges, *Alfred, ou Les années d'apprentissage de Wilhelm Meister* (Reichardt)

> A good troubadour, without any cares, can set out on his travels. Everywhere he finds pleasant shelter, everywhere happy faces. The lord of the manor has him sing, the maiden runs to hear him. What else does he want?

p. 26: Goethe, "Der Sänger," traditional *Ballade* also called "Ballade des Harfners" from *Wilhelm Meisters Lehrjahre*

> What do I hear outside the gate, what do I hear resounding on the bridge? Let us hear song ring through our halls! The king said it, the page ran; the boy came, the king called: Let the old man in!

p. 30: Goethe, "Rastlose Liebe" (Schubert)

> Against the snow, the rain, the wind, through steamy gorges, through fragrant fog, ever on, ever on, without rest or peace.

p. 30: Bélanger, "Toujours"

> Charming friend, my life belongs to you. So does my treasured faith, never betrayed. You shall be my love, my love forever more.

p. 41: Gautier, "La diva"

> For our own idiom, raucous and without prosody, distorts all music; and the bold note, colliding in its flight with some harsh word, breaks its golden wings and falls to earth.

p. 57: quoted by Castil-Blaze, *L'art des vers lyriques*

> Dry your tears, have no fears, enjoy the pleasures of a calmer life. Depend always on your husband's promise, your husband's love.

p. 59: from Offenbach, *La belle Hélène* (text by Meilhac and Halévy)

> And that is how a gallant man avoids all troubles.

p. 59: Musset, "Le lever"

> Lovely tresses which we arrange in the morning and undo together at night!

p. 67: quoted by Saint-Saëns, "La poésie et la musique," from an operetta by Lecocq

> It is a husband who runs away with his wife, a wife who flees with her husband.

p. 73: Musset, "Chanson"

> When hope and gayety are lost by some sad event, the remedy for the melancholic one is music and beauty!

p. 73: Heine, *Lyrisches Intermezzo* (No. 41)

> When I hear the sound of that little song that once my be-
> loved sang, my heart wants to burst from the fierce pain of
> longing.

p. 74: Musset, *Les marrons du feu* (Scene V)

> Poetry, you see, is good. But music is better. By God, there
> you have two delightful tunes. Language without a singing
> throat is nothing. See Dante; his gilded seraph speaks not, he
> sings. It is music that made me believe in God.

p. 74: Musset, "Lucie" (1835) and earlier, slightly varied, in "Le
saule" (1830)

> Harmony, Harmony, daughter of sadness, language invented
> by the spirit for love, you came to us from Italy and to Italy
> from Heaven.

p. 75: Musset, "Mimi Pinson"

> Mimi Pinson is a blond, a well-known blond. She owns only
> one dress, and but one bonnet.

p. 77: Lamartine, "Le vallon" (from *Premières méditations*)

> Worship here the echo that Pythagoras worshipped. With
> him lend your ear to the celestial concerts.

p. 77: Lamartine, "Ischia" (from *Nouvelles méditations*)

> She sings and at times her voice expires; and from the lute's
> more lightly struck chords the dormant echoes deliver to the
> breeze only dying sighs interrupted with silence.

p. 77: Lamartine, "La voix humaine" (from *Harmonies poétiques*)

> How can the air, modulated by the sounding cord, create
> those sublime transports in us? Why does the heart follow a
> sound that evaporates? Because there is a soul in the chords;
> because this soul, present in each of the accents modulated by
> your voice, is suddenly answered by the voices of our hearts be-
> fore the sweet sound has even faded away; and because, like a
> sound in a temple awakening a thousand echoes speaking at
> once, your soul, whose echo vibrates in each ear, will create such
> a soul wherever your voice sounds.

p. 78: Lamartine, "Désir" (from *Harmonies poétiques*)

> Holy and mysterious law! A melodious soul animates the whole universe; every being has its harmony, every star its guiding spirit, every element its consort.

p. 78: Hugo, "Que la musique date du seizième siècle" (from *Les rayons et les ombres*)

> Mighty Palestrina, old master, ancient genius, I salute you here, father of harmony, for like a great river where men drink, all that music flowed from your hands. For Gluck and Beethoven, branches under which we dream, were born to your family and made of your life sap. For Mozart, your son, took from your altars that new lyre unknown to mortals, more sensitive than the grass is to the breath of daybreak, born in the sixteenth century from your sounding fingers. For, master, all our sighs go to you whenever a voice sings and a soul responds.

p. 85: Lamartine, "Le lac," 1st stanza

> So, always impelled toward new shores, carried without return into everlasting night, shall we never be able to cast anchor in time's ocean for a single day?

p. 88: Gérard de Nerval, "Les Cydalises" (set by the poet)

> Where are the women we loved? They are in the grave, happier in a more beautiful dwelling.

> They are close to the angels, far away in the blue sky, singing the praises of the Mother of God.

> O pale betrothed, O young flowering virgin, abandoned lover blighted by sadness.

> The depths of eternity were smiling in your eyes. Extinguished torches of the world, be rekindled in Heaven!

p. 105: Hugo, "La captive" (Berlioz)

> In a bed of mosses I like to recite a Spanish air.

p. 108: Gautier, "Le spectre de la rose" (Berlioz)

> O you who caused my death, you cannot prevent my rosy ghost from coming to dance all night at your bedside. But fear nothing, I require neither Mass nor *De Profundis*. This delicate perfume is my soul and I am arriving from Paradise.

p. 114: Pierre Jean de Béranger, "Les champs" (Berlioz)

> Far from the noise of the city, let us seek a quiet refuge for happiness.

p. 121: Joseph Méry, "Sicilienne" (Meyerbeer)

> Flowers adored by beauty, sky gilded by mirth, it is summer.
>
> Full moon, shining sea, warm breath that follows it, it is night.
>
> Fire that gilds every abode and consumes every day, it is love.

pp. 129 & 131: Hugo, "Oh! quand je dors" (Liszt)

> On my gloomy brow, where perhaps is ending a dark vision that lasted too long, let your glance rise like a star ... suddenly my dream will shine.
>
> Grant a kiss, and change from angel to woman ...

p. 132: Hugo, "Enfant, si j'étais roi" (Liszt)

> And the profound chaos, with fecund womb, eternity, space, and the heavens, and the earth.

p. 176: Lamartine, "Vers sur un album" (Gounod)

> The book of life is the supreme book that one can neither close nor reopen at will. The interesting passage cannot be read twice, but the fatal leaf turns by itself: we would like to return to the page where we love, and the page where we die is already under our fingers.

p. 186: Gounod, "L'absent" (Gounod)

> O silence of nights whose voice alone is sweet when I no longer hear her voice, mysterious beams of light that glide over the moss in the shadow of these woods, tell me if her eyes gently open when all is asleep, and if my beloved, while I keep vigil, remembers the absent one.

p. 188: Boileau, "Souvenirs" (Massé)

> Here are the wonderful places where my enraptured soul used to contemplate Sylvia.

p. 195: Hugo, "Coccinelle" (Bizet)

> "Son, learn what they call me," said the insect flying in the blue sky. "Animals belong to God, but stupidity belongs to man."

p. 196: Lamartine, "Douce mer" (Bizet)

Murmur around my little boat, gentle sea whose dear waves, like a faithful lover, utter an eternal lament on its poetic remains.

p. 215: Dortzal, "Battements d'ailes" (Massenet)

Summer evenings so gentle, veiled in blue mourning, where the heart comes to die with a beating of wings, make the trees light as blond tresses on which laces would dreamily float.

The lake has redonned its colorless tones and in its water reflects the sky's single star. Let us look deep into each other's eyes, so that our love may raise its white sail.

Ah, let us be soothed by divine chance. What happiness to love each other at the very heart of things, to cast a tranquil and long look at life, to cast a handful of roses at life!

p. 216: Comte R. de Gontaut Biron, "La dernière lettre de Werther à Charlotte" (Massenet)

"We must part ...

On the edge of this abyss, the time has come for our eternal separation. And I shall go, if it is true that love is a crime, to ask God's forgiveness for it.

It is over! Forever! I undertake a voyage from which I shall not return to find you again. But in my broken heart I carry away your picture as a charm against my death!

Until the supreme moment, intoxicated by your charms, my heart will have beaten in the shadows only for you, and my last kiss, my last tears, I place at your knees.

I bid you farewell from the small room which I shall leave only in my shroud; and to console me on this December day, there is no one! I am alone!

Besides, it is growing late; in a few moments I shall prepare to leave for there ... Christmas! From afar I hear gay tunes played by flutes.

Charlotte! ... I love you! ... Farewell! We must part! (Charlotte ...

Farewell ... Farewell!)"

pp. 226 & 227: Hugo, "Le pas d'armes du roi Jean" (Saint-Saëns)

> Up there shines on that wall Yseult, young girl with innocent countenance.

> In the storm, like a bent lily, a handsome page has fallen. He faints, surrenders his soul; he calls for a priest.

p. 235: Hugo, "Puisqu'ici-bas toute âme" (Lalo)

> Since every soul here on earth gives to some one its music, fire, or fragrance ...

p. 240: Beauquier, "Humoresque" (Lalo)

> What is politics to me? Republic, royalty, are hollow words! All those who reflect turn gray. Well, see my black hair.

p. 243: Musset, "Ninon" (Franck)

> Ninon, Ninon, what are you doing with life? The hours go by, day succeeds day. Rose tonight, tomorrow wilted. How do you live, you who know not love?

p. 250: Sully-Prudhomme, "Le vase brisé" (Franck)

> Its fresh water ran out drop by drop. The flowers' moisture is drained. No one suspects it yet. Do not touch it, it is broken.

p. 257: Baudelaire, "Chant d'automne" (Fauré)

> I love the greenish light of your wide eyes, sweet beauty, but today everything is bitter to me.

p. 273: Lahor, "Chanson triste" (Duparc)

> In your heart sleeps a moonbeam, a gentle summer moonbeam, and to escape from troublesome life I shall drown myself in your light.

> I shall forget past pain, my love, when you cradle my sad heart and my thoughts in the loving quiet of your arms.

> You will take my aching head on your knees sometimes and recite me a ballad that will seem to speak about us,

> and from your eyes full of sadness, from your eyes I shall then drink up so many kisses and such tenderness that perhaps I shall be healed ...

p. 283 : Bonnières, "Le manoir de Rosemonde" (Duparc)

> With its swift and hungry tooth, like a dog, love has bitten me.
>
> I have traveled around this sad world and thus I went and died far away, far away, without discovering the blue manor of Rosemonde.

p. 285 : Gautier, "Lamento" (Duparc)

> Do you know the white tomb where, with a plaintive sound, floats the shadow of a yew? On the yew tree a white dove, sad and alone, sings its song to the setting sun.

APPENDIX VI

Song Catalogue

Remarks for the Second Edition

This catalogue was originally compiled as a personal working tool, without any view toward publication. As the book neared completion the idea grew that, in spite of many imperfections, the lists might be welcomed by readers because of the lack of any other aid of the same type. This impression was confirmed by reviewers of the first edition, who commented on the catalogue's usefulness for students of nineteenth-century French music.

For the second edition as much of the original material as was available to the editors was reexamined. Although no systematic attempt was made to search out additional material, a few new songs have been inserted. This new material and the rearrangement of the alphabetical sequence to conform to standard English practice has resulted in a different song numbering from that found in the first edition. The revision also incorporates data about the songs supplied by some extensive critical and bibliographical studies issued since the writing of the original. Publishers' plate numbers, which have diminishing importance during the nineteenth century, are omitted from the second edition, except for anonymous publishers. The abbreviations are explained on page 408.

The catalogue includes songs for one or more solo voices and piano, songs for voice and orchestra (even when piano reductions do not exist), song cycles, and separate aria-like songs not known to have been part of an opera, oratorio, or cantata. It should be noted, however, that fragments of larger works published as *mélodies* without indication of their origin are often difficult to identify, especially for the less studied composers (see, for example, Winton Dean's study of Bizet's works, where songs previously considered to be independent are now thought to be fragments of earlier unfinished dramatic works). Questionable cases are included for the sake of completeness.

Aside from such difficulties as may result from a composer having borrowed from his own works, or having revised the same work, many other confusions arise from publishers' reissuance of songs with new titles, new subtitles, or even new texts. Sometimes the songs were regrouped and issued with a collective title; they may have been advertised under the collective title, or the single songs published with the additional collective title printed on them, but never actually issued as a set (Berlioz' songs provide many such confusing examples). In other cases, songs issued together (even occasionally having a collective title that indicates an inner connection, like some of Fauré's cycles) retain individual copyright dates and plate numbers. Publishers' casualness in these respects is frequently matched by composers' consideration of their songs as mere trifles, seldom mentioned in letters or memoirs.

Such circumstances make it difficult to decide in certain instances whether a group of songs is a true cycle, with poetic unity and cohesive character that create a musical entity (although the parts may still be performed separately), or whether the songs simply *appear* to have a somewhat related nature, were possibly composed about the same time, and were put together by composer or publisher for convenience or commercial reasons. Sets of songs of the first type are indicated here by cross references within the alphabetical listing of songs, while collections in which the songs are clearly unrelated appear after the main list, with letter designations; the latter group is not intended to be complete and is supplied mainly for the convenience of performers, since many of the collections are still easily available. The song numbers assigned in this catalogue are indicated after the listing for the collection. Operatic excerpts and other irrelevant material contained in the collections are, of course, omitted. With this limitation (and when available to the editors for reexamination), the contents of collections are fully indicated, unlike the first edition, where the presence of a song was indicated only if the collection constituted the earliest publication of the song. The reader should be warned, however, that in a few cases collections transposed for another voice range may have appeared with unchanged title but with slightly varying contents.

Most of the information given here was taken directly from copies of the songs deposited in the Paris Bibliothèque Nationale and Bibliothèque du Conservatoire. The year (and sometimes month) of deposit are usually marked on the title page or cover of those copies. Unfortunately, publishers did not invariably fulfill their legal depository obligations; when they did, the act of deposit was not always simultaneous with the actual publication of the piece, but may have occurred years later, or rarely, months before. Where the two dates are known to be different, both are included here; otherwise only the publication date is given. Similarly, when the copyright and *dépôt* dates are known to be the same, only the former is given.

Besides information taken from the music itself, some additional data were secured from publishers' catalogues, bibliographic compilations such as those of Pazdirek and Hoffmeister, newspaper announcements, composers' letters and diaries, and standard biographical and critical studies. The most important of these secondary sources are mentioned under the pertinent individual composers.

Material in parentheses after many song titles includes a cross reference to the cycle of which the song may be a part, opus number, specification of setting when other than for one voice and piano, and subtitle (including generic designations when other than *mélodie*). The generic designations are translated into English only when there appears to be a chance for misunderstanding. Data that apply to all the songs in a cycle or collection are generally given only under the broader entry to which reference is made. Cross references are also made from translated or variant titles or spellings, and from text incipits or subtitles by which the songs are sometimes identified.

Names of text authors and publishers are usually given as they appear in the source, with no attempt to force them into a consistent pattern or trace the authorship of texts given anonymously or under pseudonyms. For the most famous poets (e.g., Hugo or Gautier), however, only the surname is given. Unless otherwise indicated, the place of publication is Paris. The changing ownership and variant names of most of the French publishers involved may be traced in Cecil Hopkinson's *Dictionary of Paris Music Publishers 1700–1950* (London, 1954), which may also be used to determine which works are likely to be available (i.e., publishers still operating in 1950).

Hippolyte Monpou [1804–1841]

SEPARATE SONGS

Most of the songs appeared simultaneously with guitar accompaniments, although there is no evidence that these were done by the composer.

1. "À genoux"; words Hugo; pub. J. Meissonnier, 1838.
2. "Addio Teresa" (*chanson sicilienne*); words Dumas; pub. Bernard-Latte, November 9, 1837.
3. "L'âme du bandit"; words Auguste Richomme; comp. 1840; pub. J. Meissonnier.
4. "L'Andalouse" (*boléro*); words Musset; comp. 1830; pub. Lemoine, 1830.
5. "Le beau moine"; words Bernard Lopez; pub. Lemoine *aîné*, 1834.
6. "Bergeronnette" (*romance*, duo); pub. Mme. Vve. Lemoine.
7. "Le capitaine négrier" (*marine*); words Régis de Fobriant; pub. in *L'écho musical*.
8. "La captive" (*orientale*); words Hugo; pub. J. Meissonnier, dep. 1841.
9. "C'est tout mon bien" (*romance*); words H. L. Guérin; pub. Lemoine.
10. "Les champs" (duet); words Béranger; comp. before 1830; pub. Lemoine.
11. "La chanson de la nourrice" (*romance*); poet unknown; pub. J. Meissonnier, 1835.
12. "La chanson du fou de Cromwell" (*romance*); words Hugo; pub. J. Meissonnier, 1835.
13. "Chanson du Triboulet" (*romance*; op. posth.); words Édouard Plouvier; pub. Bureaux de *La France musicale* (Schott), dep. 1843.
14. "Chauvin et Jeanneton" (*chansonnette*); comp. before 1830; pub. le Bailly (O. Bornemann, *successeur*).
15. "Un clair de lune"; pub. Romagnési, 1834; not found.
16. "Les clocheteurs des trépassés"; poet unknown; pub. Meissonnier; not found.
17. "Les colombes de Saint-Marc"; words Roger de Beauvoir; pub. J. Meissonnier, probably 1834.
18. "Dans ma gondole de Venise" (*rêverie*); words Émile Barateau adapted to the melody of no. 17; pub. J. Meissonnier, 1842.
19. "Les deux archers" (*ballade*); words Hugo; pub. J. Meissonnier, 1834.

20. "Les deux cousines" (*duettino*); words Dumas; pub. Bernard-Latte.
21. "Les deux étoiles" (*nocturne* for 2 voices); words Édouard Plouvier; pub. Bureaux de *La France musicale*, dep. 1844.
22. "Enfant, dis-moi ta romance"; words Schoeppers; comp. 1834; pub. J. Meissonnier, 1834.
23. "L'enfant perdu"; words Édouard Plouvier; pub. Bureaux de *La France musicale*, dep. 1844 (with new words; see *FM* VII, 1844, p. 201).
24. "L'espingole" (*chant de basse;* op. posth.); words Édouard Plouvier; pub. Bernard-Latte; also pub. with title "Mon espingolle."
25. "L'étoile disparue"; words Édouard Plouvier; pub. Bernard-Latte, before 1838.
26. "Exil et retour" (*nocturne* for 2 voices); pub. Bureaux de *La France musicale* (Schott), 1842.
27. "Fauvette" (*chansonnette*); probably comp. before 1830; pub. Lemoine.
28. "La femme changée en pierre" (*chronique vendéenne*, with chorus *ad lib.*); words Mélanie Waldor; pub. Lemoine.
29. "La fille de Gentilly" (*moralité*, for 1 or 3 voices); poet unknown; pub. Pétibon.
30. "Gastibelza, le fou de Tolède" (*chanson d'Espagne*); words Hugo; pub. J. Meissonnier, 1840.
31. "La gitana"; words Frédéric Soulié; pub. J. Meissonnier, 1838.
32. "La glaneuse" (*chansonnette*); pub. Lemoine; not found.
33. "Hélène" (*ballade*); words Danglemont; pub. Romagnési, dep. July 1837.
34. "L'heure où le jour s'endort" (*nocturne*, op. posth., for 2 voices); words Édouard Plouvier; pub. Bureaux de *La France musicale* (Schott), dep. 1842.
35. "Il était trois chasseurs" (*chanson des fileuses du pays de Caux*: song of the spinners from the Caux region); comp. before 1830; pub. Lemoine *aîné*.
36. "Il ne faut pas rire des sorciers"; probably comp. 1834; probably pub. Meissonnier; not found.
37. "Je ne réponds de rien" (*chansonnette*); words Robillard; pub. Lemoine.
38. "Joli cœur" (*chansonnette militaire*); comp. before 1830; pub. Lemoine.
39. "Les jolis tambours" (*chanson militaire* for 3 voices); poet unknown; pub. Mme. Vve. Lemoine.
40. "La Juive" (*cantatille*); words Hugo; probably comp. 1834; pub. J. Meissonnier, 1834, dep. 1835.
41. "J'veux m'battre encore" (*chanson militaire*); words B. Gibon; 1st ed. not found; 2nd ed., pub. unknown (PN H.954).
42. "Lamento"; words Gautier (?); pub. ann. by Bernard-Latte in 1837; not found.
43. "Les larmes du départ" (*romance*); words Édouard Plouvier; pub. Lemoine, dep. 1844.
44. "Lénore"; words Bürger; trans. by ?; not found. Monpou refers in a

letter to "'Lénore,' my most complete and important work" (quoted above in Appendix I).

45. "Le lever" (chansonnette); words Musset; pub. Lemoine aîné.

46. "La Madonna col Bambino"; words Alfred Vannault; "édition corrigée" pub. Henry Lemoine.

47. "Madrid" (cantatille); words Musset; pub. Romagnési et Lemoine, before 1838.

48. "Le mal d'amour" (chanson du temps passé: song of days past); words Édouard Plouvier; pub. Bureaux de La France musicale (Schott), dep. August 1842 (ann. as op. posth.).

49. "Marie" (ballade tirée de la légende bretonne: ballade taken from the Breton legend); words Naudet; pub. Romagnési in Étrennes lyriques, 1830.

50. "Une marine"; words Ph. de Forges; pub. Henry Lemoine.

51. "Le matelot breton" (chansonnette for 2 voices); words Évariste Boulay-Paty; pub. Lemoine.

52. "Mignon" (chanson from Wilhelm Meister); words Goethe; trans. Théodore Coussenel; pub. in La romance, no. 7, 1834; pub. J. Meissonnier, dep. 1839.

53. "La milice" (chansonnette); words Jaime; comp. before 1830; pub. Lemoine.

☐ "Mon espingolle": see "L'espingole"

54. "Mon fils charmant"; words Édouard Plouvier; pub. Schott in Album de La France musicale, 1842.

55. "Le noir"; words Roger de Beauvoir; pub. J. Meissonnier, 1834.

56. "Une nuit sur l'eau"; poet unknown; pub. Lemoine.

57. "L'oiseau du cèdre"; pub. Costallat; not found.

58. "L'onde et les beaux yeux"; words A. Romagnési, adapted to the melody of "Une nuit sur l'eau"; pub. Lemoine.

59. "Paroles d'un croyant" (chant d'exile); words Lamennais; pub. in La romance, no. 27, July 5, 1834.

60. "Pastourelles"; words M. de Manchangy; pub. Lemoine.

61. "Pauvre Hélène" (romance); words A. Gourdin; comp. 1841; pub. Schott in Album de La France musicale, 1842.

62. "Pendant l'orage" (chansonnette for 2 voices); words A. Naudet; pub. Henry Lemoine.

63. "Pour un sourire" (romance); words Édouard Plouvier; pub. Schott, Bureau central de la musique, with expurgated text, dep. 1844 (cf. FM VII, 1844, pp. 177 and 201).

64. "Prière pendant l'orage"; pub. Lemoine; not found. Probably identical with no. 62.

65. "La Psyché" (fantaisie); words Édouard Plouvier; pub. Bernard-Latte, 1843, dep. 1844.

66. "Les résurrectionnistes" (chant); words Frédéric Soulié; comp. before 1834; pub. Lemoine.

67. "Rosa"; words Mme. Melanie Waldor; pub. Henry Lemoine.
68. "Sara la baigneuse" (*cantatille*); words Hugo; comp. 1834; pub. Romagnési et Lemoine, 1834.
69. "Une sérénade"; words M. de Forges; pub. J. Meissonnier, 1835.
70. "Si je mourais!"; words Alfred Vannault; pub. in *La romance* II, 1835, p. 49.
71. "Si j'étais ange" (*bluette*); words A. de Kermainguy; probably comp. 1834; pub. Schott in *Lyre française*, no. 143.
72. "Si j'étais petit oiseau" (*chansonnette* or *nocturne* for 3 voices); words Béranger; comp. 1828; pub. Mathieu, 1828.
73. "Simple amour" (*rêveuse*); words Mme. Hermance Lesguillon; pub. Meissonnier, 1834, dep. 1835.
74. "Le soleil de la liberté" (*chant héroïque*); pub. Lemoine; not found.
75. "Le soulier dans la cheminée"; words Ed. Thierry; pub. Lemoine, 1834 or 1835.
76. "Sur la mer" (*romance* for baritone or contralto); words Gautier; pub. Bernard-Latte, before 1838.
77. "La tour de Nesle" (*ballade de l'écolier de Cluny*); words Roger de Beauvoir; pub. Henry Lemoine.
78. "Les trois marteaux" (*chanson des compagnons orfèvres du tems de la Fronde*: song of the journeymen goldsmiths at the time of the Fronde); pub. J. Meissonnier, 1838.
79. "La Varsovienne" (*chant héroïque*, for 4 voices); words Casimir Delavigne; pub. Mme. Vve. Lemoine.
80. "Venise"; words Musset; pub. Lemoine *aîné*.
81. "Vieux sergent, jeune soldat"; words Émile Barateau; pub. Romagnési in *L'abeille musicale*, dep. 1837.
82. "Vite, aimez-moi"; words M. Aumassip; pub. Lemoine, 1834 or 1835.
83. "Le vœu sur la mer"; words Roger de Beauvoir; comp. 1834; pub. Meissonnier, 1834, dep. 1835.
84. "Le voile blanc" (op. posth.); words l'Abbé de Lécluse; pub. Bureau de *La France musicale* in *Album de la France musicale*, 1841.
85. "Vous vous trompez, grand'mère" (*chansonnette*); words F. L.; comp. before 1830 (?); pub. Pétibon.
86. "Les yeux noirs" (*caprice*); words Charles Dovalle; pub. Mathieu; pub. Lemoine *aîné*.

Hector Berlioz [1803–1869]

Although Berlioz' songs have received relatively thorough bibliographical treatment and numerous autobiographical documents yield many facts concerning their composition, the picture nevertheless remains somewhat clouded by the composer's frequent habit of borrowing or arranging his own works. In spite of some limitations, the compilation of Cecil Hopkinson (*A Bibliography of the Works of Hector Berlioz*, Edinburgh, 1951) is by far the richest source of information about the various editions of Berlioz' songs.

SEPARATE SONGS

1. "Absence" (*see Nuits d'été*, op. 7/4); aut. (ms. 1180) in Bibl. Nat.; coll. A, no..4. Orchestrated Dresden, February 12, 1843; aut. ms. in Bibl. Nat.; pub. Richault, ca. 1844. (Hopkinson, no. 25)
2. "Adieu Bessy" (*romance anglaise et française; see Neuf mélodies*, op. 2/8); coll. A, no. 14. (Hopkinson, no. 10)
☐ "Amitié, reprends ton empire": *see* "L'invocation à l'amitié"
3. "L'Arabe jaloux" (*romance*); words Florian; comp. ca. 1820; aut. ms. at La Côte-Saint-André; pub. Mme. Cuchet, 1822, with title "Le Maure jaloux." (Hopkinson, no. 3)
4. "Au cimetière" (*clair de lune; see Nuits d'été*, op. 7/5); aut. ms. in Bibl. Nat.; coll. A, no. 5. Orchestrated 1856; aut. ms. at La Côte-Saint-André; pub. Winterthur, Rieter-Biedermann, 1856. (Hopkinson, no. 25)
5. "Aubade" (for soprano or tenor with 4 horns and 2 cornets); words Musset as "Le lever"; comp. after 1830; aut. ms. at La Côte-Saint-André; unpub. (cf. Hopkinson, p. 192)
☐ "Barcarolle": *see* "L'île inconnue"
6. "La belle Isabeau" (*conte pendant l'orage*: story during the storm); words Dumas; comp. 1844; aut. ms. in Bibl. Nat.; pub. Bernard-Latte, 1844; possibly incorporated in *Feuillets d'album*, op. 19/5; coll. A, no. 32. (Hopkinson, no. 33)
7. "La belle voyageuse" (*légende irlandaise; see Neuf mélodies*, op. 2/4); pub. Mme. Cuchet, 1829; coll. A, no. 10. Orchestrated 1834; pub. Richault, 1844. (Hopkinson, no. 10)
8. "Canon libre à la quinte" (*duet*); words M. Bourgerie; pub. Boieldieu jeune, 1823. (Hopkinson, no. 6)
9. "La captive" (*orientale*, op. 12); words Hugo; comp. February 1832; aut. ms. in Bibl. Nat.; coll. B, Vol. XVII, no. 12(a), 1904. 2d version for voice, 'cello and piano comp. 1834; aut. ms. in Bibl. Nat.; pub. M. Schlesinger, 1834. 3d version for voice and orchestra comp. 1848; pub. Richault, 1849. (Hopkinson, no. 16)
10. "Les champs" (*romance*); words Béranger; comp. 1834; pub. in *La romance*, I, no. 15, April 12, 1834. 2d version with subtitle *aubade* incorporated in *Feuillets d'album*, op. 19/2; coll. A, no. 28. (Hopkinson, no. 14)
11. "Le chant des Bretons" (*see Fleurs des landes*, op. 13/5); version for 4 male voices pub. Schlesinger, ca. 1833–35; coll. B, Vol. XVI, no.

7(a), 1904; coll. A, no. 26. Another version for solo voice pub. coll. B, Vol. XVII, no. 27(a), 1904. (Hopkinson, no. 18)

12. "Chant du bonheur"; words Berlioz; 1st version in *Lélio ou Le retour à la vie*, comp. 1831. 2d version for voice and piano pub. Schlesinger, 1834. (Hopkinson, no. 13)

13. "Le chasseur danois" (for bass voice); words A. de Leuven; comp. 1844; aut. ms. in Bibl. Nat.; pub. Bernard-Latte in *La mélodie, Album de chant du Monde musical*, 1845; possibly incorporated in *Feuillets d'album*, op. 19/6; coll. A, no. 31. 2d version for voice and orchestra comp. 1834; coll. B, Vol. XV, no. 8, 1903. (Hopkinson, no. 35)

14. "Le coucher du soleil" (*rêverie; see Neuf mélodies*, op. 2/1); coll. A, no. 7. (Hopkinson, no. 10)

15. "Le dépit de la bergère" (*romance*); words Mme. . . .; comp. ca. 1819; pub. Auguste Le Duc, ca. 1820. (Hopkinson, no. 1)

16. "Élégie" (*see Neuf mélodies*, op. 2/9); prose text by Berlioz, after Thomas Moore; comp. January 1830; coll. A, no. 15 with Berlioz' "Quelques mots sur le sujet de l'Élégie" and the "Termination of Emmet's Speech." Orchestration never completed (cf. Berlioz' *Mémoires*, Chap. 18). (Hopkinson, no. 10)

☐ *Feuillets d'album*, op. 19; pub. Richault, 1850; ann. as 6 songs, but probably only 1st 3 actually pub. as op. 19. Contents: (1) "Zaïde" (2) "Les champs" (3) "Le chant des chemins de fer" (solo and chorus) (4) "Prière du matin" (children's chorus) (5) "La belle Isabeau" (6) "Le chasseur danois." (Hopkinson, no. 46)

☐ "First Love's Pure Vows": *see* "Premiers transports"

☐ *Fleurs des landes, 5 mélodies*, op. 13; pub. Richault, 1850; possibly never issued in complete form. Contents: (1) "Le matin" (2) "Petit oiseau" (3) "Le trébuchet" (4) "Le jeune paysan breton" (5) "Le chant des Bretons." (Hopkinson, no. 45)

17. "Hélène" (*ballade* for 2 voices; *see Neuf mélodies*, op. 2/2); aut. ms. in Bibl. Nat.; coll. A, no. 8. (Hopkinson, no. 10)

18. "L'île inconnue" (*see Nuits d'été*, op. 7/6); aut. ms. in Bibl. Nat. with title "Barcarolle"; coll. A, no. 6. Orchestrated 1856; aut. ms. at La Côte-Saint-André; pub. Winterthur, Rieter-Biedermann, 1856. (Hopkinson, no. 25)

19. "L'invocation à l'amitié" (*romance* for soprano, descant, and tenor, with choral refrain); words Florian; comp. ca. 1820; aut. ms. at La Côte-Saint-André; pub. Boieldieu *jeune*, 1823, with title "Amitié, reprends ton empire." (Hopkinson, no. 4)

☐ *Irlande: see Neuf mélodies imitées de l'anglais*

20. "Je crois en vous" (*romance*); words Léon Guérin; pub. in *Le Protée* III, September 1834, supplement. (Hopkinson, no. 15)

☐ "Le jeune pâtre breton": *see* "Le jeune paysan breton"

21. "Le jeune paysan breton" (*see Fleurs des landes*, op. 13/4); words

August Brizeux; comp. ca. 1833; aut. ms. in Bibl. Nat. 2d version for voice, horn, and piano pub. M. Schlesinger, 1834, with title "Le jeune pâtre breton"; coll. A, no. 25. 3d version for voice and orchestra pub. Ad. Catelin, ca. 1839, with latter title. (Hopkinson, no. 17)

22. "Le matin" (see Fleurs des landes, op. 13/1); words Adolphe de Bouclon (same text as no. 28); comp. 1850; coll. A, no. 22. (Hopkinson, no. 45)

☐ "Le Maure jaloux"; see "L'Arabe jaloux"

23. "Le montagnard exilé" (chant élégiaque for 2 equal voices); words Albert Duboys; pub. Boieldieu jeune, 1823. (Hopkinson, no. 7)

24. "La mort d'Ophélie" (ballade); words E. Legouvé, after Shakespeare; comp. 1847; pub. Brandus in Album de chant de La gazette musicale, January 1, 1848; coll. A, no. 21; later incorporated in the collective work Tristia, op. 18/2 (cf. Hopkinson, no. 44). (Hopkinson, no. 40)

☐ Neuf mélodies imitées de l'anglais, op. 2; words Thomas Gounet, after Thomas Moore (except "Élégie"); comp. 1829 (except "Élégie"); pub. Schlesinger, 1830. Rev. ed. pub. Richault, 1850, with title Irlande. Contents: (1) "Le coucher du soleil" (2) "Hélène" (3) "Chant guerrier" (solo and chorus) (4) "La belle voyageuse" (5) "Chanson à boire" (solo and chorus) (6) "Chant sacré" (solo and chorus) (7) "L'origine de la harpe" (8) "Adieu Bessy" (9) "Élégie." (Hopkinson, no. 10)

☐ Les nuits d'été, 6 mélodies, op. 7; words Gautier; comp. ca. 1840 (except "Villanelle"); pub. Ad. Catelin, 1841; pub. New York, International Music Co., 1956 (with English text attached). Orchestral score pub. Winterthur, J. Rieter-Biedermann, 1856 (without "Absence"); pub. New York, E. F. Kalmus, n.d. (with French and German texts). Contents (1) "Villanelle" (2) "Le spectre de la rose" (3) "Sur les lagunes" (4) "Absence" (5) "Au cimetière" (6) "L'île inconnue." (Hopkinson, no. 25)

25. "L'origine de la harpe" (ballade; see Neuf mélodies, op. 2/7); coll. A, no. 13. (Hopkinson, no. 10)

26. ["Page d'album"]; Italian words; comp. London, November 12, 1847; aut. ms. in Bibl. Nat.; coll. B, Vol. XVII, no. 25, 1904. (Hopkinson, no. 70)

27. "Le pêcheur"; words Albert Duboys, after Goethe; 1st version in Lélio, ou Le retour à la vie, comp. 1831. 2d version for voice and piano pub. M. Schlesinger, 1834. (Hopkinson, no. 12)

28. "Petit oiseau" (see Fleurs des landes, op. 13/2); words Adolphe de Bouclon (same text as no. 22); comp. 1850; coll. A, no. 23. (Hopkinson, no. 45)

29. "Pleure, pauvre Colette" (romance for 2 equal voices and piano); words Bourgerie; comp. ca. 1820; pub. Mme. Cuchet, 1822. (Hopkinson, no. 2)

30. "Premiers transports"; words Émile Deschamps; pub. Catelin, 1840. Later incorporated in Roméo et Juliette, op. 17. Issued separately as "Strophes" and "First Love's Pure Vows." (Hopkinson, no. 23)

31. "Romance d'Estelle"; words Florian; lost ms. reconstructed by Tiersot from opening theme of *Symphonie fantastique* (cf. Tiersot, *La musique aux temps romantiques*, Paris, 1930, pp. 79–81).

32. "Romance de Marie Tudor"; a lost work (cf. Boschot, *Un romantique sous Louis-Philippe*, new ed., Paris, 1948, p. 116).

33. "Le spectre de la rose" (*see Nuits d'été*, op. 7/2); aut. ms. in Bibl. Nat. 2d version transposed from D to B major; pub. Winterthur, Rieter-Biedermann, 1856; coll. A, no. 2. 3d version for voice and orchestra; aut. ms. at La Côte-Saint-André; pub. Winterthur, Rieter-Biedermann, 1856. (Hopkinson, no. 25)

☐ "Strophes": *see* "Premiers transports"

34. "Sur les lagunes" (*lamento; see Nuits d'été*, op. 7/3); coll. A, no. 3. Orchestrated 1856; aut. ms. at La Côte-Saint-André; pub. Winterthur, Rieter-Biedermann, 1856. (Hopkinson, no. 25)

35. "Toi qui l'aimas, verse des pleurs"; words Albert Duboys; comp. ca. 1820; pub. Boieldieu *jeune*, 1823. (Hopkinson, no. 5)

36. "Le trébuchet" (*scherzo* for 2 voices; *see Fleurs des landes*, op. 13/3); words Émile Deschamps; comp. 1850; coll. A, no. 24. (Hopkinson, no. 45)

☐ *Tristia: see* "La mort d'Ophélie"

37. "Villanelle" (*see Nuits d'été*, op. 7/1); comp. March 23, 1840; aut. ms. in Bibl. Nat.; coll. A, no. 1. Orchestrated 1856; pub. Winterthur, Rieter-Biedermann, 1856. (Hopkinson, no. 25)

38. "Zaïde" (*boléro; see Feuillets d'album*, op. 19/1); words Roger de Beauvoir; aut. ms. in Bibl. Nat.; coll. B, Vol. XVII, no. 23(a), 1904. 2d version for voice, castanets, and piano pub. Bernard-Latte, 1845; coll. A, no. 27. 3d version for voice and orchestra; aut. ms. in Bibl. Nat.; pub. coll. B, Vol. XV, no. 7, 1903. (Hopkinson, no. 37)

COLLECTIONS

A. *Collection de 32 mélodies pour une ou plusieurs voix et chœur*; pub. S. Richault, 1863. The "32" later became "33." A few of the songs have English or German words as well as the French. Contains nos. 1, 2, 4, 6, 7, 10, 11, 13, 14, 16–18, 21, 22, 24, 25, 28, 33, 34, 36–38.

B. *Werke*, ed. C. Malherbe and F. Weingartner; pub. Leipzig, Breitkopf & Härtel, 1900–1907. The songs are in Vol. XIV–XVII, with texts in English, French, and German. The coll. is indicated under specific songs only where the publication is significant or unique. The edition is carefully indexed in the *MLA Index Series*, No. 2 (*An Alphabetical Index to Hector Berlioz Werke*, New York, 1964).

(N.B.: A new scholarly edition of the complete works has been initiated by the Berlioz Centenary Committee of London. The songs are scheduled to appear in Vols. XIV and XVI.)

Giacomo Meyerbeer [1791–1864]

In addition to Meyerbeer's French *mélodies*, the list includes those of his German *Lieder* and Italian *canzonette* that were translated into French with his cooperation. Some information derives from A. Pougin (*Meyerbeer*, Paris, 1864).

SEPARATE SONGS

☐ "À une jeune fille": *see* "À une jeune mère"

1. "À une jeune mère"; words Durand; comp. before August 25, 1839; pub. M. Schlesinger; coll. A, no. 20 (as "À une jeune fille").

☐ "À Venise": *see* "A Venezia"

2. "A Venezia" (*barcarolle*); words Pietro Beltramo; trans. Émilien Pacini as "À Venise"; pub. Brandus, dep. 1856.

3. "L'absence"; poet unknown; pub. Launer, 1833; not found (ann. in *RMF* XIII, no. 5, March 2, 1833, p. 40).

4. "Aimez" (*chansonnette*); poet unknown; pub. in *La France musicale*, dep. 1847.

5. "Au revoir"; poet unknown; pub. Launer, 1833; not found (ann. in *RMF* XIII, no. 5, March 2, 1833, p. 40).

6. "Ballade de la reine Marguerite de Valois"; words Marguerite de Valois; pub. Schlesinger in *Hommage aux dames*, 1829; coll. A, no. 36.

7. "Le baptême"; words Maurice de Flassan; pub. Brandus, 1849; coll. A, no. 26; pub. in *Revue des dames et des demoiselles*; dep. 1853.

8. "La barque légère"; words Naudet; pub. M. Schlesinger, 1829; coll. A, no. 16 (as "Ma barque légère").

9. "Cantique du Trappiste"; poet unknown; pub. Bureaux de *La France musicale*, dep. November 1842; coll. A, no. 17.

10. "Canzona"; Italian words N. del Santo Mano; trans. Émile Deschamps as "Délire"; pub. A. Meissonnier et Heugel, dep. May 1840; coll. A, no. 19.

☐ "C'est elle": *see* "Die Rose, die Lilie, die Taube"

☐ "Chanson des moissonneurs vendéens": *see* "Chant des moissonneurs vendéens"

11. "La chanson du Maître Floh"; words Henri Blaze; pub. M. Schlesinger, dep. 1841; coll. A, no. 23.

☐ "Chanson persane": *see* "La dame invisible"

12. "Chant de mai"; words Henri Blaze; comp. before 1838; pub. M. Schlesinger, dep. 1841; coll. A, no. 1.

13. "Chant des moissonneurs vendéens"; words Henri Blaze; pub. M. Schlesinger, dep. 1839; coll. A, no. 14.

☐ "Le chant du berger": *see* "Des Schäfers Lied"

☐ "Le chant du dimanche": *see* "Sonntagslied"

14. "Confidences"; words Maurice Bourges; pub. Brandus, dep. May 1851.

15. "La dame invisible" (*chanson persane*); words Ed. Thierry; aut. ms. in Bibl. Nat. (ms. 4704) has title "Chanson persane" (and subtitle "La prisonnière" added in another hand) with dedication "A. M. Roger," in folder marked "Institut-Académie des Beaux-Arts, Associés Etrangers, 17 X^{bre} 1834"; pub. Brandus (ann. in *RGM* XIV, no. 52, December 26, 1847, p. 428, under "Publications nouvelles, Romances" but Bibl. Nat. copy pub. in 1884); coll. A, no. 33.

☐ "De ma première amie": *see* "Hör ich das Liedchen klingen"
☐ "Délire": *see* "Canzona"
☐ "Elle et moi": *see* "Sie und ich"

16. "Fantaisie"; words Henri Blaze; pub. M. Schlesinger, dep. 1841; coll. A, no. 39.

☐ "Les feuilles de rose": *see* "Die Rosenblätter"

17. "La fille de l'air"; words Méry; comp. before August 25, 1839; pub. Chabal, dep. April 1840; coll. A, no. 22.

18. "Les fleurs de la vie"; words Crével de Charlemagne; pub. unknown (PN A.A. 41), dep. 1853.

19. "La folle de St. Joseph"; words Marquis de Custine; pub. M. Schlesinger, dep. 1837; coll. A, no. 24.

20. "Frühling im Versteck"; words Lua; trans. Émile Deschamps as "Printemps caché"; pub. Brandus, dep. September 1848; coll. A, no. 30.

21. "Der Garten des Herzens"; words Wilhelm Müller; trans. Henri Blaze as "Le jardin du cœur"; pub. M. Schlesinger, dep. 1839; coll. A, no. 9.

☐ "Guide au bord ta nacelle": *see* "Komm"

22. "Hör ich das Liedchen klingen"; words Heine; trans. Émile Deschamps as "De ma première amie"; pub. M. Schlesinger (with German text), dep. November 1837.

23. "Jamais adieu"; words Mme. Valmore; pub. Launer in the album *La première heure du 1833*; not found (ann. in *RMF* XII, no. 45, December 8, 1832, p. 260).

☐ "Le jardin du cœur": *see* "Der Garten des Herzens"

24. "Komm"; words Heine; trans. Émile Deschamps as "Guide au bord ta nacelle"; pub. M. Schlesinger, dep. December 1837; coll. A, no. 6.

25. "La lavandière" (*ballade*); words Michel Carré; pub. in *Messager des dames et des demoiselles*, October 15, 1855.

26. "Lied des venezianischen Gondoliers"; words Michael Beer; trans. Émile Deschamps as "Mina"; pub. Brandus, dep. 1849; coll. A, no. 12.

27. "Luft von Morgen"; words Knapp; trans. Maurice Bourges as "Le pénitent"; aut. ms. in Bibl. Nat. (ms. 4706bis); pub. M. Schlesinger, dep. July 1842; coll. A, no. 31.

☐ "Ma barque légère": *see* "La barque légère"

28. "La marguerite du poète"; words Henri Blaze; pub. M. Schlesinger, dep. 1841; coll. A, no. 32.

29. "Menschenfeindlich"; words Michael Beer; trans. Henri Blaze as "Seul"; pub. M. Schlesinger, dep. 1841; coll. A, no. 2.

30. "Mère grand" (*nocturne* for 2 voices); words A. Betourné; pub. M. Schlesinger; coll. A, no. 11.

☐ "Mina": *see* "Lied des venezianischen Gondoliers"

31. "Le miroir magique"; poet unknown; pub. Launer, 1833; not found (ann. in *RMF* XIII, no. 5, March 2, 1833, p. 40).

32. "Le moine"; words Émilien Pacini; comp. 1829 (?); pub. M. Schlesinger in *Hommage aux dames*, 1839 (?); coll. A, no. 8.

33. "Murillo" (*ballade*); words Aylic Langlé; comp. after 1849; pub. Brandus.

☐ "Neben dir": *see* "Près de toi"

34. "Nella" (*chansonnette*); words Émile Deschamps; comp. before August 25, 1839; pub. Chabal, dep. April 1840.

☐ "Le pénitent": *see* "Luft von Morgen"

35. "Les plus beaux jours" (*arioso*); words Crével de Charlemagne; pub. unknown (PN A.A. 42), dep. 1853.

36. "Le poète mourant" (*élégie*); words Millevoye; pub. Maurice Schlesinger in *Hommage aux dames*, 10e année, 1832 (?).

37. "Près de toi" (for tenor with 'cello obligato); words Roger and Duisberg; pub. Brandus, dep. 1857. Listed in *Grove's Dictionary* as "Neben dir."

☐ "Printemps caché" (or "Printemps en cachette"): *see* "Frühling im Versteck"

☐ "La prisonnière": *see* "La dame invisible"

38. "Rachel à Nephtali"; words Émile Deschamps; pub. Schlesinger, dep. 1839; pub. Pacini; coll. A, no. 3.

39. "Le ranz-des-vaches d'Appenzell" (*chanson suisse*, for 2 voices); words E. Scribe; comp. before August 25, 1839; pub. Schlesinger, 1839 (?); coll. A, no. 37.

40. "Le revenant du vieux château de Bade" (*ballade*, with recitation); words Méry; pub. Brandus et Dufour, dep. 1859.

41. "Le ricordanze"; words Gaetano Rossi; trans. Maurice Bourges as "Les souvenirs"; pub. (with Italian text) M. Schlesinger, dep. April 1834; pub. (with French and Italian texts) Schlesinger in *Album de chant de La revue et Gazette musicale*, 1843; coll. A, no. 18.

42. "Die Rose, die Lilie, die Taube"; words Heine; trans. Émile Deschamps as "C'est elle"; pub. Brandus, dep. 1849; coll. A, no. 5.

43. "Die Rosenblätter"; words W. Müller; trans. Émile Deschamps as "Les feuilles de rose"; pub. Brandus, dep. 1849; coll. A, no. 34.

44. "Des Schäfers Lied" (*Lied* for tenor with clarinet obbligato); words

Rellstab; trans. G. Roger and Duisberg as "Le chant du berger"; pub. Brandus, dep. 1857.

45. "Scirocco"; words Michael Beer; trans. Émile Deschamps; pub. M. Schlesinger, dep. November 1837; coll. A, no. 10.

☐ "Sérénade": *see* "Ständchen"

☐ "Seul": *see* "Menschenfeindlich"

46. "Sicilienne"; words Méry; pub. Brandus, dep. 1849; coll. A, no. 27.

47. "Sie und ich"; words Fr. Rückert; trans. Émile Deschamps as "Elle et moi"; pub. M. Schlesinger, dep. 1841; coll. A, no. 15.

48. "Sonntagslied"; words Kletke; trans. Émile Deschamps as "Le chant du dimanche"; comp. ca. 1840; pub. Heugel; coll. A, no. 35.

☐ "Les souvenirs": *see* "Le ricordanze"

49. "Ständchen"; words G. Seidl; trans. Maurice Bourges as "Sérénade"; pub. Maurice Schlesinger, dep. 1842; coll. A, no. 13.

50. "Suleika"; words Goethe; trans. Henri Blaze; pub. M. Schlesinger, dep. 1841; coll. A, no. 25.

51. "Sur le balcon" (*romance*); words Ed. Thierry; pub. Brandus, 1847 (ann. in *RGM* XIV, no. 52, December 26, 1847, p. 428); coll. A, no. 38.

52. "Le vœu pendant l'orage"; words A. Betourné; comp. before August 25, 1839; pub. M. Schlesinger; coll. A, no. 29.

☐ "Voici donc le soir": text incipit of "Le ranz-des-vaches d'Appenzell"

☐ "Zuleika": *see* "Suleika"

COLLECTIONS

A. *40 mélodies à une et à plusieurs voix, avec acc^t de piano, avec paroles françaises et allemandes*; pub. Brandus, 1849. Reprinted 1883–85 in six volumes of 20 songs each, two for each voice range. Contains nos. 1, 6–13, 15–17, 19–21, 24, 26–30, 32, 38, 39, 41–43, 45–52.

Among Meyerbeer's other German and Italian songs, the following may be noted:

Vingt romances (Lieder) pour le roman Schwarzwalder Dorfgeschichten, d'Auerbach (ms.).

Zwei geistliche Lieder; aut. ms. in Bibl. Nat. (ms. 4706); anon. ed. in Bibl. Nat. (D. 8428^43) probably printed outside France.

Dix-huit canzonnette de Métastasio (ms.).

Franz Liszt [1811–1886]

Humphrey Searle's "Catalogue of Works" (in *The Music of Liszt*, 2d rev. ed., New York, 1966, pp. 155–195, and expanded in *Grove's Dictionary*, 5th ed., London, 1954, Vol. V, pp. 263–316) is an excellent source of further information on the location of autographs, arrangements, editions, etc.

SEPARATE SONGS

1. "Comment, disaient-ils"; words Hugo; comp. St. Petersburg, 1843; coll. A; coll. D, Vol. I, no. 6. 2d version in coll. B; coll. C; coll. D, Vol. II, no. 41. (Searle, no. 276)
2. "Élégie"; words Étienne Monnier; pub. Bernard-Latte, dep. 1845; Bibl. Nat. Vm⁷ 75122 may be a unique copy; see reproduction in Appendix II. (not in Searle)
3. "Enfant, si j'étais roi"; words Hugo; comp. ca. 1844; coll. A; coll. D, Vol. I, no. 7. 2d version in coll. B; coll. C; coll. D, Vol. II, no. 42. (Searle, no. 283)
4. "Gastibelza" (boléro); words Hugo; comp. ca. 1844; coll. A; coll. D, Vol. I, no. 10. (Searle, no. 286)
5. "Il m'aimait tant"; words Delphine Gay (Mme. Émile de Girardin); comp. ca. 1840; pub. Mainz, Schott, 1843, in L'aurore, collection de morceaux de chant avec accompagnement de piano, no. 51; coll. D, Vol. I, no. 2. Liszt's arr. for solo piano pub. Mainz, Schott, 1843. (Searle, no. 271)
□ "J'ai perdu ma force": text incipit of "Tristesse"
6. "Jeanne d'Arc au bûcher" (romance dramatique); words Dumas; comp. Basle, 1845; aut. (ms. 152) in Bibl. Nat.; pub. Bernard-Latte, 1846; pub. Mainz, Schott, 1846, in L'aurore, no. 87. 2d version of 1858 unpub. 3d version of 1874 pub. Mainz, Schott, 1876; pub. New York, G. Schirmer, 1915; coll. D, Vol. III, no. 1. (Searle, no. 293)
7. "Le Juif errant"; words Béranger; comp. 1847; aut. ms. in Weimar, Liszt Museum; unpub. (Searle, no. 300)
8. "Oh pourquoi donc"; words Mme. Pavlov; comp. 1848; aut. ms. owned 1954 by Friedrich Schnapp; unpub. (Searle, no, 301a)
9. "Oh! quand je dors"; words Hugo; comp. 1842; coll. A; coll. D, Vol. I, no. 5. 2d version in coll. B; coll. C; coll. D, Vol. II, no. 40. (Searle, no. 282)
10. "S'il est un charmant gazon"; words Hugo; comp. ca. 1844; aut. ms. in Bibl. Nat. (W 6,61); coll. A; coll. D, Vol. I, no. 8. 2d version in coll. B; coll. D, Vol. II, no. 43. (Searle, no. 284)
11. "La tombe et la rose"; words Hugo; comp. ca. 1844; coll. A; coll. D, Vol. I, no. 9. (Searle, no. 285)
12. "Tristesse"; words Musset; comp. Weimar, May 28, 1872; pub. Leipzig, Kahnt, 1879; coll. C; coll. D, Vol. III, no. 11. (Searle, no. 327)
13. "Le vagabond"; words Béranger; comp. before 1848; coll. D, Vol. I, no. 1 as "Le vieux vagabond." (Searle, no. 304)
□ "Le vieux vagabond": see "Le vagabond"
N.B.: Among doubtful and lost works Searle also includes "Air de Chateaubriand" (no. 762) and "L'aube naît"; words Hugo (no. 765a).

COLLECTIONS

A. *Buch der Lieder*, Heft II; pub. Berlin, Schlesinger, 1844. Contains nos. 1, 3, 4, 9–11.
B. *Gesammelte Lieder*, Heft IV; pub. Berlin, Schlesinger, 1860. Contains nos. 1, 3, 9, 10.
C. *Gesammelte Lieder*; pub. Leipzig, C. F. Kahnt, 1908. Contains nos. 1, 3, 9, 12.
D. *Musikalische Werke*, ser. VIII: Einstimmige Lieder und Gesänge, Band I–III; pub. Leipzig, Breitkopf & Härtel, 1917–1921. Reprinted in England by Gregg Press, 1966. Contains nos. 1, 3–6, 9–13.

Richard Wagner [1813–1883]

SEPARATE SONGS

1. "Les adieux de Marie Stuart"; words Béranger; comp. March 26, 1840; coll. C.
2. "Attente"; words Hugo; comp. 1840; pub. Flaxland, 1842, in the journal *Europa*; coll. A, no. 3; coll. B; coll. C.
3. "Les deux grenadiers"; words Heine; trans. unknown; comp. 1839–1840; pub. Mainz, Schott, 1843, in *L'aurore*, no. 22 (with French and German words); coll C.
4. "Dors, mon enfant"; poet unknown; comp. 1840; pub. Flaxland, 1842, in the journal *Europa*; coll. A, no. 1; coll. B; coll. C.
5. "Mignonne"; words Ronsard; comp. 1840; pub. Flaxland, 1842, in the journal *Europa*; coll. A, no. 2; coll. B; coll. C.
6. "Tout n'est qu'images fugitives"; words Jean Reboul; comp. 1840; coll. C.

COLLECTIONS

A. *3 Gesänge*; pub. Berlin, Fürstner. Contains nos. 2, 4, 5.
B. *3 mélodies*; pub. Durand, Schoenewerk et Cie, dep. 1870. Contains nos. 2, 4, 5.
C. *Musikalische Werke*, ed. Michael Balling, Vol. XV: Lieder und Gesänge; pub. Leipzig, Breitkopf & Härtel, 1914. Contains nos. 1–6.

Félicien David [1810–1876]

SEPARATE SONGS

1. "L'absence" (*romance*); poet unknown; pub. M. Schlesinger, dep. 1842.
2. "Adieu à Charence"; words E. T.; pub. M. Schlesinger, dep. 1842; coll. B, no. 5.
3. "L'amitié"; words Charles Chaubet; coll. B, no. 13.

4. "L'amour créateur"; words Tyrtée Tastet; pub. Brandus, dep. 1847; coll. B, no. 45.

5. "Un amour dans les nuages"; words Marc-Constantin; pub. Bureau central de musique, dep. 1846.

☐ "Amour perdu": see "Bonheur d'aimer"

6. "Amour pour amour" (see Les perles d'Orient, no. 2); words Gautier; coll. B, no. 46.

7. "L'ange rebelle" (air for bass); words Eugène Hanapier; pub. Maison Boieldieu, Sylvain St.-Étienne succ^r; coll. B, no. 41.

8. "Au couvent" (romance); words Ed. Bouscatel; pub. Ancienne Maison Chabal, Gambogi frères succ^{rs}; coll. B, no. 47.

9. "La Bayadère"; words L. Escudier; undated ms. in Bibl. Nat. (no. 1805); pub. Bureau central de musique, dep. 1846; coll. B, n. 40. The song was first called "Un revers de médaille," then "Joie et tristesse" (with words by Tyrtée Tastet). When Escudier's words were finally adapted to it, the title became "La Bayadère."

10. "Le Bédouin"; words adapted from the Arabic by J. Cognat; pub. FM, 1839; pub. Bureau central de musique, dep. 1845; coll. B, no. 2.

11. "Bonheur d'aimer" (see Les perles d'Orient, no. 6); words Ed. Brazier; coll. B, no. 32 (the song is also known as "Amour perdu").

12. "Le captif"; words Sylvain St.-Étienne; pub. J. Meissonnier, dep. 1846; coll. B, no. 35.

13. "La chanson du pêcheur" (lamento); words Gautier; pub. anon; coll. B, no. 20.

14. "Le Chybouk"; words Jourdain; pub. Bureau central de musique, dep. 1845; coll. B, no. 9.

15. "Le cri de Bosphore" (chant guerrier: war song); words Charles Chaubet; pub. Maison Boieldieu, Sylvain St.-Étienne succ^r, dep. 1853.

16. "Cri de charité"; words Charles Chaubet; pub. Maison Boieldieu, Sylvain St.-Étienne succ^r, dep. 1853; coll. B, no. 21. Aut. ms. of orchestral score in Bibl. Nat. (no. 1084).

17. "Dormez, Marie" (berceuse); words Émile Barateau; coll. A; coll. B, no. 4.

18. "Dors, petit" (berceuse); poet unknown; coll. B, no. 49.

19. "L'Égyptienne" (romance); words Jacques Cognat; pub. M. Schlesinger, dep. 1842; coll. B, no. 11. Aut. ms. of orchestral score in Bibl. Nat. (no. 1810) with vocal line lacking words.

20. "En chemin" (chant du voyageur: wanderer's song); words Émile Barateau; coll. A; coll. B, no. 12.

21. "Éoline"; words Édouard Plouvier; pub. Heugel - Maison A. Meissonnier, dep. 1851; coll. B, no. 23.

22. "L'étoile du pêcheur" (marine); words Charles Chaubet; coll. A.

23. "Éveillez-vous" (sérénade); words Mme. G. de La Renaudière; pub. Bureau central de musique, dep. 1846; coll. B, no. 28.

24. "Fleur de bonheur"; words Émile Barateau; coll. A; coll. B, no. 16.
25. "La fleur et l'oiseau mouche"; words Victor Séjour; coll. A; coll. B, no. 43.
26. "Formosa"; words Tyrtée Tastet; pub. Brandus, dep. 1847; coll. B, no. 19.
27. "Le fou de Bicêtre" (*scène dramatique*); words Marc-Constantin; pub. D. Grue, *successeur de* Martin, dep. 1844.
28. "Gardez-vous, mon cœur, de l'aimer" (*rêverie*); words Émile Barateau; coll. A.
29. "Gronde, océan" (*méditation*); words Charles de Marecourt; pub. Maison Boieldieu, Sylvain St.-Étienne, *succ*[r], dep. 1853.
30. "Les hirondelles" (*romance*); words Volny l'Hotelier; pub. Lyons, J. Benacci et Peschier, dep. 1844; coll. B, no. 26.
31. "J'ai peur de l'aimer" (*rêverie*); words Émile Barateau; coll. B, no. 10.
☐ "Joie et tristesse": *see* "La Bayadère"
32. "Le jour des morts" (*méditation* for bass); words Lamartine, as "La pensée des morts"; comp. 1837; pub. Sylvain St.-Étienne; coll. B, no. 25.
33. "Magdeleine" (*chant du moyen âge*: medieval song); words Émile Barateau; coll. A; coll. B, no. 36.
34. "Mon almée" (*prière au prophète*: prayer to the prophet; *see Les perles d'Orient*, no. 3); words Marc-Constantin.
35. "Le mourant" (*élégie*); words Sylvain St.-Étienne; pub. 1846 by *RGM*; pub. Brandus, Ancienne Maison Schlesinger, dep. 1847; coll. B, no. 30.
36. "Le nuage" (*rêverie*); words Édouard Plouvier; coll. A; coll. B, no. 3.
37. "L'océan" (*scène; see Les perles d'Orient*, no. 4); words Marc-Constantin; comp. 1837 (cf. David's aut. letter in Bibl. Nat., no. 77); fragmentary aut. sketches in Bibl. Nat. (ms. 1830, pp. 3–5); coll. B, no. 14, with title "Le quart."
38. "Oubli"; words Marc-Constantin; pub. Bureau central de musique; coll. B, no. 15.
39. "L'oublier, jamais!" (*vénitienne*); words Émile Barateau; pub. J. Meissonnier *et fils*, dep. 1847; coll. B, no. 33.
40. "Partons" (*nocturne* for 2 equal voices); words Émile Deschamps; coll. A; coll. B, no. 50.
41. "Le pêcheur à sa nacelle" (*barcarolle*); words Charles Poncy; pub. D. Grue, *successeur de* Martin; coll. B, no. 8.
☐ *Les perles d'Orient, six mélodies*; pub. in *Album 1846* for subscribers to *La France musicale*, dep. December 1845. Contents: (1) "Reviens! reviens!" (2) "Amour pour amour" (3) "Mon almée" (4) "L'océan" (5) "Tristesse de l'odalisque" (6) "Bonheur d'aimer."
42. "Le pirate"; words Sylvain St.-Étienne; pub. Lemoine *aîné*; coll. B, no. 29.

43. "Une plainte" (*romance*); poet unknown; coll. B, no. 44.
44. "Plainte amoureuse"; words Fonteille; pub. Compagnie musicale, Ancienne Maison Meissonnier; coll. B, no. 48.
45. "La pluie" (*romance*); words Eugène Tourneux; comp. March 1837 (cf. David's aut. letter in Bibl. Nat., no. 77); pub. Pacini, dep. 1845; coll. B, no. 39.
46. "La providence à l'homme"; words Lamartine; pub. Al. Curiner (livraisons 76–77), dep. 1854.
☐ "Le quart": *see* "L'océan"
47. "Qui t'aime plus que moi" (*canzonetta*); words Émile Barateau; coll. A; coll. B, no. 34.
48. "Le ramier"; words Marc-Constantin; pub. Brandus, dep. 1851; coll. B, no. 22.
49. "La rêverie"; words Mme. E. Tourneaux de Voves; pub. Alex. Grus and in Lyons, J. Benacci et Peschier, dep. 1844; coll. B, no. 7.
☐ "Un revers de médaille": *see* "La Bayadère"
50. "Reviens! reviens!" (*see Les perles d'Orient*, no. 1); words Gautier; coll. B, no. 6.
51. "Le Rhin allemand"; words Musset; pub. Ancienne Maison Meissonnier, Compagnie musicale; coll. B, no. 24.
52. "La rosée"; words E. Tourneux; pub. Bureau central de musique, dep. 1845.
53. "Les roses et le printemps"; words Fonteille; pub. Ancienne Maison Meissonnier, Compagnie musicale; coll. B, no. 1 (also known as "Le vieillard et les roses").
54. "Saltarelle"; words Antony Deschamps; pub. M. Schlesinger, dep. 1842; coll. B, no. 18. Aut. ms. of orchestral score in Bibl. Nat. (no. 1819).
55. "La Savoisienne"; words Eugène l'Héritier; pub. E. Masset.
56. "Le sommeil d'enfant"; words Gabriel Monavon; pub. Lyons, J. Benacci et Peschier, dep. 1845; coll. B, no. 37.
57. "Sultan Mahmoud"; words Gautier; pub. Bureau central de musique, dep. 1846; coll. B, no. 31.
☐ "Le Tchibouk": *see* "Le Chybouk"
58. "Tristesse de l'odalisque" (*see Les perles d'Orient*, no. 5); words Gautier; coll. B, no. 17.
59. "La vengeance des fleurs"; words Fonteille; pub. Maison J. Meissonnier, Compagnie musicale, dep. 1857; coll. B, no. 42.
60. "Le ver luisant"; words Marc-Constantin; pub. Ancienne Maison A. Meissonnier, Heugel *et Cie*, dep. 1851; coll. B, no. 38.
☐ "Le vieillard et les roses": *see* "Les roses et le printemps"

COLLECTIONS

A. *Album de 10 mélodies et 3 valses expressives pour le piano*; pub. J. Meissonnier, 1847; dep. 1846. Contains nos. 17, 20, 22, 24, 25, 28, 33, 36, 40, 47.

B. *Cinquante mélodies, scènes, romances pour chant et piano*; pub. E. Gérard, dep. 1866. Contains nos. 2–4, 6–14, 16–21, 23–26, 30–33, 35–45, 47–51, 53, 54, 56–60.

Henri Reber [1807–1880]

SEPARATE SONGS

1. "À Marie"; words Hugo; pub. Richault, dep. 1858; coll. A, no. 23.
2. "À un passant" (*ballade*); words Hugo; pub. Richault, dep. 1879; coll. B, no. 20.
3. "L'absence"; words Gautier; coll. B, no. 9.
4. "L'amour"; words Louise Bertin; pub. Richault, dep. 1851; coll. A, no. 15.
5. "Au bord du ruisseau"; words Quinault; pub. Richault, dep. 1879; coll. A, no. 5.
6. "Bergeronnette" (*chansonnette*); words Dovalle; pub. Richault at Reber's expense, dep. June 1834; coll. A, no. 16.
7. "Blessures"; words Henri Toupin; pub. Colombier, dep. 1876.
8. "Le bonheur est un oiseau"; words Louisa Siefert; coll. B, no. 17.
9. "La captive"; words Hugo; pub. Richault at Reber's expense, dep. 1837; coll. A, no. 8.
10. "Chanson de Barberine"; words Musset; pub. Richault, dep. 1868; coll. B, no. 2.
11. "Chanson de Fortunio"; words Musset; pub. Colombier, dep. 1861; coll. A, no. 26.
12. "Chanson de grand-père"; words Hugo; pub. Colombier, dep. 1878.
13. "Chanson de Thibaut, Comte de Champagne"; pub. Richault at Reber's expense, dep. February 1837; coll. A, no. 19.
14. "Chanson du Duc Charles d'Orléans"; pub. Richault, dep. 1845; coll. A, no. 7.
15. "Chanson du pays"; words Marie de M. B.; pub. Richault at Reber's expense, dep. February 1837; coll. A, no. 12.
16. "Chant de Mignon"; words Xavier Marmier, after Goethe; pub. Richault, dep. 1863; coll. A, no. 33.
17. "Le départ" (*chanson*); words Malherbe; pub. Richault, dep. 1842; coll. A, no. 9.
18. "L'échange" (*ariette*); words Dumas; pub. Richault, dep. 1846; coll. A, no. 3.
19. "L'ermite" (*ariette*); words Marot; pub. Richault, dep. 1846; coll. A, no. 24.
20. "La fée Mélior" (*ballade*); words Fournier; pub. Richault, dep. 1847; coll. A, no. 17.
21. "La fleur de l'âme"; words Hugo; coll. B, no. 5.

22. "La fontaine"; words Arsène Houssaye; pub. Richault, dep. 1869; coll. B, no. 12.

23. "La fortune" (*chansonnette* for 2 voices); words Béranger; pub. Richault at Reber's expense, dep. June 1834; coll. A, no. 28.

24. "Guitare"; words Hugo; pub. Richault, dep. 1845; coll. A, no. 13.

25. "Hai luli"; words Xavier de Maistre; pub. Richault at Reber's expense, dep. February 1837; coll. A, no. 11.

☐ "L'hermite": *see* "L'ermite"

26. "Les hirondelles"; words Florian; pub. Richault, dep. 1849; coll. A, no. 27 (in 2 versions, the 2d for 2 voices).

27. "Le jardin"; words Dumas; pub. Richault, dep. 1851; coll. A, no. 2.

28. "Je te suivrai"; words Mme. Blanchecotte; pub. Richault, dep. 1879; coll. B, no. 19.

29. "Je voudrais être enfant"; words Mme. E. Pressencé; coll. B, no. 7.

30. "Lon lon la"; words Mme. Blanchecotte; coll. B, no. 16.

31. "Madeleine"; words Hugo; pub. Richault, dep. 1849; coll. A, no. 18.

32. "Mandoline"; words Théodore Massiac; pub. Richault, dep. 1849; coll. B, no. 15.

33. "Le message" (*chanson basque*); words Cte de Brayer; pub. Richault, dep. 1879; coll. B, no. 18.

34. "Mortel, ouvre les yeux"; words Corneille; coll. B, no. 8.

35. "Ninette"; words Vte Alenis de Valon; pub. Richault, dep. 1850; coll. A, no. 4.

36. "Nouvelle chanson"; words Hugo; pub. Richault, dep. 1845; coll. A, no. 25.

☐ "Où ton cœur se pose": text incipit of "Nouvelle chanson"

37. "Le papillon et la fleur"; words Hugo; pub. Richault, dep. 1847; coll. A, no. 1.

38. "Pastorale berrichonne" ("Les trois bûcherons"); words George Sand; coll. B, no. 4.

39. "Le prisonnier" (*romance* for 1 or 2 voices); words Béranger; pub. Richault at Reber's expense, dep. June 1834.

40. "Le prisonnier de guerre"; words Béranger; pub. C. Heu; coll. A, no. 29.

41. "Les proscrits" (*chant de ceux qui s'en vont sur la mer*: song of those who go to sea); words Hugo; coll. B, no. 13.

42. "Regrets"; words Mary Stuart (*fragment*); coll. A, no. 31.

43. "La rive inconnue"; words Gautier; coll. B, no. 6.

44. "Rose" (*vieille chanson du jeune temps*: old song from youthful days); words Hugo; pub. Richault, dep. 1858; coll. A, no. 6.

45. "Rosette"; words l'Abbé de l'Écluse; coll. A, no. 21.

46. "Le serment"; words Marceline Desbordes-Valmore; pub. Richault at Reber's expense, probably 1834; coll. A, no. 20.

47. "Si mes vers avaient des ailes"; words Hugo; coll. A, no. 32.

48. "Si vous n'avez rien à me dire"; words Hugo; pub. Richault, dep. 1869; coll. B, no. 10.

49. "Si vous saviez"; words Sully-Prudhomme; pub. Richault, dep. 1878; coll. B, no. 14.

50. "Sous le balcon"; words Hugo; pub. Richault, dep. 1869; coll. B, no. 11.

51. "Sous les pampres verts"; words Mme. C. Berton; coll. B, no. 3.

52. "Stances de Malherbe"; pub. Richault, dep. 1842; coll. A, no. 10.

53. "Toi et moi"; poet unknown; coll. A, no. 30.

□ "Les trois bûcherons": *see* "Pastorale berrichonne"

54. "Villanelle"; words Gautier; pub. Richault; coll. B, no. 1. Orchestrated.

55. "Vœu" (*orientale*); words Hugo; pub. Richault, dep. 1850; coll. A, no. 14.

56. "Le voile de la châtelaine"; words l'Abbé de l'Écluse; coll. A, no. 22.

COLLECTIONS

A. *Mélodies pour chant et piano, premier recueil*; pub. Richault, dep. 1863. Contains nos. 1, 4–6, 9, 11, 13–20, 23–27, 31, 35–37, 40, 42, 44–47, 52, 53, 55, 56.

B. *Mélodies pour chant et piano, deuxième recueil*; pub. Richault, dep. 1880. Contains nos. 2, 3, 8, 10, 21, 22, 28–30, 32–34, 38, 41, 43, 48–51, 54.

Charles Gounod [1818–1893]

In addition to the French *mélodies*, the list also includes songs written to English, Italian, and Spanish words. The work by J.-G. Prod'homme and A. Dandelot (*Gounod, sa vie et ses œuvres*, 2 vols., Paris, 1911) is the most important (although not always reliable) source of information.

SEPARATE SONGS

1. "À Cécile"; words G. Dubuffe; pub. H. Lemoine, dep. 1881; coll. H, no. 2.

2. "À la brise" (*madrigal*); words Jules Barbier; comp. 1875; pub. H. Lemoine, dep. 1875; coll. G, no. 11.

3. "À la Madone" (*romance* used in *Roméo et Juliette*); words Jules Barbier; coll. D, no. 8; pub. Choudens, 1874 in *L'âge d'or*, no. 9.

4. "À la nuit"; words Gounod; comp. 1891; pub. Lemoine, dep. 1891.

5. "À toi, mon cœur"; words Jules Barbier; comp. 1876; pub. Choudens, dep. 1876; coll. C, no. 3.

6. "À une bourse"; words Émile Augier; comp. 1865; pub. Choudens, dep. 1869; coll. B, no. 13.

7. "À une jeune fille"; words Émile Augier; comp. 1865; pub. Choudens, dep. 1869; coll. B, no. 1.

8. "À une jeune Grecque"; words trans. Prosper Yraven, from Sappho; comp. 1860; pub. Choudens, dep. 1862.

9. "À une sœur" (*romance*); words O. Pradère; pub. Choudens in *L'âge d'or*, no. 13; dep. 1875.

☐ "Abraham's Request": *see* "Prière d'Abraham"

10. "Absence"; words A. de Ségur; comp. 1870; pub. Choudens, dep. 1870; coll. C, no. 18.

11. "L'absent"; words Gounod; comp. 1876; pub. H. Lemoine, dep. 1877; còll. H, no. 1.

12. "Les adieux à la maison"; poet unknown; pub. Lemoine, 1885.

13. "Aimons-nous"; words Jules Barbier; comp. 1874; pub. Choudens, dep. 1874; coll. C, no. 12.

14. "L'âme de la morte"; words Théodore de Banville; pub. Imp. de Magnier, February, 1860.

15. "L'âme d'un ange"; words Théodore de Banville; comp. 1860; coll. A, no. 16. Italian version pub. London, 1865 as "La rondinella."

16. "L'ange gardien" (for 4-part chorus); words A. Quételard; comp. 1854–55; pub. Lebeau, August 1858. 2d version for voice and piano pub. Lebeau, dep. 1861; coll. I, no. 11.

17. "L'anniversaire des martyrs" (*cantique*); words Ch. Dallet; comp. 1870; coll. F, no. 5.

18. "L'arithmétique"; words Ch. Turpin; pub. Lebeau, February 1855. 2d version a *duettino* for 2 equal voices; coll. I, no. 15.

19. "Au matin"; words S. Ferrière; aut. ms. sold Paris, 1950, by dealer R. Legouix to unknown buyer; song is marked "Allegretto" (G major, 3/4) with dedication "A ma petite amie Jeanne de la Ferrière."

20. "Au printemps"; words Jules Barbier; pub. Choudens, dep. 1868; coll. B, no. 12.

21. "Au rossignol"; words Lamartine; pub. Choudens, 1867; coll. B, no. 19.

22. "Aubade"; words Hugo; pub. Brandus, February 1855; coll. A, no. 6.

☐ "Ave Maria" (*mélodie religieuse* adapted to Bach 1st prelude); see "Premier prélude de J. S. Bach"

23. "L'Ave Maria de l'enfant"; poet unknown; possibly comp. 1872–1873; pub. Lemoine, dep. 1891.

24. "L'aveu"; words Jean Rameau; pub. Heugel, © 1894 (marked "Gounod's last *mélodie*"); coll. J, no. 2.

25. "Le banc de pierre"; words Paul de Choudens; pub. Choudens, dep. 1876; coll. D, no. 1.

26. "Barcarola" (*duetto* for soprano and baritone); words Giuseppe Zaffira, French trans. by Jules Barbier; comp. 1872–73; pub. Henri Lemoine; pub. London, Goddard, dep. 1873; coll. G, no. 20.

27. "Bethléem" (*pastorale sur un noël du XVIIIe siècle*: *pastorale* on an 18th-century Christmas carol, for chorus and orchestra); comp. under title

"Dans cette étable"; poet unknown; pub. Lemoine *aîné*, 1860. 2d version entitled "Bethléem" for voice and piano or organ; pub. Lebeau, dep. 1880.

28. "Beware"; words Longfellow; comp. 1871; pub. London, Novello, Ewer, dep. 1871.

29. "Bienheureux le cœur sincère" (paraphrase of Psalm I); words Jules Barbier; comp. 1872; pub. H. Lemoine, dep. 1876; coll. H, no. 18. Pub. H. Lemoine with English words as "Blessed is the man," dep. 1873.

30. "Biondina": *see Biondina, poème musical*, no. 1.

☐ *Biondina, poème musical*; words Giuseppe Zaffira; comp. 1871–72; pub. London, Duff and Stewart, dep. 1872; pub. H. Lemoine, dep. 1873. Contents: "Prologo": "Ha qualche tempo" (1) "Biondina" (2) "Sotto un cappello rosa" (3) "Le labbra ella compose" (4) "E stati alquanto" (5) "Ho messo nuove corde al mandolino" (6) "Se come io son poeta" (7) "Siam iti l'altro giorno" (8) "E le campane hanno suonato" (9) "Ella è malata" (10) "Ier fù mandata" (11) "L'ho accompagnata."

☐ "Blessed is the man": *see* "Bienheureux le cœur sincère"

31. "Blessures"; words Henri Turpin; comp. 1885; pub. H. Lemoine, dep. 1885; coll. H, no. 3.

32. "Boire à l'ombre"; words Émile Augier; comp. 1868; pub. Choudens, dep. 1869; coll. B, no. 9.

33. "Boléro"; words Jules Barbier, English trans. B. Kett; comp. 1871; pub. London, Chappell, 1871; pub. Choudens, dep. 1877; coll. C, no. 10.

34. "Bon jour, bon soir" (for 3-part chorus); comp. 1857; words M. Spenner. 2d version for voice and piano pub. Lebeau, 1861; coll. I, no. 7.

35. "Cantique pour la première communion"; words R. P. Dulong de Rosnay; comp. 1872; pub. H. Lemoine, dep. 1874.

36. "Cantique pour l'adoration du Saint Sacrament"; words A. du Ségur; comp. 1868; pub. H. Lemoine, dep. 1888.

37. "Canzone di ringraziamento per un Prussiano avendo ritrovato la voce di petto"; words Gounod; comp. 1880; aut. ms. in Bibl. Nat. (FS 39³⁸ and attached piece).

38. "Ce que je suis sans toi"; words L. de Peyre; pub. Choudens, dep. 1868; coll. B, no. 15.

39. "Ce qu'il faut à mon âme"; words l'Abbé Félix Sédillot; comp. 1872; pub. Lemoine, dep. 1887.

40. "Les champs"; words Béranger; coll. A, no. 1.

41. "Chanson d'avril" (*sérénade* from *Le passant*); words François Coppée; comp. 1872; pub. H. Lemoine, dep. 1872; coll. B, no. 5.

42. "La chanson de la brise" (duo, sequel to the duo "La siesta");

words Ch. Ligny, English trans. Francis Turner Palgrave as "The Message of the Breeze"; comp. 1872; pub. H. Lemoine, dep. 1872; coll. H, no. 19.

43. "La chanson de la glu"; words from Jean Richepin's drama *La glu*; comp. 1883; pub. H. Lemoine, dep. 1883; coll. H, no. 4.

44. "Chanson du printemps"; words Eugène Tourneux; comp. 1860; pub. J. Meissonnier *fils*, dep. 1860; coll. A, no. 13.

45. "La chanson du pâtre"; words Émile Augier; comp. ca. 1850 and inserted in the opera *Sapho*; pub. Choudens, dep. 1878; coll. C, no. 13.

46. "La chanson du pêcheur"; words Gautier; comp. Rome, 1841; pub. Choudens, dep. 1895. Another *mélodie* with the same text was pub. by Lemoine with the title "Ma belle amie est morte."

47. "Chanson printanière"; words Jules Barbier; pub. Choudens, dep. 1895.

48. "Chant d'automne"; poet unknown; pub. Brandus, February 1855; coll. A, no. 7.

49. "Chant des saveteurs bretons"; words Anaïs Ségala; comp. 1882; pub. H. Lemoine, dep. 1882.

50. "Chanter et souffrir"; words Albert Delpit; coll. C, no. 16.

51. "Chantez Noël" (duo for soprano and contralto); words Jules Barbier; pub. Choudens, dep. 1870; coll. E, no. 10. Version for voice and piano pub. in coll. B, no. 10.

52. "Chantez, voix bénies" (*hymne* comp. in honor of His Holiness, Pius IX); words Jules Barbier, English trans. by C. J. Rowe, Italian by Giuseppe Zaffira; comp. 1870; coll. F, no. 3.

53. "Châteaux en Espagne" (duo for tenor and baritone); words Pierre Véron; aut. ms. in Bibl. Nat. (no. W² 52) dated Paris, April 9, 1858; pub. Lebeau *aîné*, July 1858.

54. "Chidiock Tichborne"; English poet unknown; comp. 1872–73; pub. Lemoine, dep. 1873.

55. "Le ciel a visité la terre" (*cantique* after communion); words A. de Ségur, English trans. Farnie; comp. 1868–69; coll. C, no. 17; coll. F, no. 1.

56. "Les cloches" (for chorus and piano); words Gounod. 2d version for voice and piano pub. in coll. H, no. 5.

57. "Clos ta paupière" (*berceuse*); words Jules Barbier, English trans. as "Peacefully Slumber"; comp. 1873; pub. H. Lemoine, dep. 1875; coll. G, no. 1.

58. "Compliment"; words Dumas *fils*; comp. 1876; pub. H. Lemoine, dep. 1876.

59. "Crépuscule"; poet unknown; comp. 1865; pub. Choudens, dep. 1866; coll. B, no. 17.

☐ "The Daisy": *see* "La Pâquerette"

☐ "Dans cette étable": *see* "Bethléem"

60. "Départ" (*scène*); words Emile Augier; comp. 1868; pub. Choudens, dep. 1869; coll. B, no. 18.

61. "Départ des missionaires" (duo); words Charles Dallet; coll. F, no. 4. Cf. Prod'homme-Dandelot, p. 263, for several other versions, the authenticity of which could not be verified.

62. "Le départ du mousse" (*barcarolle*); words Pierre Barbier; comp. 1878; pub. Choudens, dep. 1878; coll. D, no. 20.

63. "Dernières volontés"; words Louis Veuillot; comp. 1883; pub. Lemoine, dep. 1883; coll. H, no. 6.

64. "Les deux pigeons"; words from La Fontaine's fable; comp. 1883; pub. Lemoine, dep. 1883; coll. H, no. 7.

65. "Deux vieux amis" (*scène intime* for tenor and baritone); words Pierre Véron; pub. Heugel, 1856; coll. J, no. 5.

66. "Dieu partout" (duo for 2 equal voices); words Plouvier; comp. 1886; pub. Choudens, dep. 1886.

67. "La distribution des prix" (for 3-part chorus); poet unknown; comp. 1852–58. 2d version for 1 voice pub. Lebeau, dep. 1867; coll. I, no. 13.

68. "Donne-moi cette fleur"; words Léon Gozlan; comp. ca. 1867; pub. Choudens, 1869; coll. B, no. 11.

69. "D'un cœur qui t'aime" (duo for soprano and alto); words Racine; pub. H. Lemoine, dep. 1882; coll. H, no. 20.

70. "E le campane hanno suonato": *see Biondina, poème musical,* no. 8.

71. "E stati alquanto": *see Biondina, poème musical,* no. 4.

72. "L'écriture" (*duettino* for 2 equal voices); words Ch. Turpin; comp. 1854–55; pub. Lebeau, 1855.

73. "Ella è malata": *see Biondina, poème musical,* no. 9.

74. "Elle sait"; words Georges Boyer; comp. 1882; pub. H. Lemoine, dep. 1882; coll. H, no. 8.

75. "Entreat me not to Leave Thee"; words from "The Song of Ruth"; comp. 1872–73; pub. H. Lemoine, dep. 1882.

76. "Envoi de fleurs"; words Émile Augier; comp. 1865; pub. Choudens, 1869.

77. "L'Eucharistie" (*cantique,* op. posth.); words Brother Eucher; pub. Lemoine, 1895.

78. "La fauvette" (*chanson*); words Millevoye; comp. 1871–72; pub. H. Lemoine, 1872; pub. London, Novello and Ewer; coll. G, no. 2.

79. "La fête des couronnes" (duo for 2 equal voices); words Édouard Plouvier; comp. 1886; pub. Choudens, dep. 1886.

☐ "Fleur des bois": *see* "Little Celandine"

☐ "La fleur du foyer": *see* "Oh, Happy Home"

80. "Forever with the Lord"; words J. Montgomery; comp. 1872; pub. London, Philips and Page, 1886.

81. "The Fountain Mingles with the River"; words Shelley; comp. 1871; pub. London, Chappell, 1871.

82. "Fuyons, ô ma compagne" (duo); words F. Ponsard; pub. Choudens, dep. 1883.

83. "Gliding Down the River" (boat song); words H. B. Farnie; pub. London, Pitt and Hatzfeld; pub. Choudens, dep. 1887.

84. "Glory to Thee My God" (an evening song); words Bishop Ken; comp. 1872; pub. London, Philips and Page, 1884, dep. 1885.

85. "Good Night"; words Shelley; comp. 1871; pub. London, Chappell, 1871.

86. "Ha qualche tempo": see *Biondina, poème musical*, "Prologo."

87. "Heureux sera le jour"; words Ronsard; comp. 1871–72; pub. H. Lemoine, 1872; coll. G, no. 6.

88. "Ho messo nuove corde al mandolino": see *Biondina, poème musical*, no. 5.

89. "The Holy Vision"; words Frederick E. Weatherley; comp. 1886; pub. London and New York, Novello, Ewer, dep. 1888.

90. "Hommage à Madame La Comtesse Herminie de Léautaud"; words Mᵐᵉ Baëlen; comp. 1865; pub. Lebeau *aîné*, 1869.

91. "Hymne à la nuit"; words Jules Barbier; pub. Choudens, dep. 1868; coll. B, no. 14.

92. "Ier fù mandata": see *Biondina, poème musical*, no. 10.

93. "If Thou Art Sleeping Maiden, Awake"; words Longfellow; comp. 1872–73; pub. Lemoine, dep. 1873; pub. London, Chappell.

94. "Ilala" (May 1873); words Lord Houghton; comp. 1873; pub. London, Marsten and Goddard, 1873; pub. E. Gérard, 1873 as "Stances à la mémoire de Livingstone."

95. "Invocation"; words O. Pradère; comp. 1872–73; pub. Choudens, dep. 1873; coll. C, no. 15.

96. "It is Not Always May"; words Longfellow; comp. 1871; pub. London, Chappell, 1871.

97. "Je ne puis espérer" (*mélodie dramatique*); words Albert Delpit; comp. 1870; pub. Choudens, dep. 1870; pub. Lebeau; coll. C, no. 14.

98. "Je te rends grâce, ô Dieu" (*cantique*); words Paul Collin; pub. Lebeau, dep. 1892.

99. "Jésus à la crèche" (*Noël*); words R. P.; comp. 1878; pub. Lebeau, dep. 1878; coll. I, no. 6.

100. "Jésus de Nazareth" (*chant évangélique*); words A. Porte, English trans. Chorley; comp. 1856; pub. Lebeau *aîné*, May 1856. Version for chorus and orchestra pub. London, 1877.

101. "La jeune fille et la fauvette"; words Edmond de Chauvinière; comp. 1860; pub. Lebeau *aîné*, 1860; coll. I, no. 2.

102. "Les jeunes Françaises" (*duettino*); words Ernest Legouvé; comp. 1876; pub. Choudens.

103. "Le jour des prix"; words E. Scribe; pub. Lebeau, dep. 1867; coll. I, no. 4.

104. "Le Juif errant"; words Béranger; comp. 1860; pub. Choudens, 1861; coll. A, no. 12.

☐ "The King of Love my Shepherd Is": *see* "Le Roi d'amour est mon pasteur"

105. "Le labbra ella compose": *see Biondina, poème musical*, no. 3.

☐ "Lamento": *see* "Chanson du pêcheur" and "Ma belle amie est morte"

106. "Le lever"; words Musset; pub. Brandus, dep. 1855; coll. A, no. 8.

107. "L'ho accompagnata": *see Biondina, poème musical*, no. 11.

108. "Les lilas blancs" (*valse chantée*); words Paul Bourguignat; comp. 1876; pub. Lemoine, dep. 1876; coll. G, no. 18.

109. "Little Celandine" (vocal duet); words Wordsworth, French trans. by Ch. Ligny as "Fleur des bois"; comp. 1872; pub. London, Goddard; pub. H. Lemoine, dep. 1873; coll. G, no. 19, with French words only.

110. "Loin du pays"; words Gounod; comp. 1873; pub. London, Goddard; pub. Lemoine, dep. 1873; coll. G, no. 9.

111. "Ma belle amie est morte" (*lamento*; a new song set to the text of "Chanson du pêcheur"); words Gautier; comp. 1872; pub. Lemoine, dep. 1872; coll. G, no. 13.

112. "Ma fille, souviens-toi"; words Mme Louise Marie B.; comp. 1876; pub. H. Lemoine, dep. 1876; coll. H, no. 10.

113. "Maid of Athens"; words Byron (dedicated to Byron's original "Maid of Athens," Mrs. Black), French trans. J. Ruelle as "Vierge d'Athènes," Italian by A. Zanardini as "Vergine d'Atene"; comp. 1872; pub. London, Goddard, dep. 1872; pub. H. Lemoine, 1887; coll. H, no. 16, with French and Italian words only.

114. "Marguerite" (*romance*); words O. Pradère; pub. Choudens, dep. 1865; coll. B, no. 2.

115. "Medjé" (*chanson arabe*); words Jules Barbier; comp. 1865; pub. Choudens, 1865; coll. B, no. 3.

116. "Mélancolie" (*rêverie*); words François Coppée; comp. 1879–80; pub. in the journal *Gil-Blas*, dep. 1880; pub. Choudens, dep. 1884.

117. "Memorare" (duo for soprano and contralto); poet unknown; pub. Lemoine, 1883.

☐ "The Message of the Breeze": *see* "La chanson de la brise"

118. "Mignon"; words Louis Gallet, paraphrased from Goethe; comp. 1871; pub. Choudens, 1871; coll. C, no. 4.

119. "Mon amour a mon cœur"; words Jules Barbier; comp. 1875; pub. Lemoine, dep. 1875; coll. B, no. 4.

120. "Mon habit" (*chanson*); words Béranger; pub. Heugel, dep. 1855; coll. A, no. 18; coll. J, no. 3.

121. "My Beloved Spake" (with piano and 'cello acc.); words from *The Song of Solomon*; comp. 1873; pub. London, Goddard; pub. Lemoine as "Viens, mon cœur," dep. 1873.

122. "Le nid"; words A. Quételard; pub. Lebeau, dep. 1867; coll. I, no. 14.

☐ "Noël": *see* "Chantez Noël"

123. "Le nom de Marie"; words A. de Ségur; coll. D, no. 16; coll. F, no. 2.

124. "Notre Dame de France" (*hymne à la patrie*); words Georges Boyer; comp. 1888; pub. in *Le Figaro*, August 15, 1888; pub. Hartmann, dep. 1888; coll. J, no. 6.

125. "Notre Dame des petits enfants" (*cantique*); words A. de Ségur; coll. D, no. 4; coll. F, no. 6.

126. "Ô ma belle rebelle"; words Baïf; pub. Brandus, dep. 1855; coll. A, no. 5.

127. "Oh! dille tu!" (*madrigale*); words Giuseppe Zaffira; comp. 1871–1872; pub. London, Goddard, 1872.

128. "Oh, Happy Home"; words Ed. Maitland, French trans. Ch. Ligny as "La fleur des foyers"; pub. London, Rudall and Carte, 1872; pub. H. Lemoine, dep. 1872.

129. "Oh! That We Two are Maying" (with *ad lib.* acc. of harmonium and viola); words Charles Kingsley; comp. 1871; pub. London, Duff and Stewart, 1871.

130. "Où voulez-vous aller?" (*barcarolle*); words Gautier; pub. J. Meissonnier, dep. 1839; coll. C, no. 5.

☐ "L'ouvrier": *see* "The Worker"

☐ "Oyème": *see* "Prière"

131. "La paix de Dieu"; words A. L. Hettich, after Maurice Henry; pub. Alphonse Leduc, dep. 1913.

132. "La Pâquerette" (*chanson*); words Dumas *fils*, English trans. Henry Dulchen as "The Daisy"; comp. 1871; pub. Choudens, 1871; coll. C, no. 1.

133. "Par une belle nuit" (*nocturne* for soprano and contralto); words A. de Ségur; comp. 1870; pub. Choudens, 1870; coll. E, no. 2.

134. "Parlez pour moi" (*romance*); words Jules Barbier; pub. Choudens in *L'âge d'or*, no. 20, dep. 1875.

135. "Passiflora"; words Comtesse Jeanne de Chambrun; comp. 1888; pub. Lemoine, dep. 1888; coll. H, no. 11.

136. "Patte de velours" (for 3-part chorus); words Spenner. 2d version for voice and piano pub. Lebeau, dep. 1861; coll. I, no. 8.

137. "Pauvre Braga"; words Gustave Badaud; comp. 1882; pub. Imp. Ed. Delanchy, dep. 1882.

138. "Le pays bienheureux" (*question d'enfant*); words Gounod, paraphrased from Felicia Hemans' "The Better Land"; comp. 1871–1872; pub. Lemoine, 1872; coll. B, no. 3.

☐ "Peacefully Slumber" (lullaby): *see* "Clos ta paupière"

139. "Perchè piangi?"; words Corrado Marchese Paresi; comp. 1871–72; pub. London and New York, Novello, Ewer, 1872.

140. "Le premier jour de mai"; words Passerat; pub. Brandus, dep. 1855; coll. A, no. 4.

141. "Premier prélude de J. S. Bach"; words Lamartine ("Vers sur un album," from his *Recueillements poétiques*); comp. 1852; pub. Mayaud, December 1852, dep. 1853. This is the original version of the famous "Ave Maria"; coll. A, no. 3 and coll. J, no. 1 as "Ave Maria."

142. "Prends garde"; words Jules Barbier; comp. 1871 (?); pub. Choudens, dep. 1876; coll. C, no. 9.

143. "Prière"; words Sully-Prudhomme, free English trans. Marqués de Alta Villa as "Oyème"; pub. Lemoine, dep. 1876; coll. H, no. 12.

144. "Prière à la Vierge"; poet unknown; comp. 1868; pub. Lebeau, dep. 1868; coll. I, no. 12.

145. "Prière d'Abraham"; words Jules Barbier, English trans. as "Abraham's Request"; comp. 1872–73; pub. H. Lemoine, dep. 1876; pub. London, Goddard, 1873; coll. G, no. 17, with French words only.

146. "Prière du soir" (1); words Ch. Ligny; comp. 1871–72; pub. Lemoine, dep. 1872; coll. G, no. 16.

147. "Prière du soir" (2); words Eugène Manuel; comp. 1873; pub. Choudens, dep. 1873; coll. D, no. 19.

148. "Prière pour l'Empereur et la famille impériale"; words Mme Baëlen; comp. 1869; pub. Lebeau.

149. "Primavera" (*chanson*); words Gautier; comp. between 1852 and 1858; pub. Choudens; coll. B, no. 16.

150. "Quand l'enfant prie"; words Georges Boyer; comp. 1884; pub. Lemoine, dep. 1884; coll. H, no. 13.

151. "Quanti mai"; words Metastasio; comp. 1871–72; pub. London and New York, Novello, Ewer, dep. 1872; coll. G, no. 10.

152. "Que ta volonté soit faite" (*prière:* prayer); words Gounod; pub. Lemoine; coll. G, no. 15.

153. "Queen of Love"; words Francis Turner Palgrave; comp. 1871; pub. London and New York, Novello, Ewer, dep. 1871.

154. "Repentir"; poet unknown; pub. in *Revue de Paris*, December 15, 1894; pub. Choudens, 1895.

155. "Réponse de Medjé"; words Marie Barbier; comp. 1882; pub. Choudens, dep. 1882; coll. H, no. 15, as "Tu m'aimes."

156. "Un rêve" (for chorus); words Spenner. 2d version for solo voice and piano pub. Lebeau, dep. 1867; coll. I, no. 5.

157. "Rêverie"; words Jules Barbier; comp. 1878; pub. Choudens; coll. C, no. 19.

158. "Ring Out, Wild Bells"; words Tennyson; pub. London, C. Kegan

Paul, 1880, in *Songs From the Published Writings of Alfred Tennyson* (*Poet Laureate*), *Set to Music by Various Composers*, ed. W. G. Cusius (Bibl. Nat. G 5345).

159. "Le Roi d'amour est mon pasteur"; words Paul Collin, English trans. Sir Hy. W. Baker as "The King of Love my Shepherd Is"; pub. Lebeau, 1892; pub. London, Philips and Page, 1884.

☐ "La rondinella": *see* "L'âme d'un ange"

160. "Le rosier blanc" (for 3-part chorus); words Spenner. 2d version for solo voice and piano in coll. I, no. 1.

161. "Roy's Wife of Aldivalloch"; poet unknown; comp. 1873; pub. Lemoine.

162. "Se come io son poeta": *see Biondina, poème musical*, no. 6.

163. "The Sea Hath Its Pearls" (with *ad lib.* acc. of harmonium and violin); words Longfellow; comp. 1871; pub. London, Duff and Stewart, 1871.

164. "Sérénade"; words Hugo; comp. 1855–57; pub. Lebeau *aîné*, December 1857; coll. A, no. 10.

165. "Seul"; words Lamartine from his "La pensée des morts"; coll. A, no. 2.

166. "Si la mort est le but" (*stances*); words Louise Bertin; comp. 1865–1866; pub. Choudens, 1866; coll. B, no. 6.

167. "Si vous n'ouvrez votre fenêtre" (*chanson*); words Dumas *fils*; comp. 1871–72; pub. Lemoine, 1872; coll. G, no. 8.

168. "Siam iti l'altro giorno": *see Biondina, poème musical*, no. 7.

169. "La siesta" (duo); Spanish poet unknown; comp. 1871; pub. London, Novello, Ewer, dep. 1871.

170. "Le soir"; words Lamartine; comp. 1840–42; coll. A, no. 20. Aut. ms. in Bibl. Nat. (no. M 3,375) for voice and piano with horn obbligato.

171. "Soir d'automne" (op. posth.); words Gounod; pub. Henri Tellier, © 1896; coll. J, no. 4.

172. "Solitude"; words Lamartine; comp. 1865; pub. Choudens, 1865; coll. B, no. 7.

173. "Sotto un cappello rosa": *see Biondina, poème musical*, no. 2.

174. "Sous le feuillage" (duo); words Jules Barbier; coll. E, no. 5.

175. "Le souvenir"; words Joseph Collin; comp. 1871; pub. Choudens, dep. 1871; coll. C, no. 6.

☐ "Stances": *see* "Si la mort est le but"

☐ "Stances à la mémoire de Livingstone": *see* "Ilala"

176. "Sur la montagne"; words Jules Barbier; comp. 1874; pub. Choudens, coll. C, no. 2.

177. "Sweet Baby, Sleep!" (lullaby); words George Wither (1641) from Sir Roundell Palmer's *Book of Praise*; pub. London, Novello, Ewer, dep. 1871.

178. "Le temps des roses"; words Camille Roy; comp. 1885; pub. Lemoine, dep. 1886; coll. H, no. 14.

179. "Le temps qui fuit"; poet unknown; pub. Lebeau, dep. 1867; coll. I, no. 3.

180. "There is a Green Hill Far Away" (sacred song); words Mrs. C. F. Alexander; pub. London, Novello, Ewer, dep. 1871.

181. "There is Dew"; words Thomas Hood; comp. 1871; pub. London, Chappell, dep. 1871.

182. "To God, Ye Choir Above"; words Philipp Skelton (1784); comp. 1872–73; pub. London, Goddard, dep. 1873; pub. H. Lemoine.

183. "Tombez, mes ailes" (*romance*); words Ernest Legouvé; comp. 1865; pub. Choudens, 1865, dep. 1866; coll. B, no. 8.

184. "Tout l'univers obéit à l'amour"; words La Fontaine; comp. 1893; Lemoine, dep. 1893.

185. "Le travail béni" (for chorus); words Édouard Plouvier; pub. Meissonnier, dep. 1856. 2d version for 2 equal voices pub. Choudens, dep. 1886.

□ "Tu m'aimes": *see* "Réponse de Medjé"

186. "Les vacances" (duo for 2 equal voices); words L. Bigorie; pub. Lebeau, dep. 1867; coll. I, no. 9 for one voice only.

187. "Le vallon"; words Lamartine; comp. 1840–42; pub. Choudens, dep. 1861; coll. A, no. 11; pub. London, 1867 with English trans. by L. H. F. Terreaux.

188. "Venez, douces compagnes"; poet unknown; unpub. youthful work; aut. ms. in Bibl. Nat. (no. 1781).

189. "Venise"; words Musset; aut. ms. in Bibl. Nat. (no. 1755) signed and dated June 1842; coll. A, no. 9. Pub. Brandus, dep. 1855, with 4-hand acc.

□ "Vergine d'Atene": *see* "Maid of Athens"

190. "Viens, les gazons sont verts" (*chanson*); words Jules Barbier; comp. 1875; pub. Lemoine, dep. 1875; coll. G, no. 7.

□ "Viens, mon cœur": *see* "My Beloved Spake"

□ "Vierge d'Athènes": *see* "Maid of Athens"

191. "Vincenette" (*chanson provençale*); words Pierre Barbier; pub. H. Lemoine, dep. 1887; coll. H, no. 17.

192. "Vive la France" (*chant patriotique*); words Paul Déroulède; comp. 1877; pub. Lemoine.

193. "Voguons sur les flots" (*barcarolle*); poet unknown; pub. Lemoine, 1884.

194. "Voix d'Alsace-Lorraine"; words R. Rousseil; comp. 1885; pub. Lemoine, dep. 1885.

195. "Woe's Me! Woe's Me!"; words Campbell; pub. Chappell, 1871.

196. "The Worker"; words Frederick Weatherley, French trans. Charles Ligny as "L'ouvrier"; comp. 1873; pub. London, Goddard, dep. 1873; coll. G, no. 14, with French words only. Orchestrated.

COLLECTIONS

A. *Vingt mélodies pour chant et piano, 1ᵉʳ recueil*; pub. Choudens, 1867. Contains nos. 15, 22, 40, 44, 48, 120, 126, 140, 141, 164, 165, 170, 187, 189.

B. *Vingt mélodies pour chant et piano, 2ᵐᵉ recueil*; pub. Choudens, 1869. Contains nos. 6, 7, 20, 21, 32, 38, 41, 51, 59, 60, 68, 91, 119, 138, 149, 166, 172, 183.

C. *Vingt mélodies pour chant et piano, 3ᵐᵉ recueil*; pub. Choudens, 1872. Contains nos. 5, 10, 13, 33, 45, 50, 55, 95, 97, 118, 130, 132, 142, 157, 175, 176.

D. *Vingt mélodies pour chant et piano, 4ᵐᵉ recueil*; pub. Choudens, 1877. Contains nos. 3, 25, 62, 123, 125, 147.

E. *Quinze duos pour chant et piano, 5ᵉ recueil* (for 2 voices and piano); pub. Choudens, 1880 (?). Contains nos. 51, 133, 174.

F. *6 Cantiques avec accompagnement de piano ou d'orgue*; pub. Choudens, 1870. Contains nos. 17, 52, 55, 61, 123, 125.

G. *Vingt mélodies pour chant et piano*; pub. Henry Lemoine, 1877. Contains nos. 2, 26, 57, 78, 87, 145, 146, 151, 152, 167, 190, 196.

H. *Vingt mélodies pour chant et piano, 2ᵉ recueil*; pub. Lemoine et fils, 1890. Contains nos. 1, 11, 29, 31, 42, 43, 56, 63, 64, 69, 74, 112, 113, 135, 143, 150, 155, 178, 191.

I. *Quinze mélodies enfantines avec accompagnement de piano*; pub. Lebeau (later Choudens), 1878. Contains nos. 16, 18, 34, 67, 99, 122, 136, 144, 156, 160, 179, 186.

J. *Six mélodies*; pub. Heugel, © 1894. Contains nos. 24, 65, 120, 124, 141, 171.

Victor Massé [1822–1884]

SEPARATE SONGS

1. "À une femme" (*cantilène*); words Hugo; pub. Choudens, dep. 1869; coll. A, no. 1.

2. "Addio"; words Edmond Cottinet; pub. E. St. Hilaire, dep. 1850.

3. "Adieux à la France" (*see Chants d'autrefois*, no. 12); words Mary Stuart; pub. Mayaud, dep. 1850.

4. "Adieux à la vie"; words Gilbert; coll. B, no. 12.

5. "Adieux à Suzon"; words Musset; coll. B, no. 2.

6. "L'alcyon"; not found.

7. "L'âme du purgatoire"; words Casimir Delavigne; coll. B, no. 6.

8. "Amour et souffrance"; words Émile Barateau; pub. Bernard-Latte, dep. 1845.

9. "Attente"; words Gautier; pub. E. St. Hilaire, dep. 1861.

10. "Au bord de la mer"; words Gautier; coll. B, no. 11.

11. "L'aubespin" (*see Chants d'autrefois*, no. 6); words Ronsard; pub. Mayaud, dep. 1849.

12. "Aurore"; words Henri IV; pub. E. St. Hilaire, dep. 1860; coll. A, no. 13, as "La chanson du roi Henri."

13. "L'avenir de la France"; words Édouard Plouvier; pub. J. Meissonnier *et fils*.

14. "L'avenir d'un berceau" (*see Chants du soir*, later edition, no. 6); words E. Lecygne; pub. Léon Grus, dep. 1864.

15. "Aveux d'une fleur" (*see Chants du soir*, later edition, no. 11); poet unknown; pub. Léon Grus.

16. "Avril" (*see Chants d'autrefois*, no. 4); words Rémy Belleau; pub. E. Mayaud, dep. 1849.

17. "Le baiser donné" (*villanelle*); words Jean-François Regnard; pub. E. St. Hilaire, dep. 1860; coll. A, no. 5.

18. "Barcarolle"; words Gautier; pub. E. St. Hilaire, dep. 1851; coll. A, no. 16.

19. "La barque"; words Marceline Desbordes; coll. A, no. 4.

20. "Le Bengali"; words Alfred de Beauchesne; aut. ms. in Bibl. Nat. (no. W 24,188) signed and dated April 15, 1856.

21. "Berceuse"; words Marquis de Pastoret; coll. B, no. 20.

22. "Bergerie"; words Dufresny; pub. E. St. Hilaire, dep. 1860; coll. A, no. 9.

23. "Boire à l'ombre"; words Émile Augier; coll. B, no. 4.

24. "Cantique d'Athalie"; words Racine; pub. Léon Grus, dep. 1873; coll. C, no. 4.

25. "Cantique d'Esther" (for 2 female voices); words Racine; pub. Léon Grus, dep. 1873; coll. C, no. 20.

26. "Chanson de Barberine"; words Musset; coll. B, no. 10.

27. "Chanson de la gerbe" (*see Chants bretons*, no. 4); words "folk poetry."

28. "Chanson de l'alouette"; words paraphrased from Ronsard; coll. C, no. 16.

29. "La chanson de la Loïc" (*see Chants bretons*, no. 6); words Brizeux.

30. "La chanson de la reine" (*see Chants du soir*, later edition, no. 5); poet unknown; pub. Léon Grus (*see Pazdirek*).

31. "La chanson de Marie" (*see Chants bretons*, no. 8); words Brizeux.

32. "Chanson de mer"; words Sully-Prudhomme; pub. Jules Raux, dep. 1898.

33. "La chanson des lavandières" (*duettino* for soprano and mezzo-soprano); words Hugo; pub. E. St. Hilaire, dep. 1861; coll. A, no. 20.

34. "La chanson du printemps" (*see Chants bretons*, no. 2); words "folk poetry."

☐ "La chanson du roi Henri": *see* "Aurore"

35. "La chanson du vanneur de blé" (*see Chants d'autrefois*, no. 3); words Du Bellay; pub. Mayaud, dep. 1849.

36. "Chant des Caïdjis" (*orientale* for tenor and bass); words Émile d'Abancourt; pub. Flaxland, dep. 1864; coll. A, no. 19.

37. "Chante Madeleine" (*romance*); words Victor Doinet; pub. Bernard-Latte, dep. 1864; coll. B, no. 15.

☐ *Chants bretons*; pub. Cendrier, dep. 1853. Contents: (1) "Ivanoïc" (2) "La chanson du printemps" (3) "Les goëlans" (4) "Chanson de la gerbe" (5) "Le sonneur de Cornouaille" (6) "La chanson de la Loïc" (7) "La chaumière" (8) "La chanson de Marie."

☐ *Chants d'autrefois*; pub. Mayaud, dep. 1849–50. Contents: (1) "Mignonne" (2) "Félicité passée" (3) "Chanson du vanneur de blé" (4) "Avril" (5) "Icare" (6) "L'aubespin" (7) "Une fontaine" (8) "Épicurienne" (9) "Robin Gray" (10) "Consolation" (11) "Souvenirs" (12) "Adieux à la France."

☐ *Chants du soir*; first pub. separately 1850–54; the songs may never have appeared under the collective title before their publication in coll. D. Contents: (1) "Ninon" (2) "Mandoline" (3) "L'émir de Bengador" (4) "La fileuse de Manchester" (5) "Suzanne" (6) "Croyons au bonheur" (7) "Loetice" (8) "Les desseins de Dieu" (9) "La fée aux aiguilles" (10) "La peur dans les bois." In a later edition of coll. D the songs of *Chant du soir* became: (1) "Croyons au bonheur" (2) "Les desseins de Dieu" (3) "Mandoline" (4) "Loetice" (5) "La chanson de la reine" (6) "L'avenir d'un berceau" (7) "Thérésine" (8) "Ninon" (9) "La fileuse de Manchester" (10) "Suzanne" (11) "Aveux d'une fleur" (12) "Nanette" (13) "Le pêcheur de Sorrente" (14) "La fée aux aiguilles" (15) "Sara la baigneuse."

38. "Le chasseur" (for bass voice); words Gautier; comp. before 1861; pub. E. St. Hilaire; not found.

39. "La chaumière" (*see Chants bretons*, no. 7); words Brizeux.

40. "Consolation" (*see Chants d'autrefois*, no. 10); words Malherbe; pub. Mayaud.

41. "La couronne des élus"; pub. Bernard-Latte; not found.

42. "Croyons au bonheur" (*see Chants du soir*, no. 6; later edition, no. 1); words Michel Carré; pub. Bureau central de musique (ann. in 1850).

43. "Le crucifix"; words Lamartine; pub. Léon Grus, dep. 1873; coll. C, no. 7.

44. "Dans les bois"; words Nerval; coll. B, no. 5.

45. "Les desseins de Dieu" (*see Chants du soir*, no. 8; later edition, no. 2); words Jules Lorin; pub. Bureau central de musique, dep. 1850.

46. "Dieu qui sourit et qui donne"; words Hugo; coll. B, no. 1.

47. "Le doux printemps"; words Armand Silvestre; pub. Th. Michaélis, dep. 1878.

48. "Ého!"; words "folk poetry"; coll. B, no. 7.

49. "L'émir de Bengador" (*chanson indienne; see Chants du soir*, no. 3) words Méry; pub. Alexandre Grus, dep. 1854.

50. "Engagez qui vous plaira" (*romance*); words Delavigne; pub. Th. Michaélis, dep. 1878.

51. "Épicurienne" (*see Chants d'autrefois*, no. 8); words Ronsard; pub. Mayaud, dep. 1849.

52. "L'étoile" (*rêverie*); words Musset; pub. Léon Grus, dep. 1873; coll. C, no. 3.

53. "La fauvette de Calvaire"; words Hégésippe Moreau; pub. Th. Michaélis, dep. 1877.

54. "La fée aux aiguilles" (*chansonnette; see Chants du soir*, no. 9; later edition, no. 14); words Hippolyte Guérin.

55. "Félicité passée" (*see Chants d'autrefois*, no. 2); words Jean Bertaut; pub. Mayaud, dep. 1849.

56. "La feuille du chêne" (*ballade*); words Millevoye; pub. Bernard-Latte, dep. 1845; coll. B, no. 18.

57. "La fileuse de Manchester" (*ballade; see Chants du soir*, no. 4; later edition, no. 9); words trans. from English by D. Tagliafico; pub. Bureau central de musique, dep. 1850.

58. "Fleur de bruyère" (*villanelle* with piano and harmonium or organ); words Auguste Barbier; pub. E. St. Hilaire, dep. 1861; coll. A, no. 3.

59. "Une fontaine" (*see Chants d'autrefois*, no. 7); words Phillippe Desportes; pub. Mayaud, dep. 1849.

60. "Le garde-française" (*bluette*); words Eugène de Lonlay; pub. by the journal *La mode* in *Album 1850 Eugène Lonlay*, dep. 1849.

61. "Les goëlans" (*see Chants bretons*, no. 3); words Brizeux.

62. "Les hirondelles" (*rondeau*); words Florian; pub. Léon Grus, dep. 1873.

63. "L'homme au sable" (*berceuse*); words Alfred Bosquet; pub. Léon Grus, dep. 1876; coll. C, no. 15.

64. "Icare" (*sonnet; see Chants d'autrefois*, no. 5); words Philippe Desportes; pub. Mayaud, 1859.

65. "Ivanoïc" (*see Chants bretons*, no. 1); words Brizeux.

66. "Je t'aimerai"; words "folk poetry"; pub. Léon Grus; dep. 1876; coll. C, no. 12.

67. "Je veux oublier"; words Émile Augier; pub. Léon Grus, dep. 1873; coll. C, no. 8.

68. "La jeune captive"; words André Chénier; coll. B, no. 13.

69. "Lisette"; words A. Bouffier; pub. anon. (PN E.C. et Cie 2989), dep. 1863.

70. "Loetice" (*see Chants du soir*, no. 7; later edition, no. 4); words Jules Barbier; pub. Bureau central de musique, 1850.

71. "Mai"; words Joséphin Soulary; pub. Léon Grus, dep. 1876; coll. C, no. 13.

72. "Mandoline" (*sérénade; see Chants du soir*, no. 2; later edition, no. 3); words Jules Barbier; pub. Bureau central de musique, 1850.

73. "Le matin" (*tableau rustique du XVIIe siècle*: 17th-century rustic picture); words Théophile de Viau; pub. E. St. Hilaire, dep. 1860; coll. A, no. 7.

74. "La messagère" (*canzonetta*); words Auguste Barbier; pub. E. St. Hilaire, dep. 1861; coll. A, no. 17.

75. "La meunière du châtelain"; words Francis Tourte; pub. Heugel, dep. 1849.

76. "Mignonne" (*see Chants d'autrefois*, no. 1); words Ronsard; pub. Mayaud, dep. 1849.

77. "Le muletier de Calabre"; words Joseph Vimeux; pub. Bernard-Latte, dep. 1844; coll. B, no. 17.

78. "Nanette" (*see Chants du soir*, later edition, no. 12); poet unknown; pub. Bureau central de musique; pub. Léon Grus (*see* Pazdirek).

79. "Ninon" (*sérénade; see Chants du soir*, no. 1; later edition, no. 8); words Musset; pub. Bureau central de musique (ann. in 1850).

80. "Noël"; words Gautier; pub. Léon Grus, dep. 1873; coll. C, no. 9.

81. "L'oiseau bleu" (*conte de fée*: fairy tale); words Édouard Laboulaye; coll. B. no. 8.

82. "Paradis terrestre"; words Eugène de Lonlay; pub. Gambogi *frères* in *Album des contemporains à la mémoire de A. Goria*, no. 9, dep. 1861.

83. "Partenza" (*canzona*); words Malherbe; pub. E. St. Hilaire; pub. Léon Grus, dep. 1873; coll. C, no. 6.

84. "Le pêcheur de Sorrente" (*see Chants du soir*, later edition, no. 13); poet unknown; pub. Léon Grus (*see* Pazdirek).

85. "La peur dans les bois" (*duettino* for soprano and mezzo-soprano; *see Chants du soir*, no. 10); words Édouard Plouvier; pub. Alexandre Grus, dep. 1854.

86. "Pietro le lazzarone"; pub. Bureau central de musique (ann. in 1850); not found.

87. "La plainte du pêcheur"; words Brizeux; pub. E. St. Hilaire, dep. 1860; coll. A, no. 14.

88. "Pourquoi ne m'aimez-vous"; words Mathurin Régnier; pub. E. St. Hilaire, dep. 1860; coll. A, no. 8.

89. "Premier sourire du printemps"; words Gautier; coll. B, no. 3.

90. "Prenez, bergers, vos musettes" (duet or chorus for female voices); words Molière; pub. Léon Grus, dep. 1876; coll. C, no. 20.

91. "Prière de l'enfant à son réveil"; words Lamartine; pub. Léon Grus, dep. 1873; coll. C, no. 2.

92. "Le printemps" (*valse chantée*); words Philippe Gille; pub. Léon Grus, dep. 1873; coll. C, no. 10.

93. "Que le jour me dure"; words Jean-Jacques Rousseau; pub. Léon Grus, dep. 1873; coll. C, no. 1.

94. "Ramez, dormez, aimez"; words Hugo; pub. Meissonnier (Compagnie musicale), dep. 1860; coll. B, no. 13.
95. "Regrets"; words Quinault; pub. E. St. Hilaire, dep. 1860; coll. A, no. 10.
96. "Le réveil"; words Eugène de Lonlay; pub. Alex. Grus, dep. 1854.
97. "Rêverie"; words Philippe Gille; coll. A, no. 2.
98. "Riche et pauvre" (*romance*); words Francis Tourte; pub. Alphonse Leduc, dep. 1849.
99. "Robin Gray" (*see Chants d'autrefois*, no. 9); words Florian; pub. Mayaud, dep. 1849.
100. "Rozette" (*villanelle*); words Philippe Desportes; pub. E. St. Hilaire, dep. 1860; coll. A, no. 12.
101. "Sara la baigneuse" (*orientale; see Chants du soir*, later edition, no. 15); words Hugo; pub. Léon Grus, dep. 1864.
102. "Si vous voulez que j'aime encore" (*romance*); poet unknown; pub. Jules Raux, dep. 1894.
103. "Le sonneur de Cornouaille" (*see Chants bretons*, no. 5); words Michel Carré.
104. "Sous bois" (duet for mezzo-soprano and baritone); words Philippe Gille; pub. Léon Grus, dep. 1877; coll. C, no. 19.
105. "Souvenirs" (*see Chants d'autrefois*, no. 11); words Boileau; pub. Mayaud, dep. 1850.
106. "Soyez bénie"; words Jules Barbier; pub. Léon Grus, dep. 1876; coll. C, no. 11.
107. "Strophe de Psyché"; words Corneille; pub. Léon Grus, dep. 1877; coll. C, no. 14.
108. "Suzanne" (*chanson; see Chants du soir*, no. 5; later edition, no. 10); words Arsène Houssaye; pub. Bureau central de musique (ann. in 1850).
109. "Taiaut" (*chasse*: hunting song, for bass voice); words Eugène de Lonlay; pub. Bernard-Latte, dep. 1845.
110. "Te voir" (*romance*); words Eugène de Lonlay; pub. Bernard-Latte, dep. 1844.
111. "Le temps fait passer l'amour"; words Lambert Thiboust; coll. B, no. 9.
112. "Thérésine" (*see Chants du soir*, later edition, no. 7); poet unknown; pub. Léon Grus (*see Pazdirek*).
113. "Toujours"; words Sully-Prudhomme; pub. Léon Grus, dep. 1875; coll. C, no. 15.
114. "Toujours toi, toujours moi"; words Émile Barateau; coll. B, no. 16.
115. "Tristesse d'Olympio" (*méditation*); words Hugo; pub. E. St. Hilaire, dep. 1860; coll. A, no. 6.
116. "Le truand"; pub. Bernard-Latte; not found.

117. "Vivre et mourir là" (*chanson vénitienne* for 2 voices); words Musset; pub. Léon Grus, dep. 1873; coll. C, no. 18.

118. "Voix de la nuit"; poet unknown; pub. Bernard-Latte, dep. 1845; coll. B, no. 19.

119. "Voyage"; words Alfred Busquet; pub. E. St. Hilaire, dep. 1861; coll. A, no. 15.

COLLECTIONS

A. *Vingt mélodies pour chant et piano*; pub. Choudens, dep. 1869. Contains nos. 1, 12, 17–19, 22, 33, 36, 58, 73, 74, 87, 88, 95, 97, 100, 115, 119.

B. *Vingt mélodies, deuxième recueil*; pub. E. Gérard et Cie, dep. 1874. Consists of two groups of songs entitled *Mélodies nouvelles* and *Premières mélodies*, comprising nos. 4, 5, 7, 10, 21, 23, 26, 37, 44, 46, 48, 56, 68, 77, 81, 89, 94, 111, 114, 118.

C. *Vingt et un morceaux de chant*; pub. Léon Grus, ca. 1878. Contains nos. 24, 25, 28, 43, 52, 63, 66, 67, 71, 80, 83, 90–93, 104, 106, 107, 113, 117.

D. *Premières mélodies*; pub. Léon Grus, dep. 1881. Consists of three cycles, the contents of which are listed above under *Chants d'autrefois*, *Chants bretons*, and *Chants du soir*.

Ernest Reyer [1823–1909]

SEPARATE SONGS

1. "À un berceau"; words Pierre Dupont; pub. at Reyer's expense (PN E.R. N° 1) and sold by Mayaud, dep. 1853; coll. B, no. 9.

2. "Adieu Suzon"; words Musset; pub. L. Mayaud et Cie; coll. B, no. 17.

3. "Aux étoiles" (*rêverie*); words Vte Alexis de Valon; coll. B, no. 13.

4. "Berthe de Normande"; words Vte Eugène de Richemont; pub. A. Meissonnier-Heugel, dep. 1849.

5. "Chanson indienne" (*pantoum*); words Méry; pub. Alfred Ikelemer, dep. 1858; coll. A, no. 9.

6. "Le chant des sirènes" (*sonnet; see Trois sonnets de Camille du Locle*, no. 2); pub. Heugel, © 1897.

7. "La charité"; words N. P. Doubeveyer; pub. without publisher's name (PN E.C. 755).

8. "Le comte Belfégor" (*chanson espagnole*); words Dumas; pub. E. Minnier.

9. "Le dernier rendez-vous" (*sonnet; see Trois sonnets de Camille du Locle*, no. 1); pub. Heugel, © 1896.

10. "Fleur des nuits"; words Vte E. de Richemont; pub. Gérard, dep. 1861; coll. B, no. 12.

11. "Le fleuve d'oubli" (*sonnet; see Trois sonnets de Camille du Locle*, no. 3); pub. Heugel, © 1899.

12. "Les gouttes de pluie"; words paraphrased from the German by Alfred Bosquet; pub. Alfred Ikelemer, dep. 1858; coll. A, no. 8.

13. "Hiamina" (*romance imitée d'une légende arabe*); words Désirée Léglise; pub. Mayaud, dep. 1849.

14. "L'homme" (*scène lyrique*); words Georges Boyer; pub. Choudens, © 1892.

15. "Hylas" (*sonnet*); words Camille du Locle; pub. Choudens, dep. 1873; coll. B, no. 1.

16. "La jeune fille d'Inspruck"; words Pierre Dupont; pub. Houssiaux in *Collection des chants et chansons de Pierre Dupont*, dep. 1852.

17. "La Madeleine au désert" (*scène* for baritone or contralto); words Édouard Blau; pub. Choudens, dep. 1874; coll. B, no. 7. Aut. ms. of orchestration in Bibl. Nat. (Rés. Vm^a ms. 515).

☐ "Pantoum": *see* "Chanson indienne"

18. "Petite étoile" (*rêverie*); words A. de Chancel; pub. Mayaud, dep. 1849.

19. "La pluie"; words Méry; pub. Alfred Ikelemer, dep. 1858. Also known as "Prière."

20. "Pourquoi ne m'aimez-vous" (*vieille chanson*); words Mathurin Régnier; pub. Choudens, dep. 1869; coll. B, no. 2.

☐ "Prière": *see* "La pluie"

21. "Rédemption"; words Louis Bouilhet; pub. at Reyer's expense (PN E.R. N° 1) and sold by L. Mayaud, dep. 1853; coll. B, no. 4. Aut. ms. of orchestration in Bibl. Nat. (Rés. Vm^a ms. 512).

22. "Le retour" (*madrigal*); words Camille du Locle; coll. A, no. 5.

23. "Le Rhin allemand"; words Musset; pub. L. Mayaud et Cie.

24. "Salvadorita"; words Dumas *fils*; pub. without publisher's name or PN.

25. "Sérénade"; poet unknown; pub. Choudens, dep. 1889; coll. B, no. 3.

26. "Sommeil"; words paraphrased from the German by Alfred Bosquet; pub. Alfred Ikelemer, dep. 1858; coll. A, no. 1.

27. "Le sorcier du Rhin" (*ballade*); words paraphrased from Goethe by Eugène de Richemont; pub. Bernard-Latte.

28. "Sous les tilleuls"; words Pierre Dupont; pub. Alfred Ikelemer, dep. 1858; coll. A, no. 2.

29. "Tanko le fondeur"; words Vte Eugène de Richemont; pub. Mayaud, dep. 1850.

☐ *Trois sonnets de Camille du Locle*; pub. Heugel, © 1896–99. Contents: (1) "Le dernier rendez-vous" (2) "Le chant des sirènes" (3) "Le fleuve d'oubli."

☐ "Vieille chanson": *see* "Pourquoi ne m'aimez-vous"

30. "Vieille chanson du jeune temps"; words Hugo; pub. Maison Meissonnier *fils* (Compagnie musicale), dep. 1860; coll. B, no. 16.

31. "Voguons!"; words Méry; pub. Alfred Ikelemer, dep. 1858; coll. A, no. 10.

COLLECTIONS

A. *Dix mélodies pour chant et piano*; pub. Choudens. Contains nos. 5, 12, 22, 26, 28, 31.

B. *Vingt mélodies pour chant et piano*; pub. Choudens *fils*, 1889. Contains nos. 1–3, 10, 15, 17, 20, 21, 25, 30.

Georges Bizet [1838–1875]

The excellent catalogue of Bizet's works by Winton Dean (*Georges Bizet, his Life and Works*, London, 1965, Appendix B) has been used for additional information on dates of composition, location of mss., and the composer's reuse of his own material.

SEPARATE SONGS

1. "À une fleur" (*see Feuilles d'album*, no. 1); words Musset. (Dean, no. 70)
2. "L'abandonné"; comp. 1868 (?); words Catulle Mendès; coll. B, no. 16; possibly an operatic excerpt. (Dean, no. 102)
3. "Absence"; words Gautier; pub. Choudens, dep. 1872; coll. A, no. 13. (Dean, no. 85)
4. "Adieux à Suzon" (*see Feuilles d'album*, no. 2); words Musset. (Dean, no. 71)
5. "Adieux de l'hôtesse arabe"; words Hugo; comp. 1866; pub. Choudens, 1867, dep. 1866; coll. A, no. 4. (Dean, no. 66)
6. "Aimons, rêvons"; words Paul Ferrier; comp. 1868 (?); coll. B, no. 9; possibly a dramatic excerpt, later used in the duet "Rêvons." (Dean, no. 96)
7. "L'âme humaine"; words Lamartine; aut. ms. in Bibl. Nat. (a youthful unpub. work). (Dean, no. 62)
8. "Après l'hiver"; words Hugo; comp. 1866; pub. Choudens, 1866, dep. 1867; coll. A, no. 15. (Dean, no. 67)
9. "Aubade"; words Paul Ferrier; coll. B, no. 5; possibly a dramatic excerpt. (Dean, no. 93)
10. "Barcarolle"(duo for 2 sopranos, without words); aut. (?) ms. in Bibl. Nat. (ms. 422), the 2d of a set of unpub. works. The ms. says: "I was 11 years and 4 months old." (not in Dean)
11. "Berceuse sur un vieil air"; words Marceline Desbordes-Valmore; comp. 1868; aut. ms. in Bibl. Nat.; pub. G. Hartmann, dep. 1868; coll. A, no. 11. (Dean, no. 79)
12. "Chanson d'avril"; words Louis Bouilhet; comp. 1866 (?); pub. Choudens, 1867; coll. A, no. 1. (Dean, no. 69)
13. "La chanson de la rose"; words Jules Barbier; coll. B, no. 10. (Dean, no. 97)

14. "La chanson du fou"; words Hugo; comp. 1868; aut. ms. in Bibl. Nat.; pub. G. Hartmann, dep. 1868; coll. A, no. 12. (Dean, no. 80)

15. "Chant d'amour"; words Lamartine; pub. Choudens, dep. 1872; coll. A, no. 17. (Dean, no. 86)

16. "La coccinelle"; words Hugo; comp. 1868; aut. ms. in Bibl. Nat.; pub. G. Hartmann, dep. 1868; coll. A, no. 16. (Dean, no. 81)

17. "Le colibri"; words Alexandre Glan; comp. after 1867; aut. ms. in Bibl. Nat. (ms. 463). (Dean, no. 89)

18. "Conte"; words Paul Ferrier; coll. B, no. 8; possibly a dramatic excerpt. (Dean, no. 95)

19. "Douce mer" (*barcarolle*); words Lamartine; comp. 1866; pub. Choudens, dep. 1867; coll. A, no. 14. (Dean, no. 68)

20. "Le doute"; words Paul Ferrier; coll. B, no. 7; dramatic fragment used in the symphony *Roma* (comp. 1860–68). (Dean, no. 83)

☐ "En avril": *see* "Petite Marguerite"

21. "L'esprit saint" (*hymne*); poet unknown; aut. ms. in Bibl. Nat.; pub. G. Hartmann, dep. 1869; coll. A, no. 19. (Dean, no. 84)

☐ *Feuilles d'album*, 6 *mélodies*; comp. 1866; pub. Heugel, 1866, dep. 1867. Contents: (1) "À une fleur" (2) "Adieux à Suzon" (3) "Sonnet" (4) "Guitare" (5) "Rose d'amour" (6) "Le grillon."

22. "La foi, l'espérance, et la charité" (*chant religieux*); words Rousseau de Lagrave; comp. ca. 1857; pub. unknown (no PN); Bibl. Nat. copy (A.c.m. 2227) marked "Musique de Mr Georges Bizet, 1er prix du Conservatoire, élève de Mr Halévy." (not in Dean)

23. "La fuite" (duo); words Gautier; aut. ms. in Washington, D.C., Library of Congress; pub. Choudens, dep. 1872. (Dean, no. 130)

24. "Le Gascon" (*chanson*); words Catulle Mendès; comp. 1868 (?); coll. B, no. 12; possibly an operatic excerpt. (Dean, no. 98)

25. "Le grillon" (*see Feuilles d'album*, no. 6); words Lamartine. (Dean, no. 75)

26. "Guitare" (*see Feuilles d'album*, no. 4); words Hugo. (Dean, no. 73)

27. "Ma vie a son secret" (*sonnet*); words Félix Arvers; aut. ms. in Bibl. Nat.; pub. G. Hartmann, dep. 1868; coll. A, no. 8. (Dean, no. 78)

28. "N'oublions pas!"; words Jules Barbier; comp. 1868; coll. B, no. 13; possibly an operatic excerpt. (Dean, no. 99)

29. "La nuit"; words Paul Ferrier; coll. B, no. 6; an operatic excerpt later used in "Les nymphes des bois." (Dean, no. 94)

30. "Les nymphes des bois" (*duettino*); words Jules Barbier; comp. 1868; pub. Choudens, dep. 1887. (Dean, no. 127)

31. "Oh! quand je dors" (*sérénade*); words Hugo; aut. ms. in Bibl. Nat. (Dean, no. 90)

32. "Pastel"; words Philippe Gille; coll. B, no. 15. (Dean, no. 101)

33. "Pastorale"; words Jean-François Regnard; comp. 1868; pub. G. Hartmann, dep. 1868; coll. A, no. 9. (Dean, no. 76)

34. "Petite Marguerite" (*romance*); words Olivier Rolland; pub. Mme. Cendrier, dep. 1854; pub. Choudens with new words by Armand Silvestre as "En avril," dep. 1888. (Dean, no. 63)
35. "Le retour" (duo for soprano and tenor); words Jules Barbier; pub. Choudens, dep. 1887; possibly a dramatic excerpt, used earlier in "Voyage." (Dean, no. 125)
36. "Rêve de la bien-aimée"; words Louis de Courmont; comp. 1868; pub. G. Hartmann, dep. 1868; coll. A, no. 5. (Dean, no. 77)
37. "Rêvons" (duo for mezzo-soprano and baritone); words Jules Barbier; comp. 1868 (?); pub. Choudens, dep. 1887. (Dean, no. 126)
☐ "Rive d'amour"; *see* "La rose et l'abeille"
38. "Rose d'amour" (*see Feuilles d'album*, no. 5); words Millevoye. (Dean, no. 74)
39. "La rose et l'abeille" (*romance*); words Olivier Rolland; comp. 1854 (?); pub. Mme. Cendrier, dep. 1854; pub. Choudens with new words by Armand Silvestre as "Rive d'amour," dep. 1888. (Dean, no. 64)
☐ "Sérénade": *see* "Oh! quand je dors"
40. "Si vous aimez!"; words Philippe Gille; coll. B, no. 14; possibly a dramatic excerpt. (Dean, no. 100)
41. "La sirène"; words Catulle Mendès; comp. 1868; coll. B, no. 1; operatic fragment. (Dean, no. 82)
42. "Sonnet" (*see Feuilles d'album*, no. 3); words Ronsard. (Dean, no. 72)
43. "Tarantelle"; words Édouard Pailleron; aut. ms. in Bibl. Nat.; pub. Choudens, 1872; coll. A, no. 20. (Dean, no. 87)
44. "Vieille chanson"; words Millevoye; comp. 1865; "dated aut. survives" (Dean); pub. Choudens, dep. 1865; coll. A, no. 3. (Dean, no. 65)
45. "Vocalise" (for tenor); aut. (?) ms. in Bibl. Nat. (ms. 422) explains that it "may be transposed to B-flat for soprano, to G for contralto or baritone, and to F for bass"; the 1st of a set of unpub. works, marked "I was 11 years and 4 months old." (not in Dean)
46. "Vœu"; words Hugo; aut. ms. in Bibl. Nat. (ms. 464). (Dean, no. 91)
47. "Vous ne priez pas"; words Casimir Delavigne; aut. ms. in Bibl. Nat.; pub. Choudens, 1880; coll. A, no. 7. (Dean, no. 88)
48. "Voyage"; words Philippe Gille; coll. B, no. 4; possibly a dramatic excerpt later used in "Le retour." (Dean, no. 92)

COLLECTIONS

A. *Vingt mélodies pour chant et piano*; pub. Choudens *père et fils*, 1873. Contains nos. 3, 5, 8, 11, 12, 14–16, 19, 21, 27, 33, 36, 43, 44, 47.
B. *Seize mélodies*; pub. Choudens, 1886, dep. 1885. Contains nos. 2, 6, 9, 13, 18, 20, 24, 28, 29, 32, 40, 41, 48.

Léo Delibes [1836–1891]

SEPARATE SONGS

The *chansonnettes* are omitted.

1. "À ma mignonne"; words J. Renaut; pub. Heugel, dep. 1890; coll. B, no. 6.
2. "Arioso"; words Armand Silvestre; pub. G. Hartmann; coll. A, no. 15; coll. C, no. 15. Orchestrated.
3. "Avril"; words Rémy Belleau; pub. G. Hartmann; coll. A, no. 4; coll. C, no. 4; musical material borrowed from a short *a cappella* choral work dating from 1866.
4. "Blanche et rose"; words Armand Silvestre; pub. G. Hartmann; coll. A, no. 12; coll. C, no. 12.
5. "Bonjour Suzon" (*see Trois mélodies*, no. 1); words Musset; aut. ms. in Bibl. Nat. (W 8.21) dated September 15, 1861; coll. A, no. 10; coll. C, no. 7.
6. "Chanson de Barberine"; words Musset; original version for voice and harp comp. 1882; pub. Heugel, dep. 1882; coll. B, no. 2.
7. "Chanson de l'oiseleur" (*pastorale*); words Lockroy; pub. G. Hartmann; coll. A, no. 8; coll. C, no. 9.
8. "Chanson espagnole" (*boléro; see Trois mélodies*, no. 3); words Musset; coll. A, no. 6; coll. C, no. 6.
9. "Chanson hongroise"; words François Coppée, after Petőfi; pub. Heugel, dep. 1880; coll. B, no. 4.
10. "Chant de l'almée"; words Philippe Gille; pub. G. Hartmann; coll. A, no. 11; coll. C, no. 11.
11. "Chrysanthème"; words Paul Fuchs; pub. Heugel, dep. 1889; coll. B, no. 3.
12. "Départ" (*scène*); words Émile Augier; pub. Hartmann; coll. A, no. 5; coll. C, no. 5.
13. "Églogue" (*see Trois mélodies*, no. 2); words Hugo; coll. A, no. 1; coll. C, no. 1.
14. "Épithalame"; words Édouard Grenier; pub. Heugel, dep. 1888; coll. B, no. 9.
15. "Faut-il chanter?"; words Vte de Borrelli; pub. Heugel, dep. 1891; coll. B, no. 8.
☐ "Les filles de Cadix": *see* "Chanson espagnole"
16. "Heure du soir"; words Armand Silvestre; pub. G. Hartmann; coll. A, no. 7; coll. C, no. 8.
17. "Le marchand d'oublies" (*chanson* for 2 voices); words Auguste Parmentier; pub. Colombier, dep. 1868.
18. "Le meilleur moment des amours"; words Sully-Prudhomme; aut. ms. in Bibl. Nat. (ms. 1738) dated [18]72; pub. G. Hartmann; coll. B, no. 7.

19. "Myrto"; words Armand Silvestre; facsimile of a signed page in Bibl. Nat. (ms. 1743); anon. ed. in Bibl. Nat. (A 7818); pub. G. Hartmann; coll. A, no. 2; coll. C, no. 3.

☐ "Pastorale": *see* "Chanson de l'oiseleur"

20. "Peine d'amour"; words Armand Silvestre; pub. G. Hartmann; coll. A, no. 14; coll. C, no. 14.

21. "Que l'heure est donc brève"; words Armand Silvestre; pub. G. Hartmann; coll. A, no. 2; coll. C, no. 2.

22. "Regrets" (paraphrase of a theme from the ballet *La source*); words Armand Silvestre; pub. G. Hartmann; coll. A, no. 9; coll. C, no. 10.

23. "Le rossignol" (*ariette*); words "old poem"; pub. G. Hartmann; coll. A, no. 2; coll. C, no. 2.

24. "Sérénade à Ninon"; words Musset; pub. Heugel, dep. 1879; coll. B, no. 1 (Delibes' arr. of the original version for voice and mandolin or harp).

25. "Sérénade de Ruy Blas"; words Hugo; pub. Heugel, dep. 1879; coll. B, no. 5 (Delibes' arr. of the original version for voice, humming chorus, and orchestra).

☐ *Trois mélodies*; pub. Colombier, dep. 1863. Contents: (1) "Bonjour Suzon" (2) "Églogue" (3) "Chanson espagnole."

26. "Les trois oiseaux" (duo for female voices); words François Coppée; pub. Heugel, © 1891; coll. B, no. 11.

27. "Vieille chanson" (for voice and mandolin); words Hugo; pub. Heugel, dep. 1883; coll. B, no. 10; sung in the 3d act of Hugo's drama *Le Roi s'amuse.*

COLLECTIONS

A. *1er recueil: Quinze mélodies et deux chœurs*; pub. G. Hartmann (later Heugel). Contains nos. 2–5, 7, 8, 10, 12, 13, 16, 19–23.

B. *2me recueil: 16 mélodies et un chœur*; pub. Heugel. Contains nos. 1, 6, 9, 11, 14, 15, 18, 24–27.

C. *Songs*; pub. New York, G. Schirmer, © 1886–87. The same songs as coll. A, arr. in slightly different order, and with words in French and English.

Jules Massenet [1842–1912]

The work by Octave Séré (*Musiciens français d'aujourd'hui*, 9th ed., Paris, 1921, pp. 292–297, 435) was used chiefly as an additional source of information on dates of composition.

SEPARATE SONGS

The listing includes a few *mélodies* in languages other than French.

1. "À Colombine" (*sérénade d'Arlequin*); words Louis Gallet; aut. ms. in Bibl. Nat. (ms. 4316) signed and dated February 17, 1872; pub. G. Hartmann, dep. 1872; coll. A, no. 2.

2. "À deux pleurer!"; words J. L. Croze; aut. ms. in Bibl. Nat. (ms. 4336) dated "Égreville, Sunday, August 20, 1897, 9:30 a.m."; pub. Heugel, © 1899; coll. E, no. 17.

☐ "À la trépassée": *see* "Lève-toi"

☐ "À la Zuecca": *see* "Souvenir de Venise"

3. "À Mignonne" (*see Chants intimes*, no. 2); undated aut. ms. in Bibl. Nat. (ms. 4323) with dedication "To my friend Georges Hartmann, publisher of young France!!"; coll. B, no. 18.

4. "Adieu" (*see Poème d'avril*, no. 8).

5. "Un adieu"; words Armand Silvestre; comp. between 1866 and 1872; pub. G. Hartmann, dep. 1882; coll. A, no. 14.

6. "Adieux à la prairie" (*see Poème pastoral*, no. 6).

☐ "Adieux de Gilbert": *see* "Stances"

7. "Ah! du moins, pour toi je veux être" (*see Poème d'hiver*, no. 5).

8. "L'air du soir emportait" (*see Poème souvenir*, no. 2).

9. "Les alcyons"; words J. Autran; comp. 1887; pub. G. Hartmann, dep. 1887; coll. B, no. 9.

10. "L'âme des fleurs"; words Paul Delair; comp. 1891; pub. A. Quinzard et Cie, dep. 1891.

11. "L'âme des oiseaux"; words Hélène Vacaresco; comp. 1895; pub. Heugel, dep. 1895; coll. D, no. 1.

12. "Les âmes"; words Paul Demouth; comp. 1898; pub. Heugel, © 1898; in coll. E, no. 9, with acc. of piano or harp.

13. "Âmes obscures"; words Anatole France; pub. Heugel, © 1912; coll. G, no. 18.

14. "L'amour pleure" (*romance de jadis*: romance of long ago); words Madeleine Postel; pub. Heugel, © 1912; coll. H, no. 4.

15. "Amoureuse"; words Morel-Retz; comp. 1898; pub. Heugel, © 1898; coll. E, no. 2.

16. "Les amoureuses sont des folles"; words Duke of Taranto; comp. 1902; pub. Heugel, © 1902; coll. F, no. 11.

17. "Amoureux appel"; words Georges de Dubor; comp. 1900; pub. Heugel, © 1900; coll. F, no. 19.

18. "Amours bénis"; words André Alexandre; comp. 1899; pub. Heugel, © 1899; coll. E, no. 15.

19. "L'ange et l'enfant" (from *Les contes blancs*); words Marie Barbier; comp. 1899; pub. Heugel, © 1899; coll. H, no. 12.

20. "Anniversaire"; words Armand Silvestre; comp. 1880; pub. Heugel; coll. B, no. 6.

21. "Antienne" (*see Poème d'un soir*, no. 1).

☐ "L'attente": *see* "Sur une poésie de Van Hasselt"

22. "Au delà du rêve"; words Gaston Hirsch; comp. 1903; pub. Heugel, © 1903; coll. H, no. 13.

23. "Au large" (duo for mezzo-soprano and baritone); words Louisa Sieffert; aut. ms. in Bibl. Nat. (ms. 4318) dated "Valse, May 7, 1871, Sunday morning."

24. "Au très aimé"; words after Caroline Duer; comp. 1900; pub. Heugel, © 1900; coll. G, no. 3.

25. "Aubade"; words Gabriel Prévost; comp. 1877; pub. G. Hartmann, dep. 1877; coll. B, no. 7.

26. "Aube païenne"; words Lucien Rocha; pub. Heugel, © 1914; coll. H, no. 1.

27. "Aurore" (see Poème pastoral, no. 3).

28. "Automne" (see Poème d'octobre, no. 1).

☐ "Aux étoiles": see "Les belles de nuit"

29. "Ave Margarita" (prière d'amour: love prayer); words Édouard Noël; comp. 1902; pub. Heugel, © 1902; coll. F, no. 12.

30. "Avec toi"; words Julien Gruaz; comp. 1902; pub. Heugel, © 1902; coll. F, no. 10.

31. "Avril est amoureux"; words Jacques d'Halmont; comp. 1900; pub. Heugel, © 1900; coll. G, no. 17. Orchestrated.

32. "Avril est là"; words François Ferrand; comp. 1899; pub. Heugel, © 1899; coll. E, no. 20.

33. "Ballade" (from the cantata David Rizzio, for which Massenet won the Prix de Rome); words Gustave Chouquet; comp. 1863; pub. Heugel, © 1899.

34. "Battements d'ailes" (with rhythmic declamation: see Expressions lyriques, no. 4); words Jeanne Dortzal.

35. "Beaux yeux que j'aime"; words Thérèse Maquet; comp. 1891; pub. Heugel, dep. 1891; coll. C, no. 15.

36. "Les belles de nuit"; words Thérèse Maquet; aut. ms. in Bibl. Nat. (ms. 4327) dated "Paris, September 2, 1887, 2 p.m."; pub. Heugel, dep. 1892; coll. C, no. 9. Arr. for 2 voices or female chorus as "Aux étoiles"; pub. Hartmann, dep. 1891.

37. "Belles frileuses" (see Poème d'octobre, no. 4); coll. B, no. 16, as "Roses d'octobre."

38. "Berceuse" (see Chants intimes, no. 3); aut. ms. in Bibl. Nat. (ms. 4310, 4310bis) marked "revised and simplified, Paris, April 17, 1870"; coll. C, no. 11.

39. "Berceuse"; words Henri Gibout; comp. 1896; pub. Heugel, © 1896, dep. 1897.

40. "Les bois de pins" (souvenir de Douarnez; see Trois mélodies . . ., no. 2).

41. "Bonne nuit" (see Trois mélodies . . ., no. 1).

☐ "Cantique": see "Sœur d'élection"

42. "Ce que disent les cloches"; words Jean de la Vingtrie; comp. 1900; pub. Heugel, © 1900; coll. F, no. 2.

43. "Ce sont les petits que je veux chanter"; words Édouard Grieumard; comp. 1899; pub. Heugel, © 1899; coll. E, no. 8.

44. "C'est au temps de la chrysanthème" (*see Poème d'hiver*, no. 1).

45. "C'est l'amour"; words Hugo; comp. 1908; pub. Heugel, © 1908; coll. G, no. 4.

46. "C'est le printemps"; words Adrien Gillouin; comp. 1906; pub. Heugel, dep. 1906.

47. "Chanson andalouse" (on a ballet air from the opera *Le cid*); words adapted by Jules Ruelle; arr. 1891; pub. Heugel, © 1891; coll. D, no. 4.

48. "Chanson de Capri" (after a fragment of the opera *Don César de Bazan*); words Louis Gallet; comp. 1872; pub. G. Hartmann; coll. A, no. 13.

49. "Chanson désespérée"; words Edmond Teulet; comp. 1905; pub. Heugel, © 1910; coll. G, no. 5.

50. "La chanson des lèvres"; words Jean Lahor; comp. 1897; pub. Heugel, © 1897; coll. H, no. 9.

51. "Chanson juanesque"; words Félicien Champsaur; comp. 1905; pub. Heugel, © 1905; coll. H, no. 14.

52. "Chanson pour elle"; words Henri Maigrot; comp. 1897; pub. Heugel, © 1897; coll. E, no. 18.

☐ *Chansons des bois d'Amaranthe* (suite for soprano, contralto, tenor, and baritone, with piano acc.); words Marc Legrand, after Redwitz; comp. 1900; pub. Heugel, © 1901. Contents: (1) "O bon printemps" (trio) (2) "Oiseau des bois" (duet) (3) "Chères fleurs" (quartet) (4) "O ruisseau" (trio) (5) "Chantez" (quartet).

53. "Chant de guerre cosaque"; words Hélène Vacaresco; comp. 1893; pub. Heugel, dep. 1893; coll. D, no. 10.

54. "Chant de nourrice" (for singing voice and recitation); words Jean Aicard; comp. 1905; pub. Heugel, © 1905.

55. "Chant provençal" ("Mireille"); words Michel Carré; aut. ms. in Bibl. Nat. (ms. 4263) dated "Fontainebleau, July 23, 1871, 10:30 a.m."; pub. G. Hartmann, dep. 1880; coll. A, no. 7.

56. "Chantez" (*see Chansons des bois d'Amaranthe*, no. 5).

☐ *Chants intimes*; words Gustave Chouquet; comp. 1869; pub. G. Hartmann, dep. 1869. Contents: (1) "Déclaration" (2) "À Mignonne" (3) "Berceuse."

57. "Chères fleurs" (*see Chansons des bois d'Amaranthe*, no. 3).

58. "Le coffret d'ébène"; words Victor Jannet; pub. Heugel, © 1914.

59. "Come into the Garden, Maud"; words Tennyson; pub. London, C. Kegan Paul and Co., 1880, in the collection *Songs from the Published Writings of Alfred Tennyson, Poet Laureate, Set to Music by Various Composers*, ed. W. G. Cusius (Bibl. Nat. G 5345).

60. "Comme autrefois" (with rhythmic declamation; see *Expressions lyriques*, no. 6); words Jeanne Dortzal.
61. "Coupe d'ivresse"; words H. Ernest Simoni; comp. 1899; pub. Heugel, © 1899; coll. E, no. 12.
62. "Crépuscule" (see *Poème pastoral*, no. 5); coll. A, no. 15.
63. "Dans l'air plein de fils de soie" (see *Poème du souvenir*, no. 4).
64. "Dans le sentier, parmi les roses"; words Jean Bertheroy; comp. 1891; pub. Heugel, dep. 1891; coll. C, no. 4.
65. "La danse des rameaux" (see *Poème des fleurs*, no. 3).
□ "David Rizzio": see "Ballade" from *David Rizzio*
66. "Déclaration" (see *Chants intimes*, no. 1); words Gustave Chouquet, after Shelley; untitled aut. ms. in Bibl. Nat. (ms. 4307) dated "Paris, June 1866," with text incipit "Je crains tes baisers"; coll. B, no. 15.
67. "Defuncta nascuntur" (see *Poème d'un soir*, no. 3).
68. "Départ"; words Guérin-Catelain; comp. 1893; aut. ms. in Chicago, Newberry Library (ms. VM 1621 M41de), dated "Paris, April 1894" and inscribed to Frederic Grant Gleason; pub. Heugel, © 1893; coll. D, no. 18. Orchestrated.
69. "La dernière chanson"; words Louis Lefèbvre; pub. Heugel, © 1897; coll. E, no. 10.
70. "La dernière lettre de Werther à Charlotte" (with rhythmic declamation; see *Expressions lyriques*, no. 5); words Comte R. de Gontaut Biron.
□ *Deux duos et un trio*, op. 2: see *Trois mélodies, deux duos, et un trio*
71. "Devant l'infini"; words Émile Trolliet; comp. ca. 1892; pub. Heugel; coll. D, no. 7.
72. "Dialogue" (with rhythmic declamation; see *Expressions lyriques*, no. 1); words Marc Varenne.
73. "Dialogue nocturne" (duo for soprano and tenor); words Armand Silvestre; aut. ms. in Bibl. Nat. (ms. 4320) dated "Fontainebleau, 1871"; pub. Hartmann, 1872.
74. "Dieu créa le désert"; words Madeleine Grain; comp. 1910; pub. Heugel, © 1910.
75. "Dites-lui que je l'aime"; words Georges Fleury-Daunizeau; comp. 1910; pub. Heugel, © 1910; coll. H, no. 5.
76. "Dormons parmi les lis"; words Hélène Picard; comp. 1908; pub. Heugel, © 1908.
77. "Dors, Magda"; words Armand Silvestre; comp. 1905; pub. Heugel, © 1905.
□ "Le doux printemps a bu": text incipit of "Vous aimerez demain" (see *Poème d'avril*, no. 5)
78. "Effusion"; words Henri Allorge; pub. Heugel, © 1912.
79. "Élégie"; words Louis Gallet; comp. between 1866 and 1872; pub. E. & A. Girod, dep. 1875; coll. A, no. 1.

☐ "Elle": *see* "Lui et elle"

80. "Elle s'en est allée"; words Lucien Solvay; comp. 1895; pub. Heugel, © 1895; coll. D, no. 15.

81. "En chantant"; words Georges Boyer; comp. 1906; pub. Heugel, © 1906.

82. "En même temps que ton amour" (*see Quelques chansons mauves*, no. 1).

83. "En voyage"(with rhythmic declamation: *see Expressions lyriques*, no. 3); words Th. Maurer.

84. "Enchantement" (based on a ballet air from the opera *Hérodiade*); words adapted by Jules Ruelle; arr. 1890; pub. G. Hartmann, dep. 1890; coll. C, no. 2.

85. "Les enfants"; words Georges Boyer; aut. ms. in Bibl. Nat. (ms. 4325) dated "Paris, June 22, 1881"; pub. G. Hartmann, dep. 1882; coll. C, no. 1. Aut. ms. of orchestration in Bibl. Nat. (ms. 4305) dated "Paris, Saturday morning, August 4, 1883."

86. "Épitaphe" (*see Poème du souvenir*, no. 6).

87. "L'esclave" (*see Quatre mélodies*, no. 1); words Gautier.

88. "Et puis . . ." (*rondel*); words Maurice Chassang; comp. 1905; pub. Heugel, © 1905; coll. H, no. 15.

89. "Éternité"; words Marg. Girard; comp. 1899; pub. Béziers, Jules Robert, dep. 1899.

90. "Être aimé"; words Hugo; comp. 1893; pub. Heugel, © 1893; coll. H, no. 16.

91. "Éveil"; words Alfred Gassier; comp. 1906; pub. Heugel, © 1906; coll. H, no. 20.

92. "L'éventail" (*vieille chanson française*); words Stop (pseudonym for Morel-Retz); pub. Heugel, © 1892; coll. D, no. 13.

☐ Expressions lyriques; pub. Heugel, © 1913. Contents: (1) "Dialogue" (2) "Les nuages" (3) "En voyage" (4) "Battements d'ailes" (5) "La dernière lettre de Werther à Charlotte" (6) "Comme autrefois" (7) "Nocturne" (8) "Mélancolie" (9) "Rose de mai" (10) "Feux-follets d'amour."

93. "Extase printanière"; words André Alexandre; comp. 1902; pub. Heugel, © 1902; coll. F, no. 6.

94. "Les extases"; words Annie Dessirier (Jean du Clos); pub. Heugel, © 1912; coll. H, no. 3.

95. "Les femmes de Magdala"; words Louis Gallet; pub. G. Hartmann, dep. 1887; coll. A, no. 3.

96. "Feux-follets d'amour" (with rhythmic declamation; *see Expressions lyriques*, no. 10); words Madeleine Grai.

97. "Fleuramye" (*see Poèmes d'un soir*, no. 2).

98. "Les fleurs" (duo for soprano and baritone); words Jacques Normand; comp. 1894; pub. Heugel, © 1894; coll. D, no. 20. Orchestrated.

99. "Fleurs cueillies"; words Louis Bricourt; comp. 1888; pub. Rouen, A. Klein et Cie, dep. 1888.

100. "Fourvières"; words Maurice Léna; comp. 1893; pub. Heugel, © 1896; coll. D, no. 12.

101. "La gavotte de Puyjoli"; words Édouard Noël; comp. 1909; coll. G, no. 10; version for 2 voices pub. Heugel, © 1909.

102. "Guitare"; words Hugo; comp. 1886; pub. G. Hartmann, dep. 1886; coll. C, no. 5.

☐ "L'heure d'amour": see "Nuit d'Espagne"

103. "L'heure douce"; words Ernest Chabroux; comp. 1907; pub. Heugel, © 1907.

104. "L'heure solitaire" (duo for female voices); words J. Ader; comp. 1908; pub. Heugel, © 1908.

105. "Heure vécue"; words Mme. M. Jacquet; pub. Heugel, © 1912; coll. G, no. 19.

106. "L'heure volée"; words Catulle Mendès; comp. 1902; pub. Heugel, © 1902; coll. F, no. 5.

107. "L'heureuse souffrance"; words from a "chanson de cour Henri IV" found and arr. by Georges de Dubor; comp. 1902; pub. Heugel, © 1902; coll. F, no. 7.

108. "Horace et Lydie" (duo); words Musset, after Horace; aut. ms. in Bibl. Nat. (ms. 4233) signed and dated "Tuesday morning, Paris, February 23, 1886"; pub. Heugel, dep. 1893; coll. D, no. 19.

109. "Hymne d'amour"; words Paul Desachy; aut. ms. in Bibl. Nat. (ms. 1208) is a revised copy dated March 20, 1895; pub. Heugel, © 1895; coll. D, no. 6.

110. "L'hymne des fleurs" (see Poème des fleurs, no. 2).

111. "Il pleuvait" (impromptu-mélodie); words Armand Silvestre; aut. ms. in Bibl. Nat. (ms. 4313) dated "Font[ainebleau], June 8, 1871— August 2"; pub. G. Hartmann, dep. 1882; coll. A, no. 12.

112. "Immortalité" (2-voice canon); poet unknown; comp. 1909; pub. in La revue musicale IX, October 15, 1909, supplement, pp. 9–10.

113. "L'improvisatore" (rimembranza del Trastevere); words G. Zaffira; aut. ms. in Bibl. Nat. (ms. 4308) dated "Rome, October 1864—Paris, January, 1870"; pub. G. Hartmann, dep. 1872; coll. A, no. 20.

114. "Ivre d'amour"; words after the poem by Grégoire Akhtamar; comp. 1906; pub. Heugel, © 1906; coll. H, no. 17.

115. "Jamais plus!"; words Olga de Sarmento; pub. Heugel, © 1912; coll. H, no. 7.

116. "Jamais un tel bonheur" (see Quelques chansons mauves, no. 3).

117. "Je cours après le bonheur"; words Maupassant; comp. ca. 1888; pub. Heugel, dep. 1892; coll. C, no. 10.

☐ "Je crains tes baisers": text incipit of "Déclaration"

118. "Je me suis plaint aux tourterelles" (see Poème d'amour, no. 1).

119. "Je m'en suis allé vers l'amour"; words Théodore Maurer; comp. 1902; pub. Heugel, © 1902; coll. F, no. 1.

120. "Je t'aime"; words Suzanne Bozzani; comp. 1893; pub. Heugel, © 1893; coll. D, no. 3. Orchestrated.

121. "Joie" (*duetto* for 2 sopranos; *see Trois mélodies* . . ., no. 5).

122. "Jour de noces"; words Stéphan Bordèse; aut. ms. in Bibl. Nat. (ms. 4326¹) dated May 19, 1886; pub. G. Hartmann, dep. 1886; coll. D, no. 17.

123. "Larmes maternelles"; words M. C. Delines, after Nekrassoff; comp. 1893; pub. Heugel, © 1893; coll. D, no. 16. Orchestrated.

124. "Le sais-tu"; words Stéphan Bordèse; comp. 1880; pub. G. Hartmann, dep. 1880; coll. B, no. 17.

125. "La légende du baiser" (*see Trois poémes chastes*, no. 3); words Jean de Villeurs.

126. "La lettre"; words Mme. Catulle Mendès; comp. 1907; pub. Heugel, © 1907; coll. G, no. 7.

127. "Lève-toi" (*see Poème du souvenir*, no. 1); pub. New York, G. Schirmer, © 1888, as "À la trépassée."

128. "Loin de moi ta lèvre qui ment"; words Jean Aicard; comp. ca. 1888; pub. Heugel, dep. 1901; coll. B, no. 4.

129. "Lui et elle" (for 2 voices); words Th. Maquet; comp. 1891; pub. G. Hartmann, dep. 1891. Contents: (1) "Lui" (2) "Elle."

130. "Ma petite mère a pleuré"; words Paul Gravollet; pub. Hamelle, 1902 in the coll. *La chanson des enfants*, no. 1; pub. Heugel, © 1903; coll. H, no. 19.

131. "Madrigal"; words Armand Silvestre; comp. 1866–72; pub. Hartmann, dep. 1882; coll. A, no. 19.

132. "Les mains"; words Noël Bazan; comp. 1899; pub. Heugel, ©1899; coll. E, no. 7.

133. "La marchande des rêves"; words Armand Silvestre; comp. 1905; pub. Heugel, © 1905; coll. G, no. 6.

134. "Marine" (*duettino; see Trois mélodies* . . ., no. 4).

135. "Marquise"; words Armand Silvestre; comp. 1888; pub. G. Hartmann, dep. 1888; coll. C, no. 8.

136. "Les marronniers" (*see Poème d'octobre*, no. 2).

137. "Matinée d'été" (trio for female voices; *see Trois mélodies* . . ., no. 6).

138. "Mélancolie" (with rhythmic declamation; *see Expressions lyriques*, no. 8); poet unknown.

139. "La mélodie des baisers"; words André Alexandre; pub. G. Astrue et Cᵗᵉ (Éditions de la Société musicale), © 1906, dep. 1907.

140. "Manteuse chérie"; words Ludana; pub. Heugel, © 1912; coll. G, no. 20.

141. "Les mères"; words Georges Boyer; aut. ms. in Bibl. Nat. (ms. 4334)

dated "Sunday, October 29, 1891, before dinner"; pub. A. Quinzard et Cie, dep. 1892. Aut. ms. of 2d version in Bibl. Nat. (ms. 4335) dated "Égreville, July 9, 1901."

142. "Mienne"; words Ernest Laroche; comp. 1894; pub. Heugel, © 1894.

☐ "Mireille": see "Chant provençal"

143. "Mon cœur est plein de toi" (see Poème d'hiver, no. 2).

144. "Mon page"; words Maurice de Théus; comp. 1900; pub. Heugel, © 1900; coll. F, no. 18.

145. "La mort de la cigale"; words Maurice Faure; comp. 1911; pub. Heugel, © 1911; coll. G, no. 1.

146. "Mousmé"; words André Alexandre; comp. 1901; pub. Heugel, © 1901; coll. F, no. 9.

147. "Musette" (see Poème pastoral, no. 2); words Florian; coll. C, no. 6.

148. "Ne donne pas ton cœur"; words Paul Mariéton; comp 1892; pub. Heugel, © 1892; coll. D, no. 8.

149. "La neige"; words Stéphan Bordèse; comp. 1891; pub. A. Durand, dep. 1891.

150. "Le nid"; words Paul Demouth; comp. 1898; pub. Heugel, © 1898; coll. E, no. 19.

151. "Nocturne" (with rhythmic declamation; see Expressions lyriques, no. 7); words Jeanne Dortzal.

152. "Noël" (see Poème d'hiver, no. 3).

153. "Noël des fleurs"; words Louis Schneider; pub. Heugel, © 1912; coll. H, no. 18.

154. "Noël des humbles"; words Jean Aicard; comp. 1908; pub. Heugel, © 1908; coll. G, no. 8.

155. "Noël païen"; words Armand Silvestre; comp. 1866–72; pub. G. Hartmann, dep. 1886; coll. C, no. 16.

156. "Non, tu n'as pas fini d'aimer"; words Mme. Blanchecotte; aut. ms. in Bibl. Nat. (ms. 4342) dated "Biarritz, April 15, 1871, 4 p.m., splendid weather!"; pub. G. Hartmann, dep. 1882, as "Sérénade d'automne"; also thus in coll. A, no. 18.

157. "Nouvelle chanson sur un vieil air"; words Hugo; aut. ms. in Bibl. Nat. (ms. 4321) dated "Venice, September 6, 1865—Paris, March 6, 1869."

158. "Les nuages" (with free declamation; see Expressions lyriques, no. 2); words Comtesse Maurice Roch de Louvencourt.

159. "La nuit"; words Hugo; pub. Heugel, © 1914; coll. H, no. 2.

160. "Nuit d'Espagne" (based on air de ballet from orchestral suite Scènes pittoresques); words Louis Gallet; comp. 1872; pub. G. Hartmann, dep. 1874 (original title: "L'heure d'amour"); coll. A, no. 6.

161. "La nuit sans doute était trop belle" (see Poème d'amour, no. 2); aut. ms. in Bibl. Nat. (ms. 4260) dated "Paris, 1st composition written at my

table piano, the 1st day, Thursday, November 14, 1878, rue Males-
herbes—cold—snow."

162. "O bon printemps" (*see Chansons des bois d'Amaranthe*, no. 1).

163. "O ruisseau" (*see Chansons des bois d'Amaranthe*, no. 4).

164. "Oh! ne finis jamais" (*see Poème d'amour*, no. 6); aut. ms. in Bibl. Nat.
(ms. 4260) dated "Monday morning, November 24, 1879, gloomy
weather."

165. "Oh! si les fleurs avaient des yeux" (extracted from the musical
comedy *Chérubin*); words adapted by Buchillot; comp. 1903; pub.
Heugel, © 1903; coll. G, no. 2.

166. "L'oiseau de paradis"; words Jules Princet; pub. Heugel, © 1913,
dep. 1914.

167. "Oiseau des bois" (*see Chansons des bois d'Amaranthe*, no. 2).

168. "Les oiselets"; words Jacques Normand; comp. 1877; aut. ms. in
Bibl. Nat. (ms. 4328); pub. G. Hartmann, dep. 1877; coll. B, no. 3.

169. "On dit"; words Jean Roux; comp. 1901; pub. Heugel, © 1901; coll.
F, no. 13.

170. "Orphelines"; words Ludana; comp. 1906; pub. Heugel, © 1906;
coll. G, no. 9.

171. "Où que s'envole"; words Paul Bourguignat; aut. ms. in Bibl. Nat.
(ms. 4326²) dated "Paris, October 1884."

172. "Ouvre tes yeux bleus" (*see Poème d'amour*, no. 3); aut. ms. in Bibl.
Nat. (ms. 4260) dated "Sunday, September 15, 1878, 5 p.m."; coll.
C, no. 12. Orchestrated.

173. "Pareils à des oiseaux" (*see Poème d'octobre*, no. 5).

174. "Parfums"; words Jeanne Dortzal; pub. Heugel, © 1914.

175. "Passionnément"; words Ch. Fuster; comp. 1899; pub. Heugel,
© 1899.

176. "Pastorale avec chœur" (*see Poème pastoral*, no. 1).

177. "Le pauv' petit" (*see Trois poèmes chastes*, no. 1); words Georges Boyer.

178. "Paysage" (*see Poème pastoral*, no. 4).

179. "Pensée d'automne"; words Armand Silvestre; comp. 1888; pub. G.
Hartmann, dep. 1888; coll. C, no. 17. Aut. ms. of version for voice and
orchestra (written especially for Sibyl Sanderson) in Bibl. Nat. (ms.
4303) dated "Paris, Saturday, November 24, 1888."

180. "Pensée de printemps"; words Armand Silvestre; comp. 1893; pub.
Heugel, © 1893; coll. D, no. 2. Orchestrated.

181. "Le petit Jésus" (*chanson pour bercer la misère humaine*: song to cradle
human misery); words Georges Boyer; comp. 1899; pub. Heugel,
© 1899; coll. E, no. 1. Orchestrated.

182. "Petite Mireille"; words Fernand Beissier; comp. 1899; pub. Heugel,
© 1899; coll. E, no. 5.

183. "Pitchounette" (*farandole* for voice); words Jacques Normand;
comp. 1897; pub. Heugel, © 1897; coll. E, no. 16. Orchestrated.

184. "Plus vite"; words Hélène Vacaresco; comp. 1892; aut. ms. in Bibl. Nat. (ms. 1344) annotated by the composer; pub. Heugel, © 1892; coll. D, no. 9.

☐ *Poème d'amour*; words Paul Robiquet; comp. 1878–79; pub. G. Hartmann, dep. 1880. Contents: (1) "Je me suis plaint aux tourterelles" (2) "La nuit sans doute était trop belle" (3) "Ouvre tes yeux bleus" (4) "Puisqu'elle a pris ma vie" (5) "Pourquoi pleures-tu?" (6) "Oh! ne finis jamais."

☐ *Poème d'avril*, op. 14; words Armand Silvestre; comp. 1866; pub. G. Hartmann, before 1873; pub. Mainz, Schott, with French and German words. Contents: (1) "Prélude" (piano alternating with declamation) (2) "Sonnet matinal" (3) "Voici que les grand lys" (4) "Riez-vous?" (declamation followed by piano solo) (5) "Vous aimerez demain" (text incipit: "Le doux printemps a bu") (6) "Que l'heure est donc brève" (7) "Sur la source elle se pencha" (8) "Adieu" (declamation with incipit "Nous nous sommes aimés" precedes song with incipit "Je pars").

☐ *Poème des fleurs* (suite for female voices with piano acc.); words Biagio Allievo, trans. Armand Gasqui; comp. 1907; pub. Heugel, © 1908. Contents: (1) "Prélude" (2) "L'hymne des fleurs" (3) "La danse des rameaux."

☐ *Poème d'hiver*; words Armand Silvestre; comp. 1882; pub. G. Hartmann, dep. 1882. Contents: Unnumbered piano prelude (1) "C'est au temps de la chrysanthème" (2) "Mon cœur est plein de toi" (3) "Noël" (4) "Tu l'as bien dit" (5) "Ah! du moins, pour toi je veux être."

☐ *Poème d'octobre*; words Paul Collin; comp. 1876; pub. G. Hartmann, dep. 1878. Contents: "Prélude" (1) "Automne" (2) "Les marronniers" (3) "Qu'importe que l'hiver" (4) "Belles frileuses" (5) "Pareils à des oiseaux."

☐ *Poème du souvenir*; words Armand Silvestre; comp. 1868; pub. G. Hartmann. Contents: (1) "Lève-toi" (2) "L'air du soir emportait" (3) "Un souffle de parfums s'élève" (4) "Dans l'air plein de fils de soie" (5) "Pour qu'à l'espérance" (6) "Épitaphe."

☐ *Poème d'un soir*; words Georges Vanor; comp. 1895; pub. Heugel, © 1895. Contents: (1) "Antienne" (2) "Fleuramye" (3) "Defuncta nascuntur."

☐ *Poème pastoral*; words Florian and Armand Silvestre; aut. ms. in Bibl. Nat. (ms. 4261) dated "Fontainebleau, June 1872"; pub. G. Hartmann. Contents: (1) "Pastorale avec chœur" (2) "Musette" (3) "Aurore" (4) "Paysage" (5) "Crépuscule" (6) "Adieux à la prairie." Orchestrated.

185. "Poésie de Mytis"; poet unknown; pub. in the journal *Musica*, © 1902; coll. F, no. 3.

☐ "Le poète est roi"; text incipit of "Royauté"; coll. C, no. 18

186. "Le poète et le fantôme"; poet unknown; comp. 1891; pub. Heugel, © 1891; coll. C, no. 14.
187. "Le portrait d'un enfant" (*see Quatre mélodies*, no. 4); words Ronsard.
188. "Pour Antoinette"; words Paul de Chabaleyret; aut. ms. in Bibl. Nat. (ms. 4331) dated "Égreville, August 23, 1899"; pub. Heugel, © 1899; coll. E, no. 6.
189. "Pour qu'à l'espérance" (*see Poème du souvenir*, no. 5).
190. "Pourquoi pleures-tu?" (*see Poème d'amour*, no. 5); aut. ms. in Bibl. Nat. (ms. 4260) dated "Sunday, 7:30 a.m., November 23, 1879, gloomy weather."
☐ "Prélude": *see Poème d'avril* and *Poème d'octobre*
191. "Prélude" (*see Poème des fleurs*, no. 1).
192. "Première danse"; words Jacques Normand; comp. 1899; pub. Heugel, © 1899; coll. E, no. 3. Orchestrated.
193. "Premier fils d'argent"; words Marie de Valendré; comp. 1987; pub. Heugel, © 1897; coll. E, no. 11.
☐ "Prière d'amour": *see* "Ave Margarita"
194. "Printemps dernier"; words Philippe Gille; aut. ms. in Bibl. Nat. (ms. 4329) dated "Thun, Switzerland, August 6, 1884, 5:30 a.m."; pub. G. Hartmann, dep. 1885; coll. C, no. 7.
195. "Le printemps visite la terre"; words Jeanne Chaffotte; comp. 1901; pub. Heugel, © 1901; coll. F, no. 14.
☐ "Profitons bien des jours d'automne": text incipit of "Automne" (*see Poème d'octobre*, no. 1)
196. "Puisqu'elle a pris ma vie" (*see Poème d'amour*, no. 4); aut. ms. in Bibl. Nat. (ms. 4260) dated "Sunday, November 16, 1879, noon"; coll. B, no. 19.
197. "Quand nous nous sommes vus" (*see Quelques chansons mauves*, no. 2).
198. "Quand on aime" (*sérénade*); words Eugène Manuel; aut. ms. in Bibl. Nat. (ms. 4311) dated April 23, 1887; pub. G. Hartmann, dep. 1888; coll. C, no. 19.
☐ *Quatre mélodies*, op. 12; comp. 1868; pub. E. & A. Girod, dep. 1868. Contents: (1) "L'esclave" (2) "Sérénade aux mariés" (3) "La vie d'une rose" (4) "Le portrait d'un enfant."
199. "Que l'heure est donc brève" (*see Poéme d'avril*, no. 6); coll. B, no. 11.
☐ *Quelques chansons mauves*; words André Lebey; comp. 1902; pub. Heugel, © 1902. Contents: (1) "En même temps que ton amour" (2) "Quand nous nous sommes vus" (3) "Jamais un tel bonheur."
200. "Qu'importe que l'hiver" (*see Poème d'octobre*, no. 3).
201. "Regard d'enfant"; words Léon G. Pélissier; comp. 1898; pub. Heugel, © 1898; coll. E, no. 4.
202. "Retour d'oiseau"; words Paul Stuart; pub. Heugel, © 1911.
203. "Rêverie sentimentale"; words Mathylde Peyre; comp. 1910; pub. Heugel, 1910.

204. "Rêvons, c'est l'heure" (for soprano and tenor); words Paul Verlaine; aut. ms. in Bibl. Nat. (ms. 4312) dated "Fontainebleau, July 26, 1871, 9 a.m."; pub. Hartmann, 1872.

205. "Rien ne passe"; words Lucien Monrousseau; comp. 1911; pub. Heugel, © 1911; coll. G, no. 12.

206. "Riez-vous?" (see Poème d'avril, no. 4).

207. "La rivière"; words Camille Bruno; comp. 1900; pub. Heugel, © 1900; coll. F, no. 20. Orchestrated.

208. "Rondel de la belle au bois"; words Julien Gruaz; comp. 1900; pub. Heugel, © 1900; coll. F, no. 5.

209. "Rose de mai" (with free declamation; see Expressions lyriques, no. 9); words S. Poirson.

☐ "Roses d'octobre" (see Poème d'octobre, no. 4, also called "Belles frileuses"); coll. B, no. 16

210. "Royauté"; words Georges Boyer; aut. ms. in Bibl. Nat. (ms. 4330) dated "Paris, September 1889"; pub. Hartmann; coll. C, no. 18 as "Le poète est roi."

211. "Sainte Thérèse prie"; words Pierre Sylvestre; comp. 1902; pub. Heugel, © 1902; coll. F, no. 4. Orchestrated.

212. "Salut, printemps" (duo for equal voices); words L. Baillet; comp. 1872; pub. G. Hartmann, dep. 1879.

213. "Le sentier perdu" (idylle); words Paul de Choudens; comp. 1877; pub. G. Hartmann, dep. 1877; coll. B, no. 8.

214. "Séparation"; words Paul Mariéton; aut. ms. in Bibl. Nat. (ms. 4332) dated "Étretat, Friday evening, September 24, 1886, Juliette better, I suffering, autumn weather"; pub. Heugel, © 1892; coll. D, no. 14.

215. "Septembre"; words Hélène Vacaresco; comp. 1891; pub. Heugel, ©1891; coll. C, no. 3.

216. "Sérénade"; words Eugène Manuel; aut. ms. dated March 1886 in possession of Julien Torchet in 1907 (cf. L. Schneider, Massenet, Paris, 1908, pp. 354–357).

217. "Sérénade aux mariés" (see Quatre mélodies, no. 2); words Jules Ruelle.

☐ "Sérénade d'automne": see "Non, tu n'as pas fini d'aimer"

218. "Sérénade de Zanetto"; words François Coppée; comp. 1869; undated aut. ms. in Bibl. Nat. (ms. 4316); pub. G. Hartmann, dep. 1869; coll. A, no. 9 as "Sérénade du passant." Orchestrated.

☐ "Sérénade du passant": see "Sérénade de Zanetto"

219. "Sévillana" (based on the interlude from the opera Don César de Bazan); words adapted by Jules Ruelle; arr. 1895; pub. Heugel, © 1895; coll. D, no. 11. Orchestrated.

220. "Si tu l'oses"; words Daniel Garcia Mansilla; comp. 1897; pub. Heugel, © 1897; coll. G, no. 14.

221. "Si tu m'aimes"; words Anne Girard Duverne; pub. Heugel, © 1912; coll. H, no. 11.

222. "Si tu veux, Mignonne"; words Georges Boyer; comp. 1876; pub. G. Hartmann, dep. 1876; coll. B, no. 1. Aut. ms. of orchestration in Bibl. Nat. (ms. 4239) dated "Paris, Monday, December 12, 1887."

223. "Si vous vouliez bien me le dire"; words Ludana; comp. 1907; pub. Heugel, © 1907; coll. G, no. 16.

224. "Sœur d'élection"; words Émile Trolliet; comp. 1900; pub. Heugel, © 1900; coll. F, no. 17. Arr. for small orchestra as "Cantique."

225. "Le soir" (duo for female voices); words L. Baillet; aut. ms. in Bibl. Nat. (ms. 4309) dated "Easter Monday, Tuesday morning, 1870"; pub. G. Hartmann, 1872.

226. "Soir de printemps" (*déclamatorium*); words Gabriel Martin; comp. 1894; pub. Heugel, © 1894.

227. "Soir de rêve"; words Antonin Lugnier; pub. Heugel, © 1914; coll. H, no. 8.

228. "Soleil couchant"; words Hugo; pub. Heugel, © 1912; coll. H, no. 6.

229. "Sonnet"; words Georges Pradel; comp. 1869; pub. Hartmann, dep. 1869; coll. B, no. 5.

230. "Sonnet matinal" (*see Poème d'avril*, no. 2); coll. C, no. 20.

231. "Sonnet païen"; words Armand Silvestre; comp. 1866–1878; pub. Hartmann; coll. A, no. 17.

232. "Un souffle de parfums s'élève" (*see Poème du souvenir*, no. 3).

233. "Souhait"; words Jacques Normand; comp. 1880; pub. G. Hartmann; dep. 1880; coll. B, no. 13.

234. "Sous les branches"; words Armand Silvestre; aut. ms. in Bibl. Nat. (ms. 4315) dated May 13, 1868; pub. C. Hartmann, dep. 1869; coll. A, no. 10.

235. "Souvenance"; words Paul Mariéton; comp. 1897; pub. Heugel, © 1897.

236. "Souvenir de Venise"; words Musset; comp. 1865; pub. G. Hartmann, dep. 1887; coll. A, no. 16. Arr. for 2 sopranos with title "À la Zuecca"; aut. ms. in Bibl. Nat. (ms. 4319) dated "Paris, February 24, 1872, morning."

237. "Stances" (also called "Adieux"); words Gilbert; comp. between 1866 and 1872; pub. G. Hartmann, dep. 1880; coll. A, no. 4.

238. "Sur la source elle se pencha" (*see Poéme d'avril*, no. 7).

239. "Sur une poésie de Van Hasselt" (*L'attente*); comp. 1902; pub. Heugel, © 1902; coll. F, no. 16.

240. "Le temps et l'amour" (duo for tenor and baritone); words Ludana; comp. 1907; pub. Heugel, © 1907.

241. "Tes cheveux"; words Camille Bruno; comp. 1905; pub. Heugel, © 1905.

242. "Ton souvenir"; words Emile Feillet; comp. 1909; pub. Heugel, © 1909.

243. "Toujours"; words Paul Max; comp. 1910; pub. Heugel, © 1910.
244. "Tout passé"; words Camille Bruno; comp. 1909; pub. Heugel, © 1909; coll. G, no. 13.
245. "Tristesse"; words P. Carrier; comp. 1894; pub. Heugel, © 1894.
☐ *Trois mélodies, deux duos & un trio*; words Camille Distel; comp. 1868; pub. Prosper Pégiel, dep. 1872; pub. Durand as op. 2, dep. 1880. Contents: (1) "Bonne nuit" (2) "Les bois de pins" (3) "Le verger" (4) "Marine" (5) "Joie" (6) "Matinée d'été."
☐ *Trois poèmes chastes*; comp. 1903; pub. Heugel, © 1903. Contents: (1) "Le pauv' petit" (2) "Vers Bethléem" (3) "La légende du baiser."
246. "Tu l'as bien dit" (*see Poème d'hiver*, no. 4).
247. "La veillée du petit Jésus"; words André Theuriet; comp. 1876; pub. G. Hartmann, dep. 1886; coll. B, no. 20.
248. "La verdadera vida" (*coplas*); Spanish words Guillot de Saix; pub. Heugal, © 1933.
249. "Le verger" (*ancienne chansonnette; see Trois mélodies . . .*, no. 3).
250. "Vers Bethléem" (*see Trois poèmes chastes*, no. 2); words Paul le Moyne; aut. ms. in Bibl. Nat. (ms. 4337) dated "Égreville, September 1903."
251. "La vie d'une rose" (*see Quatre mélodies*, no. 3); words Jules Ruelle.
252. "Vieilles lettres"; words Jacques Normand; comp. 1898; pub. Heugel, © 1898; coll. E, no. 13.
253. "Voici que les grands lys" (*see Poème d'avril*, no. 3).
254. "Voix de femmes"; words Pierre d'Amor; comp. 1901; pub. Heugel, © 1901; coll. F, no. 8.
255. "Voix suprême"; words Antoinette Lafaix-Gontié; pub. Heugel, © 1912; coll. H, no. 10.
256. "Vous aimerez demain" (*see Poème d'avril*, no. 5).
257. "Vous qui passez"; words Paul de Chabaleyret; comp. 1899; pub. Heugel, © 1899; coll. E, no. 14.
258. "Les yeux clos"; words G. Buchillot; comp. 1905; pub. Heugel, © 1905; coll. G, no. 15.

COLLECTIONS

A. *Vingt mélodies, 1er volume*; pub. Hartmann (later Heugel). Contains nos. 1, 5, 48, 55, 62, 79, 95, 111, 113, 131, 156, 160, 218, 231, 234, 236, 237.
B. *Vingt mélodies, 2e volume*; pub. Heugel. Contains nos. 3, 9, 20, 25, 37, 66, 124, 128, 168, 196, 199, 213, 222, 229, 233, 247.
C. *Vingt mélodies, 3e volume*; pub. Heugel. Contains nos. 35, 36, 38, 64, 84, 85, 102, 117, 135, 147, 155, 172, 179, 185, 186, 194, 198, 210, 215, 230.
D. *Vingt mélodies, 4e volume*; pub. Heugel. Contains nos. 11, 47, 53, 68, 71, 80, 92, 98, 100, 108, 109, 120, 122, 123, 148, 180, 184, 214, 219.
E. *Vingt mélodies, 5e volume*; pub. Heugel. Contains nos. 2, 12, 15, 18, 32, 43, 52, 61, 69, 132, 150, 181–183, 188, 192, 193, 201, 252, 257.

F. *Vingt mélodies, 6e volume*; pub. Heugel. Contains nos. 16, 17, 29, 30, 42, 93, 106, 107, 119, 144, 146, 169, 195, 207, 208, 211, 224, 239, 254.

G. *Vingt mélodies, 7e volume*; pub. Heugel. Contains nos. 13, 24, 31, 45, 49, 101, 105, 126, 133, 140, 145, 154, 165, 170, 205, 220, 223, 244, 258.

H. *Vingt mélodies, 8e volume;* pub. Heugel. Contains nos. 14, 19, 22, 26, 50, 51, 75, 88, 90, 91, 94, 114, 115, 130, 153, 159, 221, 227, 228, 255.

Camille Saint-Saëns [1835–1922]

In addition to the French *mélodies*, the list includes songs written to English, Italian, German, and Spanish words. Two additional sources of information have been used: *Catalogue général et thématique des œuvres de C. Saint-Saëns* (2d ed., Paris, Durand, 1908) and Octave Séré, *Musiciens français d'aujourd'hui* (9th ed., Paris, 1921).

SEPARATE SONGS

1. "À la lune"; poet unknown; aut. ms. in Bibl. Nat. (ms. 911^b) dated August 10, 1856.

2. "À quoi bon entendre les oiseaux des bois"; words Hugo; undated aut. ms. in Bibl. Nat. (ms. 906^d); pub. G. Hartmann, dep. 1868; coll. B, no. 3.

3. "À Saint-Blaise" (*see Cinq poèmes de Ronsard*, no. 3); aut. ms. in Bibl. Nat. (ms. 780) dated January 1921; pub. Durand, dep. 1921.

4. "Aimons-nous"; words Théodore de Banville; aut. ms. in Bibl. Nat. (ms. 2473) dated 1892; pub. Durand *et fils*, dep. 1892; coll. D, no. 1. Aut. ms. of orchestration in Bibl. Nat. (ms. 2474) dated 1919.

5. "Alla riva del Tebro" (*madrigale*); poet unknown; comp. ca. 1860; pub. G. Hartmann, dep. 1870. In 1898 Saint-Saëns made an arr. for voice and piano of the famous madrigal comp. to the same words by Palestrina; pub. Durand, 1899.

6. "L'amant malheureux" (*see Cinq poèmes de Ronsard*, no. 5); aut. ms. in Bibl. Nat. (ms. 780) dated January 1921; pub. Durand, dep. 1921.

7. "Âme triste" (*see La cendre rouge*, no. 2).

8. "Amoroso" (*see La cendre rouge*, no. 7).

9. "L'amour blessé" (*see Cinq poèmes de Ronsard*, no. 2); aut. ms. in Bibl. Nat. (ms. 744) dated January 1921; pub. Durand, dep. 1921.

10. "L'amour oyseau" (*see Cinq poèmes de Ronsard*, no. 1); aut. ms. in Bibl. Nat. (ms. 796) dated 1907; pub. Durand, dep. 1907; inserted in the cycle in 1921.

11. "Amour viril"; words Georges Boyer; comp. 1891; pub. Durand, dep. 1891.

12. "Angélus"; words Pierre Aguétant; pub. Durand, © 1918. Aut. ms. of orchestration in Bibl. Nat. (ms. 2475) dated 1918.

13. "Antwort"; words Ludwig Uhland; undated aut. ms. in Bibl. Nat. (ms. 910ᵇ).

14. "L'arbre"; words Jean Moréas; aut. ms. in Bibl. Nat. (ms. 905) dated February 1903; pub. Durand, © 1903.

15. "Ariel"; poet unknown; aut. ms. in Bibl. Nat. (ms. 754) dated October 7, 1841.

16. "L'attente"; words Hugo; comp. ca. 1855; pub. Richault, dep. 1856; coll. A, no. 7; coll. C, no. 6; coll. E, no. 8.

17. "Au cimetière" (see Mélodies persanes, no. 5); undated aut. mss. in Bibl. Nat. (mss. 799 and 925); pub. Durand, 1872, dep. 1896; coll. D, no. 4.

18. "Avril" (see Vieilles chansons, no. 2); words Rémy Belleau; comp. 1921; aut. ms. in Bibl. Nat. (ms. 808).

☐ "Barcarolle": see "Le soir descend sur la colline"

19. "Bergeronnette"; words F. Lombard; aut. ms. in Bibl. Nat. (ms. 529) dated February 1850.

20. "La brise" (see Mélodies persanes, no. 1); undated aut. ms. in Bibl. Nat. (ms. 797); pub. Durand, 1872, dep. 1898. Orchestrated 1870; aut. ms. in Bibl. Nat. (ms. 684).

21. "Canzonetta toscana"; Italian words by unknown poet; comp. ca. 1863; aut. ms. in Bibl. Nat. (ms. 912⁶); pub. G. Hartmann, dep. 1870.

☐ La cendre rouge; words Georges Docquois; pub. Durand, dep. 1915. Contents: (1) "Prélude" (2) "Âme triste" (3) "Douceur" (4) "Silence" (5) "Pâques" (6) "Jour de pluie" (7) "Amoroso" (8) "Mai" (9) "Petite main" (10) "Reviens."

☐ "Chanson": see "S'il est un charmant gazon"

22. "Chanson à boire du vieux temps"; words Nicolas Boileau; aut. ms. in Bibl. Nat. (ms. 798) dated September 1885; pub. Durand, dep. 1885; coll. D, no. 17.

23. "Chanson de Fortunio"; words Musset; undated aut. ms. in Bibl. Nat. (ms. 911ᵈ).

24. "Le chant de ceux qui s'en vont sur la mer"; words Hugo; pub. G. Hartmann, dep. 1860; coll. B, no. 6.

25. "La chasse du Burgrave" (scène for mezzo-soprano); poet unknown; aut. ms. in Bibl. Nat. (ms. 529); pub. Richault, dep. 1854.

26. "La cigale et la fourmi"; words La Fontaine; aut. ms. in Bibl. Nat. (ms. 911ᵉ); pub. Cologne, Arno Volk Verlag, 1958, in the collection The Solo Song Outside German Speaking Countries, ed. Frits R. Noske (Anthology of Music, Vol. XVI).

☐ Cinq pœmes de Ronsard. Contents: (1) "L'amour oyseau" (2) "L'amour blessé" (3) "À Saint-Blaise" (4) "Grasselette et Maigrelette" (5) "L'amant malheureux."

27. "Clair de lune"; words Catulle Mendès; comp. ca. 1865; coll. A, no. 15; coll. C, no. 27.

28. "La cloche"; words Hugo; comp. ca. 1855; pub. Richault, dep. 1856; coll. A, no. 12; coll. E, no. 4. Orchestration pub. Durand.
29. "Les cloches de la mer"; words Saint-Saëns; comp. 1900; pub. Durand, dep. 1900. Undated ms. of orchestration in Bibl. Nat. (ms. 2469).
30. "La coccinelle"; words Hugo; comp. 1868; pub. Durand, dep. 1896.
31. "Dans ce beau mois" (*cantique*); poet unknown; aut. ms. in Bibl. Nat. (ms. 888ª).
32. "Dans les coins bleus"; words Sainte-Beuve; aut. ms. in Bibl. Nat. (ms. 800) dated August 1880; pub. Durand, dep. 1884; coll. D, no. 6.
33. "Dans ton cœur"; words Jean Lahor (Henri Cazalis); aut. ms. in Bibl. Nat. (ms. 793) dated 1872; pub. Durand, dep. 1884.
34. "Danse macabre"; words Henri Cazalis; comp. 1873; pub. Enoch, dep. 1873. 2d version for voice and orchestra (1873) pub. 1874. 3d version as symphonic poem (1874) pub. 1875.
35. "El desdichado" (*boléro* for 2 equal voices); poet unknown; trans. from Spanish by Jules Barbier; aut. ms. in Bibl. Nat. (ms. 822) dated "London 1871"; pub. Durand, dep. 1884; coll. D, no. 20. Aut. ms. of orchestration in Bibl. Nat. (ms. 2477) dated August 1873.
☐ "Deseo de amor": *see* "Désir d'amour"
36. "Désir d'amour"; French translator unknown, from the Spanish "Deseo de amor" of Don Francesco Perpiñan; comp. 1901; pub. Durand, 1901. Copied ms. of orchestration (as "Romanza" for bass and orchestra) in Bibl. Nat. (ms. 2478); *see also* "Romanza."
37. "Désir de l'Orient"; words Saint-Saëns; aut. ms. in Bibl. Nat. (ms. 782) dated "London, May 12, 1871"; pub. Durand, dep. 1895; coll. D, no. 2; inserted in the 1-act comic opera *La princesse jaune*.
☐ *Deux mélodies*; words Hugo; pub. Flaxland, dep. 1864. Contents: (1) "Extase" (2) "Soirée en mer."
☐ *Deux mélodies*; aut. ms. in Bibl. Nat. (ms. 787) dated 1914; pub. Durand. Contents: (1) "Jour de pluie" (2) "Les sapins."
38. "Douceur" (*see La cendre rouge*, no. 3).
39. "L'écho de la harpe"; poet unknown; undated aut. ms. in Bibl. Nat. (ms. 911ᶠ).
40. "Elle" (*sonnet*); words Charles Lecocq; comp. 1901; pub. Durand, dep. 1901.
41. "L'enlèvement"; words Hugo; comp. 1865; aut. ms. in Bibl. Nat. (ms. 906ᵇ) dated January 4, 1865; pub. Richault, 1866; coll. A, no. 16; coll. E, no. 5. Aut. ms. of orchestration in Bibl. Nat. (ms. 2479); pub. Durand.
42. "L'étoile"; words Prince Haïdar Pacha; comp. 1907; aut. ms. in Bibl. Nat. (ms. 775); pub. Durand, © 1907.
43. "Étoile du matin"; words Camille Distel; comp. ca. 1860; pub. Durand, 1869, dep. 1880.

44. "Extase" (see Deux mélodies, 1864, no. 1); comp. ca. 1860; coll. A, no. 11; coll. E, no. 3. Undated aut. ms. of orchestration in Bibl. Nat. (ms. 2480).

45. "Les fées" (4-hand piano acc.); words Théodore de Banville; comp. 1892; 2 aut. mss. in Bibl. Nat. (mss. 790 and 2481²); pub. Durand, dep. 1892; coll. D, no. 18. Aut. ms. of orchestration in Bibl. Nat. (ms. 2481¹).

46. "La feuille de peuplier"; words Mme. Amable Tastu; comp. 1853; undated aut. ms. in Bibl. Nat. (ms. 791); pub. Richault, dep. 1854; coll. A, no. 2; coll. C, no. 2. Undated aut. ms. of orchestration in Bibl. Nat. (ms. 2482).

47. "La fiancée du timbalier" (ballade for voice and orchestra, op. 82); words Hugo; comp. 1887; undated aut. ms. in Bibl. Nat. (ms. 505); pub. Durand, 1882. Aut. ms. of arr. for voice and piano in Bibl. Nat. (ms. 807) dated September 1887; pub. Durand, dep. 1906.

48. "Fière beauté"; words A. Mahot; aut. ms. in Bibl. Nat. (ms. 2483) dated 1893; pub. Durand, dep. 1893. Aut. ms. of orchestration in Bibl. Nat. (ms. 2484) dated July 1909.

49. "Les fleurs" (ariette); words Vᵗᵉ de Collerville; aut. mss. in Bibl. Nat. (mss. 801¹ and 801²) dated 1892.

50. "Le fleuve"; words Georges Audigier; comp. 1906; undated aut. ms. sketch in Bibl. Nat. (ms. 774); pub. Durand, dep. 1906.

51. "Une flûte invisible" (with flute obbligato); words Hugo; comp. 1885; pub. Durand, dep. 1885. Set to the same text as "Viens."

52. "La Française" (chant héroïque de la grande guerre); words Miguel Zamacoïs; pub. Le petit Parisien, 1915.

53. "Le golfe de Baya"; words Lamartine; comp. ca. 1847; undated aut. ms. in Bibl. Nat. (ms. 907ᵉ).

54. "Grasselette et Maigrelette" (see Cinq poèmes de Ronsard, no. 4); aut. ms. in Bibl. Nat. (ms. 780) dated December 1920; pub. Durand, dep. 1921.

55. "Guitare"; words Hugo; aut. ms. in Bibl. Nat. (ms. 906ᵃ) dated April 15, 1851; pub. G. Hartmann, dep. 1870; coll. B, no. 5.

56. "Guitares et mandolines"; words Saint-Saëns; comp. 1890; copied ms. in Bibl. Nat. (ms. 779) dated 1890; pub. Durand, dep. 1890; coll. D, no. 8.

57. "Heures passées"; words A. Lenfaut; aut. ms. in Bibl. Nat. (ms. 912¹⁵) dated November 15, 1865.

58. "Heureux qui du cœur de Marie" (cantique for mezzo-soprano); poet unknown; comp. ca. 1860; pub. 1865 (by Richault?).

59. "Honneur à l'Amérique"; words Paul Fournier; comp. 1917; aut. ms. in Bibl. Nat. (ms. 783); pub. Durand, dep. 1917.

60. "Hymne à la paix" (for voice and orchestra); words J. L. Faure; comp. 1919; aut. ms. in Bibl. Nat. (ms. 709) dated December 1909

[sic]. Aut. ms. of sketch for voice and piano in Bibl. Nat. (ms. 778¹);
pub. Durand, © 1920.

61. "Idylle"; words Mme. Deshoulières; aut. ms. in Bibl. Nat. (ms. 529)
dated May 12, 1852; another aut. ms. in Bibl. Nat. (ms. 911ᶜ).

62. "Jour de pluie" (*see Deux mélodies*, 1914, no. 1, and *La cendre rouge*, no.
6); words Georges Docquois; aut. ms. in Bibl. Nat. (ms. 787) dated 1914.

63. "Là-bas"; words J.-L. Croze; comp. 1892; undated aut. ms. in Bibl.
Nat. (ms. 906ᵉ); pub. Durand, dep. 1892; coll. D, no. 10.

64. "Le lac"; words Lamartine; aut. ms. in Bibl. Nat. (ms. 529) dated
December 1850; pub. Richault, dep. 1856.

65. "Lamento"; words Gautier; aut. ms. in Bibl. Nat. (ms. 529) dated
February 1850.

66. "Le lever de la lune"; words after Ossian; comp. 1855; pub. Richault,
dep. 1865; coll. A, no. 6; coll. C, no. 5.

67. "Lever de soleil sur le Nil" (for contralto and orchestra); words
Saint-Saëns; aut. ms. in Bibl. Nat. (ms. 2485) dated March 1898. Arr.
for voice and piano pub. Durand, dep. 1898.

68. "La libellule" (*valse chantée*); words Saint-Saëns; copied ms. in Bibl.
Nat. (ms. 799) dated June 1894; pub. Durand, dep. 1894. Aut. ms. of
orchestration in Bibl. Nat. (ms. 2486) dated 1894.

69. "Madeleine"; words Alfred Tranchant; aut. ms. in Bibl. Nat. (ms.
773) dated February 9, 1892; pub. Durand, 1892, dep. 1893; coll. D,
no. 9.

70. "La Madonna col Bambino" (*cantico* for mezzo-soprano); words St.
Alfonso di Liguori; comp. ca. 1855; pub. Mme. Mayens-Couvreur,
1868.

71. "Mai" (*see La cendre rouge*, no. 8).

72. "La maman"; words Mme. A. Tastu; comp. ca. 1841; undated
copied ms. in Bibl. Nat. (ms. 2460²).

73. "Maria Lucrezia"; words Ernest Legouvé; comp. 1868; pub. G.
Hartmann, dep. 1870; pub. Choudens; coll. B, no. 7.

74. "Marquise, vous souvenez-vous?" (*menuet*); words François Coppée;
comp. ca. 1869; pub. Hartmann, 1870; pub. Choudens; pub. Berlin,
Fürstner as "Menuet"; coll. B, no. 2.

75. "Le matin"; words Hugo; comp. ca. 1864; undated aut. ms. in Bibl.
Nat. (ms. 906ᶜ); coll. A, no. 17; coll. C, no. 15.

☐ "Meditazione": *see* "Rêverie"

☐ "Mélancolie": *see* "La solitaire"

76. "Mélodie" (with orchestra); words Lamartine; comp. Vichy, 1852;
aut. ms. in Bibl. Nat. (ms. 907ᵉ).

☐ *Mélodies persanes*, op. 26; words Armand Renaud; comp. 1870; pub.
Durand, 1872, dep. 1896–98. Contents: (1) "La brise" (2) "La
splendeur vide" (3) "La solitaire" (4) "Sabre en main" (5) "Au
cimetière" (6) "Tournoiement."

☐ "Menuet": *see* "Marquise, vous souvenez-vous?"

77. "La mort d'Ophélie" (*ballade*); words E. Legouvé; comp. ca. 1857; aut. ms. of 1st sketch in Bibl. Nat. (ms. 756); pub. Richault, 1858; coll. A, no. 13; coll. C, no. 11.

78. "My Land"; words F. David; comp. 1871; pub. London, Boosey, 1871.

79. "Ne l'oubliez pas"; words Mme. Félix Regnault; undated aut. ms. in Bibl. Nat. (ms. 806); pub. Durand, © 1915.

80. "Night Song to Preciosa"; words Isaac Ginner; comp. 1879; pub. London, Boosey, 1879.

81. "Nocturne"; words Quinault; aut. ms. in Bibl. Nat. (ms. 771) dated October 2, 1900; pub. Durand, dep. 1900.

82. "Nous qu'en ces lieux" (*cantique*); poet unknown; comp. ca. 1844; undated aut. ms. sketch in Bibl. Nat. (ms. 888^d).

83. "Où nous avons aimé"; words Pierre Aguétant; pub. Durand, © 1918. Aut. ms. of orchestration in Bibl. Nat. (ms. 673) dated 1918.

84. "Pallas Athène" (for soprano and orchestra); words J.-L. Croze; aut. ms. in Bibl. Nat. (ms. 2457) dated September 1894; pub. Durand, 1894.

85. "Papillons"; words Renée de Leche; aut. ms. in Bibl. Nat. (ms. 747) dated 1918; pub. Durand, dep. 1918. Aut. ms. of orchestration in Bibl. Nat. (ms. 671) dated 1918.

86. "Pâques" (*see La cendre rouge*, no. 5).

87. "Le pas d'armes du roi Jean" (*ballade*); words Hugo; comp. 1852; undated aut. ms. in Bibl. Nat. (ms. 529); pub. Richault, 1855; coll. A, no. 9; coll. C, no. 4; coll. E, no. 7. Aut. ms. of orchestration in Bibl. Nat. (ms. 2459) dated March 1864.

88. "Pastorale" (*duettino*); words Destouches; comp. 1855; pub. Richault, dep. 1856; coll. A, no. 5; coll. C, no. 18; coll. E, no. 10.

89. "Petite main" (*see La cendre rouge*, no. 9).

90. "Peut-être"; words J.-L. Croze; aut. ms. in Bibl. Nat. (ms. 748) dated 1893; pub. Durand, 1894, dep. 1895.

91. "Plainte"; words Mme. Amable Tastu; comp. ca. 1855; pub. Richault, dep. 1856; coll. A, no. 4; coll. C, no. 4. Aut. ms. of orchestration in Bibl. Nat. (ms. 670) dated 1915.

92. "Le poète mourant"; words Lamartine; aut. ms. in Bibl. Nat. (ms. 529) dated April 1851; another aut. ms. in Bibl. Nat. (ms. 860).

93. "Pourquoi rester seulette?" (*bergerie Watteau*); J.-L. Croze; comp. 1894; pub. Durand, dep. 1895; coll. D, no. 16.

94. "Pourquoi t'exiler"; poet unknown; aut. ms. sketch in Bibl. Nat. (ms. 912^4) dated March 9/10, 1858.

95. "Prélude" (*see La cendre rouge*, no. 1).

96. "Présage de la croix"; words Stéphan Bordèse; comp. 1890; pub. Durand, dep. 1891.

97. "Primavera"; words Charles d'Orléans; undated aut. ms. in Bibl. Nat. (ms. 749¹). Set to the same text as "Temps nouveau."

98. "Primavera"; words Paul Stewart; copied ms. in Bibl. Nat. (ms. 779) dated January 1893; pub. Durand, dep. 1893; coll. D, no. 11.

99. "Reçois mes hommages" (*cantique*); poet unknown; comp. ca. 1844; undated aut. ms. in Bibl. Nat. (ms. 888ᵇ).

100. "Reine des cieux"; poet unknown; comp. ca. 1860; pub. 1865 (by Richault?).

101. "Le rendez-vous"; words E. Fiéffé; aut. ms. in Bibl. Nat. (ms. 529) dated February 25, 1851.

102. "Rêverie"; words Hugo; aut. ms. in Bibl. Nat. (ms. 903) dated October 1851; another aut. ms. in Bibl. Nat. (ms. 529); pub. Richault, dep. 1852; pub. Durand; coll. A, no. 1; coll. C, no. 1; coll. E, no. 1; also pub. Durand with Italian text as "Meditazione"; pub. Berlin, Fuerstner, with German text as "Meditazione." Orchestration pub. Durand.

103. "Reviens" (*épilogue; see La cendre rouge, no. 10*).

104. "Romance pour ——" (*voix dans la coulisse*: voice behind the scenes); words Bergerat; aut. ms. for voice and harp in Bibl. Nat. (ms. 803) dated December 1892.

☐ "Romanza" ("escribida para D. Luis Pipón Conti, Las Palmas, avril 1890"); words Don Francesco Perpiñan; aut. ms. in Bibl. Nat. (ms. 908); *see also* "Désir d'amour."

105. "Ronde"; words François Coppée; aut. ms. in Bibl. Nat. (ms. 820¹) dated November 11, 1885; proof corrected by Saint-Saëns in Bibl. Nat. (ms. 820²).

106. "Le rossignol"; words Théodore de Banville; aut. ms. in Bibl. Nat. (ms. 904) dated 1892; pub. Durand, dep. 1892; coll. D, no. 12.

107. "Ruhethal"; words Ludwig Uhland; aut. ms. in Bibl. Nat. (ms. 910ᵃ) dated June 7, 1854 (the text written in German script is added by another hand).

108. "Sabre en main" (*see Mélodies persanes, no. 4*); aut. ms. in Bibl. Nat. (ms. 804); pub. Durand, 1872, dep. 1898.

109. "Les sapins" (*see Deux mélodies, 1914, no. 2*); words Paul Martin; aut. ms. in Bibl. Nat. (ms. 787) dated 1914; pub. Durand, © 1914.

110. "Sérénade" (op. 15); words L. Mangeot, adapted to Saint-Saëns' 1st version for piano, organ, violin, and viola or violoncello, comp. 1866. Aut. ms. of 2d version, for voice and piano, in Bibl. Nat. (ms. 898); pub. Choudens, dep. 1866; coll. B, no. 1. Orchestration pub. Choudens.

111. "La sérénité"; words Marie Barbier; comp. 1893; pub. Durand, 1895, dep. 1896; coll. D, no. 7.

112. "Si je l'osais"; words Alfred Tranchant; aut. ms. in Bibl. Nat. (ms. 778²) dated 1898; pub. Durand, dep. 1898.

113. "Si vous n'avez rien à me dire"; words Hugo; comp. 1870; ms. partially aut. in Bibl. Nat. (ms. 788[8]); pub. Durand, dep. 1896.

114. "S'il est un charmant gazon"; words Hugo; undated aut. ms. of 1st version, with title "Chanson," in Bibl. Nat. (ms. 911[a]). Aut. ms. of 2d version in Bibl. Nat. (ms. 752) dated 1915; pub. Durand, dep. 1915.

115. "Silence" (see La cendre rouge, no. 4).

116. "Sœur Anne"; words André Pressat; aut. ms. in Bibl. Nat. (ms. 777) dated February 1903; pub. Durand, dep. 1903.

117. "Le soir" (romance); words Mme. Desbordes-Valmore; aut. ms. in Bibl. Nat. (ms. 907[a]) dated May 15, 1841; another aut. ms. in Bibl. Nat. (ms. 754) dated June 15, 1841; a copied ms. in Bibl. Nat. (ms. 2460[1]) has notation by Saint-Saëns: "Romance offered to Mlle. Granger by her student Camille Saint-Saëns, May 10, 1841, copied by my great-aunt Mme. Charlotte Maston (née Gayard)"; coll. C, no. 2.

118. "Le soir descend sur la colline" (barcarolle for 2 voices); poet unknown; comp. 1857; pub. Richault, 1858.

119. "Soir romantique"; words Comtesse de Noailles; copied ms. in Bibl. Nat. (ms. 779) dated 1907; pub. Durand, dep. 1907.

120. "Soirée en mer" (see Deux mélodies, 1864, no. 2); comp. 1862; coll. A, no. 10; coll. C, no. 8; coll. E, no. 2.

121. "La solitaire" (see Mélodies persanes, no. 3); aut. ms. with title "Mélancolie" in Bibl. Nat. (ms. 902); pub. Durand, 1872, dep. 1896; coll. D, no. 13. Orchestrated.

122. "Le sommeil des fleurs"; words G. de Penmarch; comp. 1855; pub. Richault, dep. 1856; coll. A, no. 3; coll. E, no. 6.

123. "Sonnet" (Souvenir de Las Palmas); words Sp. c. [i.e., Saint-Saëns]; copied ms. in Bibl. Nat. (ms. 779) dated March 1898; pub. Durand, dep. 1898.

124. "Souvenances"; words Ferdinand Lemaire; comp. ca. 1858; pub. Richault, dep. 1859; coll. A, no. 14.

125. "La splendeur vide" (see Mélodies persanes, no. 2); aut. ms. in Bibl. Nat. (ms. 810) dated 1870; pub. Durand, 1872, dep. 1898; coll. D, no. 14. Aut. ms. of orchestration in Bibl. Nat. (ms. 810) dated 1910.

126. "Suzette et Suzon"; words Hugo; comp. 1888; pub. Durand, dep. 1889; coll. D, no. 15.

127. "Tandis que sur vos ans"; poet unknown; aut. ms. in Bibl. Nat. (ms. 907[b]) dated June 1844.

128. "Télesille"; words Mme. Tastu; aut. ms. in Bibl. Nat. (ms. 529) dated May 1849.

129. "Temps nouveau" (see Vieilles chansons, no. 1); words Charles d'Orléans; aut. ms. in Bibl. Nat. (ms. 749bis) dated 1921. Set to the same text as "Primavera."

130. "Thème varié"; words Saint-Saëns; comp. 1900; pub. Durand, dep. 1900.

131. "Toi" (*romance*); words Édouard St. Chaffray; pub. Richault, dep. 1856.

132. "Tournoiement" (*songe d'opium*: opium dream; *see Mélodies persanes*, no. 6); aut. ms. in Bibl. Nat. (ms. 804³); pub. Durand, 1872, dep. 1898.

133. "Tristesse" (*sonnet*); words F. Lemaire; comp. ca. 1868; pub. Richault, dep. 1877; coll. A, no. 19.

134. "Les vendanges" (*hymne populaire* for unison voices and orchestra); words S. Sicard; comp. 1898; aut. ms. in Bibl. Nat. (ms. 668). Version for voice and piano pub. Durand, dep. 1898.

135. "Le vent dans la plaine"; words Verlaine; aut. ms. in Bibl. Nat. (ms. 753) dated December 1912; pub. Durand, © 1913.

136. "Vénus" (duo for tenor and baritone); words Saint-Saëns; aut. ms. in Bibl. Nat. (ms. 792) dated February 1896; pub. Durand, dep. 1896.

137. "Victoire"; words Paul Fournier; comp. 1918; aut. ms. in Bibl. Nat. (ms. 786); pub. Durand, © 1918.

☐ *Vieilles chansons*; comp. 1921; pub. Durand, © 1921. Contents: (1) "Temps nouveau" (2) "Avril" (3) "Villanelle."

138. "Viens" (*duettino*); words Hugo; comp. ca. 1855; pub. Richault, dep. 1856; coll. A, no. 8; coll. E, no. 9. Set to the same text as "Une flûte invisible."

139. "Villanelle" (*see Vieilles chansons*, no. 3); words Vauquelin de la Fresnaye; aut. ms. in Bibl. Nat. (ms. 809) dated 1921.

140. "Violons dans le soir" (with violin obbligato); words Comtesse de Noailles; aut. ms. in Bibl. Nat. (ms. 795) dated 1907; fragment of another aut. ms. in Bibl. Nat. (ms. 924); pub. Durand, dep. 1907.

141. "Vive la France"; words Paul Fournier; comp. 1914; aut. ms. in Bibl. Nat. (ms. 785) dated November 1914; pub. Durand, © 1915.

142. "Vive Paris, vive la France" (unison song); words Alfred Tranchant; comp. 1893; pub. Margueritat, dep. 1894.

143. "Vogue, vogue la galère" (*barcarolle* for voice and piano with harmonium ad lib.); words Jean Aicard; comp. ca. 1877; pub. Richault, dep. 1877; coll. A, no. 20.

144. "A Voice by the Cedar Tree"; words Tennyson; comp. 1871; pub. London, Augener, 1871; pub. London, C. Kegan Paul, 1880, in *Songs From the Published Writings of Alfred Tennyson, Poet Laureate, Set to Music by Various Composers*, ed. W. G. Cusius (Bibl. Nat. G 5345).

COLLECTIONS

A. *Vingt mélodies pour chant & piano à 1 ou 2 voix, premier recueil*; pub. Richault, 1878. Contains nos. 16, 27, 28, 41, 44, 46, 66, 75, 77, 87, 88, 91, 102, 120, 122, 124, 133, 138, 143.

B. *Dix mélodies pour chant et piano*; pub. Choudens. Contains nos. 2, 24, 55, 73, 74, 110.

C. *1ᵉʳ recueil, Vingt mélodies et duos, nouvelle édition avec une préface de l'auteur*; pub. A. Durand & fils, 1896. Contains nos. 16, 27, 46, 66, 75, 77, 87, 88, 91, 102, 117, 120.

D. *Vingt mélodies et duos, 2ᵐᵉ recueil*; pub. Durand. Contains nos. 4, 17, 22, 32, 35, 37, 45, 56, 63, 69, 93, 98, 106, 111, 121, 125, 126.

E. *10 Songs and Duets, French and English Texts. English Text by Frances Bonner*; pub. A. Durand & fils. Contains nos. 16, 28, 41, 44, 87, 88, 102, 120, 122, 138.

Édouard Lalo [1823–1892]

SEPARATE SONGS

1. "À celle qui part" (*see Cinq Lieder*, no. 2); words Armand Silvestre; aut. ms. in Bibl. Nat. (W 264) marked "Transcription for Madame Lalo, May 22, 1882"; coll. B, no. 16.

2. "À une fleur" (for contralto; *see Trois mélodies*, 1870, no. 1, and *Six mélodies*, 1926, no. 1); words Musset; comp. 1870.

3. "Adieu désert" (*scène*); words A. Flobert; comp. 1848; pub. Launer, dep. 1848.

4. "Amis, vive, vive l'orgie" (*see Six mélodies . . . de V. Hugo*, no. 6, 1st ed.); replaced in the 2d ed. of the set by "Chanson à boire," set to the same text.

5. "Au fond des halliers" (duo for soprano and tenor); words André Theuriet; comp. 1886; pub. Choudens, dep. 1887; coll. A, no. 13; coll. B, no. 13.

6. "Aubade"; words Victor Wilder; comp. 1872 (?); undated aut. ms. in Bibl. Nat. (W 263); coll. A, no. 8; coll. B, no. 8.

7. "L'aube naît et ta porte est close" (*see Six mélodies . . . de V. Hugo*, no. 3); undated aut. ms. in Bibl. Nat. (ms. 2052). 2d version in coll. A, no. 3; coll. B, no. 3.

8. "Ballade à la lune" (*chanson humoristique*); words Musset; comp. 1860 (?); aut. ms. in Bibl. Nat. (W 435) transcribed for Mme. Lalo in December 1883; coll. A, no. 7, coll. B, no. 7. Incomplete undated aut. ms. of orchestration in Bibl. Nat. (ms. 5067).

9. "Beaucoup d'amour" (*see Six romances populaires*, no. 2).

10. "Chanson à boire" (*see Six mélodies . . . de V. Hugo*, no. 6, 2d ed.); undated aut. ms. in Bibl. Nat. (ms. 5053); coll. A, no. 6; coll. B, no. 6; substituted for "Amis, vive, vive l'orgie" in the 2d ed. of the set of songs, but set to the same text.

11. "Chanson de Barberine" (for contralto; *see Trois mélodies*, 1870, no. 2, and *Six mélodies*, 1926, no. 2); words Musset; comp. 1870.

12. "La chanson de l'alouette" (*see Cinq Lieder*, no. 5); words V. de Laprade; coll. B, no. 19.

13. "Chant breton" (with oboe obbligato; op. 31); words Albert Delpit; comp. ca. 1884; undated aut. ms. in Bibl. Nat. (ms. 5054); pub. Hamelle; coll. A, no. 9, and coll. B, no. 9 without oboe.

□ *Cinq Lieder*; pub. Mainz, Schott, 1884. Contents: (1) "Prière de l'enfant à son réveil" (2) "À celle qui part" (3) "Tristesse" (4) "Viens" (5) "La chanson de l'alouette."

□ "Comment, disaient-ils": *see* "Guitare"

14. "Dansons" (duo for soprano and mezzo-soprano; transcription (ca. 1884) of the *tambourin* from the ballet *Namouna*); poet unknown; coll. A, no. 14; coll. B, no. 14.

15. "Dieu qui sourit et qui donne" (*see Six mélodies . . . de V. Hugo*, no. 4); undated aut. mss. in Bibl. Nat. (mss. 5056 and 5057); coll. A, no. 4; coll. B, no. 4.

16. "L'esclave" (for contralto; *see Trois mélodies*, 1873, no. 3, and *Six mélodies*, 1926, no. 4); words Gautier; comp. 1872; pub. G. Hartmann, dep. 1887.

17. "La fenaison" (for contralto; *see Trois mélodies*, 1873, no. 1, and *Six mélodies*, 1926, no. 5); words Stella; comp. 1872; aut. ms. in Bibl. Nat. (ms. 5059); pub. G. Hartmann, dep. 1873; coll. B, no. 20.

18. "Guitare" (*see Six mélodies . . . de V. Hugo*, no. 1); undated aut. ms. in Bibl. Nat. (ms. 5055); pub. in the set of songs as "Comment, disaient-ils." 2d version pub. as "Guitare" in coll. A, no. 1, and coll. B, no. 1.

19. "Humoresque"; words C. Beauquier; comp. 1867 (?); undated aut. ms. in Bibl. Nat. (W 427); coll. A, no. 12; coll. B, no. 12.

20. "Marine" (op. 33); words André Theuriet; aut. ms. in Bibl. Nat. (W 437) dated December 1883; coll. A, no. 10; coll. B, no. 10.

21. "Le novice" (*scène* for baritone, op. 5); words Hippolyte Stupuy; comp. 1849; pub. Launer, dep. 1849.

22. "Oh! quand je dors" (*see Six mélodies . . . de V. Hugo*, no. 5). 2d version pub. in coll. A, no. 5, and coll. B, no. 5.

23. "L'ombre de Dieu"; words A. Lehugeur; comp. 1848; pub. Launer, dep. 1848.

24. "La pauvre femme" (*see Six romances populaires*, no. 1).

25. "Les petits coups" (*see Six romances populaires*, no. 5).

26. "Prière de l'enfant à son réveil" (*see Cinq Lieder*, no. 1); words Lamartine; comp. 1884; coll. B, no. 15.

27. "Puisqu'ici-bas toute âme" (*see Six melodies . . . de V. Hugo*, no. 2); undated aut. mss. in Bibl. Nat. (mss. 5060 and W 431). 2d version in coll. A, no. 2, and coll. B, no. 2.

28. "Le rouge-gorge" (for contralto; *see Six mélodies*, 1926, no. 6); words André Theuriet; comp. ca. 1884; aut. ms. in Bibl. Nat. (W 265) marked "Transcription for contralto, to Madame Julie Lalo, celebration of May 22, 1887"; pub. G. Hartmann, dep. 1887.

29. "Si j'étais petit oiseau" (*see Six romances populaires*, no. 4).

☐ *Six mélodies* (for contralto); pub. Heugel, 1926. Contents: (1) "À une fleur" (2) "Chanson de Barberine" (3) "La Zuecca" (4) "L'esclave" (5) "La fenaison" (6) "Le rouge-gorge."

☐ *Six mélodies sur des poésies de Victor Hugo*, op. 17; comp. 1855; pub. Maho, dep. 1856. Contents: (1) "Guitare" (2) "Puisqu'ici-bas toute âme" (3) "L'aube naît et ta porte est close" (4) "Dieu qui sourit et qui donne" (5) "Oh! quand je dors" (6) "Amis, vive, vive l'orgie" (replaced in the 2d ed. by "Chanson à boire," set to the same text).

☐ *Six romances populaires de P.-J. Béranger*; comp. 1849; pub. Launer, 1849. Contents: (1) "La pauvre femme" (2) "Beaucoup d'amour" (3) "Le suicide" (4) "Si j'étais petit oiseau" (5) "Les petits coups" (6) "Le vieux vagabond."

30. "Souvenir" (*see Trois mélodies*, 1873, no. 2); words Hugo; undated aut. ms. in Bibl. Nat. (ms. 5061); another aut. ms. in Bibl. Nat. (W 436) dated April 17, 1870; pub. G. Hartmann, ca. 1872, dep. 1887.

31. "Le suicide" (*see Six romances populaires*, no. 3).

32. "Tristesse" (*see Cinq Lieder*, no. 3); words Armand Silvestre; comp. 1884; coll. B, no. 18.

☐ *Trois mélodies*; words Musset; pub. Hartmann, 1870. Contents: (1) "À une fleur" (2) "Chanson de Barberine" (3) "La Zuecca."

☐ *Trois mélodies*; pub. Hartmann, 1873. Contents: (1) "La fenaison" (2) "Souvenir" (3) "L'esclave."

33. "Viens" (*see Cinq Lieder*, no. 4); words Lamartine; comp. 1884; coll. B, no. 17.

34. "Le vieux vagabond" (*see Six romances populaires*, no. 6).

35. "La Zuecca" (for contralto; *see Trois mélodies*, 1870, no. 3, and *Six mélodies*, 1926, no. 3); words Musset; comp. 1870; undated aut. ms. in Bibl. Nat. (ms. 5062).

COLLECTIONS

A. *Mélodies pour chant et piano*; pub. J. Hamelle, 1894. Contains nos. 5–8, 10, 13–15, 18–20, 22, 27.

B. *Mélodies pour chant et piano*; pub. J. Hamelle, © 1913. Contains nos. 1, 5–8, 10, 12–15, 17–20, 22, 26, 27, 32, 33.

César Franck [1822–1890]

Data concerning some aut. mss. are from Julien Tiersot ("Les œuvres inédites de César Franck," *La revue musicale* IV, no. 2, December 1, 1922, pp. 97–138).

SEPARATE SONGS

1. "Aimer"; words Joseph Méry; aut. ms. dated February 28, 1849; pub. Costallat; coll. B, no. 1; coll. C, no. 1.

2. "L'ange et l'enfant"; words Jean Reboul; aut. ms. dated February 7, 1846; pub. Hamelle, 1878.

3. "Blond Phébus" (*romance*); poet unknown; unsigned ms. dated January 29, 1835 (a dubious work).

4. "Les cloches du soir"; words Mme. Desbordes-Valmore; comp. 1888; pub. Bruneau, dep. 1889.

5. "L'Émir de Bengador"; words Méry; comp. 1842–43; aut. ms. dated May 18, 1846; pub. Richault (later Costallat); coll. B, no. 2.

6. "Le garde d'honneur"; words Mme. X.; comp. 1859; pub. Régnier-Canaux, dep. 1865; pub. Noël.

7. "Lied"; words Lucien Paté; comp. 1873; pub. Enoch, dep. 1893; coll. A, no. 2; coll. C, no. 4.

8. "Le mariage des roses"; words Eugène David; comp. 1871; pub. Enoch in the coll. *Le monde musical*, Vol. I; coll. A, no. 3; coll. C, no. 3.

9. "Ninon"; words Musset; comp. 1842–43; pub. Enoch (later Richault, then Costallat); coll. B, no. 3; coll. C, no. 2.

10. "Nocturne"; words L. de Fourcaud; comp. 1884; pub. Enoch, 1885, in *Album du Gaulois*; coll. A, no. 4.

11. "Notre-Dame des orages" (*cantate*); words Comte de Pastouret; work mentioned in *Mst* VI, no. 7, January 13, 1839, and seemingly lost.

12. "Paris" (*ode patriotique* for voice and orchestra); words by B. de L., a militia captain, pub. in *Le Figaro*, November 27, 1870; comp. November–December 1870; pub. B. Roudanez, 1917, with preface by Julien Tiersot (copy in New York Public Library).

13. "Passez, passez toujours"; words Hugo; comp. 1872; pub. Costallat; coll. B, no. 4.

14. "La procession" (for voice and orchestra); words Charles Brizeux; comp. 1888. Version for voice and piano pub. Bruneau; coll. C, no. 5.

15. "Robin Gray"; words Florian; comp. 1842–43; aut. ms.; pub. Richault (later Costallat); coll. B, no. 5.

16. "Roses et papillons"; words Hugo; comp. 1872; pub. Enoch in coll. *Le monde musical*, Vol. I; coll. A, no. 5.

17. "S'il est un charmant gazon" (1); words Hugo; comp. ca. 1847; 3 aut. mss.; pub. Costallat; pub. in *La revue musicale* II, no. 2, December 1, 1922, supplement, p. 1.

18. "S'il est un charmant gazon" (2); words Hugo; aut. ms. dated September 1857; pub. Costallat; pub. in *La revue musicale* II, no. 2, December 1, 1922, supplement, pp. 3–6.

19. "Souvenance"; words Chateaubriand; aut. ms. dated May 18, 1846; pub. Richault (later Costallat); coll. B, no. 6.

20. "Le sylphe" (with 'cello obbligato); words Dumas; comp. 1842–43; pub. Richault (later Costallat); coll. B, no. 7 (including separate 'cello part).

21. "Les trois exilés" (*chant national* for bass or baritone); words Colonel

Bernard Delfosse; comp. 1848; aut. ms. in Bibl. Nat.; pub. Mayaud, dep. 1849; pub. Gérard.

22. "Le vase brisé"; words Sully-Prudhomme; comp. 1879; pub. Enoch, dep. 1900; coll. A, no. 6.

COLLECTIONS

A. *Lieder & duos*; pub. Enoch. Contains nos. 7, 8, 10, 16, 22.
B. *Mélodies choisies*; pub. Costallat. Contains nos. 1, 5, 9, 13, 15, 19, 20.
C. *Six Songs, with French and English Words*; pub. Boston, Boston Music Co., 1916. Contains nos. 1, 7–9, 14.

Alexis de Castillon [1838–1873]

SEPARATE SONGS

All have texts by Armand Silvestre.

1. "Le bûcher" (*see Deux poésies*, no. 1, and *Six poésies*, no. 1); comp. 1868; pub. G. Hartmann, dep. 1869.

☐ *Deux poésies d'Armand Silvestre*; pub. G. Hartmann, dep. 1869. Contents: (1) "Le bûcher" (2) "Le semeur."

2. "La mer" (*see Six poésies*, no. 4); comp. 1868–73; undated aut. ms. in Bibl. Nat. (ms. 3883¹).

3. "Renouveau" (*see Six poésies*, no. 5); comp. 1868–73; undated aut. ms. in Bibl. Nat. (ms. 3883⁴).

4. "Le semeur" (*see Deux poésies*, no. 2, and *Six poésies*, no. 2); aut. ms. in Bibl. Nat. (ms. 3883³) dated June 28, 1869.

☐ *Six poésies d'Armand Silvestre*, op. 8; pub. Heugel. Contents: (1) "Le bûcher" (2) "Le semeur" (3) "Sonnet mélancolique" (4) "La mer" (5) "Renouveau" (6) "Vendange." Orchestrated 1920 by Charles Koechlin.

5. "Sonnet mélancolique" (*see Six poésies*, no. 3); aut. ms. in Bibl. Nat. (ms. 3883⁵) dated June 27, 1871.

6. "Vendange" (*see Six poésies*, no. 6); comp. 1868–73; undated aut. ms. in Bibl. Nat. (ms. 3883²).

Gabriel Fauré [1845–1924]

P. Fauré-Frémiet's biography of his father (*Gabriel Fauré*, new ed., Paris, 1957) has been used for additional bibliographical information. It includes a list of songs published in English-language editions.

SEPARATE SONGS

1. "À Clymène" (*see Venise*, no. 5); coll. C, no. 10.

2. "L'absent" (op. 5/3); words Hugo; signed aut. ms. in Bibl. Nat. (ms. 419ᵇ) with title "Sentiers où l'herbe se balance" and dated April 3, 1871; pub. Cloudens, dep. 1879; coll. A, no. 11.

3. "Accompagnement" (op. 85/3); words Albert Samain; comp. 1902; pub. Hamelle, dep. 1903; coll. C, no. 20.

4. "Adieu" (*see Poème d'un jour*, no. 3); coll. B, no. 6; coll. D, no. 2; coll. E, no. 19.

5. "Après un rêve" (op. 7/1); words R. Bussine; comp. ca. 1865; pub. Choudens, 1879; coll. A, no. 15; coll. E, no. 12.

6. "Arpège" (op. 76/2); words Albert Samain; comp. 1897; pub. Hamelle, dep. 1897; coll. C, no. 13.

7. "Au bord de l'eau" (op. 8/1); words Sully-Prudhomme; comp. ca. 1865; pub. Choudens, dep. 1877; coll. A, no. 17; coll. E, no. 5.

8. "Au cimetière" (op. 51/2); words Jean Richepin; comp. ca. 1889; pub. Hamelle; coll. C, no. 2; coll. E, no. 2.

9. "Au pays des rêves" (op. 39/3); words Armand Silvestre; comp. 1884; pub. Hamelle, dep. 1913; coll. B, no. 14 (as "Le pays des rêves").

10. "Aubade" (op. 6/1); words Louis Pommey; comp. ca. 1865; pub. Choudens, 1879; coll. A, no. 12.

11. "L'aube blanche" (*see La chanson d'Ève*, no. 5); comp. 1907–08; pub. Heugel, © 1908.

12. "Aurore" (op. 39/1); words Armand Silvestre; comp. 1884; pub. Hamelle; coll. B, no. 12; coll. E, no. 3.

13. "L'aurore"; words Hugo; undated aut. ms. in Bibl. Nat. (ms. 419ᶜ) is reproduced in Appendix IV of this volume; pub. Cologne, Arno Volk Verlag, 1958, in the coll. *The Solo Song Outside German Speaking Countries*, ed. Frits R. Noske (*Anthology of Music*, Vol. XVI).

14. "Automne" (op. 18/3); words Armand Silvestre; comp. ca. 1880; pub. Hamelle, dep. 1910; coll. B, no. 3; coll. E, no. 11.

15. "Avant que tu ne t'en ailles" (*see La bonne chanson*, no. 6).

16. "Barcarolle" (op. 7/3); words Marc Monnier; comp. ca. 1865; pub. Choudens, dep. 1877; coll. B, no. 20.

17. "Les berceaux" (op. 23/1); words Sully-Prudhomme; comp. 1882; pub. Hamelle, dep. 1908; coll. B, no. 7; coll. E, no. 7.

☐ *La bonne chanson*, op. 61; words Verlaine; comp. ca. 1892; pub. Hamelle. Contents: (1) "Une Sainte en son auréole" (2) "Puisque l'aube grandit" (3) "La lune blanche luit dans les bois" (4) "J'allais par des chemins perfides" (5) "J'ai presque peur, en vérité" (6) "Avant que tu ne t'en ailles" (7) "Donc, ce sera par un clair jour d'été" (8) "N'est-ce pas?" (9) "L'hiver a cessé." Arr. for voice, piano, and string quartet by Fauré in 1898; pub. Hamelle.

18. "C'est la paix" (op. 114); words Georgette Debladis; comp. December 1919; pub. Durand, © 1920.

19. "C'est l'extase" (*see Venise*, no. 4); coll. C, no. 11.

20. "Chanson" (extracted from incidental music to drama *Shylock*, op. 57, and arr. for voice and piano by Fauré); words Edmond de Haraucourt, after Shakespeare; comp. 1889; pub. Hamelle, dep. 1890; coll. C, no. 5.

21. "Chanson" (op. 94); words Henri de Régnier; comp. 1907; pub. Heugel, © 1907.

22. "Chanson d'amour" (op. 27/1); words Armand Silvestre; comp. 1883; pub. Hamelle; coll. B, no. 10; coll. E, no. 29.

☐ *La chanson d'Ève*, op. 95; words Charles van Lerberghe; pub. Heugel, © 1906–10. Contents: (1) "Paradis" (2) "Prima verba" (3) Roses ardentes" (4) "Comme Dieu rayonne" (5) "L'aube blanche" (6) "Eau vivante" (7) "Veilles-tu, ma senteur de soleil?" (8) "Dans un parfum de roses blanches" (9) "Crépuscule" (10) "O mort, poussière d'étoiles."

23. "Chanson du pêcheur" (*lamento*; op. 4/1); words Gautier; comp. ca. 1865; pub. Choudens, dep. 1879; coll. A, no. 7. Orchestrated.

24. "Chant d'automne" (op. 5/1); words Baudelaire; comp. ca. 1865; pub. Choudens, dep. 1879; coll. A, no. 9.

☐ *Cinq mélodies "de Venise": see Venise*, op. 58

25. "Claire de lune" (*menuet*; op. 46/2); words Verlaine; comp. 1887; coll. B, no. 19; coll. E, no. 22. Orchestrated (by Fauré?).

26. "Comme Dieu rayonne" (*see La chanson d'Ève*, no. 4); comp. 1907–1909; pub. Heugel, © 1909.

27. "Crépuscule" (*see La chanson d'Ève*, no. 9); comp. 1906; pub. Heugel, © 1906.

28. "Cygne sur l'eau" (*see Mirages*, no. 1); coll. D, no. 8.

29. "Dans la forêt de septembre" (op. 85/1); words Catulle Mendès; comp. 1903; pub. Hamelle, dep. 1903; coll. C, no. 18.

30. "Dans la nymphée" (*see Le jardin clos*, no. 5); coll. D, no. 6.

31. "Dans la pénombre" (*see Le jardin clos*, no. 6).

32. "Dans les ruines d'une abbaye" (op. 2/1); words Hugo; comp. ca. 1865; pub. Choudens, dep. 1869; coll. A, no. 3; coll. E, no. 26. Orchestrated.

33. "Dans un parfum de roses blanches" (*see La chanson d'Ève*, no. 8); comp. 1907–09; pub. Heugel, © 1909.

34. "Danseuse" (*see Mirages*, no. 4); coll. D, no. 10.

35. "Diane, Séléné" (*see L'horizon chimérique*, no. 3); coll. D, no. 11.

36. "Le don silencieux" (op. 92); words Jean Dominique; comp. 1906; pub. Heugel, © 1906.

37. "Donc, ce sera par un clair jour d'été" (*see La bonne chanson*, no. 7).

38. "Eau vivante" (*see La chanson d'Ève*, no. 6); comp. 1907–09; pub. Heugel, © 1909.

39. "En prière"; words Stéphan Bordèse; comp. 1890 (?); pub. Durand, 1890; coll. B, no. 16; coll. E, no. 30. Orchestrated.

40. "En sourdine" (*see Venise*, no. 2); coll. C, no. 8; coll. E, no. 4.
41. "Exaucement" (*see Le jardin clos*, no. 1); coll. D, no. 3.
42. "La fée aux chansons" (op. 27/2); words Armand Silvestre; comp. 1883; pub. Hamelle; coll. B, no. 11.
43. "Fleur jetée" (op. 39/2); words Armand Silvestre; comp. 1884; pub. Hamelle; coll. B, no. 13; coll. E, no. 23.
44. "La fleur qui va sur l'eau" (op. 85/2); words Catulle Mendès; comp. 1902; pub. Hamelle, dep. 1903; coll. C, no. 19.
45. "Green" (*see Venise*, no. 3); coll. C, no. 9; coll. E, no. 13.
46. "L'hiver a cessé" (*see La bonne chanson*, no. 9); coll. E, no. 6.
☐ *L'horizon chimérique*, op. 118; words Jean de la Ville de Mirmont; comp. 1921; pub. Durand, © 1922. Contents: (1) "La mer est infinie" (2) "Je me suis embarqué" (3) "Diane, Séléné" (4) "Vaisseaux, nous vous aurons aimés."
47. "Hymne" (op. 7/2); words Baudelaire; comp. ca. 1865; pub. Hartmann, 1871; coll. A, no. 16.
48. "Ici-bas" (op. 8/3); words Sully-Prudhomme; comp. ca. 1865; pub. Choudens, dep. 1877; coll. A, no. 19; coll. E, no. 9.
49. "Il m'est cher, Amour, le bandeau" (*see Le jardin clos*, no. 7); coll. A, no. 19.
50. "Inscription sur le sable" (*see Le jardin clos*, no. 8); coll. D, no. 7.
51. "J'ai presque peur, en vérité" (*see La bonne chanson*, no. 5).
52. "J'allais par des chemins perfides" (*see La bonne chanson*, no. 4).
☐ *Le jardin clos*, op. 106; words Charles van Lerberghe; aut. ms. in Bibl. Nat. (ms. 415) dated 1914; pub. Durand, © 1915. Contents: (1) "Exaucement" (2) "Quand tu plonges tes yeux dans mes yeux" (3) "La messagère" (4) "Je me poserai sur ton cœur" (5) "Dans la nymphée" (6) "Dans la pénombre" (7) "Il m'est cher, Amour, le bandeau" (8) "Inscription sur le sable."
53. "Jardin nocturne" (*see Mirages*, no. 3).
54. "Je me poserai sur ton cœur" (*see Le jardin clos*, no. 4); coll. D, no. 5.
55. "Je me suis embarqué" (*see L'horizon chimérique*, no. 2).
☐ "Lamento": *see* "Chanson du pêcheur"
56. "Larmes" (op. 51/1); words Jean Richepin; comp. ca. 1899; pub. Hamelle; coll. C, no. 1.
57. "La lune blanche" (*see La bonne chanson*, no. 3); coll. E, no. 15.
58. "Lydia" (op. 4/2); words Leconte de Lisle; comp. ca. 1865; pub. Hartmann, 1871; pub. Choudens, 1877; coll. A, no. 8; coll. E, no. 24.
59. "Madrigal" (extracted from incidental music to drama *Shylock*, op. 57, and arr. for voice and piano by Fauré); words Edmond de Haraucourt, after Shakespeare; comp. 1899; pub. Hamelle, dep. 1890; coll. C, no. 6.
60. "Madrigal" (vocal quartet with orchestral acc., op. 35); words

Armand Silvestre; comp. 1884. Version for voice and piano pub. Hamelle.

61. "Mai" (op. 1/2); words Hugo; comp. ca. 1865; pub. Hartmann, 1871; pub. Choudens, 1877; coll. A, no. 2; coll. E, no. 27.

62. "Mandoline" (see Venise, no. 1); coll. C, no. 7; coll. E, no. 21.

63. "Les matelots" (op. 2/2); words Gautier; comp. ca. 1865; pub. Choudens, 1876; coll. A, no. 4.

64. "La mer est infinie" (see L'horizon chimérique, no. 1).

65. "La messagère" (see Le jardin clos, no. 3).

☐ Mirages, op. 113; words Baronne de Brimont; comp. 1919; pub. Durand, © 1919. Contents: (1) "Cygne sur l'eau" (2) "Reflets dans l'eau" (3) "Jardin nocturne" (4) "Danseuse."

66. "Nell" (op. 18/1); words Leconte de Lisle; comp. ca. 1880; pub. Hamelle; coll. B, no. 1; coll. E, no. 10.

67. "N'est-ce pas?" (see La bonne chanson, no. 8).

68. "Nocturne" (for contralto; op. 43/2); words Villiers de l'Isle Adam; comp. 1886; pub. Hamelle; coll. B, no. 17.

69. "Noël" (with acc. of piano, and harmonium ad lib., op. 43/1); words Victor Wilder; comp. 1886; pub. Hamelle; coll. A, no. 20 (without harmonium).

70. "Notre amour" (op. 23/2); words Armand Silvestre; comp. 1882; pub. Hamelle; coll. B, no. 8; coll. E, no. 8.

71. "O mort, poussière d'étoiles" (see La chanson d'Ève, no. 10); comp. 1907–10; pub. Heugel, © 1910.

72. "Le papillon et la fleur" (op. 1/1); words Hugo; comp. ca. 1860; pub. Choudens, dep. 1869; pub. Hamelle; coll. A, no. 1.

73. "Paradis" (see La chanson d'Ève, no. 1); comp. 1906; pub. Heugel, © 1907.

74. "Le parfum impérissable" (op. 76/1); words Leconte de Lisle; comp. 1897; pub. Hamelle, 1897, dep. 1900; coll. C, no. 12.

☐ "Le pays des rêves": see "Au pays des rêves"

75. "Pleurs d'or" (duo for mezzo-soprano and baritone, op. 72); words Albert Samain; comp. ca. 1896; pub. Hamelle.

76. "Le plus doux chemin" (op. 87/1); words Armand Silvestre; comp. 1904; pub. Hamelle, © 1907; coll. C, no. 16.

☐ Poème d'un jour, op. 21; words Charles Grandmougin; comp. 1880; pub. Durand, 1880, dep. 1905. Contents: (1) "Rencontre" (2) "Toujours" (3) "Adieu."

77. "Les présents" (op. 46/1); words Villiers de l'Isle Adam; comp. 1887; pub. Hamelle; coll. B, no. 18.

78. "Prima verba" (see La chanson d'Ève, no. 2); comp. 1906; pub. Heugel, © 1907.

79. "Prison" (op. 83/1); words Verlaine; comp. before 1897; pub. E. Fromont as op. 51/1, dep. 1896; coll. C, no. 14; coll. E, no. 16.

80. "Puisque l'aube grandit" (*see La bonne chanson*, no. 2).
81. "Puisqu'ici-bas" (duo for sopranos, op. 10/1); words Hugo; comp. 1874; pub. Choudens, dep. 1879; pub. Hamelle.
82. "Quand tu plonges tes yeux dans mes yeux" (*see Le jardin clos*, no. 2); coll. D, no. 4.
83. "Le ramier" (op. 87/2); words Armand Silvestre; comp. 1904; pub. Milan, Gramophone Co., 1904; pub. Hamelle, 1907; coll. C, no. 17.
84. "La rançon" (op. 8/2); dedicated to Henri Duparc; words Baudelaire; comp. ca. 1865; undated aut. ms. in Bibl. Nat. (ms. 419ᵈ); pub. Choudens; pub. Hamelle, dep. 1879; coll. A, no. 18.
85. "Reflets dans l'eau" (*see Mirages*, no. 2); coll. D, no. 9.
86. "Rencontre" (*see Poème d'un jour*, no. 1); coll. B, no. 4; coll. D, no. 1; coll. E, no. 17.
87. "Rêve d'amour" (op. 5/2); words Hugo; comp. ca. 1865; pub. Choudens, dep. 1875; pub. Hamelle; coll. A, no. 10; coll. E, no. 1.
88. "La rose" (op. 51/4); words Leconte de Lisle; comp. ca. 1889; pub. Hamelle, dep. 1891; coll. C, no. 4.
89. "Roses ardentes" (*see La chanson d'Ève*, no. 3); comp. 1907–08; pub. Heugel, © 1908.
90. "Les roses d'Ispahan" (op. 39/4); words Leconte de Lisle; comp. 1884; pub. Hamelle, dep. 1908; coll. B, no. 15; coll. E, no. 14. Orchestration pub. Hamelle.
91. "Une Sainte en son auréole" (*see La bonne chanson*, no. 1); comp. 1892.
92. "Le secret" (op. 23/3); words Armand Silvestre; comp. 1882; pub. Hamelle; coll. B, no. 9; coll. E, no. 20.
☐ "Sentiers où l'herbe se balance": *see* "L'absent"
93. "Sérénade toscane" (op. 3/2); words R. Bussine; comp. ca. 1865; pub. Choudens, dep. 1879; pub. Hamelle; coll. A, no. 6.
94. "Seule" (op. 3/1); words Gautier; aut. ms. in Bibl. Nat. (ms. 419ᵃ) dated 1871; pub. Hartmann, 1871; pub. Choudens; pub. Hamelle; coll. A, no. 5.
☐ "S'il est un charmant gazon": text incipit of "Rêve d'amour"
95. "Soir" (op. 83/2); words Albert Samain; comp. before 1897; pub. Fromont as op. 68/2, dep. 1896; pub. Hamelle; coll. C, no. 15.
96. "Spleen" (op. 51/3); words Verlaine; comp. before 1889; pub. Hamelle; coll. C, no. 3.
97. "Sylvie" (op. 6/3); words Paul de Choudens; comp. ca. 1865; pub. Choudens; pub. Hamelle, dep. 1879; coll. A, no. 14; coll. E, no. 25.
98. "Tarantelle" (duo for sopranos, op. 10/2); words Marc Monnier; comp. ca. 1870; pub. Choudens, dep. 1879; pub. Hamelle. Orchestration remains in ms.
99. "Toujours" (*see Poème d'un jour*, no. 2); coll. B, no. 5; coll. E, no. 18.
100. "Tristesse" (op. 6/2); words Gautier; comp. ca. 1865; pub. Choudens, dep. 1876; pub. Hamelle; coll. A, no. 13; coll. E, no. 28.

101. "Vaisseaux, nous vous aurons aimés" (*see L'horizon chimérique*, no. 4); coll. D, no. 12.
102. "Veilles-tu, ma senteur de soleil?" (*see La chanson d'Ève*, no. 7); comp. 1907–10; pub. Heugel, © 1910.
☐ *Venise, Cinq mélodies*, op. 58; words Verlaine; comp. 1890; pub. Hamelle, dep. 1891. Contents: (1) "Mandoline" (2) "En sourdine" (3) "Green" (4) "C'est l'extase" (5) "À Clymène."
103. "Vocalise" (originally "Pièce" for oboe); without words; comp. 1907; pub. A. Leduc, 1907 in coll. *Répertoire moderne de vocalises-études*, ed. A. L. Hettich, Vol. I.
104. "Le voyageur" (op. 18/2); words Armand Silvestre; comp. ca. 1880; pub. Hamelle; coll. B, no. 2.

COLLECTIONS

A. *20 mélodies, 1er recueil*; pub. Choudens, 1879; pub. Hamelle. Contains nos. 2, 5, 7, 10, 23, 24, 32, 47, 48, 58, 61, 63, 69, 72, 84, 87, 93, 94, 97, 100.
B. *20 mélodies, 2ème recueil*; pub. Hamelle. Contains nos. 4, 9, 12, 14, 16, 17, 22, 25, 39, 42, 43, 66, 68, 70, 77, 86, 90, 92, 99, 104.
C. *20 mélodies, 3ème recueil*; pub. Hamelle. Contains nos. 1, 3, 6, 8, 19, 20, 29, 40, 44, 45, 56, 59, 62, 74, 76, 79, 83, 88, 95, 96.
D. *Douze chants pour chant et piano*; pub. A. Durand & Fils, © 1915–22. Contains nos. 4, 28, 30, 34, 35, 41, 50, 54, 82, 85, 86, 101.
E. *30 Songs for Voice and Piano*, ed. S. Kagen; pub. New York, International Music Co., © 1953. Includes English text at head of each song. Contains nos. 4, 5, 7, 8, 12, 14, 17, 22, 25, 32, 39, 40, 43, 45, 46, 48, 57, 58, 61, 62, 66, 70, 79, 86, 87, 90, 92, 97, 99, 100.

Henri Duparc [1848–1933]

SEPARATE SONGS

☐ "Absence": *see* "Au pays où se fait la guerre"
1. "Au pays où se fait la guerre"; words Gautier; comp. 1869 but probably altered later; pub. in *Journal de musique d'Armand Gouzien*, May 19, 1877; coll. A, no. 13. Orchestrated.
2. "Chanson triste" (*see Cinq mélodies*, no. 4); words Jean Lahor (Henri Cazalis); coll. A, no. 9; coll. B, no. 6; coll. C, no. 8. Orchestrated.
☐ *Cinq mélodies*, op. 2; comp. 1868; pub. G. Flaxland, dep. 1870. Contents: (1) "Soupir" (2) "Sérénade" (3) "Romance de Mignon" (4) "Chanson triste" (5) "Le galop."
3. "Élégie"; prose trans. of Thomas Moore's poem on the death of Robert Emmet; comp. 1874; pub. in *Journal de musique d'Armand Gouzien*,

January 12, 1878; pub. Rouart, Lerolle, dep. 1912; coll. A, no. 10; coll. C, no. 9.

4. "Extase"; words Jean Lahor (Henri Cazalis); comp. 1878; pub. Baudoux, dep. 1894; coll. A, no. 4; coll. B, no. 3; coll. C, no. 4.

5. "La fuite" (duo for soprano and tenor); words Gautier; comp. 1872; pub. Demets, ca. 1900.

6. "Le galop" (*see Cinq mélodies*, no. 5); words Sully-Prudhomme; pub. Durand, 1948.

7. "L'invitation au voyage"; words Baudelaire; comp. 1870; pub. Baudoux, dep. 1894; coll. A, no. 1, coll. B, no. 1; coll. C, no. 2.

8. "Lamento"; words Gautier; comp. 1883; pub. Baudoux, dep. 1895; coll. A, no. 7; coll. B, no. 4; coll. C, no. 6.

9. "Le manoir de Rosemonde"; words Robert de Bonnières; comp. 1879; pub. Baudoux, dep. 1894; coll. A, no. 6; coll. B, no. 5; coll. C, no. 5. Orchestrated.

10. "Phidylé"; words Leconte de Lisle; comp. 1882; pub. Baudoux, dep. 1894; coll. A, no. 5; coll. C, no. 1. Orchestrated.

11. "Romance de Mignon" (*see Cinq mélodies*, no. 3); words Victor Wilder, after Goethe.

12. "Sérénade" (*see Cinq mélodies*, no. 2); words Gabriel Marc; facsimile of the 1870 ed. appears on pp. 274–276 of the present volume.

13. "Sérénade florentine"; words Jean Lahor (Henri Cazalis); comp. 1880; pub. Baudoux, dep. 1894; coll. A, no. 2; coll. C, no. 3.

14. "Soupir" (*see Cinq mélodies*, no. 1); words Sully-Prudhomme; coll. A, no. 11; coll. B, no. 2; coll. C, no. 10.

15. "Testament"; words Armand Silvestre; comp. 1883; pub. Baudoux, dep. 1896; coll. A, no. 8; coll. C, no. 7. Orchestrated.

16. "La vague et la cloche" (for bass voice and orchestra); words François Coppée; comp. 1871; aut. score in Bibl. Nat. (ms. 1271). Reduction for voice and piano by Vincent d'Indy pub. Baudoux, dep. 1894; coll. A, no. 3; coll. C, no. 12.

17. "La vie antérieure" (for voice and orchestra); words Baudelaire; comp. 1884. Reduction for voice and piano pub. Rouart-Lerolle; coll. A, no. 12; coll. C, no. 11.

COLLECTIONS

A. *Mélodies, nouvelle édition complète*; pub. Rouart, Lerolle, 1911. Contains nos. 1–4, 7–10, 13–17.

B. *Album of Six Songs*; pub. Boston, Boston Music Co., © 1914. Contains nos. 2, 4, 7–9, 14.

C. *12 Songs for Voice and Piano*, ed. Sergius Kagen; pub. New York, International Music Co., © 1952. Includes English prose text trans. in preface. Contains nos. 2–4, 7–10, 13–17.

Table of Abbreviations

acc.	accompaniment
ann.	announced
anon.	anonymous
arr.	arranged or arrangement
aut.	autograph
Bibl. Cons.	Bibliothèque du Conservatoire, Paris (the pertinent material from this library was transferred in 1964 to the Bibliothèque Nationale, where the original call numbers are retained)
Bibl. Nat.	Bibliothèque Nationale, Paris
©	copyright
ca.	approximately
coll.	collection
comp.	composed
dep.	*dépôt légal* (legal deposit)
ed.	edition, editor, or edited
FM	*La France musicale*
GM	*Gazette musicale de Paris*
ms(s).	manuscript(s)
Mst	*Le ménestrel*
op.	opus or *œuvre*
PN	publisher's plate number
posth.	posthumous
pub.	published or publisher
rev.	revised
RGM	*Revue et Gazette musicale de Paris*
RMF	*Revue musicale*, founded by Fétis
trans.	translated or translator

NOTES

1. T. Gérold, *L'art du chant en France au XVIIe siècle*, Strasbourg, 1921; H. Gougelot, *La romance française sous la Révolution et l'Empire : Étude historique et critique*, 2 vols., Melun, 1938–1943, and *Catalogue des romances parues sous la Révolution et l'Empire*, 2 vols., Melun, 1937–1943.

2. J. Barzun, review of F. Noske, *La mélodie française de Berlioz à Duparc*, in *Music Library Association Notes* 2d ser. XII, no. 3, June 1955, p. 441.

3. Cf. P.-M. Masson, "Les brunettes," *Sammelbände der Internationalen Musik-gesellschaft* XII, 1910/11, pp. 347–369.

4. C. Ballard, *Brunetes ou Petits airs tendres, avec les doubles et la basse-continue, mélées de chansons à danser*, 3 vols., Paris, 1703–1711.

5. According to J.-B. Weckerlin (*Échos du temps passé*, Paris, 1853, Vol. I, pp. 88–89), who does not mention the source.

6. Cf. M. Cauchie, "La version authentique de la romance 'Plaisir d'amour'," *Revue de musicologie* XXI, February 1937, pp. 12–14. The song was first published under the title "Romance du chevrier."

7. Cf. Gougelot, *La romance*, Vol. I, Chap. I. The 2d vol. of this work, entitled *Choix de textes musicaux*, includes romances by Plantade, Blangini, and all the other composers mentioned below.

8. Thiébault, Baron de l'Empire, *Du chant et particulièrement de la romance*, Paris, 1813, p. 54.

9. A. Romagnési, *L'art de chanter les romances, les chansonnettes et les nocturnes et généralement toute la musique de salon*, Paris, 1846, p. 16. The same year another edition of the work was published with the title *La psychologie du chant*.

10. When a composer was famous, his dramatic romances were often sung during the prologue or interlude of an opera performance. Thus Meyerbeer's

"Le moine," which "has produced such a sensation in the salon," was performed in Vienna "in the midst of enthusiasm impossible to describe" by the *basse-taille* Staudigl (reported in "Nouvelles," *RGM* III, no. 20, May 15, 1836, p. 167).

11. Among romances written before the Restoration, only one appears to give the violin a role equal to that of the voice: C. d'Ennery's "La romance de Benedict." A copy of the original 1801 edition is in the private collection of Henri Gougelot.

12. Announcement of publication in "Bulletin d'annonces," *RMF* XIII, no. 11, April 13, 1833, p. 88, which also contains the above-quoted remark.

13. Publication announced in *RMF* I, no. 16, May 1827, p. 42; cf. also *RMF* II, 1828, p. 453.

14. Cf. *RMF* IV, 1829, pp. 398–399. Other romances of this type by the same composer are "Philomèle," with flute; "La montagnarde," with oboe; and "Les échos des Alpes," with horn. Cf. *Mst* XXVII, no. 13, February 26, 1860, p. 100.

15. Cf. Mme. Duchambge's obituary in *RGM* XXV, no. 22, May 30, 1858, pp. 185–186. One of her best-known romances was "À mon ange gardien" (which the publisher Pleyel issued in a 2d edition about 1829), mentioned by Flaubert in *Madame Bovary*.

16. *Mst* III, no. 3, December 20, 1835, p. 1.

17. Like Panseron, Bruguière wrote romances with concertante instrumental parts. He also applied the name *romance dialoguée* to several of his *nocturnes* (e.g., "Le faux ermite," for two voices, announced in *RMF* III, 1828, p. 384).

18. Beauplan, whose real name was Rousseau, also had some success as painter and poet (cf. C. Laforêt, *La vie musicale au temps romantique*, Paris, 1929, p. 30).

19. P. Scudo, "Esquisse d'une histoire de la romance," *Critique et littérature musicales* 1st ser., 3d ed., Paris, 1856, p. 322.

20. A. de Lasalle, *Dictionnaire de musique appliquée à l'amour*, Paris, 1868, p. 234.

21. A. Daudet, *Tartarin de Tarascon*, 1st episode, III.

22. *La mélodie* I, no. 11, October 8, 1842, p. 2.

23. J.-A. Delaire, *Histoire de la romance considérée comme œuvre littéraire et musicale*, Paris, 1845, p. 22. The author studied with the composer Reicha.

24. *Mst* III, no. 16, March 20, 1836, p. 6. Jacques (or Jacob) Strunz, a German composer of operas, ballets, and other works, was the dedicatee of Balzac's "Massimilla Doni." Strunz and Liszt were Berlioz' witnesses at his marriage to Harriet Smithson in 1833 (cf. L. Guichard, "Quels furent les témoins du premier mariage de Berlioz?", *Revue de musicologie* LII, no. 2, 1966, pp. 211–214).

25. *Mst* VI, no. 8, January 20, 1839.

26. *Mst* IV, no. 22, April 30, 1837, pp. 2–3.

27. Review (signed "R.") of "Concert de M. Panseron," *RMF* XII, no. 8, March 24, 1832, pp. 61–62.

28. Delaire, *op. cit.*, p. 24.

29. "Des auteurs de paroles de romances, des compositeurs, des chanteurs et des éditeurs," *Mst* XIV, no. 24, May 16, 1847; the article had appeared earlier in *La presse musicale.*

30. *Mst* XIV, no. 25, May 23, 1847.

31. A. Le Carpentier, *Petit traité de composition mélodique, appliqué aux valses, quadrilles et romances*, Paris, Heugel, 1843 (cf. *Mst* X, no. 35, July 30, 1843).

32. Laforêt, *op. cit.*, p. 18.

33. *Ibid.*, p. 24.

34. Cf. the catalogue of the centenary exhibition: Paris. Bibliothèque Nationale. *Le romantisme; Catalogue de l'exposition, 22 janvier – 10 mars 1930*, Bois-Colombes (Seine), 1930, p. 104.

35. Under the title "Nocturne du lac" it had been set by F. Bodin, who also composed music for "Le vallon" and "L'automne" (cf. *Journal général d'annonce des œuvres de musique* I, no. 1576–1761, Paris, 1825.

36. *Vie d'un compositeur moderne*, Paris, 1893, preface, p. vii. The biography was written by the composer's son, Baron Louis Alfred Niedermeyer, but was published without his name.

37. The catalogue of Niedermeyer's works (*ibid.*, pp. 155–156) includes 28 songs, for which Lamartine and Hugo each provided six poems, Deschamps eight, Pacini four, and Baïf, Millevoye, Delavigne, and Manzoni one each.

38. Fétis, *Biographie universelle*; T. Gautier, "Hippolyte Monpou," in *Histoire du romantisme*, Paris, 1873, pp. 254–258; and H. Bachelin, "Hippolyte Monpou," *Mst* XC, no. 19–20, May 11 and 18, 1928, pp. 205–206, 217–219. On Monpou's Romanticism, see Appendix I, p. 299.

39. In 1835 Monpou wrote "Les cris de Paris, chant burlesque à quatre parties, pour faire suite aux cris de Paris du XVIème siècle de Cl. Jannequin" (Paris Street Cries, Burlesque Song for Four Voices, A Sequel to Claude Jannequin's Sixteenth-Century Paris Street Cries). Exhibiting not the slightest trace of Romanticism, this piece conveys the impression of a badly executed school exercise; the fugato in particular, on the text "Voici la bell' Madeleine qui vend des gâteaux qui sont tout chauds" (Here is pretty Madeleine selling warm cakes), shows extreme clumsiness in the handling of the counterpoint.

40. Unsigned article, "M. Hippolyte Monpou," *GM* II, no. 32, August 9, 1835, pp. 264–265.

41. Voltaire's remark, taken from his *Remarques sur Corneille* (1764), could not have had the meaning read into it by Bescherelle, since in the eighteenth century the word *mélodie* generally meant a succession of tones, or occasionally, a musical theme.

42. T. Moore, *The Journal of Thomas Moore, 1818–1841*, ed. Peter Quennell, New York, 1964, pp. 129–130.

43. *Ibid.*, editor's introduction, p. x.

44. Article "Mélodies irlandaises," in P. Larousse, *Grand dictionnaire universel du XIXᵉ siècle*, Paris, 1873, Vol. X, p. 1483.

45. Moore, *The Journal*, p. 112.

46. Unsigned article (by Fétis?), "Sur les airs irlandais," *RMF* VII, March 6, 1830, pp. 145–150, in which Stevenson's accompaniments are severely treated. An English critic was more generous, although hardly enthusiastic. He praises the poetry and airs of the seventh number, adding, "Sir J. Stevenson scarcely at all disturbed their naïve simplicity and expression" (*Quarterly Musical Magazine and Review* I, 1818, p. 266). Bishop's accompaniments to the ninth number, however, inspired an anonymous critic in the same journal to remark that they "are so sparkling, yet so appropriate, that we are led on, as the airs are ushered in, by the light of his genius" (*ibid.* VI, 1824, p. 411). Information about the London and Dublin publications of the songs may be found in Percy H. Muir, "Thomas Moore's Irish Melodies, 1808–1834," *The Colophon* 15, 1933.

47. P. Duchambge, "Dixième mélodie, imitée de Thomas Moore," trans. Léon Halévy, Paris, Pleyel, ca. 1829, PN 2692. The copy consulted was in the Stellfeld Collection.

48. *Mélodies romantiques; choix de nouvelles ballades de divers peuples*, Paris, Janet, 1827. This rare work is not in the Bibl. Nat. Cf. M. Escoffier, *Le mouvement romantique, 1788–1850; essai de bibliographie synchronique et méthodique*, Paris, 1934, p. 162, no. 640.

49. F. Baldensperger (*Sensibilité musicale et romantisme*, Paris, 1925, p. 117), referring to a collection of verse translated by A. Fontaney (*Ballades, mélodies et poésies diverses*, Paris, Hayet, 1829), claims that Fontaney's use of the word *mélodie* in the title, along with those of other poetic forms, proves that the term also had literary significance at that time. But the *mélodie* of that title alludes specifically to the poems of Thomas Moore in the collection, so that Fontaney is not introducing a new term into the French language but simply translating a name created by Moore and intended for no other poems but his.

50. Publication of Vimeux' "Mon pauvre André, mélodie romantique" announced in *RMF* XII, no. 35, September 29, 1832, p. 280; publication of Sowinsky's *Mélodies polonaises* announced in *RMF* XIII, no. 31, August 31, 1833, p. 248; unsigned review of Bessems' *Mélodies dramatiques* in *GM* I, no. 10, March 9, 1834, pp. 81–82; and an unsigned review of Barrault de Saint-André's "Miserrimus, première mélodie hébraïque" in *RGM* III, no. 11, March 13, 1836, pp. 87–88.

51. Publication of Thalberg's "Un soupir" announced in *FM* VII, April 14, 1844, p. 113. Other instrumental *mélodies* were announced in *RMF* XIV, no. 5, February 2, 1834, p. 40 (Panseron's *Voyage en Suisse*, a collection for piano of four "favorite airs" entitled "Valse," "Air," "Ranz," and "Mélodie");

and in *FM* VII, March 3, 1844, p. 70 (Victor Magnen's four *Mélodies*, op. 44, for piano, violin, and violoncello, in which the numbers are preceded by the poetic mottoes by Lamartine, Hoffmann, Desbordes-Valmore, and Delavigne that supposedly served as the composer's themes).

52. *RMF* VII, February 13, 1830, pp. 62–63.

53. *GM* I, no. 16, April 20, 1834, p. 124 [i.e., p. 132].

54. Unsigned review of G. Carulli, *Mélodies pour trois voix égales,* "à l'usage des pensionnats," with words by Lamartine and others, in *RGM* III, no. 7, February 14, 1836, pp. 63–64. The reviewer suggests that Carulli "opens the set with a *ranz des vaches* [entitled "Les Suisses"] because of the fashion for things Swiss, even when there is little relation to Switzerland." According to G. Tarenne (*Recherches sur les ranz des vaches,* Paris, 1813, p. 7), who also gives some interesting speculations on the derivation of the word *ranz,* "a *ranz des vaches* is an air sung or played by Swiss mountain folk while guarding their herds." Cf. also the unsigned article "Notice sur les airs suisses," *RMF* VII, February 6, 1830, pp. 1–9.

55. C.-L. de Sévelinges, *Alfred, ou Les années d'apprentissage de Wilhelm Meister,* 3 vols. (with music), Paris, 1802. The names of the chief characters are changed from Wilhelm and Mignon to Alfred and Fanfan.

56. *Ibid.,* Vol. II, p. 69, translator's note.

57. *Ibid.,* Vol. I, p. 186.

58. Published in a collection entitled *Mélanges poétiques* (with music), Paris, Bouland, 1824.

59. Announced in *GM* I, no. 23, June 8, 1834, p. 188. The collection contains "La poste" ("Die Post" by Müller), "La sérénade" ("Ständchen" by Rellstab), "Au bord de la mer" ("Am Meer" by Heine), "La fille du pêcheur" ("Das Fischermädchen" by Heine), "La jeune fille et la mort" ("Der Tod und das Mädchen" by Claudius), and "Berceuse" ("Wiegenlied" by Körner). Cf. the critical bibliography in E. Duméril, *Lieds et ballades germaniques traduits en vers français,* Paris, 1934, p. 38, no. 126–131.

60. Undated publication, dep. 1834; cf. Duméril, *op. cit.,* p. 40, no. 148.

61. Undated publication, dep. 1835; *ibid.,* p. 42, no. 160–163. The four songs are "Alinte" ("Alinde" by Rochlitz), "La petite truite" ("Die Forelle" by Schubart), "La clochette des agonisants" ("Das Zügenglöcklein" by Seidl), and "Le voyageur" ("Der Wanderer" by Schmidt von Lübeck).

62. Richault alone had already published sixty *mélodies* by 1837, according to E. Legouvé ("Mélodies de Schubert," *RGM* IV, no. 3, January 15, 1837, p. 26).

63. Translated by Bélanger but lacking publisher and date; dep. 1836.

64. Translation signed "D. P." but lacking publisher and date; dep. 1838.

65. Cf. V. Haape, "Alfred de Musset in seinen Beziehungen zu Deutschland und zum deutschen Geistesleben," *Zeitschrift für französische Sprache und Literatur* XXXIV, 1909, pp. 80–84.

66. Cf. H. Blaze de Bury, "Poètes et musiciens d'Allemagne: Uhland et M. Dessauer," *Revue des deux mondes* 4th ser. V, October 15, 1835, pp. 129–158.

67. Cf. H. Blanchard, review of Dessauer's *Mélodies* in *RGM* IX, no. 5, January 30, 1842, pp. 45–46.

68. E.g., "Vous!", *Lied* by F. Hiller, words by M. Barateau, reviewed (and issued as supplement) in *GM* I, no. 20, May 18, 1834, p. 163, and *Compositions vocales* by F. Kücken on texts by M. Bourges, reviewed by G. Kastner in *RGM* XII, no. 31, August 3, 1845, pp. 254–255.

69. The three collections by Mendelssohn are: (*a*) *Album de chant* (trans. Bourges) offered to subscribers in *RGM* XIII, no. 7, February 15, 1846, pp. 49–50; (*b*) *12 Lieder* (trans. Jules Forrest), Paris, Richault, n.d. (dep. 1848); cf. Duméril, *op. cit.*, p. 71, no. 480; (*c*) *12 Lieder* (trans. Bélanger), Paris, Richault, n.d. (dep. 1849); cf. *ibid.*, no. 481.

70. L. Quicherat, *Adolphe Nourrit, sa vie, son talent, son caractère, sa correspondance*, Paris, 1867, Vol. II, p. 32. Besides Nourrit, other persons were credited with having "discovered" Schubert. Legouvé claims in his memoirs (*Soixante ans de souvenirs*, Paris, 1886–1887; 2d ed., 1888, Vol. III, p. 176) that the violinist Chrétien Urhan was the first to introduce a Schubert *Lied*, a song called "Adieu," into France. His assertion remains incorrect in any case, since the piece in question was falsely attributed to Schubert. Several years before the appearance of Legouvé's memoirs, Weyrauch was shown to have composed the so-called "Adieu" to a German text entitled "Nach Osten" (cf. T. Parmentier, "*L'adieu* de Schubert," *RGM* XLIV, no. 7, February 18, 1877, pp. 52–53, and O. E. Deutsch, *Schubert Thematic Catalogue*, London, 1951, Appendix I).

71. Cf. J.-G. Prod'homme, "Les œuvres de Schubert en France," *Bericht über den internationalen Kongress für Schubertforschung in Wien*, Augsburg, 1929, p. 92.

72. Fétis, "Société des concerts du Conservatoire: Premier concert annuel," *RMF* XV, no. 4, January 25, 1835, p. 27.

73. Quoted in Quicherat, *op. cit.*, Vol. III, pp. 27–28.

74. Quoted in Quicherat, *op. cit.*, Vol. II, p. 30, from *Le courrier de Lyon*, August 2, 1837.

75. F. Liszt, "Lettre d'un bachelier ès-musique," *RGM* V, no. 6, February 11, 1838, p. 61.

76. Quoted in Quicherat, *op. cit.*, Vol. II, p. 28 from an article by C. Rouget in *Le sémaphore de Marseille*, June 20, 1837.

77. Cf. Blaze de Bury, *Musiciens contemporains*, Paris, 1856, p. 229, and Quicherat, *op. cit.*, Vol. II, p. 35.

78. Undated letter to Monsier Ed. P. of Le Havre, written in January or February 1835, quoted in Quicherat, *op. cit.*, Vol. III, p. 7.

79. Quoted by H. Girard in the introduction to his edition of Deschamps' *Un manifeste du romantisme, La préface des Études françaises et étrangères*, Paris, 1923, p. xxxix.

80. Curiously enough, Deschamps knew no German whatsoever. He seems to have proceeded in the same manner as Nourrit, putting into verse the prose that his friend Henri de Latouche had translated from the German. Cf. H. Girard, *Un bourgeois dilettante à l'époque romantique: Émile Deschamps*, Paris, 1921 (thesis), pp. 195–196, and also Blaze de Bury, "Poètes et romanciers modernes de la France, XLIV: MM. Émile et Antony Deschamps," *Revue des deux mondes* 4th ser. XXVII, August 1841, p. 554.

81. *Revue des deux mondes* 4th ser. XVII, February 15, 1839, pp. 548–549. The anonymous author of this "Revue musicale" suggests an ideal complete edition of the *Lieder*. The best French poets would dedicate their talent to the translation, while the illustrations would be assigned to such artists as Delacroix, Boulanger, and Ziegler.

82. Blaze de Bury, *op. cit.*, p. 555.

83. Fétis, "Société des concerts ...," p. 27.

84. In his review of Nourrit's notable performance of "La jeune religieuse" at the Conservatoire (signed merely "H..."), Berlioz even went so far as to state that "Schubert's music surely contains nothing of what certain people call melody—quite fortunately!" (*Journal des débats*, January 25, 1835).

85. Legouvé, "Mélodies de Schubert," *RGM* IV, no. 3, January 15, 1837, p. 26.

86. H. Panofka, "François Schubert," *RGM* V, no. 41, October 14, 1838, pp. 406–407. Other German composers are generally judged in the same tone. An earlier review of Dessauer's *Lieder*, for example, warns of similar over-emphases: "I advise against the too-frequent use of certain academic formulae and the unrestrained abuse of modulation, which will result in the destruction of all the impetus of his thought and inspiration. It is truly strange that today German composers use modulation at every turn and that this manner of writing leads them to sacrifice everything in order to develop instrumental strength. ... Whether they are writing *Lieder* or chansons ... the voice is the servant of the fingers; at the keyboard, the voice accompanies the hands. I may be wrong, but I believe Mozart behaved differently" (Blaze de Bury, "Poètes et musiciens ...," p. 152). Cf. also Fétis' remarks about Spohr in his "Examen de l'état actuel de la musique en Italie, en Allemagne, en Angleterre et en France," *RMF* I, no. 14, May 1827, p. 356.

87. Fétis, "Société des concerts ...," *RMF* XV, 1835, p. 27; J. d'Ortigue, "Schubert," *Revue de Paris* new ser. XXX, June 1836, p. 275.

88. Anonymous article, "Les mélodies de François Schubert," *FM* I, no. 12, March 18, 1838, pp. 3–4.

89. Blanchard, "Les deux romances," *RGM* VI, no. 21, May 23, 1839, p. 170.

90. Blanchard, "Romagnési," *RGM* V, no. 41, October 14, 1838, p. 410.

91. Legouvé, *loc. cit.*

92. "Les mélodies de François Schubert," *loc. cit.*

93. Blanchard, "Le premier de l'an musical," *RGM* VII, no. 77, December 31, 1840, p. 648.

94. Published in *Mst* III, no. 15–16, March 13 and 20, 1836.

95. Undated *mélodie* published by *La France musicale* (PN F.M. 122). The same poem was set to music by César Franck and Victor Massé. An important collection of Clapisson's *mélodies* bears the title *Les chants du cœur* (Paris, Richault). For further remarks on Clapisson, see Blanchard, "Des albums; revue critique," *RGM* VIII, no. 2, January 7, 1841, p. 12.

96. In a review of the *Huit mélodies* (in *RGM* V, no. 2, January 14, 1838, p. 14), Blanchard suggests that Coussemaker (a native of Douai, in the Flemish North of France) is not sufficiently familiar with the language to set French words to music.

97. G. Donizetti, *Rêveries napolitaines, six ballades*, Paris, Bernard-Latte, 1838 (PN B.L. 1880). A reviewer prefers the name *mélodies*, suggesting that the subtitle *ballades* given them by the composer is "much too modest" (*FM* I, no. 50, December 9, 1838, p. 5); Donizetti's *Matinées musicales* (Paris, Meissonnier, 1842) is a collection of six *mélodies*, two duets, and two short vocal quartets with words by Émile Deschamps and Auguste Richomme (reviewed by G. Kastner in *RGM* IX, no. 15, April 10, 1842, pp. 153–154).

98. Unless noted to the contrary, the word "prosody" is used here to mean *musical* prosody, i.e., the metrical, rhythmic, and melodic relationship between words and music.

99. P.-M. Masson, "Le mouvement humaniste," in *Encyclopédie de la musique et Dictionnaire du Conservatoire*, Paris, 1914, Part I, Vol. III, p. 1307.

100. From G. Bataille, *Airs de différents autheurs, mis en tablature de luth*, 6th Book, Paris, 1615, fol. 5 v°. The song is also reprinted in Weckerlin, *Échos...*, Vol. II, pp. 1–2.

101. [Isaac Vossius], *De poematum cantu et viribus rythmi*, Oxford, 1673, pp. 128ff. The Latin text appears in the original French edition of this book (pp. 38–39).

102. C. Rollin (*De la manière d'enseigner et d'étudier les belles-lettres*, Paris, 1726) and the Abbé d'Olivet (*Traité sur la prosodie*, Paris, 1736) had already rejected syllabic quantity as the fundamental principle of French versification. Rollin considered rhyme and "a uniform assortment of a certain number of syllables *of equal beats*" to be the factors of prime importance. D'Olivet was the first to show the importance of the accent for the rhythm of French verse and in this regard may be considered a predecessor of Scoppa. Since neither Rollin nor d'Olivet was concerned with musical prosody, however, examination of their treatises would be out of place here.

103. J.-J. Rousseau, *Essai sur l'origine des langues où il est parlé de la mélodie et de l'imitation musicale*, Chap. VII: "De la prosodie moderne." The original title of the work was *Essai sur la mélodie*.

104. *Ibid.*

105. The testimony of foreign visitors to Paris confirms the opinion that both male and female singers of the Paris Opéra shouted rather than sang: "Although beautiful in the old style, the music first amused me somewhat because of its

novelty, but then was boring. The recitative soon became tedious in its monotony because of the shrieks uttered in unlikely places" (Casanova, *Mémoires*, new ed., Paris, 1880, Vol. II, p. 303). Twenty-five years later Mozart's judgment is even more severe: "If only that confounded French tongue were not so detestable for music. It really is hopeless; even German is divine by comparison. And then the men and women singers! Indeed, they hardly deserve the name, for they don't sing—they yell—howl—and that too with all their might, through their noses and throats" (letter from Paris, July 9, 1778 in *Letters of Mozart*, ed. E. Anderson, London, 1938, Vol. II, p. 836).

106. Rousseau, *Lettre sur la musique françoise*, Paris, 1753.

107. M.-P. Chabanon, "Lettre sur les propriétés musicales de la langue française," *Mercure de France*, January 1773, pp. 171–191.

108. Chabanon, *De la musique considérée en elle-même et dans ses rapports avec la parole, les langues, la poésie, et le théâtre*, Paris, 1785. In his "Preliminary Reflections" the author calls the book "a philosophic work written for the cause of music" (p. 7) and confesses that he attaches great importance to the study, "for after all, this book is the work of my life" (p. 8).

109. *Ibid.*, pp. 250–252.

110. L'Abbé C. Batteux, *Les beaux-arts réduits à un même principe*, Paris, 1746, p. 266.

111. A. E. M. Grétry, *Mémoires, ou Essais sur la musique*, 2d ed., Paris, 1797, Vol. II, p. 35.

112. *Ibid.*, Vol. I, p. 439, note.

113. *Ibid.*, p. 406.

114. *Ibid.*, pp. 276–277. Grétry himself is guilty of much graver errors of prosody in his famous romance "Une fièvre brûlante," from *Richard Coeur-de-Lion*.

115. Grétry discusses his first meeting with Voltaire and his decision to elide the mute *e* in his *Mémoires*, Vol. I, pp. 134 and 142.

116. "Mémoire sur 'La prosodie musicale' par M. Lamouroux," *Mémoires de la Société d'Agriculture, des Sciences et des Arts d'Agen*, meetings of 6 Floréal and 4 Prairial, Revolutionary Year XIII [April 6 and May 24, 1805], pp. 16off. The quotations from Lamouroux are all taken from this source, since a copy of the original could not be found.

117. A. Scoppa, *Traité de la poésie italienne rapportée à la poésie française ...*, Paris-Versailles, Revolutionary Year XI [1803], p. 24. Other works by the same author on related topics are: *Les vrais principes de la versification française*, Paris-Versailles, 1811 (honored by the Institut de France); *Mémoire sur les questions du rythme et de la rime*, Paris, 1815; and *Des beautés poétiques de toutes les langues sous la rapport de l'accent et du rythme ...*, Paris, 1816.

118. Scoppa, *Traité*, p. 196.

119. F. H. J. Castil-Blaze, *Molière musicien*, 2 vols., Paris, 1852, *passim*; L. Roger, "Quelques mots sur la prosodie," *La semaine musicale* I, November 2, 1865,

no. 44. On the question of displacing the tonic accent and on prosodic difficulties in general, see *Richard Strauss et Romain Rolland, correspondance, fragments de journal*, Paris, 1951, *passim*, where interesting discussions arise from problems of resetting the German translation of *Salome* into a French libretto.

120. Fétis, *La musique mise à la portée de tout le monde*, 2d ed., Paris, 1836, pp. 49–54.

121. Elsewhere (*ibid.*, pp. 57–58) Fétis adds "regularity of modulation."

122. A musical phrase that is repeated within a stanza with new words is almost impossible to prosodize correctly. At the end of the first stanza Méhul repeats the phrase quoted above with the words "Avec sa faulx démolit cette ville," thus displacing the tonic accent from the last to the penultimate syllable in the word "démolit."

123. Castil-Blaze, *Noces de Figaro de Mozart*, Paris, 1819, and *De l'opéra en France*, Paris, 1820; 2d ed., 1826.

124. Castil-Blaze, *Molière musicien*, Vol. II, pp. 10–11.

125. *Ibid.*, p. 154.

126. *Ibid.*, pp. 175–176.

127. *Ibid.*, pp. 189–190, and *L'art des vers lyriques*, Paris, 1857, p. 61.

128. Castil-Blaze, *Molière musicien*, Vol. II, pp. 260ff, and *L'art des vers lyriques*, p. 116.

129. Castil-Blaze, *L'art des vers lyriques*, p. 63.

130. *Ibid.*, pp. 66–69. Castil-Blaze even dares to fit some original lines of verse to parts of the symphony. In so doing he weakens his argument, for the rhythm of his lines does not match the musical rhythm.

131. J. Lurin, *Éléments du rythme dans la versification et la prose française*, Lyons, 1850. Another writer on the subject was the former King of Holland, Louis Bonaparte (*Mémoire sur la versification française*, Florence, 1819), who describes Giuseppe Baini's harmonico-rhythmic system, which corresponds generally with that of Castil-Blaze, although more vaguely formulated. The Italian's work did not actually appear until the next year (*Saggio sopra l'identità de' ritmi poetico e musicale*, Florence, 1820).

132. J.-A. Ducondut, *Essai de rythmique française*, Paris, 1856; A. Fleury, "Du rythme dans la poésie chantée," *Études religieuses, philosophiques* ... 30e année LX, November 15, 1893.

133. *Ibid.* Among the experts convinced of the validity of Castil-Blaze's theories was J.-B. Weckerlin ("Observations sur les vers lyriques," *Bulletins de la Société des compositeurs de musique* I (2), Paris, 1863, p. 55).

134. Fétis, "Du rhythme de la poésie lyrique et des études rhythmiques de M. A. van Hasselt," *RGM* XXX, no. 11, March 15, 1863, pp. 81–83.

135. Roger, *loc. cit.*

136. C. Beauchemin, *Méloprosodie française ou Guide du chanteur*, Paris, 1847, p. 6.

137. C. Saint-Saëns, "La poésie et la musique," in *Harmonie et mélodie*, Paris, 1885, pp. 257–266.

138. M. Bourges, "Situation mélodique actuelle," *RGM* XIII, no. 30, July 26, 1846, pp. 235–236.

139. Blanchard, "Mélodie et poésie," *RGM* XX, no. 34–35, August 21–28, 1853, pp. 293–294, 301–302.

140. M. Lussy, *Traité de l'expression musicale; accents, nuances, mouvements dans la musique vocale et instrumentale*, Paris, 1874. English translation from the 4th ed. by M. E. von Glehn, *Musical Expression, Accents, Nuances, and Tempo in Vocal and Instrumental Music*, London, [1892], p. 53.

141. R. Brancour, article "Mélodie," in *La grande encyclopédie*, Paris, n.d., Vol. 23, pp. 612–616.

142. J. Combarieu, *Les rapports de la musique et de la poésie considérées au point de vue de l'expression*, Paris, 1894, pp. 422–423.

143. V. d'Indy, *Cours de composition musicale*, 3 vols., Paris, 1903–1933. The quoted excerpts are from the 5th ed., Vol. I (1912), pp. 47, 29, and 28.

144. *Ibid.*, p. 40. A realization of musical rhyme was attempted by Charles Bordes in the *mélodie* "Le son du cor s'afflige vers les bois," where he follows the exact scheme of the Verlaine sonnet: a-b-b-a a-b-b-a c-c-d e-e-d.

145. H. Woollett, *Petit traité de prosodie à l'usage des compositeurs*, Le Havre, 1903, pp. 94–95.

146. F. Divoire, "Sous la musique que faut-il mettre? De beaux vers, de mauvais, des vers libres, de la prose?" *Musica*, No. 101–102, February–March 1911, pp. 38–40, 58–60.

147. *Saint-Saëns par lui-même, d'après ses lettres reçues et commentées par Pierre Aguétant*, Paris, 1938, pp. 32–34 (letters from Cannes, May 9, 1918; from Paris, August 26, 1918; and from Cannes, May 28, 1918).

148. Saint-Saëns, "La poésie et la musique," pp. 265–266.

149. The quotations are from "Poètes et musiciens," *FM* I, no. 36, September 2, 1838, pp. 4–5. The article was later reprinted in *Mst* VII, no. 35, July 26, 1846, with the title "Les poètes et la musique." Balzac was another victim of similar gibes from the contemporary press. When his novella "Gambara" was published, a reviewer wrote (in *Mst* IV, no. 29, August 27, 1837): "O young musicians who think you understand Beethoven and Meyerbeer, read 'Gambara' and you will realize that the author of *La peau de chagrin* is wiser than you concerning these two fine geniuses. He will teach you that Beethoven wrote a symphony in C-flat, a detail of which you were no doubt as unaware as I am. ... They say that the music industry, amazed at M. de Balzac's erudition, should send a delegation to beg him to compose an opera entitled *La physiologie du mariage*."

150. Rousseau, *Lettre sur la musique françoise*, Paris, 1753. "The origin of French criticism" is seen in this and other statements of the Encyclopedists (J. Tiersot, *Jean-Jacques Rousseau*, Paris, 1912, p. 126).

151. T. Gautier, *Caprices et zigzags*, Paris, n.d., and *Les grotesques*, Paris, 1834–1835.

152. J. Gautier, *Le second rang du collier*, Paris, n.d.

153. J. Gautier, *Le collier des jours*, 2 vols., Paris, n.d.

154. Cf. *La presse*, December 11, 1839 and A. Boschot, *Un romantique sous Louis-Philippe, Hector Berlioz, 1831–1842*, new ed., Paris, 1948, pp. 282, 291–292. Concerning the review of the *Requiem* written by Jules Janin, Berlioz wrote him: "You have done very well with my notes concerning the music."

155. H. de Curzon, "Théophile Gautier et la musique," *Mst* LXXXIV, no. 43, October 27, 1922, pp. 421–423.

156. R. L. Evans, *Les romantiques français et la musique*, Paris, 1934, p. 40 (*Bibliothèque de la Revue de littérature comparée*, tome 100).

157. Gautier, "Le nid des rossignols," first published in *L'amulette, étrennes à nos jeunes amis*, Paris, 1834.

158. Curzon, *loc. cit.*

159. Cf. the introduction to Gautier, *Poésies complètes*, ed. René Jasinski, Paris, 1932, Vol. I, p. lii.

160. *Ibid.*, p. lv. In David's collection the *mélodies* are entitled "Amour pour amour" and "Tristesse de l'Odalisque." The poem "Dans un soupir" underwent several transformations before its publication in the *Poésies complètes* (1845), where the initial words became "Dans un baiser." Another poem, "Sultan Mahmoud," was also written for Félicien David.

161. *Ibid.*, p. lvi.

162. *Ibid.*, pp. xlvi and liv.

163. Curzon, *loc. cit.*

164. Musset, "Concert de Mlle Garcia," *Revue des deux mondes* 4th ser. XVII, January 1, 1839, p. 111.

165. L. Séché, *Alfred de Musset*, Paris, 1907, Vol. II, p. 141.

166. Quoted by Evans (*op. cit.*, p. 23) from P. de Musset, *Biographie d'Alfred de Musset*, Paris, 1879.

167. Musset, "Emmeline," *Revue des deux mondes* 4th ser. XI, 1837, pp. 303–336; "Le désir" is, of course, not by Beethoven but by Schubert (*Trauerwalzer* in A-flat, op. 9, no. 2, Deutsch no. 365, 2).

168. Javotte in "Le secret de Javotte," *Le constitutionnel*, 1844; Mme. de Parnes in "Les deux maîtresses," *Revue des deux mondes* 4th ser. XII, November 1, 1837, pp. 257–304; "the first mistress" in *La confession d'un enfant du siècle*, Paris, 1836, I, Chap. 10; Tizianello in "Le fils de Titien," *Revue des deux mondes* 4th ser. XIV, May 1, 1838, pp. 313–350; Octave in *La confession d'un enfant du siècle*, V, Chap. 6.

169. The Abbé Désidério in *Les marrons du feu* (1829); Silvio and Nino in *À quoi rêvent les jeunes filles* (1832); Césario and Grémio in *André del Sarto* (1833);

Fantasio in the comedy of that title (1833); Giomo of Hungary in *Lorenzaccio* (1834); Barberine and Rosemberg in *Barberine* (1835); Fortunio in *Le chandelier* (1835); Van Buck in *Il ne faut jurer de rien* (1836); the Marquis de Valberg in *On ne saurait penser à tout* (1849); and Bettine in the comedy of the same title (1851).

170. Cf. Evans, *op. cit.*, p. 156. The poem "La nuit de juin," begun in 1836, was never completed. According to Séché (*op. cit.*, Vol. II, p. 141), "he wrote this single stanza after humming Pacini's cavatina that Liszt's fingers and Rubini's voice had just made popular."

171. Before "Lucie," the same lines, very slightly varied, had already been used in "Le saule" (1830).

172. Musset, "Concert de Mlle Garcia," *Revue des deux mondes* 4th ser. XVII, January 1, 1839, p. 113.

173. Musset, "Débuts de Mlle Garcia," *ibid.* XX, November 1, 1839, p. 440. Cf. Diderot, *Rameau's Nephew*, trans. J. Barzun, New York, 1956, p. 64: "What is the musician's or the melody's model? It is declamation if the model is alive and a thinking being; it is physical noise if the model is inanimate. Consider declamation as one line and song as another, which twists snakelike about the former." Grétry revived this idea in his *Mémoires*.

174. Musset, "Le poète et le prosateur," an article written in 1839 and published posthumously in his *Œuvres complètes*.

175. Tiersot, *La chanson populaire et les écrivains romantiques*, Paris, 1931, p. 303.

176. Lamartine, *Méditations poétiques*, edition of 1849.

177. Lamartine, "La voix humaine," in *Harmonies poétiques et religieuses*, 1830, no. 38.

178. Lamartine, "La musique de Mozart," in Entretien XXIX–XXX, *Cours familier de littérature*, Paris, 1858, Vol. V, pp. 281–440.

179. Several poems from the *Recueillements poétiques* were nevertheless destined to be sung: "Le grillon," later set by Bizet, "Le moulin de Milly," "Une fleur," and "À une fiancée de quinze ans."

180. Lamartine, "Les préludes," in *Nouvelles méditations*.

181. Lamartine, "L'homme," in *Premières méditations*.

182. Lamartine, "L'isolement," *ibid.*

183. Lamartine, "Le golfe de Baïa," *ibid.*

184. Hugo expresses the same thought with reference to Palestrina in "Que la musique date du seizième siècle":

> Car, maître! c'est à vous que tous nos soupirs vont
> Sitôt qu'une voix chante et qu'une âme répond!

185. H. Expert, "À propos de la musique française à l'époque de la Renaissance," in *Encyclopédie de la musique et Dictionnaire du Conservatoire*, Paris, 1913, Part I, Vol. III, p. 1261.

186. The concert was on December 22, 1833, according to Berlioz' letter of December 26 to his sister Adèle (quoted in his *Les années romantiques 1818–1842, correspondance publiée par Julien Tiersot*, Paris, 1904, pp. 247–251).

187. Hugo, *William Shakespeare*, Part I, Book 2, IV.

188. Hugo, *Les misérables*, Part IV, Book 5, Chap. II. Hugo names the particular chorus "Chasseurs égarés dans les bois," but it is not clear to which piece he refers.

189. Hugo, *William Shakespeare*, loc. cit.

190. Hugo, "À un riche," in *Les voix intérieures*, XIX, 1837.

191. Hugo, "Que la musique date du seizième siècle," II.

192. Hugo, *Notre-Dame de Paris*, Book 2, III; Book 9, IV; Book 3, II.

193. The descriptions of the organ are from *Notre-Dame de Paris*, Book 9, IV and from "Dans l'église de ...," in *Les chants du crépuscule*.

194. Hugo, "Carnets inédits," in *Les nouvelles littéraires* XXX, April 5, 1951, p. 1.

195. Hugo, *Notre-Dame de Paris*, Book 3, II.

196. Cf. H. Schouten, *Drie Franse Liederencomponisten, Duparc, Fauré, Debussy*, Amsterdam, 1950, p. 20. In his "Carnets inédits" Hugo wrote: "Nothing irritates me like the passion for setting beautiful verse to music" (cf. *Les nouvelles littéraires*, XXXI, February 21, 1952, p. 9).

197. Hugo, *Les orientales* (1829), and Gautier, *Poésies complètes* (1845).

198. The *Lied* is conceived here in the very broad meaning it had for the French Romantics, to include also the German *Ballade* and *Romanze*. G. Sattler (*Das deutsche Lied in der französischen Romantik*, Berne, 1932, p. 14) explains that "for the French Romantic, *Lied* meant chiefly German lyric poetry, wherever it has not acquired foreign forms; and when a French poem is entitled *Lied*, it obviously means that it was written under the influence of German lyric poetry and in the same spirit."

199. "Your centralization is apoplexy at the center and paralysis at the extremities," said Lamennais (quoted in Sattler, *op. cit.*, op. 23); Schuré complained that "our excessive centralization is the curse of poetry" (*Histoire du Lied*, 2d ed., Paris, 1876, p. 495.

200. Cf. Sattler, *op. cit.*, p. 33.

201. Hugo, preface to *Odes et ballades*, 1826, and preface to *Feuilles d'automne*, 1831.

202. Musset, preface to the reader, *Premières poésies*, 1832.

203. Quoted in Sattler, *op. cit.*, p. 116.

204. A.-I. Trannoy, *La musique des vers*, Paris, 1929, pp. 7 and 110.

205. Cf. L. Quicherat, *Petit traité de versification française*, Paris, 1839; 7th ed., 1881, p. 80. Rhythmic imitation seems also to be included in the notion of imitative harmony.

206. L. Becq de Fouquières, *Traité général de versification française*, Paris, 1879.

Quotations from the work are from pp. 219–220 and 243–245. In similar research in the field of German poetry, the philologist L. Lützeler calls the generative sound the *Leitvokal*. He even points out a kind of polyphony in poems where, in the course of a stanza, two or more generative sounds each find a resonance for itself. See his "Lautgestaltung in der Lyrik," *Zeitschrift für Aesthetik und Allgemeine Kunstwissenschaft* XXIX, 1935, pp. 193–216.

207. J. Combarieu, *Les rapports de la musique et de la poésie* ..., Paris, 1894. Quotations from the work are from pp. 190–222.

208. Trannoy, *op. cit.*, p. 113.

209. Armand Silvestre was the exception to this rule. Although he was a Parnassian, many of his poems were set to music by Delibes, Massenet, Castillon, and Fauré.

210. From the questionnaire put to composers by *Musica* (Divoire, *loc. cit.*).

211. A. Marie, *Gérard de Nerval, le poète et l'homme*, Paris, 1914.

212. Gérard de Nerval, "La Bohème galante," no. VI of "Petits châteaux de Bohème," *L'artiste*, September 15, 1852. Nerval's tune seems to be lost.

213. The hero of Balzac's novella "Gambara" (1837) is a composer who analyzes Meyerbeer's *Robert le diable* in a floridly Romantic manner. In Balzac's "Massimilla Doni" (1839) the Italian princess of the title explains the profound beauty of Rossini's opera *Mosè in Egitto* in a similar way.

214. Berlioz' remark is too interesting to be omitted, even though I have unfortunately lost the card giving its source.

215. H. Berlioz, *Mémoires*, Paris, 1870, Chap. I.

216. The resemblance was called to my attention by Henri Gougelot. It seems unlikely that Berlioz was familiar with Haydn's song.

217. Berlioz, *op. cit.*, Chap. IV. For a recent comment on this incident, see H. Macdonald, "Berlioz's Self-Borrowings," *Royal Musical Association Proceedings* 92, 1965/66, p. 29.

218. J. Tiersot, *La musique aux temps romantiques*, Paris, 1930, pp. 79–81.

219. F. Stoepel, review of Berlioz, *Neuf mélodies*, *GM* I, no. 21, May 25, 1834, p. 170.

220. H. Boschot, *La jeunesse d'un romantique*, new ed., Paris, 1946, p. 214.

221. Announcement of Schlesinger's publication of Berlioz, *Neuf mélodies*, *RMF* VII, March 6, 1830, p. 160.

222. Stoepel, *loc. cit.*

223. Boschot, *loc. cit.*

224. Berlioz, *op. cit.*, Chap. LX (4th letter, written from Leipzig to Stephen Heller).

225. Cf. Berlioz' "Remarks on the subject of the elegy," in his *Werke*, ed. C. Malherbe and F. Weingartner, Leipzig, 1904, Ser. VII, Vol. XVII, Pt. 2, pp. 46–47. The translation of the song text into French prose was made by the composer.

226. One of Berlioz' biographers, Tom Wotton, suggests that "For Harriet Smithson," taken by French writers as the meaning of the "F. H. S." heading the first edition of the "Elegy," is incorrect. He proposes instead the motto "Farewell Harriet Smithson." Wotton suspects, admittedly "entirely without evidence," that although Berlioz still spoke of his suffering from Harriet's absence in February 1830, Marie Moke "was already attracting him in spite of himself" (T. Wotton, *Hector Berlioz*, London, 1935, p. 129).

227. Berlioz, *Mémoires*, Chap. XVIII.

228. *Ibid.*

229. Stoepel, *loc. cit.*

230. Berlioz had previously set "Chanson de pirates," another *orientale* by Hugo, but this work has been lost (cf. Boschot, *op. cit.*, p. 186).

231. Berlioz, *op. cit.*, Chap. XXXIX.

232. É. Fétis, "Concert donné par M. Berlioz," *RMF* XIV, no. 48, November 30, 1834, p. 382.

233. Boschot, *Un romantique sous Louis-Philippe*, new ed., Paris, 1948, p. 131.

234. Cf. the catalogue *Musik-Autographen, Auktion, 10. Oktober 1951 in Stuttgart*, Eutin & Stuttgart, 1951, p. 19, no. 13. The present owner of the ms. is not known. Another aut. ms. in the Bibl. Nat. is undated.

235. Cf. Boschot, *Un romantique*, p. 131. The irony of fate prescribed a single instance in which a text radically contradicted reality. The orchestral score of "Absence" ("Return, return, my beloved") was dedicated to Marie Recio barely a month after the composer's flight from Frankfurt (cf. Boschot, *Le crépuscule d'un romantique*, new ed., Paris, 1950, pp. 8 and 15).

236. At the time a collection of his songs was published, Berlioz wrote to his good friend Joseph d'Ortigue, who was replacing him as critic of the *Journal des débats* during his absence from Paris: "If you can find a way of saying, in a column and a half, anything important about my songs, do so; if not, leave them for another opportunity. I merely wish people to know that they exist, that the music in them is not trumpery, that I do not write simply to sell, that only a consummate musician, singer, and pianist can interpret these small compositions faithfully, and that they take neither in form nor in style after those of Schubert" (letter from London, May 5, 1852, quoted in Berlioz, *Life and Letters*, trans. H. Mainwaring Dunstan, London, 1882, Vol. I, p. 212). So far as is known, no review appeared.

237. The first quotation is from an anonymous review of *Keepsake lyrique* (Paris, Pacini), an album of thirty romances, *chansonnettes*, and *nocturnes* by various composers (*RMF* XV, no. 2, January 11, 1835, p. 15); the second is by A. Thurner, "Étude comparée sur la chanson, la romance, et le Lied," *RGM* XXXIV, no. 41, October 13, 1867, p. 327.

238. Berlioz, unsigned review of Meyerbeer, "Le moine" in *GM* II, no. 6, February 8, 1835, pp. 50–51.

239. Cf. L. Dauriac, *Meyerbeer*, Paris, 1913, p. 65 (note 2), and H. de Curzon, *Meyerbeer*, Paris, 1910, p. 45.

240. Berlioz, "Chants pour le piano, de Meyerbeer," *GM* II, no. 42–43, October 18–25, 1835, pp. 342–343 and 351.

241. Autograph letter (Berlin, February 6, 1842) in the Bibl. Nat. Meyerbeer is referring to "Luft von Morgen," which was translated by Maurice Bourges. The composer was evidently unable to prevent its publication, since it appeared with the incorrect title in the collection *40 mélodies* (Brandus, 1849).

242. Dauriac considered the appellation *Tondichter* (tone-poet) hardly applicable to Meyerbeer, since "the musical imagination must contain a grain of poetry. ... Meyerbeer is as incurably a prose writer as was our Voltaire" (Dauriac, *op. cit.*, p. 191).

243. M. Bourges, "Quarante mélodies à une et à plusieurs voix par G. Meyerbeer," *RGM* XVII, no. 19, May 12, 1850, p. 159.

244. Autograph letter (Berlin, November 27, 1841) in the Bibl. Nat.

245. Autograph letter (Boulogne-sur-Mer, August 28, 1839) in the Bibl. Nat.

246. Dauriac, *op. cit.*, pp. 182–183.

247. "Le poète mourant" appears to have been the only piece that did not entirely satisfy contemporary critics. One of them described it as a mediocre composition and maliciously added that "when you reach the last measure you gladly believe that it is not the author who is dying, but the composer" (*FM* I, no. 6, February 4, 1838, p. 4). Berlioz referred euphemistically to "Meyerbeer's tour de force." He considered Millevoye's poem obsolete and entirely unsuited for musical setting (*RGM* V, no. 5, February 4, 1838, p. 54 [i.e., 44]).

248. F.-J. Fétis, review of Meyerbeer, *Douze mélodies*, in *RGM* VIII, no. 21, March 14, 1841, p. 166. The composer thanked Fétis for the article even before he had read it! (Cf. Tiersot, *Lettres de musiciens écrites en français*, Paris, 1924, Vol. II, p. 134).

249. Cf. L. Ramann, *Franz Liszt als Künstler und Mensch*, 3 vols., Leipzig, 1880–1894; E. Reuss, *Franz Liszts Lieder*, Leipzig, 1906; and J. Wenz, *Franz Liszt als Lyriker*, Frankfurt am Main, 1921 (unpublished thesis).

250. Liszt considered only four of the *mélodies* worthy of publication in his *Gesammelte Lieder* (1860) and even those he revised completely: "Comment, disaient-ils," "Oh! quand je dors," "S'il est un charmant gazon," and "Enfant, si j'étais roi," all with words by Hugo. Later the composer added "Tristesse" (Musset). The dramatic romance "Jeanne d'Arc au bûcher," first published in 1846, was revised in 1858 but this version remained in ms. Sixteen years later Liszt arranged the piece for piano and orchestra and the score was published by Schott. "La tombe et la rose" (Hugo), "Gastibelza" (Hugo), and "Il m'aimait tant" (Delphine Gay) were not republished during the composer's lifetime; they are available in his *Musikalische Werke*, Leipzig,

1917, Ser. VII, Vol. I, together with the unpublished "Le vieux vagabond" (Béranger).

251. Quoted by P. Raabe in his preliminary remarks (*ibid.*, Leipzig, 1922, Ser. VII, Vol. III, p. v).

252. A letter that Wagner wrote to Émile Deschamps suggests the possibility that the composer wrote other songs to French texts besides these six:

> Paris, September 28, 1840
> Monsieur, the extreme willingness with which you agreed to my request to write some verses for me makes me bold enough to ask you to attend to the matter as soon as possible, because M. Pillet is going to grant me a short audition in a few days, at which time I would like to let him hear the music in question.
> Be assured, Monsieur, of the very high regard with which I have the honor of being your most obliging servant.
> Richard Wagner, 25 rue Helder.

(Quoted in H. Girard, *Un bourgeois dilettante* ..., Paris, 1921, Vol. II, p. 95).

253. The suggested resemblance between this *mélodie* and the "Spinnerlied" from *Der fliegende Holländer* appears quite farfetched to me. Cf. J. Kapp, *Richard Wagner*, Berlin, 1910, p. 132; M. Koch, *Richard Wagner*, Berlin, 1907, Vol. I, p. 291; and C. F. Glasenapp, *Das Leben Richard Wagners*, 4th rev. ed., Leipzig, 1905, Vol. I, p. 348.

254. Wagner wrote to Schumann on December 29, 1840 (quoted in Koch, *loc. cit.*): "I hear that you have set Heine's 'Grenadiers' and that the 'Marseillaise' appears at the end of it. Last winter I also set it and brought the 'Marseillaise' in at the end too. This must have some significance. ... I hereby rededicate my piece to you privately, even though it is already dedicated to Heine. Likewise, I inform you that I accept the private dedication of your 'Grenadiers' and await the dedication copy."

255. Comparing the two settings of the "Grenadiers," Koch (*loc. cit.*) calls Wagner's "surely a composition of equal quality." Kapp (*loc. cit.*) states even more positively that in Wagner's version the "Marseillaise" sounds stronger and results in a more artistic effect. Glasenapp (*loc. cit.*) sees hints of *Tristan* and *Parsifal* already present in the French *mélodies*.

256. Cf. Combarieu, *Histoire de la musique*, new ed., Paris, 1947, Vol. III, p. 111. On this subject, a significant comment by David expresses his reaction to the *première* of *Benvenuto Cellini*: "This man [Berlioz] lacks inspiration, melody; his work certainly has undeniable talent, but it is all forced, strained" (David, autograph letter no. 82, Bibl. Nat.)

257. Cognat was the composer's traveling companion in the Orient; this "adaptation," however, does not ring quite true.

258. Fauré himself wrote a song on another version of this *orientale*, calling it "Seule" (op. 3, no. 1).

259. David, autograph letters no. 77–78, Bibl. Nat.

260. This paradoxical use of the major mode, also found in Niedermeyer (see Example 4) and Schubert (e.g., 2d stanza of "Der Wegweiser"), is characteristic of musical Romanticism. Analogous phenomena may be observed in the literature of the period, as for example the sad lines of "La pensée des morts," written "to the sound of a blind piper's bagpipes, dance music for a peasant wedding." Lamartine wonders why this spectacle awakens sad feelings in him: "There was nothing there to suggest sadness and death. What was it then that led me to this thought? I know nothing about it, but I imagine it was precisely the contrast, the pressure of the pleasurable sensation on the heart, pushing it too strongly and expressing too thoroughly the power of pleasure and love, and making it feel that all would soon be over, and that the last drop of that sponge of the heart which drinks and surrenders life is a tear. Perhaps it was simply the sight of one of those beautiful immobile cypresses outlined in black against the striking blue of the sky, and recalling the tomb" (Lamartine, *Harmonies poétiques et religieuses*, commentary on "La pensée des morts," 1849).

261. David's occasional nonchalance toward his texts is demonstrated in one of his letters to Sylvain Saint-Étienne (autograph letter no. 90, November 27, 1841, Bibl. Nat.): "I have written one of these choruses without words; I give you the task of putting some to it. I have adapted some words to it after a fashion, to show you the prosody and the construction of the phrases. I have enough faith in your musical intelligence to believe that you will take care of it in the proper way. It does not matter if the lines are equal, provided that there is a rhyme to them."

262. Saint-Saëns, "Henri Reber," in *Harmonie et mélodie*, pp. 283–284. Legouvé's portrait of Reber, published almost forty years earlier, confirms the picture: "Reber is not of this age; without any effort, without searching, his music has the strangeness of works from another period; he is the contemporary of Haydn, the Boccherini of our day" (Legouvé, "Reber," *FM* VI, no. 13, March 26, 1843, pp. 98–99).

263. Cf. *FM* I, no. 8, February 18, 1838, p. 4 and Legouvé, *loc. cit.*

264. M. Ravel, "Les mélodies de Gabriel Fauré," *La revue musicale* III, no. 11, October 1, 1922, p. 215, and T. Klingsor, "Les musiciens et les poètes contemporains," *Mercure de France* XXXVI, November 1900, p. 430.

265. G. Servières, "Charles Gounod, compositeur de mélodies," *Mst* C, no. 15, April 15, 1938, p. 105.

266. Cf. the fragment of "La plainte du barde" by Henri Montan Berton, cited in Gougelot, *La romance française* ..., Vol. I, p. 184.

267. Saint-Saëns, "La poésie et la musique," in *Harmonie et mélodie*, Paris, 1885, pp. 261–262.

268. One unusual license should be noted. In the vowel group -*ie*-, the rules of French versification allow the poet to apply either synaeresis or diaeresis, depending on the needs of the situation. Although Gounod claims this right for the composer also, his handling of the versification in the *mélodie* "Tombez mes ailes" nevertheless seems curious. He twice scans the word "hier" as a

disyllable even though in Legouvé's lines the words has only a single syllable. Gounod undoubtedly took this liberty for purely musical reasons.

269. Servières, *loc. cit.*

270. According to Boschot, *Un romantique* ..., p. 338. Gounod's *mélodie* is in the third collection published by Choudens.

271. Cf. Gounod, *Mémoires d'un artiste*, Paris, 1896, pp. 84–85.

272. Quoted in J.-G. Prod'homme and A. Dandelot, *Gounod*, Paris, 1911, Vol. I, p. 80.

273. *Ibid.*, pp. 63–68.

274. "Report from Paris" in *Allgemeine musikalische Zeitung* V, no. 37, September 14, 1870, p. 295 and VI, no. 1, January 4, 1871, p. 14. Cf. also Prod'homme-Dandelot, *op. cit.*, Vol. II, pp. 121 and 123, notes.

275. Servières, *loc. cit.* It would be more accurate to say that in England Gounod spoiled his artistic integrity. His purely musical faculties were surely formed too long before to be so easily lost.

276. Byron had been inspired to write the poem "Maid of Athens" by Mrs. Black, who by 1872 was quite elderly and poverty-stricken. When a fund for her relief was started, Gounod contributed his rights to the *mélodie*. Cf. Prod'homme-Dandelot, *op. cit.*, Vol. II, p. 274.

277. *La musique* (gazette of *FM*) I, 1849, p. 148.

278. M. Bourges, review of Massé, *Chants d'autrefois* in *RGM* XVI, no. 26, July 1, 1849, p. 206.

279. Curzon, *Ernest Reyer, sa vie et ses œuvres*, Paris, 1924, p. 4.

280. Several of these *mélodies* appear to have been borrowed from unfinished operas. Cf. W. Dean, *Georges Bizet, His Life and Works*, London, 1965, pp. 152–157, 266–269.

281. Letter of September 1866 to Edmond Galabert, in G. Bizet, *Lettres à un ami, 1865–1872*, Paris, 1909, p. 77.

282. The F-minor chorus also appears in an arrangement for solo voice and piano in the first volume of Bizet's *mélodies*, published by Choudens. The relation between the two pieces misled Pigot, Bizet's first biographer. He twice speaks of "Pastorale" as an "arrangement for solo voice and piano of the lovely chorus in F-sharp minor from *L'Arlésienne*," obviously confusing it with the second number of the collection, where the arrangement in question appears under the title "Le matin" (cf. G. Pigot, *Georges Bizet et son œuvre*, Paris, 1886, pp. 193 and 318).

283. Considering the interval between 1828 when Hugo wrote the poem and 1866 when Bizet set it to music, one might conclude that for the *mélodie* Orientalism was forty years behind. See also Appendix III.

284. Romagnési, *L'art de chanter*, Paris, 1846, pp. 16–17.

285. R. Hahn, *Thèmes variés*, 10th ed., Paris, 1946, p. 180.

286. *Ibid.*, p. 179, quoted from Fernand Ochsé.

287. The heroine of Claude Farrère's widely read novel *Mademoiselle Dax, jeune fille* (1907) is the prototype of the young bourgeoise at the turn of the century.

288. Hahn, *loc. cit.*

289. J. d'Udine [pseud. of Albert Cozanet], *L'art du Lied et les mélodies de Massenet*, Paris, 1931.

290. C. Bellaigue, "Les mélodies françaises," *Revue des deux mondes* 6th period, 89th year, LIII, September 15, 1919, p. 468.

291. Words between parentheses were added by Massenet.

292. In spite of this resemblance, Saint-Saëns states in the preface of his first song collection (1878) that at the time he did not know "Die Krähe."

293. M. Bourges, review of *Six fables de La Fontaine, mises en musique par J. Offenbach*, in *RGM* IX, no. 15, April 10, 1842, p. 155. Pauline Garcia's setting of the fable "Le chêne et le roseau" and Théodore Ymbert's *Sept fables de La Fontaine* were much more favorably received (cf. *La mélodie* I, no. 19, December 3, 1842, p. 2, and *RGM* XXIX, no. 26, June 29, 1862, pp. 211–212). Another of Offenbach's critics, although conceding his skill as a 'cellist, ridiculed him unmercifully as a composer (T. Labarre, "Concert fabuleux!!! donné, le 16 avril, dans les salons de M. Pleyel, par M. Jacques Offenbach," *FM* V, April 24, 1842, pp. 158–159): "The most astounding part of the announcement was the promise to perform five or six of La Fontaine's fables, all set to music by the same Offenbach. The good La Fontaine hardly expected to see his name ever attached to such a business. Everyone knows that Rameau boasted of being able to set the prose of the *Gazette de Hollande*, should the opportunity arise. M. Offenbach, no doubt taking seriously this comical idea (the realization of which would be excused by the transcendent merit of the master), started from this principle: since a Frenchman did not fear to use a Dutch newspaper as text for his music, he, a German, could indeed be inspired by French fables to lend wings to his genius."

294. Cf. E. Baumann, *Les grandes formes de la musique*, new ed., Paris, 1923, p. 333. Baumann's enthusiasm for "La sérénité," however, is difficult to understand, since the piece suffers from its oratorical style.

295. Servières, *Saint-Saëns*, Paris, 1923, pp. 196–197.

296. *RGM* XXIII, no. 36, September 7, 1856, p. 291.

297. *Ibid.* The *Cinq Lieder* were published in 1884 by Schott in Mainz.

298. A. Giacomelli, review of Lalo, *Six mélodies* in *FM* XX, no. 40 and 51, October 5 and December 21, 1856, pp. 320–321 and 408–409.

299. Lalo's "Veni Creator," a *cantique* that is an arrangement for soprano and organ of the Andante from Schubert's Piano Sonata, op. 42, in A minor (Deutsch no. 845) is mistakenly included as an original work in Hamelle's 1913 publication of twenty Lalo *mélodies*.

300. J. Tiersot, "Les œuvres inédites de César Franck," *La revue musicale* IV, no. 2, December 1, 1922, p. 108.

301. Anonymous review in *Mst* VI, no. 7, January 13, 1839.

302. V. d'Indy, "La première manière de César Franck," *Revue de musicologie* VII, February 1923, p. 5.

303. d'Indy, *César Franck*, 5th ed., Paris, 1910, p. 245; English trans. Rosa Newmarch, London, 1909, pp. 258-270 (Dover reprint, 1965).

304. Cf. d'Indy, "La première manière ...," p. 6.

305. Cf. P. Landormy, *La musique française de Franck à Debussy*, 9th ed., Paris, 1943.

306. C. Koechlin, *Gabriel Fauré*, new ed., Paris, 1949; L. Aguettant, *Fauré*, Lyons, 1924; N. Suckling, *Fauré*, London, 1946; P. Fauré-Frémiet, *Gabriel Fauré*, rev. ed., Paris, 1957; G. Servières, *Gabriel Fauré, étude critique*, Paris, 1930; C. Oulmont, *Musique de l'amour, II: Henri Duparc*, Paris, 1935; F. L. Merle, *Psychologie et pathologie d'un artiste: Henri Duparc*, Bordeaux, 1933 (thesis).

307. V. Jankélévitch, *Gabriel Fauré, ses mélodies, son esthétique*, new ed., Paris, 1951; C. Rostand, *L'œuvre de Gabriel Fauré*, Paris, 1945; S. Northcote, *The Songs of Henri Duparc*, New York, 1950; H. Schouten, *op. cit.*

308. Cf. the "Bibliographie de l'œuvre de Gabriel Fauré," in *La revue musicale* III, no. 11, October 1, 1922, pp. 304–308.

309. Among his biographers, only Servières (*op. cit.*, p. 84) mentions the ms.

310. The simpler meters (2/4, 3/4, and 4/4) are best suited to this type of syncopation, the compound ternary meters (6/8, 9/8, and 12/8) offering fewer possibilities. Thus the practice does not appear at all in "Le papillon et la fleur," "Dans les ruines d'une abbaye," "Sérénade toscane," "Chant d'automne," "Hymne," "Tarantelle," and "Barcarolle."

311. Cf. Koechlin, *op. cit.*, p. 110.

312. *Ibid.*, p. 115.

313. N. Boulanger, "La musique religieuse [de Fauré]," *La revue musicale* III, no. 11, October 1, 1922, p. 298.

314. Jankélévitch, *op. cit.*, pp. 44–45. But where are the derided vocalises in "Chanson du pêcheur"?

315. *Ibid.*, p. 47.

316. Cf. Oulmont, *op. cit.*, p. 12: "Thirteen *mélodies* constitute Duparc's entire glorious production"; Northcote, *op. cit.*, p. 13: "Some fourteen songs, a symphonic poem, an orchestral nocturne, and a three-part motet comprise almost the whole of his existing compositions" (see also p. 43). Among some other errors in Northcote's work is the statement (on p. 53) that "Apart from *Au pays où se fait la guerre* and *Elégie*, which were printed in a musical journal about 1878, Duparc's songs were not published until 1910." The author was apparently unaware of the *Cinq mélodies* published in 1870, as well as the separate songs issued in 1894 and 1895 by Baudoux.

317. The final page of "Romance de Mignon" is lacking, but exists in an autograph ms. belonging to Charles Panzéra.

318. Northcote, *op. cit.*, p. 45.

319. P. de Bréville, "Henri Fouques-Duparc," in *Larousse mensuel illustré* IX, no. 315, May 1933, pp. 403–404.

320. By Jankélévitch (*op. cit.*, p. 47), who also mentions "Hébé," a "Greek" song in the Phrygian mode by Ernest Chausson.

321. Merle, *op. cit., passim.*

322. Ravel, *op. cit.*, p. 215.

323. R. Hahn, *Journal d'un musicien*, Paris, 1949, pp. 16–17.

324. A. Ringer, review of F. Noske, *La mélodie française de Berlioz à Duparc*, in *Amercian Musicological Society Journal* XV, 1955, pp. 217–221.

325. T. Gautier, "Hippolyte Monpou," in *Histoire du romantisme*, Paris, 1873, pp. 254–258.

326. H. Bachelin, "Hippolyte Monpou, musicien romantique," *Mst* XC, no. 20, May 18, 1928, p. 217.

327. Quoted by G. Grand, "Hippolyte Monpou," *Revue de Paris* new ser. IX, January 15, 1868, p. 299. Bachelin (*op. cit.*, p. 218) says that Monpou received only twenty-five francs for "L'Andalouse."

328. Grand, *op. cit.*, p. 298.

329. Quoted in Grand, *op. cit.*, pp. 303–305.

330. An unsigned review of a "Concert de M. H. Monpou" also calls "Lénore" the composer's "most important work" (*RMF* XIII, no. 11, April 13, 1833, p. 86).

331. After 1830 Monpou no longer wrote religious music (with the possible exception of "Paroles d'un croyant," on a prose text by the Romantic priest Lamennais, whose works were condemned by the Church, and *La chaste Suzanne*, an opera that is more erotic than religious).

332. The edition contains many typographical errors, most of which may be corrected without any difficulty (e.g., the C-sharp instead of C-natural on the sixth beats of measures 30 and 32).

333. Donizetti's romance "Les yeux noirs et les yeux bleus" and Gabussi's duet "Les petits Savoyards," both with words by Monnier, were pub. in the *Album du Monde musical*, 1845.

334. Quittard, "L'orientalisme musical. Saint-Saëns orientaliste," *La revue musicale* VI, no. 5, March 1, 1906, pp. 107–116, from which all references to Quittard are taken.

335. Since the publication of the original edition of this book, the song has appeared in Vol. XVI of the series *Anthology of Music: The Solo Song Outside German Speaking Countries*, ed. F. Noske, Cologne, 1958, pp. 79–80.

BIBLIOGRAPHY

Nineteenth-Century Periodicals Consulted

Les annales du théâtre et de la musique, Paris, 1875–1916.

L'art musical, Paris, 1860–1894.

Bulletins de la Société des compositeurs de musique, ed. J. B. Weckerlin, Paris, 1863–1870.

La chronique musicale, Paris, 1865–1876.

Le contemporain, Paris, founded 1892.

Le correspondant, Paris, 1843–1933.

Le courrier musical et théâtral, Paris, 1897–1935.

Le dilettante, Journal de musique, Paris, 1833–1834.

La France musicale, Paris, 1837–1870. Abbreviation: *FM*.

Gazette musicale de Paris, 1834–1835. Abbreviation: *GM*. United with *La revue musicale* (Fétis) to form *Revue et Gazette musicale de Paris*.

Le guide musical, Brussels-Paris, 1855–1918.

Journal des débats, Paris, founded 1789.

Journal général d'annonce des œuvres de musique, gravures, lithographies, etc. publiées en France et à l'étranger, Paris, 1825–1827.

La mélodie, Paris, 1842–1843.

Le ménestrel, Paris, 1833–1940. Abbreviation: *Mst*.

Mercure de France, Paris, 1672–1820; 1890– .

Le monde musical, ed. Mangeot, Paris, 1889–1940.

La musique, gazette de La France musicale, Paris, 1849–1850.

Revue de Paris, Paris, 1829–1845.

Revue de Paris, Paris, 1866–1869.

Revue des deux mondes, Paris, 1829–1944.

Revue et Gazette musicale de Paris, 1835–1880. Abbreviation: *RGM*.

Revue hebdomadaire, Paris, 1892–1939.

Revue internationale de musique, Paris, 1898–1899.

La revue musicale, ed. Fétis, Paris, 1827–1835. Abbreviation: *RMF*. United with *Gazette musicale de Paris* to form *Revue et Gazette musicale de Paris*.

La romance, Paris, 1834–1835.

La semaine musicale, Paris, 1865–1867.

Books, Articles, and Musical Works Not in the Song Catalogue

Aguettant, Louis, *Fauré*, Lyons, 1924.

Aubry, Georges Jean, *La musique française d'aujourd'hui*, Paris, 1916; English trans. by Edwin Evans, *French Music of Today*, London, 1919.

Bachelin, Henri, "Hippolyte Monpou, musicien romantique, 12 janvier 1804 – 10 août 1841," *Mst* XC, no. 19–20, May 11 and 18, 1928, pp. 205–206, 217–219.

Baini, Giuseppe, *Saggio sopra l'identità de' ritmi poetico e musicale*, Florence, 1820.

Baldensperger, Fernand, *Sensibilité musicale et romantisme*, Paris, 1925 (*Études romantiques*, ed. Henri Girard, I).

——— *Orientations étrangères chez H. de Balzac*, Paris, n.d. (*Bibliothèque de la Revue de littérature comparée*, tome 31).

Ballard, Christophe, *Brunetes ou Petits airs tendres, avec les doubles et la basse-continue, mélées de chansons à danser*, Paris, 1703–1711.

Balzac, Honoré de, *Gambara*, first pub. in *RGM* IV, July–August 1837.

——— *Massimilla Doni*, first pub. Paris, 1839 (and in part in *FM* II, 1839).

——— *La peau de chagrin*, first pub. Paris, 1831.

Barat, E., *Le style poétique et la révolution romantique*, Paris, 1904.

Barzun, Jacques, review of Frits Noske, *La mélodie française de Berlioz à Duparc* in *Music Library Association Notes* 2d ser. XII, no. 3, June 1955, pp. 441–442.

Bataille, Gabriel, *Airs de différents autheurs mis en tablature de luth*, 9 vols., Paris, 1609–1620.

Batteux, l'Abbé Charles, *Les beaux-arts réduits à un même principe*, Paris, 1746.

Baumann, Émile, *Les grandes formes de la musique. L'œuvre de Camille Saint-Saëns*, new ed., Paris, 1923.

Beauchemin, Charles, *Méloprosodie française ou Guide du chanteur*, Paris, 1847.

Becq de Fouquières, Louis, *Traité général de versification française*, Paris, 1879.

Bellaigue, Camille, "Balzac et la musique," *Revue des deux mondes* 7th period, 97th year, XXIII, October 1, 1924, pp. 682–697.

——— "Les mélodies françaises," *Revue des deux mondes* 6th period, 89th year, LIII, September 15, 1919, pp. 448–468.

——— "La musique et la poésie (d'après l'ouvrage de M. Combarieu)," *Le correspondant* new ser. CXXXVIII, March 25, 1894, pp. 1118–1132.

——— *Paroles et musique*, Paris, 1925.

Berlioz, Hector, *Les années romantiques 1819–1842, correspondance publiée par Julien Tiersot*, Paris, 1904.

—— "Chants pour le piano, de Meyerbeer," *GM* II, no. 42–43, October 18–25, 1835, pp. 342–343 and 351.

—— *Life and Letters*, trans. H. Mainwaring Dunstan, 2 vols., London, 1882.

—— *Mémoires*, Paris, 1870.

—— review of Meyerbeer, "Le moine," in *GM* II, no. 6, February 8, 1835, pp. 50–51.

—— review of Meyerbeer, "Le poète mourant," in *RGM* V, no. 5, February 4, 1838, pp. 53–54 [i.e., 43–44].

—— [signed "H . . ."], "Société des concerts du Conservatoire: Premier concert," *Journal des débats*, January 25, 1835.

"Bibliographie de l'œuvre de Gabriel Fauré," *La revue musicale* III, no. 11, October 1, 1922, pp. 304–308 (also numbered 112–116).

Biche-Latour, A., review of F. David, *Romances et mélodies* in *RGM* IX, no. 47, November 20, 1842, p. 458.

Bizet, Georges, *Lettres à un ami, 1865–1872*, Paris, 1909.

Blanchard, Henri, "Des albums; revue critique," *RGM* VIII, no. 2, January 7, 1841, pp. 11–13.

—— "Les deux romances," *RGM* VI, 1839, no. 21, May 23, 1839, pp. 170–171.

—— "Mélodie et poésie," *RGM* XX, no. 34–35, August 21–28, 1853, pp. 293–294, 301–302.

—— "Le premier de l'an musical," *RGM* VII, no. 77, December 31, 1840, pp. 647–649.

—— review of E. de Coussemaker, *Huit mélodies* in *RGM* V, no. 2, January 14, 1838, pp. 13–14.

—— review of J. Dessauer, *Mélodies* in *RGM* IX, no. 5, January 30, 1842, pp. 45–46.

—— "Romagnési," *RGM* V, no. 41, October 14, 1838, pp. 409–412.

Blaze, François Henri Joseph: see Castil-Blaze, François Henri Joseph

Blaze de Bury, Henri, *Musiciens contemporains*, Paris, 1856.

—— "Poètes et musiciens d'Allemagne: Uhland et M. Dessauer," *Revue des deux mondes* 4th ser. V, October 15, 1835, pp. 129–158.

—— "Poètes et romanciers modernes de la France, XLIV: MM. Émile et Antony Deschamps," *Revue des deux mondes* 4th ser. XXVII, August 1841, pp. 545–573.

—— *Tableaux romantiques de littérature et d'art*, Paris, 1878.

Boîte à musique, "Sur les mélodies de Henri Duparc," *Le courrier musical* III, no. 1, January 6, 1900, pp. 1–4.

Bonaparte, Louis, *Mémoire sur la versification française*, Florence, 1819.

Bonnerot, Jean, *Saint-Saëns, sa vie et son œuvre*, Paris, 1914.

Borren, Charles van den, *L'œuvre dramatique de César Franck: Hulda, et Ghiselle*, Brussels, 1907.

Boschot, Adolphe, *Le crépuscule d'un romantique; Hector Berlioz, 1842–1869*, new ed., Paris, 1950.

———— *La jeunesse d'un romantique; Hector Berlioz, 1803–1831*, new ed., Paris, 1946.

———— *Un romantique sous Louis-Philippe, Hector Berlioz, 1831–1842*, new ed., Paris, 1948.

Boulanger, Nadia, "La musique religieuse [de Fauré]," *La revue musicale* III, no. 11, October 1, 1922, pp. 296–303 (also numbered 104–111).

Bourges, Maurice, "Quarante mélodies à une et à plusieurs voix par G. Meyerbeer," *RGM* XVII, no. 18–19, May 5–12, 1850, pp. 149–150, 158–159.

———— review of Massé, *Chants d'autrefois*, in *RGM* XVI, no. 26, July 1, 1849, p. 206.

———— review of Offenbach, *Six fables de La Fontaine*, in *RGM* IX, no. 15, April 10, 1842, pp. 154–155.

———— "Situation mélodique actuelle," *RGM* XIII, no. 30, July 26, 1846, pp. 235–236.

Bouteron, Marcel, *Danse et musique romantiques*, Paris, 1927.

Bouyer, Raymond, "Chateaubriand et la musique," *Mst* LXXX, no. 8 and 10–19, February 21 to May 9, 1914, *passim*.

Brancour, René, article "Mélodie," in *La grande encyclopédie*, Paris, 1885–1902, Vol. 23, pp. 612–616.

———— *Félicien David*, Paris, 1911.

———— *Massenet*, Paris, 1931.

Brenet, Michel, *Dictionnaire pratique et historique de la musique*, Paris, 1926.

Bréville, Pierre de, "Henri Fouques-Duparc," in *Larousse mensuel illustré* IX, no. 315, May 1933, pp. 403–404.

Bruneau, Alfred, *Massenet*, Paris, 1935 (*Les grands musiciens*, no. 6).

Burja, A., "Sur les rapports qu'il y a entre la musique et la déclamation," *Mémoire de l'Académie de Berlin*, Paris, 1803.

Cahen, Abraham, *Littérature et musique françaises*, Cahors, 1902.

Casanova de Seingalt, Giacomo Girolamo, *Mémoires*, 8 vols., new ed., Paris, 1880.

Castil-Blaze, François Henri Joseph, *L'art des vers lyriques*, Paris, 1857.

———— *De l'opéra en France*, 2 vols., 2d ed., Paris, 1826.

———— *Dictionnaire de musique moderne*, Paris, 1821.

———— *Molière musicien*, 2 vols., Paris, 1852.

———— *Noces de Figaro de Mozart*, Paris, 1819.

Catel, Charles, *Traité d'harmonie*, Paris, 1802, English trans. by C. Clarke, London, 1854.

Catalogue général et thématique des œuvres de Saint-Saëns, 2d ed., Paris, 1908.

Cauchie, Maurice, "La version authentique de la romance 'Plaisir d'amour,'" *Revue de musicologie* XXI, February 1937, pp. 12–14.

Chabanon, Michel Paul Guy de, *De la musique considérée en elle-même et dans ses rapports avec la parole, les langues, la poésie et le théâtre*, Paris, 1785.

—— "Lettre sur les propriétés musicales de la langue française," *Mercure de France*, January 1773, pp. 171–191.

Chantavoine, Jean, *Camille Saint-Saëns*, Paris, 1947.

Choron, Alexandre Étienne, *Rapport...sur un ouvrage intitulé: Les vrais principes de la versification, développés par un examen comparatif entre les langues française et italienne, etc.*, par M. A. Scoppa..., Paris, 1812.

Clapisson, Louis, *Album contenant 12 mélodies, paroles de F. de Courcy*, Paris, J. Meissonnier, n.d.

—— *Les chants du cœur*, Paris, Richault, n.d.

Clément, Félix, *Les musiciens célèbres depuis le seizième siècle jusqu'à nos jours*, Paris, 1868.

Cœuroy, André, *Appels d'Orphée; nouvelles études de musique et de littérature comparées*, Paris, 1929 (*Essais critiques*, 1).

—— "Gérard de Nerval; critique musicale," *La revue musicale* V, no. 11, October 1, 1924, pp. 205–218.

Colling, Alfred, *Musique et spiritualité*, Paris, 1941.

Combarieu, Jules, *Histoire de la musique*, 5 vols., rev. ed., Paris, 1946–1960.

—— *Les rapports de la musique et de la poésie considérées au point de vue de l'expression*. Paris, 1894 (thesis); also pub. (Paris, 1895) as *Les rapports entre la musique et la poésie*.

Cooper, Martin, *French Music from the Death of Berlioz to the Death of Fauré*, London, 1951.

Coquard, Arthur, "Étude sur les mélodistes: Schubert," *Le contemporain*, September 1, 1872.

Cozanet, Albert: *see* his pseud., Udine, Jean d'

Curzon, Henri de, *Ernest Reyer, sa vie et ses œuvres*, Paris, 1924.

—— *Léo Delibes, sa vie et ses œuvres*, Paris, 1926.

—— *Meyerbeer*, Paris, 1910.

—— "Théophile Gautier et la musique," *Mst* LXXXIV, no. 43, October 27, 1922, pp. 421–423.

Dandelot, Arthur, *La vie et l'œuvre de Saint-Saëns*, Paris, 1930.

Dandelot, Arthur, and J.-G. Prod'homme: *see* Prod'homme, Jacques-Gabriel.

Daubresse, Mathilde, review of three Duparc *mélodies* in *Le guide musical* (Paris), LIX, no. 2, January 12, 1913, pp. 31–32.

Dauriac, Lionel, *Meyerbeer*, Paris, 1913.

Davenson, Henri, *Introduction à la chanson populaire*, Neuchâtel, 1942.

Davies, Laurence, *The Gallic Muse*, London, 1967.

Dean, Winton, *Georges Bizet, His Life and Works*, London, 1965.

Delaire, Jacques-Auguste, "Des amateurs de musique et des concerts d'amateurs," *Annales de la Société libre des beaux-arts* VI, Paris, 1836, pp. 120–135.

—— *Histoire de la romance considérée comme œuvre littéraire et musicale*, Paris, 1845.

Delmas, Marc, *Georges Bizet*, Paris, 1930.

Demuth, Norman, *César Franck*, London, 1949.

────── *Introduction to the Music of Gounod*, London, 1950.

Deschamps, Émile, *Un manifeste du romantisme, La préface des Études françaises et étrangères*, ed. Henri Girard, Paris, 1923.

────── *Œuvres complètes*, 6 vols., Paris, 1872–1874.

Destranges, Étienne, *L'œuvre lyrique de César Franck*, Paris, 1896.

Deutsch, Otto Erich, "Schubert et la reine Hortense," *La revue musicale* X, no. 2, December 1928, pp. 23–30.

────── *Schubert Thematic Catalogue of All His Works in Chronological Order* (in collaboration with Donald R. Wakeling), London, 1951.

Diderot, Denis, *Rameau's Nephew*, trans. Jacques Barzun, New York, 1956.

Divoire, Fernand, "Sous la musique que faut-il mettre? De beaux vers, de mauvais, des vers libres, de la prose?" *Musica* no. 101–102, February–March 1911, pp. 38–40, 58–60.

Donizetti, Giacomo, *Matinées musicales*, Paris, Meissonnier, 1842.

────── *Rêveries napolitaines, six ballades*, Paris, Bernard-Latte, 1838.

Dorchain, Auguste, *L'art des vers*, Paris, n.d.

Duchambge, Pauline, "Dixième mélodie imitée de Thomas Moore," trans. Léon Halévy, Paris, Pleyel, ca. 1829.

Ducondut, Abel, *Examen critique de la versification française, classique et romantique*, Paris, 1863.

Ducondut, Jean-Ambroise, *Essai de rhythmique française*, Paris, 1856.

Dufourcq, Norbert, *César Franck, le milieu, l'œuvre, l'art*, Paris, 1949 (*Euterpe*, no. 5).

Duméril, Edmond, *Le Lied allemand et ses traductions poétiques en France*, Paris, 1934 (*Bibliothèque de la Revue de littérature comparée*, tome 98).

────── *Lieds et ballades germaniques traduits en vers français; essai de bibliographie critique*, Paris, 1934 (*ibid.*, tome 99).

Dumesnil, René, *La musique romantique française*, Paris, 1944.

────── *Le rythme musical, essai historique et critique*, Paris, 1921; rev. ed., 1949.

Eckardt, Hans, *Die Musikanschauung der französischen Romantik*, Kassel, 1950 (*Heidelberger Studien zur Musikwissenschaft*, Bd. III).

Emmanuel, Maurice, *César Franck*, Paris, 1930.

Escoffier, Maurice, *Le mouvement romantique, 1788–1850, essai de bibliographie synchronique et méthodique*, Paris, 1934.

Escudier, Léon and Marie, *Dictionnarie de musique*, 5th ed., Paris, 1872.

Evans, Raymond Leslie, *Les romantiques français et la musique*, Paris, 1934 (*Bibliothèque de la Revue de littérature comparée*, tome 100).

Expert, Henry, "XVIᵉ siècle; à propos de la musique française à l'époque de la Renaissance," in *Encyclopédie de la musique et Dictionnaire du Conservatoire*, Paris, [1913], Part I, Vol. III, pp. 1261–1298.

Farrère, Claude, *Mademoiselle Dax, jeune fille*, Paris, 1907.

Fauré-Frémiet, Philippe, *Gabriel Fauré*, rev. ed., Paris, 1957.

Fétis, Édouard, "Concert donné par M. Berlioz," *RMF* XIV, no 48, November 30, 1834, pp. 381–383.

Fétis, François-Joseph, *Biographie universelle des musiciens*, 8 vols., 2d ed., Paris, 1867–1870.

―――― "Du rhythme de la poésie lyrique et des études rhythmiques de M. A. van Hasselt," *RGM* XXX, no. 11, March 15, 1863, pp. 81–83.

―――― "Examen de l'état actuel de la musique en Italie, en Allemagne, en Angleterre et en France; 7ᵉ article," *RMF* I, no. 14, May 1827, pp. 347–356.

―――― *La musique mise à la portée de tout le monde*, 2d ed., Paris, 1836.

―――― review of Meyerbeer, *Douze mélodies*, in *RGM* VIII, no. 21, March 14, 1841, pp. 166–167.

―――― "Société des concerts du Conservatoire: Premier concert annuel," *RMF* XV, no. 4, January 25, 1835, pp. 25–28.

―――― "Sur la romance," *RMF* IV, 1829, pp. 409–417, 433–439.

―――― (?) "Sur les airs irlandais," *RMF* VII, March 6, 1830, pp. 145–150.

Fleury, l'Abbé Alexandre, "Du rythme dans la poésie chantée," *Études religieuses, philosophiques* ... 30ᵉ année LX, November 15, 1893.

Fontaney, A., trans, *Ballades, mélodies et poésies diverses*, Paris, Hayet, 1829.

Gail, Jean François, *Réflexions sur le goût musical en France*, Paris, 1832.

Gallet, Mme. Maurice, *Schubert et le Lied*, Paris, 1917.

Gautier, Judith, *Le collier des jours*, 2 vols., Paris, n.d.

―――― *Le second rang du collier*, Paris, n.d.

Gautier, Théophile, article on Berlioz in *La presse*, December 11, 1839.

―――― *Caprices et zigzags*, Paris, n.d.

―――― *Les grotesques*, Paris, 1834–1835.

―――― "Hippolyte Monpou," in *Histoire du romantisme, suivi des notices romantiques et d'une étude sur la poésie française 1830–1868*, Paris, 1873, pp. 254–258.

―――― *Les jeune-France*, Paris, 1833.

―――― *La musique*, Paris, 1911 (articles reprinted from various journals).

―――― "Le nid des rossignols," in *L'amulette, étrennes à nos jeunes amis*, Paris, 1834.

―――― *Poésies complètes*, ed. René Jasinski, 3 vols., Paris, 1932.

George, Albert J., *Books by Balzac; a checklist of books by Honoré de Balzac, compiled from the papers of William Hobart Royce, presently in the Syracuse University Collection*, Syracuse, N.Y., 1960.

Gérold, Théodore, *L'art du chant en France au XVIIᵉ siècle*, Strasbourg, 1921.

―――― "Monodie et Lied," in *Encyclopédie de la musique et Dictionnaire du Conservatoire*, Paris, 1930, Part II, Vol. V, pp. 2757–2865.

Giacomelli, A., review of Lalo, *Six mélodies*, in *FM* XX, no. 40 and 51, October 5 and December 21, 1856, pp. 320 and 408.

Girard, Henri, *Un bourgeois dilettante à l'époque romantique: Émile Deschamps (1791–1871)*, 2 vols., Paris, 1921. Vol. II has title: *Émile Deschamps*, *dilettante; relations d'un poète romantique avec les peintres, les sculpteurs et les musiciens de son temps (Bibliothèque de la Revue de littérature comparée,* tome 2).

Giraud, H., *L'école romantique française,* Paris, n.d.

Glasenapp, Carl Friedrich, *Das Leben Richard Wagners,* 6 vols., 4th rev. ed., Leipzig, 1905–1911; English trans. by W. A. Ellis, *Life of Richard Wagner,* London, 1900–1906.

Gougelot, Henri, *Catalogue des romances françaises parues sous la Révolution et l'Empire,* 2 vols., Melun, 1937–1943.

———— *La romance française sous la Révolution et l'Empire: Étude historique et critique,* 2 vols., Melun, 1938–1943.

Goujon, Henri, *L'expression du rythme mental dans la mélodie et dans la parole,* Paris, 1907 (thesis).

Gounod, Charles, *Mémoires d'un artiste,* 5th ed., Paris, 1909; English trans. by Annette E. Crocker, *Memoirs of an Artist,* New York, 1895.

Grand, Georges, "Hippolyte Monpou," *Revue de Paris* new ser. IX, January 15, 1868, pp. 297–309.

Grétry, André Ernest Modeste, *Mémoires, ou Essais sur la musique,* 3 vols., 2d ed., Paris, 1797.

Guichard, Léon, "Quels furent les témoins du premier mariage de Berlioz?", *Revue de musicologie* LII, no. 2, 1966, pp. 211–214.

Haape, V., "Alfred de Musset in seinen Beziehungen zu Deutschland und zum deutschen Geistesleben," *Zeitschrift für französische Sprache und Literatur* XXXIV, 1909, pp. 80–84.

Hahn, Reynaldo, *Du chant,* Paris, 1920.

———— *Journal d'un musicien,* Paris, 1949.

———— *Thèmes variés,* Paris, 1945.

Hall, James, *The Art Song,* Norman, Okla., 1953.

Harding, James, *Saint-Saëns and His Circle,* London, 1965.

Höweler, Caspar, *Rhythme in vers en muziek,* Amsterdam, 1952.

Hofmeisters Handbuch der Musikliteratur, Leipzig. Pub. under this and variant titles by Anton Meysel, C. F. Whistling, or Friedrich Hofmeister since 1817.

Hopkinson, Cecil, *A Bibliography of the Musical and Literary Works of Hector Berlioz (1803–1869) with Histories of the French Music Publishers Concerned,* Edinburgh, 1951.

———— *A Dictionary of Parisian Music Publishers 1700–1950,* London, 1954.

Hugo, Victor, "Carnets inédits," *Les nouvelles littéraires* XXX, April 7, 1951 and XXXI, February 21, 1952.

———— *Œuvres complètes,* 48 vols., Paris, 1880.

Imbert, Hugues, *Nouveaux profils de musiciens,* Paris, 1892 (includes chapters on Gounod, Lalo, and Reyer).

———— *Profils d'artistes contemporains,* Paris, 1897 (includes chapters on Castillon and Massenet).

Indy, Vincent d', *César Franck*, 5th ed., Paris, 1910; English trans. by Rosa Newmarch, London, 1909 (Dover reprint, 1965).

────── *Cours de composition musicale*, 3 vols., Paris, 1903–1933.

──────"La première manière de César Franck," *Revue de musicologie* VII, February 1923, pp. 5–6.

Jankélévitch, Vladimir, *Gabriel Fauré, ses mélodies, son esthétique*, new ed., Paris, 1951.

Jansen, Albert, *Jean-Jacques Rousseau als Musiker*, Berlin, 1884.

Jasinski, René, *Les années romantiques de Théophile Gautier*, Paris, 1929.

Jullien, Adolphe, *Ernest Reyer*, Paris, 1909.

Kahl, Willi, "Schuberts Lieder in Frankreich bis 1840," *Die Musik* XXI, 1927, pp. 22–31.

Kapp, Julius, *Hector Berlioz*, Berlin, 1917.

────── *Richard Wagner*, Berlin, 1910.

Kastner, Georges, *Parémiologie musicale de la langue française*, Paris, 1866.

────── review of F. Kücken, *Compositions vocales*, in *RGM* XII, no. 31, August 3, 1845, pp. 254–255.

────── review of G. Donizetti, *Matinées musicales*, in *RGM* IX, no. 15, April 10, 1842, pp. 153–154.

Kling, Henri, "Lamartine et la musique," *Rivista musicale italiana* XVII 1910, pp. 91–112.

Klingsor, Tristan, "Les musiciens et les poètes contemporains," *Mercure de France* XXXVI, November 1900, pp. 430–444.

Koch, Max, *Richard Wagner*, 3 vols., Berlin, 1907–1918.

Koechlin, Charles, *Gabriel Fauré*, new ed., Paris, 1949; English trans. by Leslie Orrey, 2d rev. ed., London, 1946.

Labarre, Théodore, "Concert fabuleux!!! donné, le 16 avril, dans les salons de M. Pleyel, par M. Jacques Offenbach," *FM* V, April 24, 1842, pp. 158–159.

Laforêt, Claude, *La vie musicale au temps romantique (salons, théâtres et concerts)*, Paris, 1929 (also appeared in part in *La revue musicale* X, May–June 1929, pp. 16–24 and September–October 1929, pp. 218–231.

Lamartine, Alphonse de, *Cours familier de littérature*, 28 vols., Paris, 1856–1869.

────── *Harmonies poétiques et religieuses*, Paris, 1830.

────── *Méditations poétiques*, Paris, 1820 (= *Premières méditations*).

────── *Nouvelles méditations*, Paris, 1823.

────── *Recueillements poétiques*, Paris, 1839.

Landormy, Paul, *Gounod*, Paris, 1942.

────── "Les mélodies de Gounod," *Mst* CII, no. 2–3, January 12 and 19, 1940, pp. 9–10.

────── *La musique française de Franck à Debussy*, 9th ed., Paris, 1943.

Landry, Eugène, *La théorie du rhythme et le rhythme du français déclamé, avec une étude expérimentale de la déclamation de plusieurs poètes et comédiens célèbres du rhythme des vers italiens et des nuances de la durée dans la musique*, Paris, 1911 (thesis).

Larousse, Pierre, *Grand dictionnaire universel du XIXe siècle*, 15 vols., Paris, 1865–1876.

Lasalle, Albert de, *Dictionnaire de la musique appliquée à l'amour*, Paris, 1868.

Le Carpentier, Adolphe, *Petit traité de composition mélodique, appliqué aux valses, quadrilles et romances*, Paris, Heugel, 1843.

Ledhuy, Adolphe and Henri Bertini, *Encyclopédie pittoresque de la musique*, 2 vols., Paris, 1835.

Legouvé, Ernest, "Mélodies de Schubert," *RGM* IV, no. 3, January 15, 1837, pp. 26–27.

―――― "Reber," *FM* VI, no. 13, March 26, 1843, pp. 98–99.

―――― *Soixante ans de souvenirs*, 4 vols., Paris, 1886–1887; 2d ed., 1888.

Lemaire and Lavoix, *Le chant, ses principes, son histoire*, Paris, 1881.

Lichtenthal, Pietro, *Dictionnaire de la musique*, 2 vols., trans. and enlarged by Dominique Mondo, Paris, 1839.

Liszt, Franz, "Lettre d'un bachelier ès-musique," *RGM* V, no. 6, February 11, 1838, pp. 57–62.

Littré, Émile, *Dictionnaire de la langue française*, 7 vols., Paris, 1963 (1st ed., 1887).

Locke, Arthur Ware, *Music and the Romantic Movement in France*, Paris, 1920.

Lockspeiser, Edward, "The French Song in the 19th Century," *Musical Quarterly* XXVI, no. 2, April 1940, pp. 192–199.

Lützeler, L., "Die Lautgestaltung in der Lyrik," *Zeitschrift für Aesthetik und Allgemeine Kunstwissenschaft* XXIX, 1935, pp. 193–216.

Lurin, J., *Éléments du rythme dans la versification et la prose française*, Lyons, 1850.

Lussy, Mathis, *Traité de l'expression musicale; accents, nuances, mouvements dans la musique vocale et instrumentale*, Paris, 1874; English trans. from the 4th ed. by M. E. von Glehn, *Musical Expression, Accents, Nuances, and Tempo in Vocal and Instrumental Music*, London, 1892.

Macdonald, Hugh, "Berlioz's Self-Borrowings," *Royal Musical Association Proceedings* 92, 1965/66, pp. 27–44.

Mallarmé, Stéphane, *La musique et les lettres*, Cambridge-Paris, 1895.

―――― "Vers et musique en France," *Entretiens politiques et littéraires* IV, 1892, p. 237.

Marie, Aristide, *Gérard de Nerval, le poète et l'homme*, Paris, 1914.

Marrow, Henri Irenée: see his pseud., Davenson, Henri

Masson, Paul-Marie, *Berlioz*, Paris, 1923.

―――― "Les brunettes," *Sammelbände der Internationalen Musikgesellschaft* XII, 1910/11, pp. 347–369.

―――― "Les chants anacréontiques de Méhul," *Revue de musicologie* XVIII, August 1934, pp. 129–140.

―――― "Le mouvement humaniste," in *Encyclopédie de la musique et Dictionnaire du Conservatoire*, Paris, 1914, Part I, Vol. III, pp. 1298–1342.

Mauclair, Camille, *Histoire de la musique européenne*, Paris, 1914.

────── "Le 'Lied' français contemporain," *Musica* VII, no. 74, November 1908, pp. 163–164.

Mélanges poétiques, Paris, Bouland, 1824.

"Les mélodies de François Schubert," *FM* I, no. 12, March 18, 1838, pp. 3–4.

Mélodies romantiques; choix de nouvelles ballades de divers peuples, Paris, Janet, [1827].

"Mémoire sur 'La prosodie musicale,' par M. Lamouroux," *Mémoires de la Société d'Agriculture, des Sciences et des Arts d'Agen*, 6 Floréal and 4 Prairial, Revolutionary Year XIII [April 6 and May 24, 1805], pp. 16off.

Mendel-Reissmann, *Musikalisches Konversations-Lexikon*, 11 vols., Berlin, 1870–1879; 2d ed. with supplementary vol., 1880–1883.

Mendelssohn-Bartholdy, Felix, *Album de chant*, trans. M. Bourges, Paris, *RGM*, 1846.

────── *12 Lieder*, trans. Bélanger, Paris, Richault, [1849?].

────── *12 Lieder*, trans. Jules Forrest, Paris, Richault, [1848?].

Merle, F. L., *Psychologie et pathologie d'un artiste: Henri Duparc*, Bordeaux, 1933 (thesis).

Moch, F., "Réflexions sur l'esthétique, la poésie et la prosodie," *La revue musicale* X, September–October 1929, pp. 232–241.

Monnais, Édouard, "Voltaire, la musique et les musiciens," *GM* II, no. 43, October 25, 1835, pp. 345–348.

"Monpou, M. Hippolyte," *GM* II, no. 32, August 9, 1835, pp. 264–265.

Moore, Thomas, *The Journal of Thomas Moore, 1818–1841*, ed. Peter Quennell, New York, 1964.

Mozart, J. C. W. A., *Letters*, 3 vols., ed. Emily Anderson, London, 1938.

Muir, Percy H., "Thomas Moore's Irish Melodies, 1808–1834," *The Colophon* 15, 1933.

Music Library Association, *An Alphabetical Index to Hector Berlioz Werke*, New York, 1964 (*MLA Index Series*, No. 2).

Musik-Autographen, Auktion, 10. Oktober 1951 in Stuttgart, Eutin and Stuttgart, 1951.

Musset, Alfred de, *Œuvres complètes*, Paris, 1879. See also his many articles in various issues of the *Revue des deux mondes*.

Musset, Paul de, *Biographie d'Alfred de Musset*, Paris, 1879.

Nerval, Gérard de, "La Bohème galante, Petits châteaux de Bohème VI," *L'artiste*, September 15, 1852.

[Niedermeyer, Louis Alfred], *Vie d'un compositeur moderne*, Paris, 1893.

Northcote, Sidney, *The Songs of Henri Duparc*, New York, 1950.

Noske, Frits, ed., *Dix romances françaises*, Amsterdam, 1951.

────── "La mélodie et la romance," *Cahiers musicaux* (Brussels) III, no. 17, 1958, pp. 11–17.

———— *The Solo Song Outside German Speaking Countries,* Cologne, 1958 (*Anthology of Music,* XVI).

Olivet, l'Abbé d', *Traité sur la prosodie,* Paris, 1736.

Orrey, Leslie, "The Songs of Gabriel Fauré," *The Music Review* VI, 1945, pp. 72–84.

Ortigue, Joseph d', "Revue du Monde musical: Schubert," *Revue de Paris* new ser. XXX, June 1836, pp. 271–275.

Oulmont, Charles, *Musique de l'amour,* 2 vols., Paris, 1935 (Vol. I: Chausson; Vol. II: Duparc).

Panofka, Henri, "François Schubert," *RGM* V, no. 41, October 14, 1838, pp. 406–409.

Paris. Bibliothèque Nationale. *Le romantisme; Catalogue de l'exposition, 22 janvier – 10 mars 1930,* Bois-Colombes (Seine), 1930.

Parmentier, Théodore, "*L'adieu* de Schubert," *RGM* XLIV, no. 7, February 18, 1877, pp. 52–53.

Passy, Paul, *Les sons du français,* Paris, 1932.

Pazdirek, Franz, *Universal-Handbuch der Musikliteratur aller Zeiten und Völker,* 14 vols., Vienna, [1904–1910?].

Pennington, Kenneth D., *A Historical and Stylistic Study of the mélodies of Gabriel Fauré,* Ann Arbor, 1961 (thesis, Indiana University).

Pigot, Charles, *Georges Bizet et son œuvre,* Paris, 1886.

"Poètes et musiciens," *FM* I, no. 36, September 2, 1838, pp. 4–5 and with the title "Les poètes et la musique," *Mst* VII, no. 35, July 26, 1840.

Poueigh, Jean: *see* his pseud., Séré, Octave

Pougin, Arthur, *Meyerbeer,* Paris, 1864.

Prod'homme, Jacques-Gabriel, "Les œuvres de Schubert en France," *Bericht über den internationalen Kongress für Schubertforschung in Wien,* Augsburg, 1929, pp. 89–110.

———— and Arthur Dandelot, *Gounod, sa vie et ses œuvres,* 2 vols., Paris, 1911.

Quicherat, Louis Marie, *Adolphe Nourrit, sa vie, son talent, son caractère, sa correspondance,* 3 vols., Paris, 1867.

———— *Petit traité de versification française,* Paris, 1839; 7th ed., 1881.

Quittard, Henri, "L'orientalisme musical. Saint-Saëns orientaliste," *La revue musicale* VI, no. 5, March 1, 1906, pp. 107–116.

Ramann, Lina, *Franz Liszt als Künstler und Mensch,* 3 vols., Leipzig, 1880–1894; English trans. by E. Cowdrey, *Franz Liszt, Artist and Man, 1811–1840,* 2 vols., London, 1882.

Ravel, Maurice, "Les mélodies de Gabriel Fauré," *La revue musicale* III, no. 11, October 1, 1922, pp. 214–219 (also numbered 22–33).

Reber, Henri, *Traité d'harmonie,* Paris, 1862.

Reuss, Eduard, *Franz Liszts Lieder,* Leipzig, 1907 (also in *Bayreuther Blätter* no. 7/9 and 10/12, 1906).

Reuter, Evelyn, *La mélodie et le Lied,* Paris, 1950.

Riemann, Hugo, *Dictionnaire de musique*, 3d ed., trans. G. Humbert, Paris, 1931.

Ringer, Alexander, review of Frits Noske, *La mélodie française de Berlioz à Duparc*, in *American Musicological Society Journal* XV, 1955, pp. 217–221.

Roger, Louis, "Quelques mots sur la prosodie," *La semaine musicale* I, November 2, 1865, no. 44.

Rolland, Romain, *Richard Strauss et Romain Rolland, correspondance, fragments de journal*, Paris, 1951 (*Cahiers Romain Rolland*, III).

Rollin, Charles, *De la manière d'enseigner et d'étudier les belles-lettres*, Paris, 1726.

Romagnési, Antoine, *L'art de chanter les romances, les chansonnettes et les nocturnes et généralement toute la musique de salon*, Paris, 1846. The same year another edition appeared with the title *La psychologie du chant*.

Rostand, Claude, *L'œuvre de Gabriel Fauré*, Paris, 1945.

Rouchès, Gabriel, "Le sentiment musical chez les écrivains de 1830: Alfred de Musset," *Le courrier musical* VII, no. 14 and 15, July 15 and August 1, 1904, pp. 424–427, 441–446.

Rousseau, Jean-Jacques, *Dictionnaire de musique*, 2 vols., Geneva, 1767; English trans. by William Waring, *A Complete Dictionary of Music*, London, 1770.

———— *Essai sur l'origine des langues où il est parlé de la mélodie et de l'imitation musicale*, in *Œuvres complètes*, Paris, 1825. The essay, written about 1760, was originally called *Essai sur la mélodie*.

———— *Lettre sur la musique françoise*, Paris, 1753.

Saint-Saëns, Camille, "Henri Reber," in *Harmonie et mélodie*, Paris, 1885, pp. 283–296.

———— "La poésie et la musique," *ibid.*, pp. 257–266.

———— *Portraits et souvenirs*, Paris, 1903 (includes essays on Berlioz, Liszt, Gounod, Massé, and Bizet).

———— *Saint-Saëns par lui-même, d'après ses lettres reçues et commentées par Pierre Aguétant*, Paris, 1938.

Samazeuilh, Gustave, "Un maître du Lied français," [i.e., Duparc] *Revue hebdomadaire*, March 18, 1933.

Sattler, Gertrud, *Das deutsche Lied in der französischen Romantik*, Berne, 1932.

Schneider, Louis, *Massenet*, Paris, 1908.

Schouten, Hennie, *Drie Franse Liederencomponisten: Duparc, Fauré, Debussy*, Amsterdam, 1950.

Schuré, Édouard, *Histoire du Lied*, 2d ed., Paris, 1876.

Scoppa, l'Abbé Antonio, *Des beautés poétiques de toutes les langues sous le rapport de l'accent et du rythme*, Paris, 1816.

———— *Mémoire sur les questions du rythme et de la rime*, Paris, 1815.

———— *Traité de la poésie italienne rapportée à la poésie française dans lequel on fait voir la parfaite analogie entre ces deux langues, et leur versification très ressemblante: on y découvre la source de l'harmonie des vers français, qui est l'accent prosodique; et la langue française y est garantie de toutes les imputations injustes, faites par J. J. Rousseau, dans sa lettre sur la musique*, Paris-Versailles, 1803.

—— *Les vrais principes de la versification française*, Paris-Versailles, 1811.

Scudo, Paolo, "Esquisse d'une histoire de la romance," *Critique et littérature musicales* 1st ser., 3d ed., Paris, 1856, pp. 322–354.

Searle, Humphrey, *The Music of Liszt*, 2d rev. ed., New York, 1966.

Séché, Léon, *Alfred de Musset*, 2 vols., Paris, 1907.

Séré, Octave, "César Franck, Chausson et Duparc," *Musica* XII, no. 130, July 1913, p. 138 (a special number entirely devoted to the *Lied*).

—— *Musiciens français d'aujourd'hui*, 9th ed., Paris, 1921.

Servières, Georges, "Charles Gounod, compositeur de mélodies," *Mst* C, no. 15, April 15, 1938, pp. 105–106.

—— *Édouard Lalo*, Paris, 1925.

—— *Gabriel Fauré, étude critique*, Paris, 1930.

—— "Lieder français, II: Henri Duparc," *Le guide musical* (Paris), XLI, no. 6, February 10, 1895, pp. 126–129.

—— *Saint-Saëns*, Paris, 1923.

Sévélinges, Charles-Louis de, *Alfred, ou Les années d'apprentissage de Wilhelm Meister de Goethe … traduit de l'allemand*, 3 vols., Paris, 1802.

Stevens, Denis, ed., *A History of Song*, New York, 1961.

Stoepel, François, review of Berlioz, *Neuf mélodies*, in *GM* I, no. 21, May 25, 1834, pp. 169–171.

Strauss, Richard: *see* Rolland, Romain

Suckling, Norman, *Fauré*, London, 1946.

"Sur les airs irlandais," *RMF* VII, March 6, 1830, pp. 145–150.

Tarenne, G., *Recherches sur les ranz des vaches*, Paris, 1813.

Ténint, Wilhelm, *Prosodie de l'école moderne*, Paris, 1844.

Thiébault, Baron de l'Empire, *Du chant et particulièrement de la romance*, Paris, 1813.

Thurner, Auguste, "Étude comparée sur la chanson, la romance et le Lied," *RGM* XXXIV, no. 28–41, July 14 – October 13, 1867, *passim*.

Tiersot, Julien, "Berliozana," *Mst* LXX, no. 1 – LXII, no. 48, January 3, 1904 – December 1, 1906, *passim*.

—— *La chanson populaire et les écrivains romantiques*, Paris, 1931.

—— *Un demi-siècle de musique française*, 2d ed., Paris, 1924.

—— *Jean-Jacques Rousseau*, Paris, 1912.

—— *Lettres de musiciens écrites en français*, 2 vols., Paris, 1924.

—— *La musique aux temps romantiques*, Paris, 1930.

—— "Les œuvres inédites de César Franck," *La revue musicale* IV, no. 2, December 1, 1922, pp. 97–138.

Tournemire, Charles, *César Franck*, Paris, 1931.

Toyen, Paul de, *La musique en 1864 (documents relatifs à l'art musical)*, Paris, 1864.

—— *La musique en 1865 (documents relatifs à l'art musical)*, Paris, 1865.

Trannoy, A.-I., *La musique des vers*, Paris, 1929.

Udine, Jean d', *L'art du Lied et les mélodies de Massenet*, Paris, 1931.

Voltaire, *Remarques sur Corneille*, 1764.

[Vossius, Isaac], *De poematum cantu et viribus rhythmi*, Oxford, 1673.

Vuillemin, Louis, *Gabriel Fauré et son œuvre*, Paris, 1914.

────── review of three Duparc *mélodies* in *Comoedia*, I, no. 1923, January 6, 1913, p. 3.

Vuillermoz, Émile, *Gabriel Fauré*, Paris, 1960.

Weckerlin, Jean-Baptiste, *Échos du temps passé*, 3 vols., Paris, 1853–1855.

────── "Observations sur les vers lyriques," *Bulletins de la Société des compositeurs de musique* I (2), 1863, pp. 49–56.

Wenz, Joseph, *Franz Liszt als Lyriker*, Frankfurt a/M, 1921 (unpublished thesis).

Woollett, Henri, *Petit traité de prosodie à l'usage des compositeurs*, Le Havre, 1903.

────── *René Lenormand, un mélodiste français*, Paris, 1930.

Wotton, Tom, *Hector Berlioz*, London, 1935.

INDEX

The index includes names of persons (except publishers named in imprints), as well as selected subjects. Appendix V (poetic quotations) and the Bibliography are not indexed; for Appendix VI (song catalogue) only the Remarks and prefatory material are indexed. For the Notes (pages 409–431) the index lists only those items which have not already appeared in the text to which the notes refer.

A CATALOG OF SELECTED
DOVER BOOKS
IN ALL FIELDS OF INTEREST

A CATALOG OF SELECTED DOVER BOOKS IN ALL FIELDS OF INTEREST

DRAWINGS OF REMBRANDT, edited by Seymour Slive. Updated Lippmann, Hofstede de Groot edition, with definitive scholarly apparatus. All portraits, biblical sketches, landscapes, nudes. Oriental figures, classical studies, together with selection of work by followers. 550 illustrations. Total of 630pp. 9⅛ × 12¼.
21485-0, 21486-9 Pa., Two-vol. set $25.00

GHOST AND HORROR STORIES OF AMBROSE BIERCE, Ambrose Bierce. 24 tales vividly imagined, strangely prophetic, and decades ahead of their time in technical skill: "The Damned Thing," "An Inhabitant of Carcosa," "The Eyes of the Panther," "Moxon's Master," and 20 more. 199pp. 5⅜ × 8½. 20767-6 Pa. $3.95

ETHICAL WRITINGS OF MAIMONIDES, Maimonides. Most significant ethical works of great medieval sage, newly translated for utmost precision, readability. Laws Concerning Character Traits, Eight Chapters, more. 192pp. 5⅜ × 8½.
24522-5 Pa. $4.50

THE EXPLORATION OF THE COLORADO RIVER AND ITS CANYONS, J. W. Powell. Full text of Powell's 1,000-mile expedition down the fabled Colorado in 1869. Superb account of terrain, geology, vegetation, Indians, famine, mutiny, treacherous rapids, mighty canyons, during exploration of last unknown part of continental U.S. 400pp. 5⅜ × 8½. 20094-9 Pa. $6.95

HISTORY OF PHILOSOPHY, Julián Marías. Clearest one-volume history on the market. Every major philosopher and dozens of others, to Existentialism and later. 505pp. 5⅜ × 8½. 21739-6 Pa. $8.50

ALL ABOUT LIGHTNING, Martin A. Uman. Highly readable non-technical survey of nature and causes of lightning, thunderstorms, ball lightning, St. Elmo's Fire, much more. Illustrated. 192pp. 5⅜ × 8½. 25237-X Pa. $5.95

SAILING ALONE AROUND THE WORLD, Captain Joshua Slocum. First man to sail around the world, alone, in small boat. One of great feats of seamanship told in delightful manner. 67 illustrations. 294pp. 5⅜ × 8½. 20326-3 Pa. $4.50

LETTERS AND NOTES ON THE MANNERS, CUSTOMS AND CONDITIONS OF THE NORTH AMERICAN INDIANS, George Catlin. Classic account of life among Plains Indians: ceremonies, hunt, warfare, etc. 312 plates. 572pp. of text. 6⅛ × 9¼. 22118-0, 22119-9 Pa. Two-vol. set $15.90

ALASKA: The Harriman Expedition, 1899, John Burroughs, John Muir, et al. Informative, engrossing accounts of two-month, 9,000-mile expedition. Native peoples, wildlife, forests, geography, salmon industry, glaciers, more. Profusely illustrated. 240 black-and-white line drawings. 124 black-and-white photographs. 3 maps. Index. 576pp. 5⅜ × 8½. 25109-8 Pa. $11.95

THE BOOK OF BEASTS: Being a Translation from a Latin Bestiary of the Twelfth Century, T. H. White. Wonderful catalog real and fanciful beasts: manticore, griffin, phoenix, amphivius, jaculus, many more. White's witty erudite commentary on scientific, historical aspects. Fascinating glimpse of medieval mind. Illustrated. 296pp. 5⅜ × 8¼. (Available in U.S. only) 24609-4 Pa. $5.95

FRANK LLOYD WRIGHT: ARCHITECTURE AND NATURE With 160 Illustrations, Donald Hoffmann. Profusely illustrated study of influence of nature—especially prairie—on Wright's designs for Fallingwater, Robie House, Guggenheim Museum, other masterpieces. 96pp. 9¼ × 10¾. 25098-9 Pa. $7.95

FRANK LLOYD WRIGHT'S FALLINGWATER, Donald Hoffmann. Wright's famous waterfall house: planning and construction of organic idea. History of site, owners, Wright's personal involvement. Photographs of various stages of building. Preface by Edgar Kaufmann, Jr. 100 illustrations. 112pp. 9¼ × 10.
23671-4 Pa. $7.95

YEARS WITH FRANK LLOYD WRIGHT: Apprentice to Genius, Edgar Tafel. Insightful memoir by a former apprentice presents a revealing portrait of Wright the man, the inspired teacher, the greatest American architect. 372 black-and-white illustrations. Preface. Index. vi + 228pp. 8¼ × 11. 24801-1 Pa. $9.95

THE STORY OF KING ARTHUR AND HIS KNIGHTS, Howard Pyle. Enchanting version of King Arthur fable has delighted generations with imaginative narratives of exciting adventures and unforgettable illustrations by the author. 41 illustrations. xviii + 313pp. 6⅛ × 9¼. 21445-1 Pa. $5.95

THE GODS OF THE EGYPTIANS, E. A. Wallis Budge. Thorough coverage of numerous gods of ancient Egypt by foremost Egyptologist. Information on evolution of cults, rites and gods; the cult of Osiris; the Book of the Dead and its rites; the sacred animals and birds; Heaven and Hell; and more. 956pp. 6⅛ × 9¼.
22055-9, 22056-7 Pa., Two-vol. set $20.00

A THEOLOGICO-POLITICAL TREATISE, Benedict Spinoza. Also contains unfinished *Political Treatise*. Great classic on religious liberty, theory of government on common consent. R. Elwes translation. Total of 421pp. 5⅜ × 8½.
20249-6 Pa. $6.95

INCIDENTS OF TRAVEL IN CENTRAL AMERICA, CHIAPAS, AND YUCATAN, John L. Stephens. Almost single-handed discovery of Maya culture; exploration of ruined cities, monuments, temples; customs of Indians. 115 drawings. 892pp. 5⅜ × 8½. 22404-X, 22405-8 Pa., Two-vol. set $15.90

LOS CAPRICHOS, Francisco Goya. 80 plates of wild, grotesque monsters and caricatures. Prado manuscript included. 183pp. 6⅝ × 9⅝. 22384-1 Pa. $4.95

AUTOBIOGRAPHY: The Story of My Experiments with Truth, Mohandas K. Gandhi. Not hagiography, but Gandhi in his own words. Boyhood, legal studies, purification, the growth of the Satyagraha (nonviolent protest) movement. Critical, inspiring work of the man who freed India. 480pp. 5⅜ × 8½. (Available in U.S. only)
24593-4 Pa. $6.95

THE BLUE FAIRY BOOK, Andrew Lang. The first, most famous collection, with many familiar tales: Little Red Riding Hood, Aladdin and the Wonderful Lamp, Puss in Boots, Sleeping Beauty, Hansel and Gretel, Rumpelstiltskin; 37 in all. 138 illustrations. 390pp. 5⅜ × 8½.   21437-0 Pa. $5.95

THE STORY OF THE CHAMPIONS OF THE ROUND TABLE, Howard Pyle. Sir Launcelot, Sir Tristram and Sir Percival in spirited adventures of love and triumph retold in Pyle's inimitable style. 50 drawings, 31 full-page. xviii + 329pp. 6½ × 9¼.   21883-X Pa. $6.95

AUDUBON AND HIS JOURNALS, Maria Audubon. Unmatched two-volume portrait of the great artist, naturalist and author contains his journals, an excellent biography by his granddaughter, expert annotations by the noted ornithologist, Dr. Elliott Coues, and 37 superb illustrations. Total of 1,200pp. 5⅜ × 8.
Vol. I 25143-8 Pa. $8.95
Vol. II 25144-6 Pa. $8.95

GREAT DINOSAUR HUNTERS AND THEIR DISCOVERIES, Edwin H. Colbert. Fascinating, lavishly illustrated chronicle of dinosaur research, 1820's to 1960. Achievements of Cope, Marsh, Brown, Buckland, Mantell, Huxley, many others. 384pp. 5¼ × 8¼.   24701-5 Pa. $6.95

THE TASTEMAKERS, Russell Lynes. Informal, illustrated social history of American taste 1850's–1950's. First popularized categories Highbrow, Lowbrow, Middlebrow. 129 illustrations. New (1979) afterword. 384pp. 6 × 9.
23993-4 Pa. $6.95

DOUBLE CROSS PURPOSES, Ronald A. Knox. A treasure hunt in the Scottish Highlands, an old map, unidentified corpse, surprise discoveries keep reader guessing in this cleverly intricate tale of financial skullduggery. 2 black-and-white maps. 320pp. 5⅜ × 8½. (Available in U.S. only)   25032-6 Pa. $5.95

AUTHENTIC VICTORIAN DECORATION AND ORNAMENTATION IN FULL COLOR: 46 Plates from "Studies in Design," Christopher Dresser. Superb full-color lithographs reproduced from rare original portfolio of a major Victorian designer. 48pp. 9¼ × 12¼.   25083-0 Pa. $7.95

PRIMITIVE ART, Franz Boas. Remains the best text ever prepared on subject, thoroughly discussing Indian, African, Asian, Australian, and, especially, Northern American primitive art. Over 950 illustrations show ceramics, masks, totem poles, weapons, textiles, paintings, much more. 376pp. 5⅜ × 8.   20025-6 Pa. $6.95

SIDELIGHTS ON RELATIVITY, Albert Einstein. Unabridged republication of two lectures delivered by the great physicist in 1920–21. *Ether and Relativity* and *Geometry and Experience*. Elegant ideas in non-mathematical form, accessible to intelligent layman. vi + 56pp. 5⅜ × 8½.   24511-X Pa. $2.95

THE WIT AND HUMOR OF OSCAR WILDE, edited by Alvin Redman. More than 1,000 ripostes, paradoxes, wisecracks: Work is the curse of the drinking classes, I can resist everything except temptation, etc. 258pp. 5⅜ × 8½.   20602-5 Pa. $3.95

ADVENTURES WITH A MICROSCOPE, Richard Headstrom. 59 adventures with clothing fibers, protozoa, ferns and lichens, roots and leaves, much more. 142 illustrations. 232pp. 5⅜ × 8½.   23471-1 Pa. $3.95

AMERICAN CLIPPER SHIPS: 1833–1858, Octavius T. Howe & Frederick C. Matthews. Fully-illustrated, encyclopedic review of 352 clipper ships from the period of America's greatest maritime supremacy. Introduction. 109 halftones. 5 black-and-white line illustrations. Index. Total of 928pp. 5⅜ × 8½.
25115-2, 25116-0 Pa., Two-vol. set $17.90

TOWARDS A NEW ARCHITECTURE, Le Corbusier. Pioneering manifesto by great architect, near legendary founder of "International School." Technical and aesthetic theories, views on industry, economics, relation of form to function, "mass-production spirit," much more. Profusely illustrated. Unabridged translation of 13th French edition. Introduction by Frederick Etchells. 320pp. 6⅛ × 9¼. (Available in U.S. only)
25023-7 Pa. $8.95

THE BOOK OF KELLS, edited by Blanche Cirker. Inexpensive collection of 32 full-color, full-page plates from the greatest illuminated manuscript of the Middle Ages, painstakingly reproduced from rare facsimile edition. Publisher's Note. Captions. 32pp. 9⅜ × 12¼.
24345-1 Pa. $4.50

BEST SCIENCE FICTION STORIES OF H. G. WELLS, H. G. Wells. Full novel *The Invisible Man,* plus 17 short stories: "The Crystal Egg," "Aepyornis Island," "The Strange Orchid," etc. 303pp. 5⅜ × 8½. (Available in U.S. only)
21531-8 Pa. $4.95

AMERICAN SAILING SHIPS: Their Plans and History, Charles G. Davis. Photos, construction details of schooners, frigates, clippers, other sailcraft of 18th to early 20th centuries—plus entertaining discourse on design, rigging, nautical lore, much more. 137 black-and-white illustrations. 240pp. 6⅛ × 9¼.
24658-2 Pa. $5.95

ENTERTAINING MATHEMATICAL PUZZLES, Martin Gardner. Selection of author's favorite conundrums involving arithmetic, money, speed, etc., with lively commentary. Complete solutions. 112pp. 5⅜ × 8½.
25211-6 Pa. $2.95

THE WILL TO BELIEVE, HUMAN IMMORTALITY, William James. Two books bound together. Effect of irrational on logical, and arguments for human immortality. 402pp. 5⅜ × 8½.
20291-7 Pa. $7.50

THE HAUNTED MONASTERY and THE CHINESE MAZE MURDERS, Robert Van Gulik. 2 full novels by Van Gulik continue adventures of Judge Dee and his companions. An evil Taoist monastery, seemingly supernatural events; overgrown topiary maze that hides strange crimes. Set in 7th-century China. 27 illustrations. 328pp. 5⅜ × 8½.
23502-5 Pa. $5.00

CELEBRATED CASES OF JUDGE DEE (DEE GOONG AN), translated by Robert Van Gulik. Authentic 18th-century Chinese detective novel; Dee and associates solve three interlocked cases. Led to Van Gulik's own stories with same characters. Extensive introduction. 9 illustrations. 237pp. 5⅜ × 8½.
23337-5 Pa. $4.95

Prices subject to change without notice.
Available at your book dealer or write for free catalog to Dept. GI, Dover Publications, Inc., 31 East 2nd St., Mineola, N.Y. 11501. Dover publishes more than 175 books each year on science, elementary and advanced mathematics, biology, music, art, literary history, social sciences and other areas.